The red line drawn on the map (opposite) is intended to follow the following lines:

A–B–The frontier defined by the Treaty of Berlin of 13th July 1878 and by the Treaty of San Stefano of 3rd March 1878.

B–C–frontier demarcated by the Turco-Persian Frontier Commission in 1913-14 on the basis of the Protocol signed at Constantinople on the 4(17) November 1913 excepting in sectors *a–b* and *c–d* where the red line is intended to follow the line of the previous *de facto* frontier described on page 139 and 140 of the Minutes of the Frontier Commission in a note dated the 1/14th October 1914 by the Russian and British Commissioners.

C–D–E–The limit of territorial waters of the Arabian peninsula excepting the Sultanate of Koweit and the Farsan Archipelago.

E–F–The frontier defined by the Anglo-Turkish convention of 1st October 1906.

F–G–The red line is intended to follow the decision of the Conference of London on the 13th February 1914 in execution of Article 5 of the Treaty of London of 17/30th May 1913 and Article 15 of the Treaty of Athens of the 1/14th November 1913.

G–H–The frontier as defined by the Treaty of Constantinople on the 16/29th September 1913.

H–A–The limit of the territorial waters of Turkey in the Black Sea.

The Books of Edwin Black

www.edwinblack.com

**British Petroleum and
The Red Line Agreement**
*The West's Secret Pact
to Get Mideast Oil*
www.redlineagreement.com
2011

The Farhud
*Roots of the Arab-Nazi Alliance
in the Holocaust*
www.farhudbook.com
2010

Nazi Nexus
*America's Corporate Connections
To Hitler's Holocaust*
www.nazinexus.com
2009

The Plan
*How to Rescue Society When
the Oil Stops—or the Day Before*
www.planforoilcrisis.com
2008

Internal Combustion
*How Corporations and Governments
Addicted the World to Oil
and Derailed the Alternatives*
www.internalcombustionbook.com
2006

Banking on Baghdad
*Inside Iraq's 7,000 Year History of
War, Profit, and Conflict*
www.bankingonbaghdad.com
2004

War Against the Weak
*Eugenics and America's Campaign to
Create a Master Race*
www.waragainsttheweak.com
2003

IBM and the Holocaust
*The Strategic Alliance Between Nazi
Germany and America's
Most Powerful Corporation*
www.ibmandtheholocaust.com
2001

The Transfer Agreement
*The Dramatic Story of
the Pact Between the Third Reich
and Jewish Palestine*
www.transferagreement.com
1984, 2001, and 2009

Format C:
A Novel
www.formatnovel.com
1999

BRITISH PETROLEUM
AND THE
REDLINE AGREEMENT

EDWIN BLACK

DIALOG PRESS
WASHINGTON, DC

To a World Without Oil

This book includes updated and expanded research, archival, and textual materials produced for Edwin Black's earlier books, *Banking on Baghdad*, *Internal Combustion*, *The Plan*, and *The Farhud*.

This book is printed on acid-free paper.

ISBN 978-0914153153

Printed in the United States of America

15 14 13 12 11   5 4 3 2 1

Cover designed by Tallgrass Studio

Modern book text is produced using a variety of collaborative software, including spell-checkers and text revision tools. It is possible for such software to create typographical errors or other textual changes beyond the control of the author, editors, or publisher. Any changes, corrections, or additions to this book should be reported to, and/or can be found at http://www.redlineagreement.com.

Web site addresses (URLs) were accurate as of press time. Neither the author nor the publisher is responsible for URLs that have expired or moved since the manuscript was prepared.

Contents

INTRODUCTION

We are trapped. Our world is dependent upon oil for its very strength and breath. Without oil, the life we know would collapse. Where compulsive addiction meets utter dependence, the dynamics of supply and demand rule. Every day, our decisions ensure our sons and daughters will be as addicted as their mothers and fathers are to this flammable condition. This is no sudden predicament, but a hard-fought, century-long process to ensure that modern society would drink one fuel and one fuel only as its main source of energy—and that this thirst would be quenched despite all consequences: environmental, economic, military, or political. The dominant source for the crude we crave is the extended Middle East, a font still too incendiary to touch.

In the turbulent history of Mideast oil, one company and one secret pact stand above all others as the pivotal force that, by muscle and maneuver, delivered that region's petroleum to the West. Despite, and by virtue of, bloody wars to claim, commercialize, and control that oil, the combustible flow rarely, if ever, stopped. That company, operating under many prior names, was British Petroleum, now BP. The secret monopoly British Petroleum engineered on behalf of itself, a consortium of other oil companies, and three Western governments was the Redline Agreement. The terms of this secret pact were defined by a simple red line carefully marked upon a map to demarcate the cartel's oil kingdom. Once sketched, that thin red line created the most fabulous concession in the history of the world, worth billions of dollars, and worth the many earth-shattering wars, long lines of coffins, and gruesome coups its ink circumscribed.

Mideast oil and its incendiary petropolitics dictate much of our life and too much of our death. This book is not about a history or a future of oil spills or industrial accidents. Those chapters have yet to be written. This book is about a cataclysmic continuum that began more than a century ago, before commercial oil was a reality in the Mideast, before governments and gunpowder created much of the petroliferous world that we inherited. This octane world drives us to the tops of mountains, to the furthest depths of the Gulf of Mexico, and into the belly of the petropolitical beast, sacrificing any person, government, and society to obtain precious supplies of the fluid that powers our lives.

When you chase the winds of Mideast oil history, the view is often obstructed by sandstorms and mirages. To assemble this challenging story, I reached into my own research and textual sources assembled for my earlier book, *Banking on Baghdad*, plus subsequent works, such as *Internal Combustion*, *The Plan*, and *The Farhud*. In doing so, I was able to carve out the reality of British Petroleum and the Redline Agreement. The actual agreement was maintained as a mythical secret until I obtained it and published it for the first time. Readers will see the actual agreement on the inside cover of this book.

My research team worked around the world accessing original documents and obscure materials in archives, repositories, and libraries in five nations. I also pored over the private files of British Petroleum, Turkish Petroleum, Anglo-Persian Oil Company, Anglo-Iranian Oil Company, and Iraqi Petroleum, all organically connected entities. The resulting trove of documents yielded the dots that connected it all into a recognizable line. That line was red.

BP cooperated in every aspect of my investigation, granting me unrestricted access to its sensitive archival papers. While space prevents listing the several dozen researchers and technicians who valiantly aided my work, I offer special kudos to Carol DiSalvo, Eve Jones, Nick Charles, Paul Dwyer, Elizabeth Black, Ben Ratner, and Eli Pridonoff.

I ask my readers to read the entire book without skipping around—or not read it at all. The red line of this saga encompasses an enormous continuity—one that has irrevocably shaped our life today and will do so for the foreseeable future. Only when we understand that unbroken continuity can we comprehend the many ways our world was sculpted by the company that became British Petroleum and the secret pact known as the Redline Agreement.

PART I

BEFORE IRAQ

CHAPTER ONE

FLAMING
WATERS

Suddenly, magenta warning lights began flashing across the computer screen. Not just one. Not just two. The whole screen lit up in a frightening magenta array. The Deepwater Horizon drilling rig was in catastrophic trouble.

Gargantuan and muscular, the Deepwater Horizon, operated by BP—that is, British Petroleum, towered 320 feet toward the sky. She existed virtually in a class of her own. Designed for ultra-deepwater subsea drilling, the Deepwater Horizon was already famous for its celebrated prior accomplishment, the September 2009 drilling of the deepest oil well in history. That feat was off the Texas coast, where the Deepwater Horizon's drill plunged more than 35,050 feet down.

Now, on April 20, 2010, in the star-splattered ocean night, the massive Deepwater Horizon was positioned off the Louisiana coast at Macondo Prospect, where it forced its sophisticated, electronically-supervised drill five miles down to siphon the precious petroleum that lay beneath the Gulf floor. Kept steady in 5,000 feet of water by complex computer-controlled dynamic positioning, the Deepwater Horizon's careful positioning was aided by the rig's own array of thrusters, capable of making minor adjustments for breeze and current.

Andrea Fleytas was the dynamic positioning officer on duty that night. A recent 2008 graduate of the California Maritime Academy, Fleytas was responsible for keeping the rig properly positioned and monitoring all the alarms. A complex leviathan like the Deepwater Horizon, drilling deep below the water and far into the earth, is wired throughout its structure to detect any trouble anywhere. Engine alarms, ballast control alarms, mud pull alarms, fire alarms, thruster alarms—hundreds of sensors were primed to flash alerts should any small operational detail go awry.[1]

Fleytas thought her shift was little more than ordinary. Earlier that day, a gaggle of BP executives and engineers celebrated the successful completion of a battery of safety tests, beating cost estimates. Weather at the Deepwater Horizon's location was mild and the seas were calm. Fleytas came to the bridge at about 5:30 PM that night. Ordinary it was. But shortly after 9:30 PM, everything calm and ordinary would abruptly terminate into an out-of-control nightmare of mud, flames, death, and destruction. Around 9:30 PM, the careful balance of pressure and mud collapsed in the Deepwater Horizon's risers. Drilling mud is needed to maintain the delicate wellbore stability that permits the drill bits to securely scour deeply through the earth and into subterranean oil formations.[2]

With the pressure dropping, mud suddenly started to flow up through the risers. At 9:44 PM, mud and combustible methane began to gusher out of those risers showering the entire rig. Within seconds, a rigworker known as a "tool-pusher" sent an urgent message to the well site leader. Mud was coming up. Workers, he said, "diverted to the mud gas separator" and were now closing the annular preventer to squeeze off and seal the flow, thus limiting the damage. It did not work. Moments later, the assistant driller yelled a terrifying message to the senior toolpusher: "The well is blowing out . . . shutting it in now."[3]

Within moments, a dreadful hissing sound filled the air like an exhaling beast ready to pounce. Seconds later, it happened. Magenta alarms started to display. First, alarms lit for the so-called shaker house and drill shack, where workers tended to drilling operations. Then, the drill floor alarm went off followed by a mighty vibrating jolt that shot through the entire infrastructure as though the rig itself angrily convulsed.[4]

Fleytas had been trained to respond to a few magenta lights, but never dreamed they would all go off at once. Dozens of them were flashing across her screen. Suddenly, everything went black as all power shut down. Five seconds later, the first explosion ripped through the Deepwater Horizon. Ten seconds later, a much larger explosion roared through the rig.[5]

Running to the panel, Fleytas hit the distress buttons, sounding the general alarm. She broadcast a radio distress call: "Mayday! Mayday!" Moments later, the captain issued orders to abandon the rig. Escaping ahead of the accelerating firestorm, Fleytas jumped into a nearby lifeboat. The descent motor clicked on and began lowering. But when the lifeboat hit the surface, Fleytas was thrown out. She swam for her life as the Deepwater Horizon derrick became engulfed in fiery orange flames shooting hundreds of feet into the night sky. A roiling mushroom cloud billowed at the apex of the flames, ascending thousands of feet further toward the stars.[6]

Shrieks of "Fire! Fire!" filled the corridors of the shuddering rig. Firefighter Chris Choy scrambled from his quarters, thinking he would never survive. "I'm fixing to die," he thought. "This is it. We're not gonna get off of here." Disregarding the danger, Choy suited up in his firefighting gear and began to execute his training. From the force of the explosion, a crane operator had been tossed down the stairs to a spot about 50 feet below. He lay helpless as flames scorched closer. Choy went for the trapped man, but was stopped by a searing fireball that blocked his way. He realized he could not save the life of the man before him, the very man he was trained to save.[7]

"It just killed me that I knew I couldn't get to him," Choy remembered. "That's probably the hardest decision I've ever had to make in my life—that we had to … leave him there." Choy himself managed to clamber into a lifeboat, where he found a confined Hades of screams, burning flesh, moaning broken bodies, and panicked men jumping into the cramped boat built for sixty.[8]

The lifeboat's motor wasn't working. Unwilling to incinerate in the paralyzed lifeboat, Choy yanked off his seat belt and prepared to jump. Just then, a maintenance worker turned the engine over. Amid the screams and anguish of its occupants, the boat began descending to the waves below. Choy remained aboard.[9]

Others never made it to a lifeboat. People began jumping off the burning furnace. They sailed 30 to 50 feet down to the dark waters below, going airborne just ahead of the immolating flames and heat that was consuming all of the Deepwater Horizon. Either by jumping or escaping, 115 men and women survived. Eleven perished in the watery depths or within the conflagration.[10]

So powerful were the explosions that the intense shock wave smacked a man aboard a vessel watching from what he thought was a safe distance. The crew of that vessel marveled in awe as the water itself was aflame. The Deepwater Horizon was now an all-powerful, raging inferno.[11] Nothing could stop the flaming fury until the blazing rig was completely consumed by its own burning rage.

On April 22, 2010, despite a ring of water-shooting firefighting boats that sprayed the fire for a day and half, the smoldering and fiery Deepwater Horizon wrenched and heaved its last. Its iconic helipad slowly pivoted perpendicular to the ocean like an unbearable shield lowered to eye-level. The smoking steel behemoth then toppled completely into the water, sizzling to its final disappearance and destruction.[12]

Like the fireball of all oil exploration, the afterflow seemed unstoppable. Hour after hour, day after day, a fast gurgling torrent of oil spewed from the uncapped well. Eventually, about 4.5 million barrels, or 190 million gallons, of crude petroleum fouled the entire Gulf coastline and decimated the livelihoods of an entire generation of Gulf residents whose very existence depended upon the region's natural beauty and abundant seafood.[13] Petroliferous slime was slathered across the wildlife and wetlands, and indeed into the veins of a simple society of people who demanded little, possessed even less, but gave much to a greater society by virtue of their saltwater-soaked muscles and quiet will.

The broiling fire of the Deepwater Horizon was quickly replaced by a furnace of litigations, financial negotiations, and public relations. Rig operator British Petroleum, quickly under the spotlight, seemed to trigger all the wrong responses at all the wrong times as a shore-shocked America demanded answers.

At one point, on May 30, 2010, BP chief executive officer Tony Hayworth tried to show his concern for the awesome devastation his company had inflicted by blurting out in the midst of a spill-ravaged coastline and families, "I'd like my life back." That seemingly insensitive, solipsistic remark provoked outrage from all quarters. On June 17, 2010, to undo the reverberating damage, BP Chairman Carl-Henric Svanberg led a company delegation to the White House. After a meeting with President Barack Obama, Svanberg made clear how compassionate the company felt. "We care about the small people," he said.[14]

Who was and what was this giant company that viewed the lives of an entire region as "small people?" The company mobilized decamillions of dollars and an armada of PR men, lobbyists, and attorneys to portray itself as just an ordinary, caring company, being a good corporate citizen in a horrible moment. Indeed, BP went on a virtual war-footing to protect its assets, its image, and its future.

War is something British Petroleum knows well. The company was invented for wars. The enterprise was the very basis for wars. It actively participated in wars, determined the size and shape of wars, and was, in fact, a war company from the moment of its inception and through most of its wartorn history. Oil invented the political Middle East as we know it, creating nations that never existed before, for the sole purpose of becoming fuel states to supply this company. Oil was the ignition device for World War I, which saw the death and dismemberment of millions on all sides. Oil lubricated the Nazi war machine that savaged humanity. Oil has intoxicated and addicted the world as we know it today.

The history of Mideast oil and the reddened black puddles it has created in so many countries is in fact the parallel history of one company that hinged much of its success upon a single secret agreement. That story spans a century: British Petroleum and the Redline Agreement.

CHAPTER TWO

BIRTH OF
THE OIL AGE

British Petroleum was created to bring the oil of a far off land to a nation that had none and desperately craved it. Without oil, Britain believed it could not attain the military and industrial might its sense of civilization required. Oil was needed for Britain's ships to fight war more effectively and to enable its factories to churn more profitably. Indeed, Britain believed the future viability of its modern civilization depended upon oil.

But man knew oil long before man knew civilization. Many millennia before ancient Mesopotamia organized the city of Uruk, cavemen understood the usefulness of a thick black tar, later called *bitumen*. As far back as 60,000 years ago, bitumen had already become a magical substance for prehistoric society, used as an adherent on spear points and tool blades, a salve on wounds, a lubricant for heavy objects, a sealant for construction, and a decoration on surfaces. Eventually, its flammable qualities were discovered, providing heat and light for even the most primitive cave dwellers and nomads.[1]

Bitumen was easily obtainable because it oozed up from the rocks, hence its eventual name, *petroleum*, which means "rock oil." Petroleum's usefulness is amply documented throughout the inscriptions of the first civilizations, the Bible and other ancient writings. Babylon's ziggurats, its towers of Babel, were built of bricks coated in bitumen. According to tradition, Sargon the Great and Moses the Prince, as infants, were both sent floating down the river in cradles sealed with bitumen.[2]

In the ancient Mesopotamian region, pressure beneath vast deposits of bitumen sometimes forced jets of the flammable substance high into the air. Broiling summer heat regularly ignited the spray into awesome flaming towers equal to any a dragon could exhale. No wonder angry fire gods inhabited the mind of ancient man.[3]

As civilization advanced, new and better industrial and medicinal uses were found for bitumen. The thick residue from evaporated bitumen, called *asphalt*, could be used to pave roads. Gaseous, liquefied, and distilled forms of petroleum, such as naphtha, could be set aflame to light the darkness and scorch the enemy. Cyrus the Great, in the sixth century BCE, planned to use such flammables to burn out street resistance during his famous invasion of Babylon. A thousand years later, terrifying flamethrowers from Byzantine warships at Constantinople sprayed an almost inextinguishable naphtha-based mixture called "Greek Fire."[4]

In 1846, a Canadian geologist working in the United States created a new flammable he named *kerosene,* distilled from asphalt and other hydrocarbons. A wonderful new illuminant, kerosene efficiently brought light into the shadows and darkness of city streets and their great buildings. Within a few years, thousands of gallons per day were being distilled for commercial use in major American cities. Everything changed when a safe, smokeless kerosene lamp with a glass chimney vent was invented, allowing kerosene to become a household necessity—rural and urban—both in Europe and America.[5]

Most of the slow seepages and great sprays of "rock oil," from the Americas to Asia Minor, were never efficiently captured. Oil-gathering was a rudimentary operation, and included such methods as wringing oil from soaked rags, hauling buckets of the slimy crude, and simply siphoning the runoff into containers lashed to donkeys. Ultimately, oil gatherers could only watch most of their precious product simply flow away, blackening the nearby environment and constantly spurring commercial explorers to devise the better technologies for oil conquest. During the first half of the nineteenth century, natural wells had been excavated, deep holes had been bored, taps had been injected into the surface flows, but no one had yet drilled into an oil pool hidden beneath strata of earth and then industrially mastered its contents.[6]

In the 1850s, medicinal oil entrepreneurs began drilling for rock oil at Oil Creek in rural Pennsylvania, where petroleum was migrating into salt layers. Travelers had noted seepages in the area for more than a hundred years. Although the main drillers at Oil Creek sought a new source of medicinal oil, many others craved an abundant supply of commercially exploitable illuminant.[7]

On the afternoon of August 29, 1859, in the woodlands of northwestern Pennsylvania, at Oil Creek, just south of tiny Titusville, at a depth of 69.5 feet, an exploratory drill finally struck oil. Oil Creek spawned "Oil City," which overnight became one of several wild and rambunctious Pennsylvania drilling towns where fortunes were furiously made and lost as fast as oil could spill.[8]

Once struck, oil could be efficiently managed–controlled with pumps and caps, stored in tanks or other holding areas, and then transported by wagon, pipeline, and ship. An industry waiting to be born was finally brought to life. The oil business—like its product—became the most useful undertaking on earth, and also the most explosive, both chemically and politically.

The oil business was far more complicated than just exploiting endlessly gushing streams of black gold. Finding oil, determining its grade, selling it, relying on the source, transporting it, and profiting from the enterprise required a volatile and perilous chain of events. Supply and demand is the mischievous devil of commercial oil—as it is in all commerce. At first, demand soared. America's Civil War and the country's increasingly mechanized and industrial society powered an immediate, monumental need for kerosene, lubricants, sealants, and numerous other petroleum products. Titusville and the surrounding so-called oil regions experienced a frantic "gold rush" but for gold that was black. Endless wooden-sided drilling towers, waiting teams of mules and horses, wagon-clogged service roads, as well as the omnipresent pipes, barrels, tanks, and pumping gear transfigured Pennsylvania's pastoral northwestern woodlands into a grimy, black-soaked industrial oilscape.[9]

In 1860, within a year of the Titusville strike, western Pennsylvania was producing 450,000 barrels of oil. Two years later, production had multiplied to seven times that level. The market gladly gulped every barrel. Oil barges and other hauling ships floated down the Allegheny River in packs of 150 to 200 at a time. Drilling and distribution ran around the clock.[10]

But quickly, demand, compared to uncoordinated supply, became erratic and maddening. In January 1860, a barrel of oil fetched $10. By June of 1860, due to oversupply, the price had dropped to 50 cents per barrel, and at year's end a barrel sold for a mere dime. A year later, once supply was controlled, the price zoomed back up to $4 per barrel, and during 1863 a barrel sold for as much as $7.25.[11]

Manipulating supply and stimulating demand emerged as the fulcrum of success in the wild world of oil. Creating strategic shortages to keep prices high and occasional oversupplies to drive out competition, as well as everything in between, became the special craft of oil's robber barons. That challenge became all the more complicated as oil became a worldwide commodity. By 1878, oil production in Pennsylania and other states, such as Ohio and West Virginia, reached 15.5 million barrels annually, of which about half was exported. The volume about tripled by 1890. Indeed, oil became America's number one nonagricultural industrial export. Distribution became all-important. Crude had to be pumped, transported, and refined in a series of coordinated steps from oil wellhead to end user, whether in the neighboring county or across the oceans.[12]

Timing was everything. Nobody wanted to drown in unused oil. They wanted to float on the lucrative flow. Massive pipelines traversing hundreds of miles, as well as tanker trucks and oil-hauling ships, were constructed to bring the crude to refineries and the refined oil to users—from the subterranean depths of Pennsylvania to the kitchen stoves, bedroom nightstands, and industrial cogwheels a world away. It was a logistical miracle.[13]

Moreover, the pool of oil beneath a wellhead was hardly perpetual. One Titusville-area boomtown, at Pithole Creek, was just a lush tract of Allegheny forest when, on January 7, 1865, an oil speculator brought in a gusher. Within a few months, a nearby farm was transformed into bustling "Pithole City," roiling with 15,000 excited oil zealots. The overnight population attracted more than 50 hotels and boardinghouses. The Astor House hotel was built in a day. A daily newspaper sprang up. Telegraph lines were strung. The town's brand-new post office, processing some 10,000 letters and packages per day, ranked just behind those in Philadelphia and Pittsburgh. Pithole farmland rocketed in value. One parcel sold for $1.3 million during the summer of 1865, and by the time the financing closed in September, the cost had inflated to $2 million. Pithole was for millionaires—for a while. But by January 1866, the tempestuous gusher had been pumped dry. Most people left as suddenly as they had rushed in. Vacant buildings were mercilessly dismantled for firewood. A typical tract of that $2 million farmland was snatched up for a mere $4.37. The Danforth House hotel, which had cost $30,000 to build, was sold for firewood for just $16. Pithole, an instant urban success, just as instantly became an abandoned city.[14] That was the power of oil—from greatness to ghost town in the blink of a barrel.

In those first heady years, Pennsylvania catapulted to become the world's prime supplier of cheap, commercially extracted oil. Near-monopolistic control made Titusville and western Pennsylvania legendary across the financial and governmental centers of the world. As the geologic know-how, drilling acumen, and refining technology streamed into neighboring American states that possessed oil reserves, cheap commercial oil became an almost uniquely American commodity, generating gargantuan fortunes for oil barons such as John D. Rockefeller.[15] But quickly, the lure of petrodollars brought others to the well.

Nature placed oil beneath the ground in many regions around the world and on every continent. One of the richest oil fields was in Baku, a much-contested trans-Caucasian realm on the Caspian Sea, considered Persian by some, Georgian by others, and Azerbaijani by its inhabitants. But in 1813,

Baku had been ceded by the Persian Shah to Czarist Russia. Baku had always been renowned for oil—seeping up from crevices and sometimes exploding into untapped gushers, hundreds of feet tall that easily ignited into fountains of fire. The city's very air was permeated with the sting of petroleum. Overhanging clouds of naphtha fumes constantly inebriated those who worked in or dwelled near the fields, creating a surreal oleic enclave.[16]

Baku's petroleum, though abundant, had always been a manual, hand-wrought industry. For centuries, petroleum effluent was carted off in buckets and baskets, and then channeled into holding tanks for transport to rudimentary, still-like refineries located nearby. One natural well, 100 feet deep, dates back to 1594. In the early 1800s, production in the area was merely several thousand tons per year. The first primitive oil drilling efforts are said to have occurred in 1844. In 1858, organized kerosene distillation began in Baku. But when Pennsylvania struck oil in 1859, it became cheaper to import high-grade American kerosene into Russia from across the ocean than to truck in the smelly product from Baku.[17]

In 1872, the czar broke with economic custom, releasing Baku from state control and allowing private entrepreneurs to drill using American techniques. Land was leased. Scores of wells were sunk around the perimeter of those land lots on the theory that a well would not only draw petroleum from beneath one man's acreage, but from his neighbor's as well. It was true. Every well drew from the common stratum underlying everyone's plots.[18]

Baku boomed. The Nobel brothers, famous for torpedo boats and dynamite, brought in modern oil techniques. What's more, they created an efficient distribution network that included pipelines, railroad tank cars, and storage bunkers, plus they commissioned the first oil tanker, named the *Zoroaster,* to transport their commodity across the Black Sea. Baku's population increased from 12,000 in 1870 to 100,000 in 1890, while production zoomed from 10,000 tons annually to 2.7 million tons by 1890. The intoxicating flammable was openly "cooked" in dozens of open refineries. Russian oil was challenging Pennsylvania's supremacy.[19]

The euphoric fumes of Baku attracted a young Turkish man late in 1890. The 22-year-old had been traveling for several weeks, first by ship from London to Istanbul, and from there by a long, arduous train trip to the trans-Caucasian region of Baku. Frequent stops along the way to discover local ethnic groups and their customs made the journey more exciting and tolerable. But the last 400 miles of mountainous terrain from the Black Sea seaport of Batum required a grueling 24-hour segment. Late in the day, the young man finally disembarked at Baku. When he arrived in the refinery district, he beheld a stark oilscape he called hideous. "Everything is black," he wrote in his journal, "the walls, the earth, the atmosphere, the sky. One feels the oil, breathes the vapors, the acrid smell seizes you by the throat … You walk among clouds of smoke that obscure the atmosphere." Indeed, that refining district was known as "the Black City." He called it "the kingdom of oil." [20]

Not long after the young man arrived, he experienced Baku's mythic temperament. The earth rumbled and shook, and then suddenly a giant atomized jet of black oil exploded high into the air, expelling dirt and rocks that fell into a berm around its portal. Even from a distance, the soaring oil reached him, bathing him from head to toe with a fine mist that trickled between his fingers and soaked into his shoes.[21]

Oil was now in his nostrils and lungs, streaming over his skin, and saturating his clothes. Soon oil would be in his blood. Oil would dominate the rest of his life, and in turn, during the next six decades, he would dominate the life of oil. The young man's name was Calouste Sarkis Gulbenkian. Ultimately, the mightiest oil conglomerates and the world's greatest nations would bow to his demands. All the oil in Mesopotamia, and nearly in the entire Mideast, would be controlled by him–not by virtue of any monopoly or majority, but by virtue of his powerful fraction and his tenacious personality. Called "incredibly cruel" by some of those closest to him, and a "mystery man" by many who later discovered his pivotal role, in the end, Gulbenkian was one thing above all: the legendary Mr. Five Percent.

*   *   *   *

Who was Gulbenkian?

The Gulbenkians were descended from Armenian nobility, tracing their roots back to the fourth century, to the feudal princes of Rechduni, who dwelled in the disputed Asia Minor land of Vaspurkan. Once Hittite, later Persian, and eventually the Roman province named Cappadocia, the region of Vaspurkan became one of the earliest realms of Christianity—even before Constantine declared it Rome's state religion. During the Christian Byzantine centuries, the family was known as "Vart Badrik." When the Ottomans conquered Cappadocia in the 1600s, the family name was Turkified to *Gulbenkian*. The Gulbenkians continuously intermarried among their own, creating a distinct Armenian clan.[22]

In the 1800s, the family business was typical of Armenian traders in the Ottoman Empire: the Gulbenkians bought and sold, operating as commercial functionaries and go-betweens. Calouste's uncle sold fine Oriental rugs. His father, Sarkis, became wealthy as a leading importer of Russian kerosene and as a collector of revenues in Mesopotamia for the Sultan's private treasury called the "Privy Purse" or the *Civile Liste*. The *Civile Liste,* that is, the Sultan's personal fortune, was distinct from the state treasury, although in the feudal Ottoman Empire, the two often intersected. For his service, the Sultan rewarded Sarkis with the governorship of Trabzon, the Black Sea capital that dominated the Eurasian trade bridge between Asia, the Caspian Sea, the Black Sea, and Asia Minor. Indeed, Gulbenkian's father controlled the kerosene markets of Baku and their provisioning to the Sultan—hence the Gulbenkian family's petroleum fortune.[23]

Calouste Sarkis Gulbenkian was born near Istanbul, in March 1869, almost 10 years after the modern oil industry was born in Titusville. As a boy, Gulbenkian was tutored in English and French, which he reasonably mastered. Of course, he was equally at ease speaking Turkish to the Ottoman society at large and Armenian to his family at home.[24]

Young Gulbenkian did not live an easy life. Schoolmates tormented him, calling him "spotty face," since the Turkified surname of Gulbenkian translated to "rose pimple." Sickly and unathletic, the withdrawn lad was thought by some to be a hypochondriac because he went to extremes to remain healthy. Gulbenkian took refuge in the bazaars, where he was surrounded by and took a liking to the art of sly deal making.[25]

At age 16, he was shipped off to Kings College in London, where in 1887 he earned a degree in civil engineering. Of course, Gulbenkian displayed a fascination for oil, coming from a kerosene-importing family. So his graduation thesis focused on petroleum engineering. His prediction about the future of oil exploration struck reviewers as nothing less than prophetic—not for any technological insights, which it lacked, but for its astute economic forecasts of world modernization.[26]

Early on, it became clear; Gulbenkian was destined to be an oil baron. He would not become a technocrat, that is, not a geologist, discoverer or driller. Rather, he would emerge as a magnificent go-between who would connect the wealth beneath the ground to needy consumers worldwide. In exchange, all he asked was to become fabulously wealthy.

To help him understand the family petroleum business, Gulbenkian's father sent him in 1890 on a long trip from his Kings College campus in London to the exotic oil fields of Baku. As he traveled, competing with Pennsylvania was certainly on young Gulbenkian's mind. He noted that the small Apcheron Peninsula, the seat of Baku, "consists of scarcely 2,000 square kilometers, yet annually produces almost half the quantity in all of America." But, he wrote in his journal, in spite of the progress made by the numerous wells managed by the Nobel brothers, most of the oil was still being wasted. Primitive methods, lack of management technology, and simple sabotage among rivals squandered too much oil. He contrasted Baku's situation to that of the United States, where "the American exploitation is admirably organized. There, not a drop of oil is lost."[27]

Gulbenkian concluded, "Let us hope that, in time, all these clouds will be dispelled and soon the oil of the Caucasus will triumph, as it deserves, over all its competitors in Asia and Pennsylvania."[28]

Gulbenkian was so enthusiastic about the prospects for Russian oil that he produced a series of articles on the subject for the eminent French magazine, *Revue des Deux Mondes*. Some months later, he organized his journal notes into a book, also written in French, detailing his colorful travels to Baku and his estimates for its great economic promise. His well-circulated writings included revealing geological findings assembled not by him but by others, since he had spent only a few days in Baku, with no time to conduct surveys. No matter, young Gulbenkian, barely 23 years of age, quickly became the foremost published expert on Russian and Eurasian oil.[29] Suddenly, Gulbenkian was in demand.Among the first to call was Hagop Pasha, the minister of the *Civile Liste*, a close Armenian friend of Gulbenkian's father, and Selim Effendi, the Turkish state minister of mines. The two officials jointly asked Gulbenkian to produce a comprehensive survey of the oil prospects for Mesopotamia. In 1892, Gulbenkian quickly cobbled together a highly polished report filled with geological specifics, engineering suggestions, and enticing economic projections—all based not on his own expertise but on morsels picked up from the unverified writings, observations, and conversation points of others. Later, Gulbenkian even bragged, "I elaborated a comprehensive report, which was nothing else than a compilation of various travelers' books … and particularly what I had heard from different engineers of the Anatolia Railway who had been in Mesopotamia." Ironically, Gulbenkian himself never set foot in Mesopotamia before his report—or after.[30]

Sultan Abdulhamid II, later known as "Abdul the Damned," enthusiastically received Gulbenkian's news that Mesopotamia might proffer great oil deposits. Anticipating that his land might hold petroleum riches, Abdulhamid had already begun quietly transferring masses of Mesopotamian land into his private treasury, that is, the *Civile Liste*, hoping to sell oil concessions. The first was on April 8, 1889, in preparation for a railway proposal. It covered "the whole province of Mosul." After Gulbenkian's promising report, Abdulhamid transferred vast additional sections of Mesopotamian land to the *Civile Liste*. Palace officials sent telegrams to the provincial governors advising that the Sultan wanted the lands for himself. In many cases, the governors filed *tapous*, that is, cadastral or land registry certificates, which formalize land ownership. No payment was required. The *tapous* were easy enough to file when done correctly. The mere filing of the paperwork created legal property rights—this in a region where land laws were obscure and known to very few. Peasants and most of the others who lived on Mesopotamian lands understood them the least. One day the lands were simply unregistered; the next day, Abdulhamid owned them by virtue of the *tapous*. Where others owned the lands that Abdulhamid desired, the palace requested a prompt sale. Their owners formally ceded such properties to Abdulhamid's royal estates for just a token fee.[31] Those secret land transfers created powerful billion-dollar factors in the subsequent disposition of the prodigious Mesopotamian petroleum rights and the determination of who actually owned the oil fields.

*   *   *   *

Like their other efforts to join advancing societies, the Ottomans were quite late in approaching the potential of modern oil exploration. For a full generation before Gulbenkian's report to the Sultan, the petroleum business had been thriving. Indeed, the formative late nineteenth-century decades of oil exploitation—and the industrial power and opportunity for wealth it conveyed—simply bypassed the Turkish regime and the Mideast lands it controlled.

The mighty industry created by the 1859 Titusville strike quickly spread to other American states, spawning a venous network of pipelines, railroad spurs, and horse-drawn wagon routes across America. Within about a decade, John D. Rockefeller became the richest man in the world by creating a conspiratorial trust made up of numerous secret corporations and fronts calculated to drive all competitors out of business. By the 1870s, his maze of Standard Oil enterprises controlled nearly all the refineries, pipelines, and other channels of distribution in the United States, as well as in several foreign lands. So immense was this one man's power that Congress took action to craft antitrust legislation with him in mind. The courts would later dismantle Rockefeller's empire into 22 smaller companies, although each resulting splinter was a giant commercial presence in its own right.[32]

Modern industrial oil operations soon appeared across the world. For example, in the Indian Ocean, the islands of Sumatra, Borneo, and Java were long known for medicinal oil seepages and hand-dug wells dating back a thousand years. A decade after Titusville, geologists counted no fewer than 44 seepages in Java alone, and by 1872, commercial drilling began. By 1890, with the blessing of the king of Holland, the Royal Dutch Oil Company had been founded as an international company to refine and sell Indonesian products, mainly kerosene.[33]

That same year, 1890, a British city alderman and exporter named Marcus Samuel, accustomed to shipping cheap knickknacks between Japan and Europe, stepped up to transporting a more lucrative commodity: petroleum. He built the world's first true oceangoing oil tanker to shuttle Baku crude from its outlet on the Black Sea, through Turkey's Bosphorus straits, into the

Mediterranean and then through the Suez Canal to ready markets in Singapore. Samuel was fascinated with the seashell-encrusted jewel boxes and trinkets he exported. So his first tanker was aptly named the *Murex*, after the murex seashell. The next three ships were named *Conch*, *Turbo*, and *Clam*. Soon he established a newly organized oil shipping company named Shell Transport and Trading. Shell began transporting Royal Dutch oil from Sumatra to destinations everywhere. The production-distribution partnership became so important that the two companies merged to become Royal Dutch Shell.[34]

Oil enterprises also appeared across Europe. In Poland, oil from the Carpathian Mountains had been used extensively since the 1500s, when the foul-smelling crevice seepage was scooped up and used to light streetlamps in the town of Krosno. In 1852, pharmacist and oil pioneer Ignacy Lukasiewicz began refining the seepage to create illuminants safe enough to light the interior of an entire Lvov hospital. In fact, it was the Polish petroleum guru Lukasiewicz who invented the cheap kerosene lantern that became a worldwide household appliance found everywhere, from the American prairies to the castles of Vienna. Soon, primitive Polish wells replaced handscooping. Lukasiewicz's first rudimentary refinery for seepage opened in 1859, the same year Titusville reinvented the oil industry with modern deep drilling. Poland quickly began using improved methods to exploit a large number of oil fields throughout Polish Galicia. By 1873, the fabulous oil district of Drohobycz alone was using enough American, Canadian, and native drilling technology to support 12,000 oil derricks. That year, some 900 companies and 12,000 individuals were engaged in Poland's oil industry. By 1857, the Carpathian oil that made Poland a famous petroleum center was also creating an industry in Romania that would be developed into the most bountiful oil deposits in Europe, centered in Ploiesti.[35]

In Australia, rich oil shale deposits were being mined and refined from the 1860s. Canada's thriving oil center in Petrolia, near Ontario, was engaged in commercial excavation of abundant seepages as early as 1858 and moved into advanced drilling about the time of Titusville's strike. By 1861, some 400 wells were operating in Petrolia. The next year, more than 100 powerful gushers had coated everything in town with oil. For the next decades, Canada derived some 90 percent of its household and industrial oil from this one center. Petrolia engineers then fanned out to develop similar finds in other distant parts of the world, such as the Gobi desert in China and regions of South America.[36]

In the early 1880s, the advent of Thomas Edison's electric lightbulb adopted immediately in North America and throughout Europe did nothing to slow petroleum's expanding market. True, by 1886, nearly 200,000 incandescent light bulbs were in use worldwide, and millions more soon after. This certainly reduced the need for illumination kerosene. But at that very time, horseless carriages, which had operated on steam and electric batteries for decades, were being outfitted with exciting new German-designed internal combustion machines. Those engines required fuel oil. An infant automobile industry was born and it would grow up rapidly.[37]

By 1890, when Gulbenkian arrived in Baku, the oil business was indeed a worldwide phenomenon—but not in the Middle East. Doing business in the region just seemed a barrier too high to hurdle. Systemic corruption and graft meant that business suitors approaching the authorities were compelled to grease a long line of outstretched palms, from the lowliest doorman to the aides and assistants of key advisors to ministers and finally to the monarchs themselves. Moreover, the lack of roads, railroad tracks, and other modern conveniences made every industrial endeavor trebly more expensive and daunting.[38]

It isn't that some did not dabble in the potential. By the 1870s, Russia's oil fields, including those in Baku, were challenging Standard Oil's supremacy in Europe. Russia's ascendancy in natural resources disrupted the strategic balance of power in Europe and troubled Britain. Preliminary British Geological Society observations, as early as 1855, suggested the vast Baku oil field might extend to neighboring Persia, located just to the south. Of course, those Persian bitumen seepages had been famous since antiquity.[39]

The first to try to establish a Middle East oil industry was Baron Julius de Reuter, founder of Reuters News Service. He approached the Shah of Iran in 1872. Reuter secured a notorious "exclusive concession" to develop a railroad, plus all riparian mining and mineral rights in the country, including oil, for the next 70 years. This was a virtual takeover of the main commercial future of the country. The price: a mere down payment of £40,000 plus a 20 percent cut for the Shah of the so-called "profits." The Shah took Reuter's money, but then almost laughingly frustrated all further efforts to acquire the development permits.[40]

Reuter's company protested: "It is obvious that in a country like Persia, with an autocratic government and all authority directly emanating from the Shah, no commercial enterprise of a new and strange [unusual] character can be profitably carried on." Instead of assistance to carry out the concession, "the Corporation meets with direct hostility," Reuter executives railed. Calling the whole endeavor "fruitless," Reuter demanded his money back, but the Shah was giving nothing back. Soon, an embittered Reuter dissolved his concern, and the London investment market quickly dismissed Persia as a completely unreliable kingdom for investment. Even the Foreign Office rebuked Reuter for wasting his time and money on Persia.[41]

In Turkish Mesopotamia, throughout the first half of the 1800s, the Ottomans had kept its three frontier provincial regions—Basra in the south, Baghdad in the mid-section, and Mosul in the north—socially and commercially undeveloped, with little attention to the needs of its inhabitants. The centu-ries-long process of self-inflicted ruin and incessant war expenditure and rep-arations had wrought the expected result. By 1875, after 14 foreign loans, the Ottoman Public Debt Administration was compelled to admit it could not repay its multimillion-pound obligations and the attendant debt service. The Ottoman Empire declared bankruptcy. The empire created a Public Debt Administration in 1881, employing some 5,000 revenue agents, who for-warded Turkish tax revenues directly to European creditors.[42] Consequently, there was little development in Mesopotamia—only the continued extraction of what value existed for tribute, tax, and foreign levy.

But there was a brief three-year period when Mesopotamia appeared ready to catapult into a golden age of reform and modernization. Midhat Pasha, a charismatic, youthful Turkish reformer, was determined to bring the empire into modern times with recognition of individual rights. For six months in the late 1850s, Midhat traveled to the great capitals of Europe, studying their con-stitutions and judicial systems. In 1860, Midhat pushed for similar reforms and modern advances throughout the Turkish provinces, from east to west. As governor of the Danube province of Nis, encompassing Bulgaria, he built some 2,000 miles of roads and 1,500 bridges within a short period of time. He erected schools and hospitals and brought that neglected territory into the nineteenth century.[43]

The palace was uncomfortable with Midhat's emphasis on service to the citizenry and emphasis on human rights. With typical Ottoman intrigue, Mid-hat was kicked upstairs, recalled to serve as a minister in Istanbul under the palace's close scrutiny, and then transferred to distant Mesopotamian prov-inces. Midhat arrived in Baghdad as governor on April 30, 1869. He immedi-ately permitted the establishment of *Al Zawra*, the first newspaper in Baghdad. Hence, several thousand years after Mesopotamia endowed the world with the gift of writing, its capital finally had its own printed newspaper. Midhat intro-duced land reforms that would allow peasants to register the lands they had lived on for generations, thus acquiring legal ownership. He tried to settle the traditionally nomadic tribes into villages and provide them with land rights as well. Land ownership would be inviolable and would pass from father to son as an inheritance. His efforts encouraged some tribes to abandon millennia of looting and wandering to enter a new way of life.[44]

Turning to health, Midhat insisted the Persians stop sending moist, freshly deceased corpses to Najaf for sacred Shi'a burial, this to reduce the risk of infection from decomposing bodies. He was willing to accept the bod-ies, but only after they had dried and reposed for a year. Determined to bring the provinces into the modern age, he built a tramway in Baghdad, plus an orphanage, factories, a hospital, a secondary school for boys, and other public institutions. Moreover, the outspoken Midhat openly criticized corrupt Ottoman administrators and successfully conspired with his fellow Young Turks to depose despotic officials—even those in the palace.[45]

Midhat was dangerous. In 1872, after only three years, his forward momentum in Baghdad was abruptly stopped. He was transferred to imperial positions in Istanbul and then moved from province to province. No matter. In 1876, he was determined to bring European democracy to the empire. Midhat was the chief architect of a revolutionary national constitution along the European model. On December 23, 1876, Sultan Abdulhamid was pushed, pressured, and cajoled into publicly accepting a sweeping, purely democratic constitution that promised to change everything Ottoman—from Basra to Bulgaria.[46] If successful, democracy would come to the Middle East and other Ottoman lands.

Midhat's constitution was a model of egalitarian democracy. Article 8: All subjects of the empire are without distinction called Ottomans no matter what religion they profess. Article 9: All Ottomans enjoy individual liberty so long as they do not attack the liberty of other people. Article 10: Individual liberty is absolutely inviolable. Article 12: The press is free. Article 17: All Ottomans are equal before the law. Article 22: The domicile is inviolable. Article 26: Torture in all its forms is completely and absolutely prohibited. In 119 terse articles, Midhat outlined complete separation of church and state and respect for all religions, while maintaining an Islamic national identity. Separation of powers between court, palace, and legislature, checks and balances, and the right of all men to live in freedom and equality were all guaranteed.[47]

Not stopping, Midhat challenged Abdul the Damned himself. Nothing less than total democracy would do—and quickly. About a month after the constitution was accepted, Midhat wrote a January 30, 1877, letter to Sultan Abdulhamid, chastising the royal reluctance to speedily inaugurate the reforms. "It is now nine days, Sire, since you have abstained from giving a favorable answer to my petition. You thereby refuse to sanction laws indispensable to the welfare of the country."[48]

Such impudence was intolerable to Abdulhamid. A few days later, the Sultan exiled Midhat, and then, once again, shuffled him from one temporary appointive position to another, from one territory to another. In 1881, Midhat was falsely tried for murder and conspiracy, but not imprisoned. The trial, however, gave Midhat a platform to denounce the inequities of the regime. Nothing would stop the visionary Midhat, who dreamed of an Ottoman Empire and a Middle East of freedom, enlightenment, and democracy. By 1884, Midhat had been removed to Taif, a distant province in the Arabian Peninsula. In May of that year, at age 72, Midhat suddenly died. At first, the palace declared that a terrible swift disease had struck Midhat.[49]

However, a few years later, a trusted sergeant of the Taif pashas came forward to reveal what he asserted was his eyewitness account. The sergeant confessed that he was instructed by the recently installed local governor, Muhammad Nuri Pasha, an official loyal to the Sultan, to summon Midhat to the Taif governor's private room. Midhat seemed to be unnerved by the unexpected request and muttered the classic Islamic prayer of distress: "There is no help nor strength except in the Almighty God." The prayer soothed him, and Midhat calmly accompanied the sergeant into the royal chamber. When Midhat entered, Governor Nuri was there to greet him. Six other soldiers were in attendance. Governor Nuri saluted Midhat and then exited. The door was locked.[50]

Midhat turned to the squad of soldiers and spoke calmly, with dignity, "You have been ordered to kill me, my children." He commonly referred to all citizens as "my children." They replied, "Yes, your excellency." The father of Turkey's brief march toward democracy was a man who stood for everything that could cure "the Sick Man of Europe." The once-mighty Ottoman Empire was dying of its own festering corruption, economic instability, popular unrest, political chaos, and endless warfare, hence its derogatory international label as "the Sick Man of Europe." As a regime addicted to its own self-destruction, it could not help but murder its best and brightest. Midhat rose above the fate inflicted upon him. The man who crusaded for the rights of all men, no matter how high or low, was profoundly pacific in his final moments. Midhat's serenity in the face of death overcame his executioners. The sergeant fought his tears, but still visibly wept. Midhat asked simply, "How am I to die?" The men replied, "The orders are by strangulation."[51]

Midhat promptly replied, "I die for my efforts to give you, my children, and all the people of the Empire, more liberty. Children, you can carry out your orders." As tears traveled down their cheeks, and after debating whether they could mutiny, the squad decided to obey the lawful order of Abdul the Damned. They carefully tied Midhat's hands and feet, and gently laid him on his back. Four men held him down. Two others then wrapped their hands around his neck, and strangled him until he breathed no more.[52] With this execution, the last chance for democracy in Mesopotamia was smothered as well.

Midhat's constitution, previously accepted, was now discarded as an inert document. Progress in Mesopotamia slowed to a crawl. Abdulhamid was now free to systematically usurp the land reform laws intended to benefit the common man. He used the registration laws to legally transfer vast oil-endowed provincial lands to the *Civile Liste*. The April 8, 1889, transfer of all of Mosul's oil rights and revenues was just the first. On September 24, 1898, Abdulhamid added all of Baghdad province.[53]

The Sultan was now ready for any business Gulbenkian cared to transact. The petropolitical Oil Age as we know it had been born. The company that became British Petroleum would become its godfather.

CHAPTER THREE

DUELING
MONOPOLIES

N o one will ever know the true legal owner of Mesopotamia's multibillion-dollar petroleum resources. Some almost owned it. Some should have owned it. Some believed they owned it. A few just demanded it.

Was the oil German? Was it British? Was it Turkish? Was it government-owned, corporately-owned, or privately owned? The answer is probably all of the above and none of the above. Mesopotamian oil was governed by the doctrine that possession is nine-tenths of the law. Still, it is the nagging tenth that haunts the millionaires, billionaires, and corporate heirs of Mideast oil who still wonder who the rightful owner is.

To be sure, a torturous cavalcade of near misses and "almost" ownerships played out for 15 years through the corridors of European commerce, diplomacy, and government. The combative claims and disputes zigzagged through the ever-shifting dunes of Ottoman legality amidst the ravages of an international bidding war, subtle deceptions, not-so-subtle blackmail, roller-coaster negotiations, moment-to-moment compromises that evaporated as soon as they were accepted, and the unpredictable and often unseen actions of one man: Calouste Sarkis Gulbenkian, Mr. Five Percent.

The tangled, confusing, seemingly impossible saga began as the twentieth century neared and as Europe slowly drifted toward a great war that many expected and all feared.

The Sick Man of Europe was on his deathbed. Throughout the last decades of the nineteenth century, the Ottoman Empire and its neighbors had been fighting one bloody war and one insurrection after another, from Bulgaria and Greece to Armenia and Russia. Turkish finances were a mirage of mirrors. The so-called "Eastern Question"—that is, who would inherit, lead, profit from, or be damaged by the inevitable collapse of the Ottoman Empire—was being answered simultaneously by all the leading European powers. They all had plans—and plans to realize their plans.

Some capitals wanted to dominate the soon-to-be dismantled territories as their own spheres of interest. Some merely wanted to prevent others from doing so. A few wanted to see new, friendly nations emerge in the aftermath of Turkey's disintegration. Certainly, local populations throughout the empire were rising up angry and demanding an end to their dynastic, ecclesiastic, and purely monarchial regimes. The seams of Europe were unraveling.

To keep them stitched together, endless overlapping alliances, pacts, and secret agreements were sewn among friends and enemies alike, as London, Paris, Berlin, Vienna, Moscow, and Istanbul tried to maintain the so-called balance of power in Europe. War was to be avoided because the rapid mechanical, scientific, and industrial advances of recent decades had created a new style of modern warfare that could kill millions. But if war could not be avoided, steeled preparation was needed.

Hence, as the nineteenth century drew to a close, Turkish Mesopotamia, and indeed the entire extended Middle East, suddenly catapulted in importance—especially to England. No longer were the three provinces of Mesopotamia considered mere transit corridors and geographic stepping-stones to India and Asia. Now Mosul, Baghdad, and Basra were coveted for their legendary but unexploited oil.

Quite simply, as the twentieth century opened for business, the world needed much more oil. Petroleum was no longer merely a fluid to illuminate lanterns, boil stew, and lubricate moving parts. Modern armies and navies demanded vast new supplies of fuel and petroleum by-products.

Among the first to recognize the need for fuel-burning vessels was Admiral John Fisher, a visionary British naval leader with a decidedly imperialistic outlook. He knew the future of England's navy lay in a fleet of swift battleships that could maneuver sharply and fire torpedoes and long-range guns from a distance. Speed required oil-burning vessels that could be refueled quickly and cleanly—even at sea. These advanced ships would make obsolete the messy coal-burning monstrosities that required throngs of sooty dockside laborers hefting coal baskets into holds and gangs of grimy, engine-room stokers. Fisher's revolutionary new battleships would be called *dreadnoughts*, and they would be the anchor of a rapidly expanding, well-financed modern

armada of fast and deadly vessels. Britain pursued a "two power" naval policy, that is, its fleet should be as large as the two next largest fleets combined.[1]
Only an oil-powered flotilla could achieve that.

As England's fleet needed oil, the prospects for finding it were troubling.
Baku's petroleum industry was certainly expanding and by century's end represented more than half the world's supply. It had already surpassed even
Standard Oil, which was suffering under legal restraints and now controlled
only 43 percent of the world market. Russian oil was dominant in Europe.
Royal Dutch Shell—still majority Dutch-owned—was also emerging. Germany had secured control over the vast fields of Romania. But Britain's new
source of supply could not be controlled by any potential adversaries, such
as Russia, which was expanding into Eastern Europe, or Germany, which
was threatening to sever the intercontinental routes held sacred by the British
Empire, or Holland, which even then was fighting the bloody Boer War with
England in South Africa.[2]

The most logical candidate for new source was, of course, the Persian
Gulf. Britain could have chosen the United States or Mexico or Poland as a
trusted new supplier. But Persia had been within the sphere of British influence since the days of the East India Company. Persia was halfway to India.
Persia it was.

Clearly, Persia had promise. Continuing geological exploration, such as
a two-year French government survey in the 1890s, suggested good deposits.
What's more, some in Britain harbored the mistaken impression that Baku's
massive deposits were soon to be depleted. A British diplomat in Teheran in
1890 was typical as he reported, "The virgin oil fields of Persia promise a good
fortune as they may be made to engage the whole of western markets in a short
time." Many of Russia's oil workers in Baku were actually trained Persians,
endowing Persia a ready source of semi-skilled workers. Consumption of household kerosene had doubled and tripled in some Persian towns in recent years.[3]

As the new century debuted, it was time to relegate to the past Baron de
Reuter's bad oil concession experiences with Persia. Representatives of the
cash-strapped, high-living Persian Shah, unable to secure a loan in any foreign bank, informed British diplomats that the kingdom was still interested in
selling a proper oil concession. With strategic military needs pressing, Britain
was eager to try anew.[4]

In 1900, Australian mining entrepreneur William D'Arcy heard of the
opportunity and stepped forward to take the risk. D'Arcy's representative had
suggested to the Persians that "an [oil] industry may be developed that will
compete with that of Baku." After paying several thousand pounds to all the
right go-betweens, D'Arcy secured a powerful and seemingly safe concession.
His concession, dated May 28, 1901, required that a functioning petroleum

company be founded within two years or the deal would be rescinded. To forfend a repeat of the Reuter debacle, the Persian government openly agreed to "take all necessary measures" to facilitate D'Arcy's exploration. For this arrangement, D'Arcy would pay the monarch £20,000 and sign over £20,000 in shares, but only after successful exploration justified a proper petroleum company. In addition, the Shah would receive 16 percent annually, but only from "net profits," a term which—conveniently—was never defined.[5]

The ornate concession document, replete with British consular service stamps certifying the French, English, and Persian translations, plus the shah's royal indicia interlaced with green knotted twine secured by sealing wax, granted D'Arcy the exclusive oil rights to all but the five northern provinces. To mollify Russia, these five provinces were excluded because they were too close to the neighboring Baku field. D'Arcy's concession would run 60 years—until 1961.[6]

Quickly, D'Arcy dispatched a geologist who confirmed the prior French estimates and reported "ample justification" to expect "a highly profitable industry of immense magnitude." Soon thereafter, cash-short D'Arcy made arrangements with Burmah Oil, a Scottish oil firm operating in India, to bring Polish, Canadian, Russian, and other workers to drill in the most promising Persian sectors.[7]

The work and terrain were dangerous and challenging. Since roads did not exist, D'Arcy's people built their own. Marauders were everywhere. D'Arcy paid volatile and scruffy Bahktiari tribesmen, bullet belts crisscrossing their waists and chests, to guard the riggers from attack. Sometimes their leaders failed to distribute the cash, causing more than one edgy encounter. But nothing could protect the drillers from the incessant fleas, foul water, and searing heat.[8]

Ironically, months before D'Arcy's experts began scrambling over the rough-hewn Persian valleys, Ottoman Sultan Abdulhamid's own expert, Paul Ghrostopnine, was undertaking a secret survey just over the border in Mesopotamia. Ghrostopnine left Istanbul for Mesopotamia on January 4, 1901. During the next weeks, he made careful assessments of the numerous existing but completely undeveloped bitumen wells throughout the three provinces. Many in the Mosul, Kirkuk, and Baghdad areas were so well endowed, oil pooled on the ground or gurgled beneath tributary creeks. "I have visited several oil wells all over the world, both before and after exploitation," Ghrostophnine reported enthusiastically, "but none of these have proved to be so rich ... I have never seen the like as yet." However, the existing surface-scooping operations were little more than anemic. One typical well's refining output was measured in "gallons per day," another in "donkey-loads per day."[9]

Abdul the Damned well understood that his lands might hold fabulous reserves of oil. But no effort was made to organize a national drilling enterprise or a Turkish petroleum company for the good of his nation. That would have taken much investment and long-term effort. Instead, the Sublime Porte, that is, the Ottoman Empire, opted to extract whatever value it could for the moment, thereby forestalling total economic collapse yet another day. Mortgaging the future and selling off segments of the realm was the Ottoman way. Oil wealth was not something to develop as a national treasure, but to auction off to industrial others.

Employing the tactics of the bazaar, the Sultan patiently, but excruciatingly, juggled the several offers before him, maneuvering for the best price. Many came calling. The Germans were especially interested and stepped forward as part of an effort to create a sphere of interest in Turkey. Kaiser Wilhelm's state visit to Istanbul in 1898—his second—was a momentous occasion for the Sultan. Abdulhamid staged enormous banquets wherever in the empire the Kaiser traveled. The Sultan even removed a section of Jerusalem's Old City wall to make way for Kaiser Wilhelm to enter on his magnificent white stallion. The cost of these festivities—a staggering 1 million Turkish pounds—prompted Ottoman government officials to protest, inasmuch as "civil and military officers are literally starving."[10]

The Ottoman Mining Law of 1882 and 1886 had undergone changes so that only narrow, one-year permits of research were issued—but these were not concessions, merely the bought-and-paid-for right to survey and return in a year for another round of tedious discussions and paid permits. Nonetheless, German interests applied for such rights. In 1888, the Deutsche Bank, working through its essentially captive Anatolia Railway Company, acquired a concession to build a short railroad line to Ankara in central Turkey. In 1902, this right was extended all the way through Mesopotamia to Baghdad and ultimately to Basra on the Persian Gulf. This railroad line was not seen by the European powers as a mere industrial improvement bettering transportation in the region, but also as a profound German military threat and a move to grab the region's oil. The railroad was seen as a land-based challenge to England's naval supremacy.[11]

Influential German writer Paul Rohrbach explained in his well-read pamphlet, *Bagdadbahn*, later expanded into a book of the same name, "England can be attacked and mortally wounded on land in Egypt. The loss of Egypt will mean to England not only the loss of control over the Suez Canal and its connections with India and Asia, but probably the sacrifice of its possessions in Central and Eastern Africa as well. Moreover, an Islamic power like Turkey could exercise a dangerous influence over England's 60 million Islamic subjects in India, Afghanistan and Persia, that is, if Turkey should conquer Egypt. However, Turkey can subjugate Egypt only if it possesses an extended system of railroads in Asia Minor and Syria, and if by an extension of the Anatolian Railway, it is able to ward off an English attack upon Mesopotamia."[12]

With the Baghdad railroad concession came mineral and oil rights extending 20 kilometers on either side of the track. About the still undeveloped Kirkuk oil fields, Rohrbach wrote: "We ought to attach the greatest importance to the circumstance that the Baghdad Railway will pass close to the petroleum districts. The only thing to be feared is ... foreign speculators securing a preferential right in the exploitation of Mesopotamian naphtha before any effective German initiative."[13]

Britain followed every vicissitude of German and Russian expansion into the Ottoman Empire and the wider Middle Eastern region. London undertook strategic precautions and counterchecks everywhere it could. For example, in late 1898 and early 1899, the German Kaiser tried to assist Abdulhamid in reasserting control over Kuwait, a distant and only nominally Ottoman territory in the Gulf. To thwart that, on January 23, 1899, the British sealed a pact with the Kuwaiti Sheikh. In exchange for a one-time British payment of 15,000 Indian rupees, the Sheikh agreed not to transfer or lease any part of his territory without London's approval. As part of the pact, India would send troops should the Turks attempt to invade. Kuwait became a British protectorate, and remained one for more than 60 years.[14]

Pacts and political promises were only part of the *realpolitik* of the day. The beginning of the twentieth century was so serpentine a period in Europe that the great powers also found it expedient to project their power and interest via strictly commercial corporations. Hence, the Deutsche Bank's Baghdad Railway project, through the Anatolia Railway Company, was little more than a surrogate for imperial Germany. In fact, in 1903, the Anatolia Railway Company restated its rights in an actual treaty, the 1903 Baghdad Railway Convention. Article 22 specified the mineral rights. This then elevated the commercial agreement to an international covenant.[15]

The next year, in 1904, Abdulhamid's *Civile Liste* bestowed upon the Anatolia Railway far more than the original 40-kilometer corridor. It granted a one-year research permit for any oil in the provinces of Mosul and Baghdad. The railway's concession was promptly transferred to the true owner: Deutsche Bank. If oil were to be discovered, a 40-year concession would be activated.[16] With that concession, Mesopotamian oil seemed destined to be German.

However, while Germany was securing the vast oil resources of Mesopotamia, Britain's thirst for naval fuel only magnified. In 1903, Admiral Fisher, increasingly known as the "oil maniac," headed up the Admiralty's Oil Fuel Committee. That body later declared it "inexpedient to depend in peace time upon resources which would probably fail in wartime." Moreover, when Fisher became First Sea Lord, he commissioned a number of oil-only destroyers and torpedo boats, again increasing England's strategic requirement for petroleum.[17] But the source for all this needed oil was still unknown.

Meanwhile, D'Arcy's company had made little progress in Persia. He was running out of money, time, and patience in the struggle to bring in a gusher. Fisher met D'Arcy quite by accident while the two were visiting a Czech medical facility, and their oil interests naturally blended. D'Arcy wanted cash from the Admiralty to prop up his failing enterprise. Fisher wanted the oil. But after several applications by D'Arcy, the Admiralty declined because D'Arcy's efforts were simply too speculative. He had not yet brought in even one well. Instead, the Admiralty reached out to its existing contacts with Burmah Oil, a proven oil-producing concern. Burmah was already working with D'Arcy in Persia in the exploration effort. So the British navy, in late 1905, awarded Burmah a lucrative fuel contract for its existing oil in India, and then encouraged Burmah to take over in Persia as well. With enough lawyers, bankers, and official sponsorship, that happened. Burmah now pursued the Persian project, with D'Arcy scheduled to receive a cash settlement should the project achieve success.[18]

In 1904, D'Arcy was fundamentally out of the Persian project and, therefore, free to make new inquiries in Mesopotamia. He had tried and failed once before. In late 1901, just after signing the Persian concession, D'Arcy's negotiator had hoped to seal a similar agreement in Istanbul. He was unsuccessful. Now, three years later, D'Arcy received secret Foreign Office encouragement to try again and this time to secure for Britain a concession from the Sultan calculated to undercut the Deutsche Bank and Anatolia Railway. D'Arcy sent his trusted agent, Herbert Nichols, to Istanbul.[19]

Anatolia Railway's oil concession contract was issued on July 17, 1904. Within a week, D'Arcy's chief negotiator, Nichols, petitioned the palace in the saccharine idiom of concession seekers: "Your Majesty's only endeavor, since His accession to the Imperial Throne, has been the progress of trade and industry, the increase of the prosperity and richness of His vast country. Since that happy day [of the Sultan's accession], so much has been done to this effect and consequently we humbly pray you let us give our humble help to your Imperial projects by granting us the right of working, through a new Ottoman corporation, to be floated by us, the mines of Mosul and Baghdad, from which up to now no benefits or profits have been drawn."[20] Fawning was a language the palace understood.

Nichols's supplication went on to promise exploration within two years, and if successful, a going concern shortly thereafter would export petroleum, generating vast wealth for all. If given permission for the privilege of exploration, the offer promised that "the sum of three million francs would be paid to the Ministry of the *Civile Liste*, half (say 1.5 million) in cash and half (1.5 million) in shares of the new corporation. As a guarantee, a sum of 250,000 francs will be paid the Ministry of the *Civile Liste*" immediately upon signature. The

Civile Liste was the Sultan's personal treasury. Should the new company not come to pass, the Sultan could keep the down payment. Once petroleum was being pumped, 15 percent of the oil or its value would be kicked back to the *Civile Liste*, that is, to Abdulhamid. This deal would continue for 60 years, thus considerably multiplying the Sultan's wealth, now and for his subsequent generations.[21]Clearly, this was a good deal.

But the Germans and their Anatolia Railway had already been granted the oil rights in Mosul and Baghdad on July 17, 1904—just days earlier. No matter. Palace officials scrutinized the language of the Anatolia agreement, taking special note of Article 1, which required drilling studies to take place within one year, and these to be forwarded to the Ministry of the *Civile Liste*. In the bazaar, all things come to he who is patient. Abdulhamid was patient.

Conditions in Mesopotamia were challenging. Communications and connections were poor. Anatolia Railway knew trains, not oil wells. Organizing industrial exploration and proper geological studies would not be easy or expeditious. As expected, Anatolia Railway was a little late. But late they were. However, the Ministry was on time. One year and a week after the July 17, 1904 agreement was signed, Minister of the *Civile Liste* Ohannès Effendi Sakisian dispatched a carefully worded letter to the Anatolia Railway Company.[22]

"Following the settlement of the Agreement concluded with your honorable management," wrote Sakisian, "you were required within one year's time to undertake the necessary studies related to the petroleum deposits in the provinces of Baghdad and Mosul, and then confirm to the Minister of the *Civile Liste* that a technical Commission has been directed to the sites for studies." That was not done. But just in case it had been done, nothing was actually submitted to the Ministry as the agreement called for. Therefore, Sakisian cleverly added, "Even if the necessary studies have been done, the set time limit has already passed—and the result has not been communicated to our Ministry as of today."[23]

True, Anatolia Railway was late. But the company had been earnestly working on the project with an international team of experts. Mail and other communications between Europe and Mesopotamia were slow. On September 4, 1905, several days after getting the unexpected letter from the *Civile Liste*, Anatolia's assistant general manager replied with a degree of honest enthusiasm. He attached a just-received and encouraging letter from their chief geologist. "We have the honor to bring to your Excellency's attention," the railway director wrote, "a letter that we have just received from Professor Dr. Porro, chief specialist of the mission sent to Mesopotamia to evaluate the petroleum deposits and their future exploitation. Only now, after enormous difficulty and long delays, have the geologic and other samples, numerous and heavy, arrived in Europe."[24]

The railway director explained, "The original [one-year] timeframe determined at the outset was too short." He continued, "Because of its great importance ... all samples will be analyzed with minute care, and the supplementary studies which these analysis require will be carefully assessed by the knowledgeable specialists." The railway almost routinely requested an additional "ten to twelve months."[25]

That was a mistake. Sakisian was unyielding. Where were the reports? He began papering the file to demonstrate a breach. "I request that you send me the reports concerning the petroleum deposits of the regions of Baghdad and Mosul, so that my Department can study the results of the studies ... this based upon the written and executed terms of the Agreement relating to these deposits."[26]

Meanwhile, the British were finding more reasons to believe Mesopotamia would be their best source for oil. The Persian project in 1905 was floundering beneath burning deserts, swarms of gnats, and swirling dust storms, yielding dry hole after dry hole. At the same time, esteemed Foreign Office official Mark Sykes filed a secret and very enthusiastic summary of commercial, geological, and economic forecasts, titled *The Petroliferous Districts of Mesopotamia*, in which he asked Britain's consuls in the region to preempt other European competitors.[27]

The world may have been frantically seeking oil. But negotiations in the Ottoman Empire progressed glacially. Tedious correspondence and evidentiary papers to document a breach were needed because foreign corporations in the Ottoman Empire were more than mere associations of businessmen; they were surrogates for and protectorates of their foreign offices. Moreover, the Ottomans observed a "capitulation" system that basically created detached colonies of foreign businessmen, dwelling and dealing within the empire but virtually immune from Ottoman jurisdiction. Some called these "capitulation communities" an empire within an empire. Indeed, all foreign businessmen relied on pressure tactics from their foreign offices, as well as competent attorneys who were quite capable of litigating against the Ministry for the *Civil Liste*. Upon judgment, any victorious plaintiff could join the many creditors seizing and sometimes controlling Ottoman assets, debt, taxes, and duties.[28]

Lacking the funds and the studied geologic proof of exactly where to drill, the Germans, in 1906, were now biding their time. They tried not to respond to *Civil Liste* pressures to admit that the concession had been breached. But the demands from Ottoman officials kept coming.[29]

In late July 1906, the *Civile Liste* sent yet another careful, self-serving letter to the Anatolia Railway Company, this one reminding, "As stipulated in Article 1 of the preliminary agreement concluded and exchanged with your management ... concerning the petroleum deposits in the regions of Mosul and Baghdad, the necessary studies and statements were to be completed in a timeframe of one year ... and all the results of these studies ...were to be made available in detail to my Department. I hereby [again] request ... that you send me the related reports and documents." Noting Anatolia's silence and failure to respond to the previous letter, the Ottoman letter warned, "My Ministry has the power to authorize a different exploitation of the deposits in question, if your Company no longer wishes to do so ... Let me know, as soon as possible, and formally, if your management will or will not undertake the exploitation of the deposits in question."[30]

Several more demand letters were sent, but Anatolia remained mum until August 22, 1906. Anatolia cautiously replied that it had received a positive and promising expert analysis and was now sharing a copy of those results with the Ministry as required. But before proceeding with additional investment, new assurances were needed. "The expenses for this expedition were 340,000 francs," Anatolia advised, and test drilling based on the preliminary geologic analyses would cost much more. "Our Company can only take on this heavy job after the establishment of an equitable accord between the *Civil Liste* and our company."[31]

The *Civile Liste* seemed determined to disallow the German concession and maneuver for a better offer from the British. It rejected the German-language studies and messengered them back unread, insisting, "They must be translated into Turkish and French." At the same time, the *Civile Liste* demanded a whole new contract to replace the old concession agreement. Puzzled, the German group simply did not know what to do. Mesopotamian petroleum deposits were fabulously valuable. The reports proved that. So the German company's attorneys drew up another proposed contract, this one upping the offer by virtue of a new company worth 12.5 million francs. At incorporation, 2,100 shares would be issued and 1,400 of these would be allocated to the *Civile Liste* to extract annual profit.[32]

Not good enough. The *Civile Liste* replied in January 1907, formally notifying Anatolia that the time for talk was over. There would be no further negotiation. Their concession had been officially "abrogated." Anatolia's representatives shot back a letter reminding the palace that it had already spent 340,000 francs on a preliminary survey, moved as expeditiously as science would permit, and from the company's point of view, "Our rights ... are still intact and we can exercise all powers in those rights."[33] The Germans were not giving up their oil without a fight.

Legally, however, Anatolia Railway was weak. *Civile Liste* officials had sufficiently papered the file to show protracted noncompliance over a period of many months. Confidently, the Sultan's people sent Anatolia a curt note calling its claims "pretentious" and dismissing the 1904 concession for Baghdad and Mosul as completely "null and void."[34]

Meanwhile, D'Arcy's people, ever trying to finalize their offer, also encountered frustration after frustration. Nichols was said to be "still hammering away at the Mesopotamian oilfields, but [just] as he is on the point of closing, something [always] goes wrong and the *Civile Liste* slips out."[35]

In the wings were other smaller venture groups from the United States and Europe. These syndicates and venture capitalists were vying for a concession as well.[36] It seems many were laying claim, or hoping to lay claim, to the same oil deposits. Yet no one was successful.

But the more suitors who came knocking, the more the Sultan knew he possessed an extraordinarily valuable property, and the more the stakes were raised. Abdulhamid sensed he needed to wait out the offers, allowing the several competitors to continuously outbid each other. Moreover, the longer Mesopotamian petroleum was not extracted from the ground, the more valuable it became. Europe was edging toward war. Abdulhamid understood that he owned what the great powers needed—oil. The longer he delayed, the more it all appreciated, and the more precious his oil became.

Following developments closely was the cleverest of them all: Gulbenkian. Family friends controlled the Ministry of the *Civile Liste*. Since the turn of the century, Gulbenkian had been working with the Royal Dutch Shell companies as they expanded into Baku and other territories. Now, in 1907, he convinced Royal Dutch Shell to enter the Mesopotamian oil fray. The bazaar always craves more bidders. Royal Dutch Shell opened an office in Istanbul as Gulbenkian suggested, and they appointed as director none other than Gulbenkian.[37]

Gulbenkian later wrote that during these years, "Solid foundations were laid for keeping prices high and assuring big profits."[38] He now felt certain he could create an enormous monopoly in Mesopotamia—one step at a time.

As Gulbenkian was edging Shell in, and as the exasperated Germans were trying to understand why their generous offers were being spurned, the *Civile Liste* was meeting with D'Arcy's representative Nichols to iron out the most lucrative offer yet. In previous exchanges, the escalating down-payment demands had been fixed at 50,000 Turkish pounds and later inflated to 80,000. Now, on August 27, 1907, *Civile Liste* negotiators offered Nichols something new. Upon signature, the *Civile Liste* would receive 100,000 Turkish pounds "as an advance," but, also, a generous royalty per 1,000 kilos of oil, paid twice annually—regardless of profit, net or gross. Moreover, the Sultan was offering only a narrow, nine-month option, after which a new concession would have to be renegotiated.[39]

The latest offer was too rich for D'Arcy. For several months, the matter was discussed with no resolution. In December 1907, Nichols returned to London empty-handed, hoping to return one day soon to secure a Mesopotamian concession that was affordable and reasonable.[40]

At 4 A.M., May 26, 1908, everything changed. Exploration in Persia was about to be canceled for lack of results and the utter depletion of operating cash. But just as the enterprise was folding and staff being dismissed, Burmah Oil's drill at the Masjid-i-Suleiman site pierced beyond 1,180 feet of desert strata. The bore unleashed a monster gusher rising 75 feet toward the sky, soaking everything with black gold. D'Arcy, waiting years to be reimbursed for his investment, declared, "If this is true, all our troubles are over." Several months later, additional wells came in, including a sudden, unexpected, and bounteous oil spout on September 18. A new corporation named the Anglo-Persian Oil Company was created. Excitement on London's financial markets could barely be contained. All available shares were purchased within 30 minutes.[41] Britain was now assured of an abundant supply of Mideast petroleum.

Throughout 1908, the dynamics of regional oil played out. Did the Persian oil strike outmode the quest for Mesopotamian oil, or merely increase the frenzy to find it? Some could have easily argued that Anglo-Persian's oil was the answer to Britain's needs. On the other hand, abundance in business rarely satiates—it only whets the appetite for more.

The promising Mosul and Baghdad fields were, after all, just miles from the lush Persian fields. If the British did not control those fields, who would? The Germans? The French? The Russians? If the British did control them, England would possess a monopoly on the enormously wealthy deposits across an entire region. Moreover, a pipeline could transit Persia directly to the Turkish ports on the Mediterranean, avoiding the perilous mountain route to the Gulf. Hence, Mesopotamia remained directly in London's sight-line even as England sped toward a feared armed conflict with its rivals over the Eastern Question and any number of linked crises.

The equation was sudden altered again that year when, in the summer of 1908, Turkish agitators in Greece rose up against the Sultan. Since the days of Midhat Pasha and his visionary but stillborn constitution in 1876, the flame of reform had been kept alive in secret Ottoman societies. Most of these reformers were military men and oppressed Christians in distant provinces, or disillusioned ex-patriots who had settled throughout Europe. All were determined to end the generation-to-generation corruption of the sultanate and the unending decay of the empire. Various dissident groups coalesced into the Committee of Union and Progress. One of the Parisian groups published a journal that became emblematic of the movement. The journal was named *La Jeune Turquie*—The Young Turk.[42]

By the early years of the century, many of these "Young Turks," especially those in Salonica, Greece, became convinced only a coup could save Turkey. Indeed, several attempts had been aborted. But by 1908, the agitators believed they were finally ready. They focused on September 1, the anniversary of

Abdulhamid's accession. But rumors and leaks again compromised their plans. Instead, a bloodless coup was staged in the summer. Reformist pashas invaded the ministries to place them on a businesslike basis. A key demand made of the Sultan was to restore Midhat Pasha's 1876 constitution, and the parliament. Abdul the Damned told the militants he had always intended to do so—of course. Now was a perfect time. In July, he reintroduced the constitution and the parliament with great fanfare as though they were his long-delayed pet projects. That only bought him some time. The Sultan remained in an imperial limbo even as the entire Ottoman government was being resculpted in the image of reform, union, and progress.[43]

The Sick Man was going through a new stage. The Young Turks were eager to cement intelligent commercial and military alliances in Europe that would strengthen the empire. That meant closer strategic economic and military cooperation with Germany.

London's concerns were summarized precisely in one key dispatch from the British embassy in Istanbul to British Foreign Secretary Edward Grey: "During the last few years," the embassy stated, "our policy, if I may call it so, in Turkey has been, and for some time to come will be, to attempt the impossible task of furthering our commercial interests while pursuing a course ... which the Sultan interprets as preeminently hostile in aim and tendency. These two lines are diametrically opposed and consequently incompatible with one another. In a highly centralized theocracy like the Sultanate and Caliphate combined, with its pre-economic conceptions, every big trade concession is regarded as an Imperial favor to be bestowed on the seemingly friendly, a category in which, needless to say, we are not included."[44] As the Sultan was being dislodged from power, even if not from his throne, the Turkish tendency to sidestep Britain intensified.

An idea emerged at Whitehall: the National Bank of Turkey. In reality, this financial institution would be neither Turkish nor national. Instead it would be a commercial creature of Britain's projected foreign policy, employing British money, managed by Britons, and operating for British interests. Similar banks had been created during the previous century in Teheran with the British-owned and -operated Imperial Bank of Persia, which was a by-product of Reuter's debacle. British financiers had also established the Egyptian National Bank in Cairo as part of its sphere of influence at the Suez Canal.[45]

Now, in November 1908, the Foreign Office brought together a number of influential British businessmen to found yet another "national bank" in the Near East, this one, the National Bank of Turkey. Private by all its paperwork, this bank was strictly tied to official British desires. "It seems to me very desirable that there be an independent British financial interest in Constantinople [Istanbul]," wrote Foreign Secretary Grey as the bank was being established.

The Foreign Office asked Henry Babington-Smith to resign from his current position with the post office to become the new bank's director. Babington-Smith carried fiscal gravitas in Istanbul since he was formerly the British representative on the Ottoman Public Debt Administration. The internationally recognized businessman and diplomat, Sir Ernest Cassel, became president. Such eminent men as Lord Revelstoke and Lord Farrington joined as principal financial backers. The main office address was 50 Cornhill, located in a well-known London banking district.[46]

But now Britain needed a fixer, someone with good Turkish connections. That would be Gulbenkian, now living in London and a naturalized British subject since 1902. Gulbenkian regularly circulated among a monied crowd as a result of his close associations with Shell. Moreover, Gulbenkian was, at that very time, serving as a financial consultant to both the Paris and London embassies of the new Ottoman government. He was placed on the bank's board. Soon, Gulbenkian became more than just a notable board member—he emerged as a central figure in the structure and operation of the bank.[47]

At first, there was much discussion about financing for many noble and profitable projects in Mesopotamia, such as irrigation canals, a tramway in Baghdad, and electrical grids, as well as municipal bonds for Istanbul and Baghdad. These loans would only enhance Britain's standing, especially in the reshaping and reform-minded empire dominated by a coterie of Young Turks and technocrat pashas. Ultimately, some of these loans were finalized, providing the bank with a profitable loan repayment stream. But quickly, Gulbenkian's attention turned to Mesopotamian oil. Gulbenkian contacted his friends at Shell and asked them to apply for the concession, since a new administration was in power. During 1908, Shell sought Foreign Office support for the move.[48]

But the Foreign Office was put off. Royal Dutch Shell, even though partly owned by Londoner Marcus Samuel and run by Dutch citizen Henri Deterding, was still considered an alien company. Only 40 percent of its stock was actually British-owned, with the 60 percent majority owned and controlled by Dutch interests represented by Deterding. An unreceptive Foreign Office dismissed Shell executives, asking them to scrap their own initiative and instead work with the Anglo-Persian Oil Company. The government explained it had been backing Anglo-Persian for years.[49]

Meanwhile, the Young Turks and their Committee of Union and Progress were rapidly reorganizing the entire Ottoman government along twentieth century lines. By October 1908, the Committee of Union and Progress made clear its priority to deprive Abdul the Damned of the many properties transferred to his *Civile Liste*. These included the Mesopotamian oil concessions. Encouraged, D'Arcy's group elected to start all over again and negotiate with what they hoped would be level-headed bureaucrats. D'Arcy's agent contacted the Ministry of Mines.[50]

But the newly empowered pashas who had taken over the government were not certain exactly which ministry should acquire the sultan's oil concessions. Should it be the Ministry of Mines, the Ministry of Public Works, or the Ministry of Finance? Moreover, a vexed Ministry of the *Civile Liste* complained that some of its properties could not be legitimately transferred to governmental ownership for disposition because preexisting concessions, debt, and other obligations encumbered them. Perfect examples were the oil assets, which included the Anatolia agreements, that is, both the contested 1904 concession and the earlier and completely uncontested mineral rights grant within the 40-kilometer railway corridor. Indeed, those 40-kilometer rights were enshrined under international law in the Baghdad Railway Convention.[51]

With the oil properties soon to be—but not quite yet—transferred out of the Sultan's hands, a new impetus for a fast deal gripped the parties. Possession was still nine-tenths of the law. In February 1909, the oil concession reclaimed from the Germans, desired by the Dutch and Americans, but still possessed by Abdulhamid, was available to the British—for the right price. The new terms: 10,000 Turkish pounds up front, a so-called loan of 100,000 Turkish pounds, plus a 15 percent cut of the net profits, defined simply as revenues minus working costs, plus fixed depreciation and other itemized costs. The exploration period would be two years.[52]

D'Arcy's agents, jointly with Anglo-Persian Oil Company negotiators, moved quickly now. After some casbah haggling, a new contract was drawn up March 11 securing a four-year exploration period and dividing the demanded "loan" of 100,000 Turkish pounds into two phases—half now and half after oil was struck.[53]

Deal.

The Grand Vizier, that is, the Ottoman prime minister, approved as well, thus signifying governmental acceptance. On April 13, 1909, applications were filed for the Sultan to sign the actual decree. Those were approved. Finally, after years of exasperation and maneuvering, the Mesopotamian oil fields were to be Anglo-Persian's and Britain's. The next day, April 14, 1909, the minister of the *Civile Liste* and the Grand Vizier assembled all the paperwork and scheduled an immediate visit to Abdulhamid's office to obtain his signature.[54]

However, everything was now moment to moment. For days, Istanbul, the foreign press, and the great capitals of the world were burning with wild reports that Abdul the Damned would soon be deposed and perhaps even put to death. So many thousands of palace spies patrolled so many institutions throughout the empire that military men and government officials were afraid to smile at each other, lest they be accused of conspiracy. The nervous Sultan, his dry, wrinkled, and worried face a living banner for the anxious moment, took refuge behind a corps of 16,000 ethnically diverse bodyguards stationed throughout his palace grounds. Yet undeterred rebel soldiers kept streaming into the capital pledging a bloody confrontation and a coup. Some swore to hang the tyrant from the lamppost outside his palace. Others wanted him tried for corruption. Still others were readying a pro-palace mutiny to maintain the status quo. Intrigues were everywhere, as revolution and counter-revolution edged toward an explosion.[55]

April 14, 1909, documents were readied. The Grand Vizier was prepared. The Sultan was ready to sign. The Foreign Office continuously monitored reports by telegraph. Anglo-Persian emissaries waited in suspense.[56]

But riots broke out in the city early in the day and could not be contained. Thousands of soldiers loyal to the Sultan stormed into the main square. The counter-revolutionary mob invaded parliament and killed two deputies. Young Turks moved against them in armed conflict. The palace locked down. Nothing came in or out.[57]

Anglo-Persian's all-important oil documents were not signed.[58]

In the days that followed, Istanbul deteriorated into complete chaos as contending armies and political factions clashed, and the fate of the barricaded Sultan changed hour to hour. Germany, France, and Great Britain dispatched warships to protect their interests and their citizens. Day after day dragged on, and Anglo-Persian's documents were still not signed. All parties tensely hoped to just wait out the crisis. At the time, Abdulhamid was rumored to be hiding in the British embassy—no, the Russian embassy—now it was the French Embassy—no, actually on a warship steaming away from Turkey. In fact, he was cowering in the palace, where food and electrical supplies had been cut off by the plotters in an effort to starve the royal household into surrender.[59]

On April 27, after tense negotiations between the angry factions, revolutionaries finally broke into the beleaguered palace. There they found a trembling Abdul the Damned, surrounded by 20 black eunuchs, pathetically pleading for his life. It was agreed not to execute the Sultan who had executed so many thousands, nor even to subject him to a divisive trial. Instead, Abdulhamid would simply be dethroned and exiled with his several wives to a small villa in Salonica. His harem would be dispersed. The chief eunuch would be hung from a local bridge for all to see. Abdul the Damned's personal fortune—some guessed it to be $25 million, others guessed $200 million—was reclaimed. "His property, acquired illegally, will be confiscated by the state," the new Turkish prime minister declared to reporters. Within days, the billion-dollar oil properties were transferred to the Ministry of Finance.[60]

Yet from the Anglo-Persian point of view, the company had a bankable deal. True, the decree had not been signed that April 14, 1909. But the lawful owner of the moment, the Sultan, had come to final terms, confirmed by the prime minister, and the agreement was scheduled for execution, this only as a formality. Once the shouting subsided in Istanbul, Nichols and his group reapplied to the new possessor, the Ministry of Finance. The officials there, eager to industrialize the empire, saw the wisdom of Anglo-Persian's contract. A government analysis had confirmed that the deposits were probably superior to those in Baku and even America. In late June, ministerial officials agreed to resurrect the contract. A number of verbal assurances to finalize were exchanged in both directions, and it seemed Anglo-Persian finally had the oil.[61]

Just one thing. The newly appointed finance minister requested, from among all these rivers of oil, the "reservation of a few springs for government purposes." A few springs? That is not how oil exploration and geological strata work. Anglo-Persian objected and the fractious debate over terms resumed. But the contract terms were quickly tweaked until both sides accepted them. Now in July, verbal assurances were again conveyed that the matter was final, once and for all, and ready to be granted—this time for sure.[62]

Just one other thing. Following the avarice and corruption of the Sultan, contracts would now be let on an open and progressive administrative basis. Under the new mining law, the concession would have to be advertised in the newspapers for 30 days to allow others to bid. That would necessitate a three-month procedural delay. Advertising? Anglo-Persian saw its carefully negotiated plan unraveling yet again. Company negotiators protested strenuously, but the concession opportunity was subjected to public advertising as a sign of open government. The sole redeeming advantage, by agreement, was that only sealed bids would be accepted.[63]

As feared, a flood of fresh offers and exhumed claims began pouring in: from Romania, America, England, and from within the empire. A gallery of individuals, syndicates, aristocrats, and corporations coveted the oil.[64]

Moreover, the Germans and the Anatolia Railway demanded that their original rights be recognized. The Ministry of Finance reviewed Anatolia's files and declared the demand baseless. Actually, the Germans knew their claim was flimsy because they had, in fact, exceeded the time limit. One telling letter exchanged between railway officials in Berlin and Istanbul confidentially confessed, "Legally, our rights to the petroleum wells are very weak." But Anatolia kept up its staunch argument. On August 4, 1909, Anatolia threatened legal action if the Ottoman government did not confirm the railway's concession within 15 days.[65]

Just when it seemed the bedeviled concession competition could become no more complex, it did. Things were happening in London.

*   *   *   *

Winston Churchill's zeal for oil exceeded Admiral Fisher's.

Churchill had become intimately familiar with the commercial thickets surrounding oil during his stint from 1908 to 1910 as president of Britain's Board of Trade. In late October 1911, Churchill became First Lord of the Admiralty, where he intensified the race to build more ships, all faster and more powerful, all of them oil guzzlers.

When Churchill arrived at the Admiralty, he discovered that some 189 vessels, from torpedo boats to dreadnoughts, had been or were being built, every one fueled by oil, not coal. Those ships—let alone the new ones envisioned—would consume more than 200,000 tons of oil annually. Yet Britain possessed a mere four-month reserve.[66]

Anglo-Persian's oil venture was making progress. But it was hardly a reliable source. True, eight wells were pumping. But a working refinery was still needed. Construction on the refinery at Abadan on the Persian coast began in 1910. But would that refinery distill kerosene for stoves, fuel oil for battle cruisers, or some of both? It all depended on the market and contracts. A gargantuan, nearly 150-mile pipeline was being constructed to link the distant oil wells with that refinery. Sixty miles of 5-inch pipe and 80 miles of 8-inch pipe had been ordered, and these would be erected by backbreaking labor under heatstroke conditions, 16- and 22-foot segments at time. Erratic personnel, periodic worker rebellions, management conflicts, engineering problems, construction mishaps, and an unexpectedly smelly and sulfurous crude oil, not to mention gnats and dysentery, plagued the entire project, from wellhead to refinery. The oil business entailed more than just bringing in a gusher. Oil: Anglo-Persian had it. But now it lacked the cash and investors to pump it, pipe it, refine it, and then ship it to market and siphon off a profit.[67]

In December 1911, Churchill summoned a departmental oil committee to forecast the Navy's needs. Estimated 1912 consumption was fully 225 times that of a decade earlier. Moreover, the study committee concluded that at least a one-year reserve supply was needed to sustain fleet operations. But where was this fuel to come from? Churchill established a more sweeping Royal Commission on Fuel and Engines and appointed the recently retired oil maniac himself, Fisher, to locate that fuel.[68]

In June 1912, Churchill wrote, "My Dear Fisher ... You have got to find the oil: to show how it can be stored cheaply, how it can be purchased regularly and cheaply in peace; and with absolute certainty in war."[69]

But now, Shell was purchasing Anglo-Persian's oil for other markets. The first 15,000 barrels had already been loaded onto a Dutch tanker in May 1912. Moreover, cash-strapped Anglo-Persian was contemplating a buy-out from Shell—exactly what the Admiralty and Foreign Office did not want. Shell was not British controlled, it was Dutch controlled. A perfect example of the problem played out in front of the Royal Commission for Fuel in spring 1912, during testimony from both Shell executives, British subject Samuel and Dutch citizen Deterding. Samuel was nicely reassuring the committee that if given an extended contract, Shell would certainly promise a million tons per year. But Deterding interrupted and corrected Samuel in front of the committee saying: Make that a half a million.[70]

What was driving Deterding and Shell?

A threatened Shell takeover of Anglo-Persian was now more than dominating the stage in the unfolding oil drama. Such a takeover meant a foreign-controlled monopoly of virtually all known Mideast oil. Minority Shell owner Samuel was asked point-blank by the Royal Commission for Fuel whether foreign directors would not control the oil? His response was noted by commission members as "absolutely." Samuel carefully added, "but … fortunately, they are extremely pro-British."[71]

How long could pro-British sentiment be relied upon if war broke out?

The attitude of Anglo-Persian Oil Company also turned alarming. Its executive, Charles Greenway, bluntly told the Foreign Office his company wanted more than diplomatic support and a willing customer in the Royal Navy. Unless Anglo-Persian received a large contract and cash infusion from the British government, the company would become a Royal Dutch Shell operation.[72] That sounded like blackmail.

Undersecretary of State Louis Mallet wrote bitterly, "I do not like the attitude of the Anglo-Persian Oil Company who have hitherto posed as being ultra-imperialist. Mr. Greenway first comes to me and hints that if Shell obtains the Mesopotamian oilfields, it will be difficult for the Anglo-Persian Oil Company to resist coming to an agreement with them—unless the Admiralty can give them a contract. I did not at that time understand that an agreement meant more than an understanding as to the sale price of oil. Greenway now threatens complete absorption with the Shell unless the Admiralty gives him a contract."[73]

Shortly thereafter, Foreign Secretary Grey sent the Anglo-Persian oilmen a message in plain words. "The support which His Majesty's Government have given your company in the past," he asserted, "both in obtaining their concession in Persia, and in other ways, was given on the understanding that the enterprise would remain British and that it would be a matter of great surprise and regret if your company made any arrangement whereby a syndicate, predominantly foreign, got control of their interests in that country." If that occurred, the Foreign Office insisted, "Your company could not, of course, hope to get from His Majesty's Government the same support as in the past."[74]

As the British government was being squeezed, astonished officials could only wonder what had caused such a turn of events.

A Shell takeover meant a huge oil price gouging campaign against the British government. "It is clear," Undersecretary Mallet wrote, "... the Shell group are aiming at the extinction" of Anglo-Persian "as a competitor—one of their objects being to control the price of liquid fuel for the British Navy."[75]

Greenway audaciously admitted as much to the Royal Commission for Fuel when he testified, "We know very well that if we join hands with the Shell Company, we shall probably make very large profits, and that it will result in their securing a practical monopoly of oil in the Eastern Hemisphere if not in the whole world."[76]

The concept of price gouging by a Shell-directed monopoly clearly was fixed in Churchill's mind. The price of fuel oil was skyrocketing, having more than doubled during the previous 18 months, from 37 shillings 6 pence per ton to 77 shillings 6 pence per ton. "Daily, the prices of oil are rising," proclaimed a memo given to Churchill.[77]

A new approach would be needed to avoid what Churchill termed, "being mercilessly fleeced at every purchase."[78]

Anglo-Persian had been angling for a cash infusion and a reliable contract that would not only secure their Persian petroleum, but would finance the acquisition and development of the Mesopotamian lands. The many departments of the British government converging on the question—Admiralty, Foreign Office, Board of Trade, and the India Office, to name a few—were coming closer to agreeing that some special economic relationship was needed for Anglo-Persian. That would solve everything.

Not everything.

On August 6, 1912, the Foreign Ministry received a cable from its embassy in Istanbul advising there was a major new group threatening to take over the Mesopotamian oil concessions. This group suddenly appeared out of nowhere. Moreover, it was a potent alliance of the Deutsche Bank—contributing their Anatolia Railway oil concession—and the National Bank of Turkey. The group seemed intent on creating a monopoly controlled by non-British interests. In truth, the syndicate had been operating for some months behind the scenes.[79] And who was responsible for this sudden debacle?

Soon it would become clear: C. S. Gulbenkian, Mr. Five Percent.

CHAPTER FOUR

MR. FIVE PERCENT

Gulbenkian loved to annoy people. He was wealthy enough to get away with it. In his posh London residence, Gulbenkian regularly slammed doors and snarled at the butlers. At the theater, if Gulbenkian disapproved, he might loudly blurt, "The play is stupid!" When nearby rows would shush him, Gulbenkian would just start conversing with himself even more loudly. One time, he even purchased tickets closer to the stage, just to more audibly razz an actor whose performance he disliked.[1]

He was stern and unforgiving with his family. Gulbenkian once punished his six-year-old daughter, Rita, with a week's diet of bread and water for behaving badly toward another little girl he wanted her to emulate. His son, Nubar, was terrified of his father. Once, Nubar was placed on bread and water for running away from his nanny. Another time, Nubar became sick and vomited while riding in the coach sitting in the compulsory backward position reserved for him. He was spanked for "disgracing the equipage." When the children were told to dress for dinner, they were compelled to sit motionless on a high table until summoned for display among the adults. None dared disobey the protocol.[2]

Gulbenkian fancied himself a collector of fine art. If he wanted a rare coin or a statuette, he would simply demand it—and was willing to pay any amount. In one case, he insisted on preempting a scheduled auction for a pair of miniatures. "No price is too high for me!" he chastised the owners before the auction. "I want these miniatures and I'll have them fetched this evening.

Good day, sir!" He treated the art he owned as a sultan would his women. He once declined to show some favorite paintings to an intrigued guest, exclaiming, "What! Would I unveil the women of my harem to a stranger?"[3]

Gulbenkian's own harem in London, Paris, and Lisbon included dozens of young women over the years, each no older than 18 or 19. He replaced them annually until he was 80. "While it is very unkind on a young girl to have sexual relations with an old man because she loses her youth," his son recalled him bragging, "it does rejuvenate the sexual functions of the old man."[4]

Most of all, Gulbenkian was a tenacious scrapper, especially in the murky business of petroleum. He once quipped, "Oil men are like cats." Gulbenkian knew how to win a catfight. What he termed, "rousing great jealousies" among contenders was a specialty of his. It "worked both ways, to my advantage and to my disadvantage," he conceded. Gulbenkian happily confessed that as he maneuvered between the captains of oil, his "position ... was delicate ... and not in any way a pleasant one." No matter. His goal was not to be liked, but to create an enormous oil monopoly.[5]

The cantankerous Gulbenkian employed any number of high-powered attorneys ready to litigate. At the same time, he was a patient man when it came to achieving his objective—patient beyond all reason and to the point of intractable obstinence. Once, the billionaire lost a tiny, almost insignificant piece of rental property because he failed to pay local taxes. For years, Gulbenkian's enterprise continuously filed lawsuits and motions to regain the lot, and pressured any number of foreign authorities to intervene as though it were the most important matter in his life.[6] He could outlast the best of them.

Gulbenkian's effort to create an oil monopoly in Mesopotamia began long before August 6, 1912, when the Foreign Office first learned of the endeavor. In fact, the machinations began at the end of 1910 as new groups of highly nationalistic Young Turks emerged in Istanbul. Some of these new ministerial figures continued to favor Germany and Holland over Britain. This was something Gulbenkian, an experienced oil financier, could exploit. As Britain edged ever closer to securing its concession in a company it could rely upon—Anglo-Persian, Gulbenkian brought together the key dissident parties to undermine the plan.[7]

Sir Ernest Cassel, a director of the National Bank of Turkey, was on good terms with German circles, being of dual British-German citizenship. In late 1910, amid the fluid state of Young Turk politics, as a new regime was taking hold in Istanbul, Gulbenkian convinced Cassel to open negotiations with Anatolia Railway and its parent, the Deutsche Bank. Anatolia Railway, at this point, was cash-hungry for its transportation construction program. The company was more interested in securing some other entity to work the Mesopotamian oil fields, preferring to just profitably transport the products and services. Next, Gulbenkian turned to his contacts among prominent pashas in the government who, despite their reformist temperament, were not above keeping old Ottoman traditions of baksheesh alive. Naturally, Gulbenkian's good friend Deterding and Shell would also want to join in.[8]

New money and new political connections had been successfully attached to Anatolia's decade-old oil rights, real and disputed. Now, a new oil alliance was created, albeit still unnamed and unincorporated.

Gulbenkian lost no time in inventing a legal entity for his new alliance. With so many foreign syndicates competing for the concession, speed was obviously a factor. Moreover, amid the sifting, shifting dynamics of Ottoman concession politics, Gulbenkian wanted to act before Anatolia changed its mind. So, on January 31, 1911, one of Cassel's South African mining companies, named African and Eastern Concessions, was registered in London as a shell corporation for the new oil enterprise.[9]

Gulbenkian quietly worked throughout 1912 to lay the groundwork for the regional monopoly he envisioned. By early August 1912, the Foreign Office learned that the National Bank of Turkey—an institution the British government had helped sponsor—was intruding into the oil concession being groomed for Anglo-Persian. London immediately worried that Gulbenkian's group might genuinely pose a threat. When asked, British Embassy Counselor Charles Marling in Istanbul admitted in a September 10 message, "This financial alliance with German interests ... [is] most disquieting." Paramount in that fear was National Bank of Turkey's "disagreeable political favor through its relations with the Committee [of Union and Progress]," that is, the Young Turks.[10]

The Foreign Office replied to Marling in Istanbul, "After consulting with the Admiralty, who do not at all like the idea of a foreign syndicate having control of large oil supplies in Mesopotamia, we have ... told the National Bank that we are unable to support their request for a concession. Of course, our main reason is that we have already advocated and supported the demands of the Anglo-Persian Oil Co. ...The reason which we have given to the National Bank is simply that we have already pledged ourselves to support Mr. D'Arcy and company, and that it is, therefore, impossible at a late hour to encourage another competitor, but we are going to verbally tell [the bank] confidentially that, after considering the whole matter, our Government does not like the idea of entrusting to a syndicate which, though nominally British, is in reality composed of two very powerful foreign syndicates, the control of so large a supply of oil fuel."[11]

Rather than submitting to British desires to desist, Gulbenkian accelerated. On September 25, 1912, Gulbenkian held an extraordinary shareholder meeting in London—really just a gathering of the circle of personalities, to formally change the name of the paper corporation to Turkish Petroleum

Company [TPC]. The address of the new entity was identical to that of the National Bank of Turkey: 50 Cornhill in London. Of course, the company engaged in no real business except to speculate in Mesopotamian oil. Gulbenkian's intent was now perfectly clear.[12]

At that September 25 meeting, the bylaws were also changed. By the power of the papers they drew up, the group created 80,000 shares of value, each worth £1. The first 40,000-share block, called "Group A," controlled four directors on the board. The next 20,000 shares, called "Group B," controlled two directors, as did the final 20,000 shares of "Group C." Clearly, Group A shares controlled the company by virtue of its four directors.[13]

A month later, October 23, 1912, the major economic dimensions of the TPC were formally structured in an important agreement that permanently changed the face of petroleum in the Middle East. Meeting at TPC's titular London address, 50 Cornhill, in the actual offices of the National Bank of Turkey, the representatives of Deutsche Bank, the National Bank of Turkey, and Gulbenkian signed a contract specifying TPC's value. What's more, they hammered out the ownership segments that would regulate TPC's single important asset: the oil concessions. Deutsche Bank received Group C shares, numbered 60,001 through 80,000, in exchange for transferring any and all of its oil concessions. These included both the still-valid original 40-kilometer right of way concession and the dismissed but disputed general province-wide concessions. Deutsche Bank's only contribution for its quarter ownership was its concession.[14]

Of the first 60,000 shares, the National Bank of Turkey, corporately, and its officer, Cassel, individually, divided 28,000 shares. Since Cassel was president of National Bank of Turkey, he wielded a double vote. That left 32,000 shares. These went to Gulbenkian personally. *Gulbenkian initially owned 40 percent.*[15]

While Gulbenkian was quietly creating Turkish Petroleum Company as a formidable challenger to be reckoned with, the British government was more focused on the threat of the moment--that Royal Dutch Shell would absorb nearly bankrupt Anglo-Persian. "I think we should go [to] every length in supporting the independence of the Anglo-Persian Oil Company," insisted Foreign Office Assistant Undersecretary Mallet, "and subsidize them if necessary."[16]

Britain's sense of urgency only intensified when the so-called Balkan Wars erupted across Greece, Macedonia, Serbia, Thrace, Albania, and other territories in Europe. Guerrilla forces raiding Turkish installations in bayonet charges and long, 40-car trains wending across the region, packed to the rooftops with eager soldiers, were only the latest fuses in the explosive Eastern Question. Right now, only the Balkans were aflame. But no one was certain how many other powers would be drawn into the broadening conflicts, creating a massive war.[17]

As Churchill and the Admiralty continued their public inquiries on the urgent need for new oil sources, news emerged of Gulbenkian's hitherto unknown German-dominated oil axis in Mesopotamia, which, although not yet named, was in fact Turkish Petroleum. Headlines in the November 14 *Financial News* were typical: "Will Germany control the oil supply for our Navy?"[18]

Now the struggle for oil became a three-way battle among Britain, Holland, and Germany—being fought in London's corridors of power. Gulbenkian stood at the hub, playing the contenders off each other.

His next move only further complicated an already complex situation. Gulbenkian secretly leveraged most of his 32,000 shares in TPC. Under the terms of original issuance as part of the National Bank of Turkey's block, Gulbenkian could distribute some of those 32,000 shares to another oil company. So he parceled off 20,000 of his 32,000 shares to yet another participant. "In view of my connection with the Royal Dutch Shell group, and the urgent necessity to have an oil organization capable of carrying out practical work ... I therefore offered them 20,000 shares, that is to say, 25 percent of the company ... keeping for myself 12,000 shares."[19] *Gulbenkian now owned just 15 percent.*

By late 1912, TPC possessed everything it needed: Germany's oil concession; Shell's ability to explore, refine, and market; the economic wherewithal of both the National Bank of Turkey and Deutsche Bank; and the political connections of Gulbenkian. Moreover, through an exchange of binding letters of self-restriction among all the parties, TPC shareholders all agreed not to engage in petroleum exploration, refinement, or distribution anywhere in Mesopotamia except through their jointly owned Turkish Petroleum Company.[20]

Gulbenkian's Mesopotamian oil monopoly-in-waiting was now up and running.

TPC promptly began applying for research permits all over the Ottoman Empire: at the Sea of Marmora, in central Syria, and even at the Dead Sea in Palestine. In Mesopotamia, its concession application covered "[anywhere] surface indications of petroleum exist," beginning with the Anatolia Railway's right-of-way from Mosul to Tikrit. By mid-November, the Foreign Office began seeing TPC for what it was: a viable contender for the future of all Mideast oil—before, during, and after any war.[21]

Ironically, even if Anglo-Persian was left intact in Persia and price gouging was made unlikely by competition, prices could still be unstable. If TPC and Shell succeeded in controlling Mesopotamian oil, warned the Foreign Office, "it would enable the Shell Transport Company to cut prices." What was wrong with cutting prices? Shell could then artificially push prices so radically downward via an oil price war that the loss of stable income would cripple the Anglo-Persian just the same. Then Anglo-Persian would again be ripe for takeover.[22] The British government did not want oil prices too high or too low—but "just right."

Before it could address its competitive viability, Britain was first fiercely determined that Anglo-Persian not be absorbed by Shell, either directly or through the TPC. Foreign Secretary Grey understood, "our position, both commercial and political, will be seriously jeopardized if the most important British concession in Persia, the Anglo-Persian Oil Company, is allowed to pass under foreign control by absorption in the Shell Company."[23] The question was how to prevent a commercial takeover.

Anglo-Persian continually pleaded for long-range contracts and advance payment for oil not yet delivered—or even pumped. But the government simply could not justify paying millions of pounds to a financially wracked company on the verge of being devoured by rivals. Admiralty contracts people pointedly asked, "Whether the money would be repaid," in the event of an oil failure, adding, the whole thing is "a business subject to much speculative risk."[24]

Instead of financial aid, the Foreign Office instructed its embassy in Istanbul to do whatever it could to prop up Anglo-Persian and D'Arcy against the TPC and the Germans. After all, in April 1909, the paperwork granting the Sultan's concession to D'Arcy had been all but signed. Did that not carry weight?[25]

Ambassador Gerald Lowther sent back a disparaging rebuff: "As a matter of fact, I do not believe that D'Arcy [has] a leg to stand on." On the other hand, he added, "the Germans have their rights legally assured," based on the 1903 Baghdad Railway Convention, an international treaty that granted the oil concession for 20 kilometers on either side of the track.[26] Hence, even if the 1904 Anatolia concession for Baghdad and Mosul was voided for lateness, Anatolia's earlier concession for the 20 kilometers on either side of its railroad track was quite solid.

What about D'Arcy's so-called claim of a proper 1909 concession from the Sultan that was completely written but never actually signed? That had even been tentatively endorsed later that year by the Council of Ministers, subject to as yet unresolved "stipulations." Lowther deprecated the whole theory as "mere waste paper." He added, "If D'Arcy's [group] do not take the trouble to come out here and work their business, the impression is naturally created that they do not care about it." Adding that D'Arcy's agent in Istanbul was "quite useless," Lowther emphasized, if "I am only to frame my protests on 'rights,' I am afraid I shall be done for."[27]

In early January 1913, the British were so worried about the prospects for oil that Whitehall policymakers debated whether they should return to the less militarily effective but more reliable realm of coal. Speed at sea would be sacrificed, but at least Britain possessed its own coal. Budget planners even calculated the cost of coal retro-conversion: £150,000 per ship.[28]

At the end of February 1913, just before the Royal Commission on Oil Fuel concluded its second series of hearings, Deterding offered more testimony. He tried to attenuate the fear that a Dutch-controlled oil company could not be trusted by England during a war with Germany. Asked whether German money was not already in his enterprise, he parried, "Not a penny!" And what if Germany tried to pressure Holland and its oil enterprise? "We could snap our fingers at Germany," Deterding wisecracked. "What can the German Government do? They can write very nasty letters and say anything they like to the Dutch Government, but that has not anything to do with us."[29] His braggadocio was not persuasive.

A few weeks later, as if to prove Churchill's point, Deterding revised his own guarantee of Shell's annual fuel capability for the navy in the event Shell was tapped for oil. Months earlier, when Samuel spoke, he had pledged a million tons per year, only to see that number instantly halved by Deterding during commission testimony. But now Deterding promised only a fifth of even that reduced amount, that is, 100,000 tons annually. Even that 100,000 tons included no assurances about grade or quality. Navy officials clearly saw what was happening with each passing week, writing "In the meantime [since Deterding's last estimate], prices have risen very greatly and he has pledged all his oil supplies for years ahead." Ironically, Deterding only worsened official apprehension when he promised what he thought was a saving grace. He offered any volume of oil if the navy paid enough. "It is entirely a question of price," he declared. "If the Admiralty pays [a premium rate] ... you will always get supplies with no difficulty."[30]

At the same time, Turkish officials in Istanbul were wondering just how much currency would salve their own palms. Those in the Sublime Porte wielding administrative powers over Mesopotamia's petroleum now regularly mentioned multimillion-pound loan offers from oil speculators, plus lucrative commissions and participations—some real, some imaginary. Waters were tested and anxieties probed in search of personal reward for those in the Turkish government aiding the process. It was hard for fretful concession-chasers from the United States, the United Kingdom, and other countries to determine a genuine competitor from the shades of commercial dissimulation.[31]

Ironically, TPC officials fully comprehended that much of the value they attached to Anatolia's most promising asset, the concession for the provinces of Baghdad and Mosul, was fundamentally worthless puffery. Shortly after the TPC agreement was signed, Turkish National Bank president Babington-Smith confessed to a colleague at Shell, "It is quite true ... the Anatolia Railway Company Concession is somewhat vague, and of this we have of course been aware all along." TPC's Istanbul attorney echoed those reservations, advising in a private opinion, "The situation of the Anatolia Railway Company [Concession for Mosul and Baghdad] is not what I should call a 'strong case.' The exploration work was not done and the reports not rendered within the time allowed."[32]

But in the volatile realm of Turkish concessions, appearances were as important as facts. Both changed continually and interactively. Threats, veiled and explicit, spiced every dialogue on the topic. The Turks threatened to grant the concession to TPC, or to unnamed others, and sometime the mysterious "others" were in fact TPC under one guise or another. For their part, the British threatened to withhold approval of badly needed increases in Turkish customs and duties. Britain ironically maintained a veto over those revenues due to the capitulation system and the Ottoman debt. Hence, any Ottoman attempt to profit from any oil concession other than Anglo-Persian's would cost the regime dearly once taxes were tallied.[33] On April 25, 1913, Ambassador Lowther grimly reported that his efforts on behalf of D'Arcy had "now reached a point not far from deadlock and I am apprehensive lest the pressure" cause the Turks "not give the exclusive rights to either group."[34]

In spring 1913, frustrated Foreign Office officials suggested a radical solution: TPC should merge with Anglo-Persian, as long as Anglo-Persian retained majority control. This would take TPC's concession threat off the table, shunt a share of the Mideast oil profits to TPC's corporate owners, yet maintain Anglo-Persian as a "British concern" that the government could still support financially and diplomatically. Throughout the spring, endless, unnerving negotiations roiled between Anglo-Persian executives and Babington-Smith of the Turkish National Bank and TPC. Anglo-Persian offered Babington-Smith a financial majority, but a rubber-stamp minority vote— reducing TPC to a silent partner. Rejected. By June 12, Anglo-Persian suggested a clean fifty-fifty split, but mandated a British chairman to ensure true control. Likewise, rejected.[35]

Periodic appeals by Anglo-Persian executives to the Foreign Office for intervention were fruitless. As negotiations stalled, the National Bank of Turkey was proving its potency. It became active in financing oil infrastructure, principally ports and railways, not only in Mesopotamia, but beyond. For example, the bank had already become involved in port facilities at Trabzon, the Turkish gateway to the rich oil fields of Baku.[36]

By mid-June 1913, the stalemate of threat and counter-threat, offer and counter-offer, and accelerating actions by the TPC combine forced Churchill and his colleagues to revise their strategy. On June 16, 1913, Churchill filed a secret memo with the cabinet admitting that Persian oil was "more important than anticipated." He argued that Anglo-Persian must be awarded a substantial advance contract, plus some form of government financing to ensure the company's survival. "The future of the oil market is so uncertain," wrote Churchill, "and the present prices are so unfavorable." He insisted, "Action is urgent as the future oil supplies are being increasingly bought up ... and the oil market is being rapidly contracted both from natural and artificial causes." The cabinet began studying just how far Britain would go to protect its favored oil company.[37]

If Whitehall assured Anglo-Persian of lucrative long-term contracts, and even offered advance payment, what would prevent another foreign company from buying the company anyway? England would then be supplying up-front cash and contracts to the very foreign firms they hoped to resist—and still be at their mercy. The answer: On July 11, the cabinet decided that the government "should acquire a controlling interest" in Anglo-Persian. The British government would buy the company.[38]

A few days later, Churchill explained to Parliament: "Our ultimate policy is that the Admiralty should become the independent owner and producer of its own supplies of liquid fuel ... to make us safe in war, and able to override price fluctuations in peace ... We must become the owners, or at any rate the controllers at the source ... of [the] natural oil which we require."[39]

British officials were now contemplating both long-term contracts and a £2.2 million cash infusion in exchange for 51 percent of Anglo-Persian's stock, plus two government-appointed seats on the board, an assurance that the chairman would be British, and a sure policy that Anglo-Persian would forevermore operate as a captive quasi-governmental British corporation.[40]

To certify that the government was purchasing a worthwhile company and dependable reserves, a five-man team of experts, headed by Rear Admiral Sir Edmond Slade, director of naval intelligence, embarked on a three-month expedition to Persia. Their job: Investigate and verify those fabulous Persian oil fields and APOC's ability to exploit them. Dressed in classic safari suits and stereotypical British India pith helmets, periodically stopping for a civilized spot of tea served on a portable table and chairs in the desert wilderness, the five men were dazzled by the bountiful oil deposits they surveyed. "It seems to be a thoroughly sound concession," reported Slade, "which may be developed to a gigantic extent." However, he stressed, Britain must "control the company," and warned that "it would be a national disaster if the concession were allowed to pass into foreign hands ... All possible steps should be taken to maintain the company as a British undertaking."[41]

Even as the Slade Commission was poking around Persia, Undersecretary Mallet received a new assignment. He was abruptly transferred to Istanbul as Britain's new ambassador. There he continued to importune the various Turkish ministers about the concession.[42]

Quickly, Mallet's high-powered diplomacy was seen in action. First, he settled a strategic border issue. For centuries, the fuzzy frontier between Mesopotamia, Persia, and Russia had been contentious and disputed—often militarily. As part of the many efforts to forestall the expected chain-reaction war in Europe, a border commission had been established during the previous year to permanently set a mutually recognized boundary. After 18 sessions, the delegates finally fixed the international border, placing some of the richest oil-producing lands of Persia into Ottoman Mesopotamia. A treaty was drawn up to delineate the so-called Transferred Territories. But once those Persian lands were incorporated into Turkey, what would become of Anglo-Persian's concession, which was legal only within Persia? Through Mallet's pressures and persuasions, the new Turco-Persian Frontier Protocol included a unique provision recognizing Anglo-Persian's still largely unexploited concession as an international geopolitical fact that transferred with the land itself.[43] Mideast oil now proved it was bigger than international borders.

Clearly, Britain expected Anglo-Persian and D'Arcy to extend their control from Persia farther into all of Mesopotamia. The Turco-Persian Frontier Protocol proved that. Discussions about amalgamating Turkish Petroleum and Anglo-Persian now resumed in earnest, this time with German and British diplomats interceding. Germany was as eager as Britain to resolve the problem in exchange for a share of the oil. A compromise emerged. The National Bank of Turkey—established as a fundamentally British financial institution—would sell its approximate 50-percent share of TPC, held by the bank and its officers individually, to Anglo-Persian. Thus, Anglo-Persian would acquire majority control of TPC—ending the controversy. Germany would then receive a sizable portion of the extracted oil by virtue of its co-ownership of the TPC. Babington-Smith, president of the National Bank of Turkey, and his counterparts in the Deutsche Bank were both amenable, if only to stay on good relations with the governments in question. Little money had changed hands. After all, the distribution of bank shares had been fundamentally a paper transaction. So the bank officials were willing to cede their stock.[44]

Both British Foreign Office and German Foreign Ministry officials were feeling relieved, as neither wanted to tangle over the issue. But then, in the last days of November 1913, just as the merger deal was to be finalized, a bank official contacted British diplomats. There was just one other thing. In point of fact, while the main bank executives were indeed willing to simply relinquish their stock, which had cost little, if anything, in cash, one shareholder, whose name did not appear anywhere on the corporate rolls, was not cooperating. They had tried convincing him, to no avail.[45]

Who was that one shareholder whose name did not appear on the corporation registrations? Gulbenkian—and he was not budging.

Hence, the National Bank of Turkey was not free to just relinquish its share in TPC—that is, not without Gulbenkian's permission, since he controlled 15 percent. As far as duty to the British or German government, Gulbenkian did not feel obligated to either. When the Foreign Office telegraphed Gulbenkian asking him to join the compromise, he sneered at the very idea. His view: "It was for *me* to decide with the Royal Dutch Shell group what we should do." He later wrote "I was a private individual who had worked so persistently [to establish TPC] without remuneration and had invested in cash in the company." In fact, the most Gulbenkian could have paid for his 12,000 shares was £12,000, but no one could find any indication of just how that £12,000 might have been paid and to whom—if ever paid at all. No matter. Gulbenkian had his paper share and it was now invaluable.[46]

British officials were astonished and furious.

On December 1, 1913, the Foreign Office summoned their main Ottoman contact, former Turkish prime minister Hakki Pasha, sent by the Turkish government to London to resolve matters. During a four-and-half-hour meeting, Hakki Pasha revealed he was fully aware that the German and British settlement was blocked because Gulbenkian still held 15 percent of TPC's Group A shares from the original bank distribution. Moreover, the Group A shares that Gulbenkian had proffered to Shell were just as important to him because Gulbenkian had much of his personal fortune in Shell.[47] Gulbenkian had even invested his children's allowance money in Shell stock.[48]

Moreover, if anyone tried to work around him, Gulbenkian vociferously promised a lawsuit. Hakki Pasha asked embassy officials, "What was to happen if the Shell Company, or [Mr.] Gulbenkian, brought an action … for an illegal transfer of some of their holdings." The Foreign Office was not amused by or worried about Gulbenkian. Hakki Pasha was answered bluntly that the British government, if need be, would "[paralyze] partially, if not entirely, the operations of the Turkish Petroleum Company in Mesopotamia."[49]

By now, Whitehall riled at the very mention of Gulbenkian's name and felt the National Bank of Turkey itself could not be trusted. They saw it all as subterfuge preceding a shakedown. "The upshot of this seems to be that the National Bank is not behaving very well," wrote one Near East desk foreign officer on December 2, 1913. His colleague replied, "*That* is putting it very mildly … The failure of the National Bank to disclose this important feature [Gulbenkian's 15 percent share] when entering the [merger] negotiation has made a painful impression upon [Foreign Secretary] Sir E. Grey."[50]

Shell stood equally guilty in British eyes. Foreign Office diplomats also castigated Shell for being "selfish and utterly unscrupulous." Before any more surprises emerged, the Foreign Office demanded a written statement that "no voting power attached" to those original shares "held at first by Gulbenkian and now … transferred to the Shell." The imperative now: "It is of importance that we know exactly where we are as regards the Gulbenkian shares."[51]

Whitehall was convinced the Turkish government was prepared to grant the concession to whomever London designated, if only to keep the tax and customs duty increase intact. Whitehall continually threatened to veto those if the concession imbroglio was not resolved in Anglo-Persian's favor. Indeed, in early January 1914, foreign officers repeatedly reassured themselves about the concession given Istanbul's precarious financial situation. For example, the January 15, 1914 handwritten minutes of the Foreign Office on the oil concession asserted the Turks "are very short of money." This was based on a telegram that same day from Ambassador Mallet in Istanbul, which used similar language: "They are very hard up for money."[52]

At the same time, British officials tried to keep Anglo-Persian executives in London from constantly trying to take advantage of and better the subsidy Britain was willing to extend. One request by Anglo-Persian managing director Charles Greenway for a special Mesopotamian exploration company funded by a million-pound government subvention was met with an irked warning from Foreign Office staffers: "Enter into an arrangement on the terms which have been communicated" or "stand out of the Mesopotamian concession altogether."[53] In other words, "Take or leave it."

Greenway took it. In a January 31, 1914, letter, he replied, "Seeing that in the opinion of the Foreign Office no better terms are obtainable ... my colleagues, after careful examination and discussion, are willing to accept the proposals made."[54]

Everyone could agree to everything. But not Gulbenkian. Defiant, he met with Hakki Pasha, in London, reminding him that he, Gulbenkian, owned 15 percent, or about a third of the Bank's half ownership in TPC. Gulbenkian's point was that he and only he by virtue of his powerful fraction controlled the destiny of oil in Mesopotamia. Hakki Pasha went to the Foreign Office and related the exchange: "He [Gulbenkian] was not going to allow the National Bank of Turkey to bargain away his rights, and if they attempted to do so he would send a solicitor to see them, and they would be involved in a lawsuit, in which he was sure to win."[55]

Unfortunately, the Foreign Office was not responding to the threats. Feeling left out despite his key ownership, Gulbenkian wanted to discuss the matter in person. But alienated British officials simply refused to meet with the man. So Gulbenkian was reduced to passing messages through others, such as Hakki Pasha. Ironically, sometimes the messages were conciliatory, offering to reduce his percentage and relinquish voting rights to permit the merger. Other times, they were all threats and belligerence.[56]

Finally, after repeated urgings from Hakki Pasha, Whitehall reluctantly agreed to meet with Gulbenkian. On February 13, 1914, a nattily dressed Gulbenkian strode into the Foreign Office and met with Near East expert Sir Llewellyn Smith. Self-laudatory and alternating between a spirit of compromise and a penchant for combativeness, Gulbenkian cleared up any question that he—and he alone— was the prime "creator of Turkish Petroleum

Company." It was he who had put the parties together—the National Bank of Turkey, the Deutsche Bank, and Shell. Gulbenkian stated that, of course, he enjoyed a great friendship and "intimate acquaintance" with Deterding at Shell—yet was willing to act independently of Deterding if need be. In other words, he could be either a steadfast ally of his friend Deterding or undercut him as required. Gulbenkian indicated he was willing to be helpful to the government, but "very unwilling to be cut out of the Mesopotamian enterprise." Smith recorded, "He is evidently disposed to be very tenacious of what he regards as his rights."[57]

The next day, German delegates visited Mideast expert Alwyn Parker at the Foreign Office. They were anxious that the matter be settled, thereby amicably dividing Mesopotamian oil between the two nations. But the one obstacle remained: "the position of Mr. Gulbenkian, his desire to remain interested in the concession, and his contention that the National Bank could not legally transfer his shares without his consent." This stymied all plans to create an enlarged Anglo-Persian Oil Company in Mesopotamia. One Deutsche Bank official, Emil Strauss, disingenuously claimed "that the Deutsche Bank only learned a few weeks ago of this sub-participation of Mr. Gulbenkian." Had Deutsche Bank known of Gulbenkian's involvement, Strauss averred, "they never would have joined the Turkish Petroleum Company." Strauss was now explicit. "It is necessary, in order to clear the way, that either Mr. Gulbenkian's interest be eliminated, or that the Turkish Petroleum Company be wound up."[58]

Alwyn Parker and his colleagues at the Foreign Office agreed. They insisted the National Bank of Turkey treat the situation as an "internal matter" and simply "eliminate Mr. Gulbenkian's interest." Unknown was Shell's response, since it held stock through Gulbenkian, who remained a longtime friend and associate of Deterding. But by any measure, if Gulbenkian and his alliances with Shell presented so many obstacles to the Turkish Petroleum Company merging with Anglo-Persian, the governments concluded it was up to "that Company to remove them."[59]

So assured was the British government that it would prevail, the cabinet voted on February 18 to authorize £2.2 million to fund the acquisition of Anglo-Persian and to forward the measure to Treasury for approval.[60]

Gulbenkian undoubtedly now sensed he might have overplayed his position. Matters were moving forward without him. He urged Babington-Smith to contact Parker at the Foreign Office to arrange another meeting. On March 2, 1914, Babington-Smith telephoned and "asked me if I wanted to see Gulbenkian again. I said 'No,'" reported Parker, who took a tough stand, knowing the Germans and British were now unified against Gulbenkian. Even when Babington-Smith passed on a message that Gulbenkian was willing to reduce his percentage from 15 percent, Parker was not moved. As Babington-Smith pressed ahead with more compromise ideas, Parker bluntly threatened, "The German and British governments had it in their power to prevent the Ottoman [government] giving the concession to anyone of whom they [the two governments] did not approve, and neither ... [Shell] nor Mr. Gulbenkian could attach much importance to being shareholders in a paralytic company." Babington-Smith agreed on that point.[61]

A few days later, March 5, after conferring with Gulbenkian, Babington-Smith telephoned Parker again with a new proffer: Perhaps Gulbenkian could relinquish control of his 15 percent but "retain the profits." A sorely tried Parker later made a note of his reply: Once again, "I said 'NO,'" making sure he typed NO in capital letters. Babington-Smith retorted that the Gulbenkian negotiations were therefore now in deadlock. Later, Gulbenkian himself called and appealed for a meeting. Parker replied, "This was impossible, useless and undesirable," telling Gulbenkian that if he had anything to say, "He had better put in writing."[62]

The next day, a handwritten instruction from the Board of Trade was sent over to Parker: "The time has come when the F.O. should formally tell the Turkish Petroleum Company that this is the final decision." The word formally was underlined. Immediately thereafter, a curt and official letter was typed and delivered to Babington-Smith. "I am directed by the Secretary Sir E. Grey to inform you ... the proposal that Mr. Gulbenkian should retain his interest...is not one which [we] can ... accept." It continued, "His Majesty's Government have reached a final decision that a 50 per cent interest [by Anglo-Persian] ... must be obtained."[63]

Europe was beset by regional military clashes at that very moment, and alliances with the greater powers were being called into play. The Continent could break into war at any time. Hence, the formal letter from the Foreign Office to Babington-Smith concluded: "The matter is one which cannot be longer delayed without grave inconvenience, and consequently, if the Turkish Petroleum Company cannot see their way to participate in such [a merger] arrangement, His Majesty's Government will feel compelled to take such steps as they may think proper to secure the interest of the D'Arcy group."[64]

As for Shell, according to Gulbenkian, the whole idea of relinquishing shares to Anglo-Persian set Deterding "into a state of frenzy." Deterding detested Anglo-Persian and its executives. Gulbenkian related, "He became wild" at the very mention of yielding. In fact, during the back-and-forth negotiations, Deterding was difficult to gauge. He swung from offering sincere cooperation to the Admiralty to hard-nosed offers of ever-diminishing amounts of oil. Shell's position shifted at every turn. But why? "I was in daily contact with Mr. Deterding," explained Gulbenkian, "and, although I did not appear [so], I was, in fact, the pilot of his negotiations."[65]

All the self-assuredness of the Foreign Office abruptly crumbled when it received reports on March 10, 1914, that "the Germans are working with the Turks behind our backs." A syndicate of wealthy Ottoman pashas and businessmen had created an alliance of politically potent Young Turks to seize the concession as soon as the paperwork could be drawn up. More than just a paper consortium, the group was meeting frequently, making advanced plans, and was quite earnest about overpowering the entire oil business in Mesopotamia. Embassy officials warned London that this consortium seemed too powerful, moneyed, and determined to stop.[66]

The Foreign Office unsheathed its fiscal sword once more the following day. Foreign Secretary Grey dispatched a cable to Mallet in Istanbul: "You may state categorically that if concession for these fields is given to any company in which D'Arcy group does not receive 50% of the whole, I shall be compelled to break off all negotiations with Hakki Pasha and to reconsider terms on which HMG could consent to customs increase and monopolies."[67]

At the same time, the cabinet had obtained Treasury's approval for the £2.2 million investment in Anglo-Persian. The next step was parliamentary approval. Toward this end, a special cabinet committee was appointed to oversee the final acquisition of Anglo-Persian—public and private. Churchill, on March 17, 1914, went before a parliamentary naval committee to establish the core principle of the Admiralty securing its own Mideast oil supply.[68]

It was uncertain how long the rest of heavily armed and intricately allianced Europe could remain aloof from regional tensions and conflicts such as those that had recently set the Balkans ablaze. Millions of men could be thrown into a great war that would not only span the continent but also engulf colonies across the world. If the concession were not obtained immediately, no one could predict who would devour it once war commenced. Regardless of when—or where—war broke out, it would be at least a year before oil could be drilled and transported for use. But from Churchill's point of view, "A year gained over a rival might make the difference. Forward, then!"[69]

Britain's sense of urgency suddenly became a sense of immediacy on Thursday, March 19, 1914. London circles learned that Istanbul could no longer resist the powerful new Turkish syndicate that had formed to acquire the concession. Greenway sent a note to D'Arcy indicating that Turkish authorities had at first delayed "in view of the strong representation made by the British and German Ambassadors," but no more. How much time was left? Until Monday. "The Turkish Government have agreed not to commit themselves to other parties," explained Greenway, "until after Monday next, but will consider themselves as free to dispose of the concession as they please after that date. The matter must therefore be settled, one way or the other, between us and the T.P.C. before then."[70]

Quickly, that same day, March 19, 1914, the oil concerns—TPC, Shell, and Anglo-Persian, as well as the German diplomats and Deutsche Bank, plus the National Bank of Turkey, converged on the Foreign Ministry. Gulbenkian was not invited, although he had signaled his willingness to reduce his share from 15 percent to something smaller to advance the process. The remaining contentions regarding structure and methodology were hastily debated, and finally a secret contract was propounded, titled "Arrangements for Fusion of the Interests in Turkish Petroleum Concessions of the D'Arcy Group and the Turkish Petroleum Company."[71]

The ownership of the restructured Turkish Petroleum would now be 50 percent "D'Arcy's group," a synonym for Anglo-Persian, 25 percent Shell and 25 percent Deutsche Bank. Half of the eight-man board of directors was to be appointed by D'Arcy's group, with two by Shell and two by Deutsche Bank. The original 1912 monopoly would be retained. "The three groups participating in the Turkish Petroleum [Co.]," the document required, "shall give undertakings on their own behalf and on behalf of the companies associated with them not to be interested directly or indirectly in the production or manufacture of crude oil in the Ottoman Empire in Europe and Asia ... otherwise than through the Turkish Petroleum [Co.]" The specified exceptions recognized prior British commitments in Egypt, Kuwait, and in the recently "Transferred Territories" on the Turco-Persian frontier.[72]

TPC's corporate restructuring process was succinctly delineated in the document. Step 1: The shares of TPC were doubled from 80,000 to 160,000, still valued at £1 each, creating an enlarged company now worth £160,000. Step 2: Those additional 80,000 shares were allocated to D'Arcy's group. Hence, D'Arcy and Anglo-Persian now each owned half of TPC. Step 3: National Bank of Turkey transferred all of its shares to Shell and the Deutsche Bank. That completely eliminated the involvement of the National Bank of Turkey, which included Gulbenkian's 15 percent. In place of Gulbenkian's prized 15 percent, D'Arcy's group and Shell each carved out 2.5 percent of their holdings to create a conjoint 5 percent beneficial share for Gulbenkian. Both 2.5 percent blocks would be registered in the names of D'Arcy's group and Shell, which would each hold and control the stock. Gulbenkian would enjoy the beneficial 5 percent interest during his entire lifetime.[73]

Signing the document were ranking diplomats of the German Embassy in London, the Foreign Office, plus the director of the Deutsche Bank, Babington-Smith for the National Bank of Turkey, Greenway for Anglo-Persian, and Deterding for Shell.[74]

What began by paper was reduced by paper. It was all the power of paper. *Now Gulbenkian owned 5 percent.*

CHAPTER FIVE

THE FUSE IGNITES

ulbenkian wrote, "When I saw this document, I immediately protested to Mr. Deterding whom I had myself brought into the Turkish Petroleum Company—and the whole participation of this group was, in fact, due to me." He bitterly damned the entire fusion agreement, cobbled together by the Foreign Office on March 19, 1914 as a "preposterous usurpation of power crushing a minority without even consulting or asking the latter's advice."

Gulbenkian later railed, "Mr. Deterding, although he was then my friend—but oil friendships are very slippery—assured me that he had done his level best but that the [two] governments and the Anglo-Persian Company had compelled him to accept it. He stated, at the same time, that as it was a preposterous arrangement as far as I was concerned, I certainly ought not to accept an illegality."[1]

Immediately, Gulbenkian did as promised. He called his lawyers—one more esteemed than the next. Sir Wilfrid Greene, later Lord Greene, was an expert in corporate liquidation law. Sir Douglas Hogg, later Lord Hailsham, was the attorney general who had championed the Trade Disputes Act through Parliament. Sir John Simon, later Viscount Simon, had just served as solicitor general, then attorney general. The next year, in 1915, Viscount Simon became home secretary and, years later was tapped as foreign secretary. Greene, Hogg, and Simon were just the leading edge of a powerful legal team.

There were others. They "all assured me," recalled Gulbenkian, "that this was an inconceivable decision and that I should not worry myself because, not being a party to the Foreign Office agreement, my rights could not be in any way affected and that, sooner or later, I could rely on the signatories of the Agreement making satisfactory arrangements with me."[2]

Ironically, while Gulbenkian stewed and steamed over his disenfranchisement, he openly contradicted his own grievance when he later confessed that he voluntarily allowed his share to be diminished. "In order to show my genuine desire for peace and satisfactory arrangements," he wrote later, "I placed at the disposal of Deterding two-thirds of my participation in the Turkish Petroleum Company… Out of my 15%, I authorized him to dispose of 10% if a basis could be found for a general arrangement. This is how my 15% became 5%." Those sentences were written directly under an all-capitals heading: "VOLUNTARILY REDUCED MY PARTICPATION FROM 15% TO 5%."[3]

Even as Gulbenkian fumed over his new fraction, cables and telegrams flew from London and Berlin to Istanbul instructing the British and German diplomats there, as well as the designated commercial agents, to immediately inform the Ottoman ministries. Turkish Petroleum now enjoyed the full backing of both the German and British governments, and this new, enlarged entity was officially applying for a sweeping concession for the entire Baghdad and Mosul provinces. By the deadline of Monday, March 23, the Turkish authorities were presented with all the documentation they required to issue the concession.[4]

Just one other thing. The revised Turkish Mining Law now prohibited monopolies. Hence, the requested concession was just too broad. It clearly encompassed the entire provinces of Mosul and Baghdad; and in some correspondence with the TPC parties, this coverage was stretched to include Basra. Some discussion even suggested the concession might include the entire Ottoman Empire, crossing three continents. Indeed, there were so many other contenders, the matter would now have to be "studied." While it was being studied, the Young Turks followed in the footsteps of some older Turks before them, constantly asking when their baksheesh would be tendered. Compulsory loans, special commissions, and consultation fees running into six digits once more were suggested, or even demanded, in order for the right papers to pass to the right places at the right velocity.[5]

Throughout April 1914, arcane historical facts of the Anatolia concession and the sultan's *Civil Liste* were debated back and forth between officials of Britain, Germany, and Turkey. Every petition from London and Berlin that invoked the *Civil Liste* was answered by the pashas with a reminder that those original, early-century concessions predated the recent mining law and its anti-monopoly provisions. So many different legal theories were expounded that the juridical haze seemed impenetrable. One solution suggested was to cement a secret understanding with the Turks that while a monopoly would not be ordained in law, it would be granted *in fact*. Hence, other syndicates could apply, but none would actually be approved—just endlessly delayed.[6]

Regardless of what was happening with the Mesopotamian concession and TPC, the acquisition of Anglo-Persian was proceeding. On May 11, Churchill advised officials in both the Treasury and the Admiralty that the legal technicalities had been mostly worked out. An agreement was typed up.[7]

On May 20, 1914, the Treasury and the Admiralty together with Anglo-Persian signed a three-page, 14-point contract, adorned at the top with the words "An Agreement" in large gothic script. In doing so, the government essentially sealed the government's acquisition of 51 percent of the shares and, hence, control of the board of directors and the firm's commercial destiny in exchange for £2.2 million. That same day, a private letter from the government was issued to Anglo-Persian stating that the day-to-day commercial affairs of the company would be left to the management. No veto would be invoked unless any action affected naval contracts, sales to foreign entities, the geo-political territories of drilling, or corporate status.[8]

While the specifics of the oil contracts with Anglo-Persian would remain secret, like any other military supply contract, the £2.2 million funding itself was a public expenditure that would need ratification by an act of Parliament. Rather than subject the measure to an elaborate and protracted parliamentary process, Churchill prepared for a single significant public presentation before legislators, with an up or down vote.

Meanwhile, in Istanbul, the Council of State reviewed TPC's Mesopotamian concession application as well as the whole question of monopoly. The pashas ruled that no monopolistic concession could be granted—regardless of London's threats of a tax increase veto.[9] This refusal opened the door for influential and cash-flush competitors to continue peddling their influence and push for petroleum. Mesopotamia's concession was again spun round within the maze.

As Churchill prepared to conclude a deal with Anglo-Persian in Persia, to the exclusion of Shell, its executives went on the offensive. Shell's reluctant involvement in TPC was in pursuit of a project for the future. There was oil to be sold to the British navy in the here and now. Therefore, at the end of May 1914, Shell's Samuel and Deterding circulated a series of letters attacking the plan to acquire Anglo-Persian as governmental market rigging, injecting intolerable favoritism into the oil business. Churchill denounced those criticisms as nothing more than vile efforts by unscrupulous Shell to "keep prices up to the present blackmailing levels."[10]

Indeed, pressures from Shell only reinforced Churchill's drive to acquire

Anglo-Persian—and quickly. All that remained was Parliament's vote. The culminating day was June 17, 1914, when Churchill made a long, impassioned, and often sarcastic speech. His goal was to ignite the simmering animosities of the members of Parliament against monopolies, trusts, and even Jews in defense of the navy and its quest for fuel at a fair price.

"We have experienced, in common with private consumers, a long steady squeeze by the oil trusts all over the world," declared Churchill in cynical tones, "and we have found prices and freights raised steadily against us until we have been pressed to pay more than double what a few years before we were accustomed to pay... For many years it has been the policy of the Foreign Office [and] the Admiralty... to preserve the independent British oil interests of the Persian oil-field ... and, above all, to prevent it being swallowed up by the Shell or by any foreign or *cosmopolitan* companies."[11]

The term *cosmopolitan* was a snide contemporary code word for manipulative immigrant Jewish businessmen, a clear reference to Marcus Samuel, 40 percent owner of Shell. This provoked a sharp response from MP Watson Rutherford: "I think it is a very great pity that the First Lord of the Admiralty... should have gone out of his way to attack the Shell Company, or Sir Marcus Samuel." Rutherford added that Churchill obviously knew that he "would have every great difficulty with some of his own followers ... and that the best course of action to get them to support it [the funding of Anglo-Persian] was to raise the question of monopoly and to do a little Jew-baiting." Rutherford added, "There is a world shortage ... of an article which the world has only lately begun to see is required for certain special purposes. This is the reason why prices have gone up, and not because evilly-disposed gentlemen of the Hebraic persuasion—I mean *cosmopolitan* gentlemen—have put their heads together in order to try and force prices up."[12]

More than sarcastic appeals, Churchill unabashedly made the case for state-controlled capitalism. "We knew that by our contract we confer upon the Anglo-Persian Company an immense advantage which, added to their concession, would enormously strengthen the company and increase the value of their property. If this consequence arose from the necessary action of the State, why should not the State share in the advantage, which we created? ... Why should we not go a step further? Was it not wiser ... to acquire control of an enterprise ... on which, to a large extent, we must rely? That was the process of reasoning by which the Admiralty and the Cabinet were drawn from the making of a simple supply contract to the definite acquisition and control of the company and its concessions ... We have to pay for the oil, but the Treasury will recover the profits."[13]

Churchill again and again slammed the ruthless oil monopolies. "Look out upon the wide expanse of the oil regions of the world! Two gigantic corporations—one in either hemisphere—stand out predominantly. In the New World, there is the Standard Oil ... In the Old World, the great combination of the Shell and the Royal Dutch, with all their subsidiary and ancillary branches, has practically covered the whole ground ... Amongst British companies who have maintained an independent existence ... the Anglo-Persian Oil Company, is almost the only noticeable feature."[14]

He concluded: "It is for Parliament to balance ... an independent oil supply against the extortion of which the taxpayer would otherwise be the victim." [15]

Hecklers and adversaries in the House let loose. More than a few criticized the plan because oil in far-off Persia was clearly not defensible. "Nobody denies that the properties are valuable," asserted fellow member of Parliament George Lloyd, "but ... the whole of that country and the whole of your properties is surrounded by material which is far more flammable than the oil which you seek ... I am absolutely in favor of our seeking an oil supply independent of all trusts, in any part of the world, outside or inside the British Empire, where it can be found and properly controlled. I say, 'properly controlled,' which this cannot be."[16]

Lloyd emphasized, "Those places [in Persia] are situated in a country which has no central control whatever ... in a country which is surrounded by war-like tribes ... which is in the hands of turbulent tribesmen whose influence is proportionate locally for their capacity to terrorize and raid, and whose policy is directed by no respect for foreign undertakings or treaties."[17]

Another member declared, "It is as if he had stored his gunpowder near some furnace."[18]

Some members wondered how Britain could morally meddle in another nation's territory without regard for the inhabitants. "It is almost amusing," charged MP Arthur Ponsonby, "the way the great powers, when discussing a matter of this sort, consider that they are conferring an untold benefit on the country in question, and the interests of that country, so far as its population is concerned, are entirely disregarded. I suppose the Persian Government has been consulted, although I daresay that would be considered an unnecessary formality. It has been the policy of the British Government too often to concentrate attention on the material development of a country without sufficient regard to the welfare and liberties of the inhabitants to whom that country belongs ... It is a matter of small moment to any honorable member in this House how the Persians will fare. We think in our arrogance that, of course, British capital and British enterprise can do nothing but confer an immediate benefit and advantage on a country in such a backward state as the Persian Empire. That may or may not be the case. Persia had a complete civilization when we were walking about in skins."[19]

At the end of the day, the tempestuous debate over the bill known as

"Anglo-Persian Oil Company—Acquisition of Capital," culminated in a vote of 254 ayes against only 18 nays. When Greenway asked, "How did you manage to carry the House with you so successfully," Churchill readily admitted that it was the "attack on monopolies and trusts that did it."[20]

The next day, the press energetically cross-examined the just-ratified measure. "The real issue," blasted the *Times*, "is whether the Government have, by this new enterprise, entered upon a fresh and dangerous policy in the Middle East, which may in the end lead them into responsibilities of a character which Ministers still seem unable to comprehend." The *Times* did not quibble with the need for oil. But "we do not quite understand why he [Churchill] went to Persia for it." The newspaper repeated MP George's question: "How are these properties to be defended?"[21]

Finally, in one editorial, the *Times* warned, "We want the Navy to have oil. But we do not want to run the risk of fresh embroilment anywhere in the Middle East; and it is for this reason that we fear the country may come to regret an impetuous and careless undertaking."[22]

On June 18 and 19, 1914, with Parliament's vote still fresh and even as the headlines raged, identical coordinated telegrams were sent to the Turkish prime minister by the British and German governments applying maximum pressure in pursuit of the long-awaited and decade-delayed concession. These two communications only reinforced a barrage of telegrams earlier that month reminding that Turkish tax increases were completely contingent on the concession.[23]

On June 28, 1914, London received the requested definitive and positive response. "The Ministry of Finance, which has taken over from the *Civil Liste* matters concerning petroleum deposits already discovered or to be discovered in the *villayets* [provinces] of Mosul and Baghdad agrees to lease them to the T.P.C. and reserves the right later on to fix its own share as well as the general terms of the agreement."[24]

There was just one other thing. Worried over claims that Gulbenkian and others might launch, the Turkish prime minister added a sentence: "It is understood that the Company must indemnify, in case of necessity, the third parties who may be interested in the petroleum deposits situated in those two *villayets* [provinces]."[25]

Indemnification? Once again the concession was not final—just *almost* final. The Foreign Office was about to mount yet another démarche on that June 28, when the world's attention was suddenly riveted on Sarajevo in the tiny realm of Bosnia. Bosnia was one of those tiny emerging post-Ottoman realms swirling at the heart of the Eastern Question and the Balkans Wars.

Archduke Francis Ferdinand, heir apparent to throne of the Austro-Hungarian Empire, and his wife were on an official state visit to mountain-cradled

Sarajevo that June 28, 1914. About a month earlier, while sipping tea beneath a flickering gaslight at Belgrade's Café Zlatna Moruna, three fanatical Serbian nationalists from an organization called the "Black Hand," had read a short newspaper notice about the impending state visit. They immediately organized a conspiracy of some 22 individuals. A vanguard of three assassins slowly made their way to Sarajevo.[26]

June 28, 1914. Approximately 10 A.M. Riding in an open car as part of a six-vehicle motorcade, with a wealthy loyal supporter riding upright on the sideboard, the archduke's attention was drawn by a loud crack. It was a hand grenade, thrown by one the conspirators. The grenade bounced off the vehicle, exploding harmlessly away from the car. Archduke Ferdinand and his wife Sofia sped off to their destination, City Hall, to complain to the Mayor about an assassination attempt. Believing the attack to be over, and deciding to stand up to fanatics, the archduke and his wife sat patiently through the Mayor's trite speech. They were *en route* to their next stop when the driver took a wrong turn, accidentally cruising right into the sight lines of the second conspirator Gavrilo Princip. Princip approached the car, aimed, and shot twice.[27]

Princip was wrestled to the ground by guards and placed in shackles. At first, it was uncertain how seriously injured the couple was. But as the vehicle drove on, blood spurted from the archduke's mouth. His pregnant wife slumped to the floor in pain. The archduke, himself mortally wounded, turned to her and pleaded: "*Sterbe nicht! Bleibe am Leben für unsere Kinder!* Don't die, my love! Stay alive for our children!" Shortly thereafter, she died. Then he died.[28]

Europe was thrown into chaos. Throughout a tumultuous and nerve-wracking July, Vienna charged Serbia with trying to start a war. The many alliances that had been revving darkly for decades began lining up on either side of the conflict. The Eastern Question was about to be answered on a global scale.

One month after the murders, July 28, 1914, Austria-Hungary invaded Serbia. On August 1, 1914, as the czar rushed to bolster his ally Serbia, Germany declared war on Russia and, the next day, on Russia's ally, France. Britain demanded the Kaiser respect Belgium's neutrality; and when he invaded Belgium on August 4, 1914, London declared war on Germany. Within days, Japan, too, declared war on Germany. The conflict deployed great new modes of warfare: submarines, airplanes, massive trenches, tanks, long-range cannons, and many more devices and methods of terrible devastation. The Great War was on.

During those fiery weeks of July, August, September and October, frantic efforts were nonetheless undertaken to save the Mesopotamian oil concession, even as Istanbul and London sped toward the abyss of war. On October 29,

1914, the Ottoman Empire entered the war on Germany's side. Within a week, Britain was at war with Turkey as well.

The captains of industry and the leaders of nations had walked through the intoxicating vapors of Middle East petroleum, some for country, some for avarice, many for both. But two gunshots in Sarajevo ignited a fuse that exploded into a monstrous conflict that killed millions. Thereafter, fuel and fuse would be inseparable throughout the world. One would beget the other for decades.

CHAPTER SIX

BLOOD
FOR OIL

World War I: 8 million dead; 21 million wounded, 2 million missing in action, $180 billion spent.[1]

The Great War that many thought would be concluded within weeks dragged on mercilessly for nearly half a decade. In numbers that defy the darkest imagination, young men continually climbed out of muddy trenches to valiantly charge barbed wire, mines, and machine-gun fire. They were blown to bits, poisoned, and starved en masse in the irrepressible bloody conquest, loss, and bloody reconquest of mere meters of territory.

The disastrous 1915 Gallipoli campaign killed more than a half million men from both sides. During the Battle of the Somme in 1916, about a million men died from all countries. On the first day alone, there were 58,000 British casualties, a third of who were killed. At Verdun in 1916, the dead and missing were generally estimated to be nearly a million. Russia lost more than any country: mobilizing 12 million, suffering 1.7 million fatalities, 5 million wounded, and 2.5 million missing or taken prisoner. Germany's numbers were almost as staggering.[2] The best explanation of why the nations of Europe went to war and sacrificed so many men was this: They just wanted to.

But long before most of World War One's deadliest battles were fought, the British invaded Mesopotamia with a real purpose. Britain declared war on Turkey on November 5, 1914. Weeks before, however, sealed orders had been sent to Bombay for Indian Expeditionary Force D to sail to the Persian

Gulf. Not a single barrel of commercial oil had been pumped in Mesopotamia, nor had a single drill been sunk or a concession even granted. Yet Admiral Edmond Slade had urged the government to protect Anglo-Persian's recently completed refinery at Abadan, Persia, located directly downstream from Basra on the Shatt al-Arab waterway at the head of the Persian Gulf. Admiral Slade was the man who headed Churchill's fuel expedition to Persia in advance of acquiring government control of Anglo-Persian Oil Company. Shortly thereafter, Slade was appointed as one of two *ex officio* government board members of the company. He was now able to call for military action in his dual role as an advocate for Anglo-Persian and the British navy.[3]

When it appeared that the transport of Anglo-Persian's oil through the Gulf would be imperiled as part of general hostilities, the British took action. On October 31, 1914, after the Ottoman Empire joined the war on Germany's side, but before war with Turkey had been officially proclaimed, the Admiralty in London dispatched a coded telegram to Indian naval forces laying in wait near Abadan: "Commence hostilities against Turkey."[4]

Pre-positioned Indian forces promptly secured Anglo-Persian's facilities on November 6, 1914, just 24 hours after Whitehall actually declared war. British and Indian forces then pressed on toward Basra, which they occupied on November 23, 1914. The British arrived in Basra to witness thousands of Turks rapidly retreating. One senior British officer recalled, "We found the lower-class Arabs busily employed in looting and burning the houses and murdering the occupants." Order was restored only after several agitators were hanged. Thereafter, Basra became the center of a British occupation that steadily penetrated north.[5]

Now came a confluence of economic, political, and military invasions that established Britain as the new power in Mesopotamia. Indeed, as millions of young men hurtled back and forth across the ghastly trenches of Europe's battlefields, so diplomats, oil executives, and occupation officials jockeyed across Mesopotamia's commercial landscape. Millions died in Europe. But in far-off Mesopotamia, the military-industrial oil complex survived and eventually prospered beyond anyone's dreams.

*   *   *   *

The war for Mesopotamia's strategic location and resources began in London even before the first troops landed in the Persian Gulf. The law enabling the British government to acquire Anglo-Persian Oil Company passed on June 17, 1914, but did not receive the obligatory Royal Assent until August 10. By then, England had been at war with Germany for a week.[6]

In early September 1914, "Trading with the Enemy" proclamations made it illegal to transact business with German companies. In early November, as war was extended to the Ottoman Empire, Turkish entities were included. But the government now owned a majority of Anglo-Persian Oil Company, which, on March 19, 1914, had been fused with a reorganized Turkish Petroleum Company, which itself was 25 percent owned by an enemy corporation—Deutsche Bank. Hence, any and all commercial transactions, even routine business communications, with TPC were illegal.[7]

Nonetheless, on November 2, 1914, Anglo-Persian chairman Charles Greenway pleaded with the Foreign Office to permit the fusion agreement to go forward "without delay in order that the interests of the D'Arcy group (i.e., of the Anglo-Persian Oil Co. Ltd.) may be preserved, no matter how the present war may eventuate." Greenway added that failure to allow certain consummating transactions, such as the exchange of stock and resolutions necessitated by the fusion agreement, would mean that "we fail now to complete the agreement ... [and] lose all claim to an interest in these [petroleum] rights." In such a case, "whatever the result of the war," Greenway warned, "... these rights between the Baghdad Railway Company and the Turkish Petroleum Company will doubtless hold good, inasmuch as it was concluded long before the war with a company of an ostensibly British character [the National Bank of Turkey]."[8] In other words, the German-Turkish group engineered by Gulbenkian would still own much of Mesopotamian oil. Britain, without a concession, would own nothing.

Several weeks of legal deliberations throughout the Foreign Ministry and other departments forced an unwanted conclusion. The government's lead petroleum official, Maurice de Bunsen, curtly informed Greenway that the government had ruled "that the agreement of March 19, 1914 has, in the circumstances, no longer any legal validity." He added that the government "will decline to take this agreement into account when the moment comes to arrange for the future of the oil areas in these [Mesopotamian] districts." De Bunsen stressed, "Take no steps to carry out the arrangements embodied in the agreement." However, in a not so subtle wink and a presage, de Bunsen appended, "But I am to add that the necessity of safeguarding ... the interests of the British parties to that agreement will not be lost sight of."[9] Possession remained nine-tenths of the law. Britain intended to possess Mesopotamia's oil.

At the same time, the British executives of the National Bank of Turkey scrambled to resign from the bank's board because they felt their positions were meaningless and, in view of Gulbenkian's deal with the Germans, probably illegal. But a government exemption permitted the National Bank of Turkey to continue its affairs in non-Turkish-controlled territories, thus allowing it to formally divest itself of its ownership of Turkish Petroleum Company in favor of Deutsche Bank. This divestiture would later prove fateful.[10]

For his part, Gulbenkian resigned from the board of Turkish Petroleum as an individual in his own name in January 1915. He immediately rejoined as a representative of Dutch Shell, lest he officiate as a director representing himself in his own disenfranchisement. At about that time, Gulbenkian met with Greenway and other APOC executives about Anglo-Persian contributing its share of some of TPC's minor operating expenses. After all, APOC was now half owner of TPC. The meeting was both tense and telling. As Gulbenkian asked commercial questions, Greenway, mindful of Trading with the Enemy provisions, declined to answer directly and suddenly turned the conversation to "Persian pottery." A colleague chimed in about "Persian miniatures." A riled Gulbenkian later recalled, "The whole conversation was very cute, but I felt helpless." Gulbenkian, along with Shell's chief, Deterding, then paid for various routine operational expenses out of their own pockets.[11] That irritating episode only further entrenched Shell and APOC forces as bitter adversaries in the battle for Turkish Petroleum.

As Britain prosecuted the war, Anglo-Persian's oil contributed a mere 20 percent of its fuel needs. The remainder was imported chiefly from the United States. Yet by January 1915, a full British division—some 10,000 men—had occupied Basra, and thousands of additional British, Indian, and other colonial units were stationed nearby along the Persian Gulf.[12] Thus, the massive expenditure of men, materiel, and fuel was disproportionate to protecting the Anglo-Persian refinery at Abadan. Britain was locking down not the present strategic advantage, but the future of Mesopotamian oil and Gulf commercial routes.

Charles Hardinge, the British viceroy of India, complained that the massive investment of Indian troops and military resources was completely unjustified, since most of Britain's oil was coming from sure and safe sources in America. He wrote, "How I do hate that pipeline," which had been sabotaged by local Persian tribesmen. "It is inconceivable," he added, "that the Admiralty can be in any way dependent upon the supply of oil derived from Abadan."[13]

But when Hardinge visited the Abadan refinery on February 3, 1915, and witnessed its commercial value, he changed his mind. "In the first instance," he admitted to a Foreign Office colleague, "I was strongly opposed to the acquisition by the Admiralty of so large a share in this undertaking [the Anglo-Persian Oil Company], since I realized that the responsibility for its defense would fall upon India. Now I am delighted that we have so large a stake in Abadan, since it makes it absolutely certain that we can never give up Basra, which I regard as the key of the Gulf ... It is therefore absolutely essential from every point of view that we should remain at Basra where we shall have complete control over the trade of Mesopotamia, and we ought to be able to make the Basra *vilayet* [province] into a second Egypt." Just weeks before, Britain had unilaterally declared Ottoman Egypt a British protectorate, assuming all civil and military authority for the region.[14]

The Foreign Office in London concurred with Hardinge's enthusiasm. On March 31, 1915, Hardinge received an assurance from a London colleague, "I quite agree with you that we should certainly possess the Basra *vilayet* [province], and have perhaps some kind of autonomous province at Baghdad more or less under our protectorate."[15]

By the fall of 1915, the road from Basra to Baghdad was clearly foreseen. Hardinge flippantly suggested to the British palace, "My little show in Mesopotamia is still going strong and I hope that Baghdad will soon be comprised within the British Empire."[16]

However, making Mesopotamia a British satellite required more than just defeating the Turks. It meant allying with the tradition-infused, insular Arabs who lived there. That brought Britain face-to-face with the rising tetrahedron of Arab nationalism—a fractious jumble of tribal rivalries and alliances, kings without constituents, and constituents without kings, all churning across obscure landscapes of impenetrable political intrigue.[17]

Arab nationalism began in earnest as an early-century surge of Arab-Christian and Islamic intellectuals who envied Christian Europe's international movement to achieve self-determination, autonomy, and national independence for its ethnic and religious groups. Arab activists, however, were completely disunified on the geopolitical form for their aspirations. Some craved a network of decentralized, locally ruled Islamic states stretching across the Middle East. Others preferred a Turco-Arabian federation, akin to the Austro-Hungarian Empire. Still others wanted territorial independence at home linked to economic dependence on an industrialized foreign power, such as France or Great Britain. Large tribal groups yet to be swayed could not decide which nationalist expression was best—if any. But many Arabs were quite simply loyal to Istanbul as the traditional seat of the Islamic caliphate.[18]

More important, which part of the Arab domain was to be liberated? Just the Hejaz region of the coastal Arabian Peninsula? Egypt? Palestine? Syria? Some of it? All of it? None of it? The struggle was contentious and competitive. But independence-minded Arabs leaders all concluded: The long-crumbling Ottoman Empire that had ruled them for centuries was now too weak to retain domination. Soon the Sick Man would collapse. With the Great War raging, the Arab national moment had finally arrived.[19]

Nationalist yearnings, percolating for years, manifested most fiercely beginning with the newest iteration of the Ottoman Empire. True enough, Turkey's revolution, in 1908 and 1909, had brought administrative reform to the corrupt ways of the sultans. But soon thereafter, the Committee for the Union and Progress—that is, the Young Turks—had turned repressively chauvinistic. The ruling pashas decided that all the diverse ethnic groups within the empire should become one people—Turkish. They should speak one language—Turkish. Mostly, they should live with one identity—Turkish. Those who would not change willingly would be changed forcibly. The much-resented Turkification campaign of Arab lands throughout the Middle East administratively and economically favored those Arabs who assimilated into the modern Turkish culture and bowed to Istanbul's authority. The campaign snubbed the Arabic language and customs.[20]

However, the whole bundle of Arab wartime resentment toward the Turks also tore at the fabric of Islamic sensibilities. To side with.the British against the Turks meant siding with the Christian infidel against other Muslims, and indeed the modern center of the Islamic world, Turkey. After all, for all their harems and moral decay, the sultans were still the caliphs of Islam, that is, the supreme leaders of all Muslims. For better or worse, Istanbul was the seat of the caliphate.[21] Thus, all Arab alliances were uneasy. Like so many mirages and dust devils in the desert, one minute an alliance with the Arab potentates was visible and furious, the next it was gone, only to reappear a moment later.

Ironically, amid all the agitation for Islamic independence burning throughout the Mideast during World War I, the one key marginalized region was Mesopotamia. Why?

Mesopotamia's peripheral place in the wartime quest for Arab national-ism was intrinsically affected by the composition of the various Arab national parties. In response to repressive and insensitive Turkification, several con-tending parties and secret societies emerged throughout the Middle East—but these were mainly outside Mesopotamia. These included the Literary Club in South Lebanon, comprising disaffected former Arab spies and privileged functionaries of the Sultan. In Cairo, the groups included the Arab Association and the Decentralized Party, which sprang from Lebanese and Syrian immi-grants favoring separate Arab states federated with the Ottoman Empire. The two enduring societies that eventually subsumed the nationalist movement were al-Fatat and al-Ahd, which mainly operated in Paris, Istanbul, and the Arab capitals beyond the Mesopotamian provinces.[22]

For a few years before the war, the three Mesopotamian provinces did host several nationalist, revolutionary, and/or reform societies, some secret, some open. Mosul's Green Flag organization, the Basra Reform Society, and Baghdad's National Scientific Club were among them. But these groups were frequently compromised by Ottoman spies and police agents, or co-opted in the traditional Ottoman fashion by elevating the organizers to lucrative posi-tions. The main agitation within the three provinces was left to the local chap-ters of al-Ahd and al-Fatat in Baghdad and Basra, which advanced pan-Arab issues. However, this agenda was necessarily focused on Syria, Lebanon, and Egypt, where those groups were headquartered, plus the holy sites of the Hejaz.[23]

Demographics in the three main Mesopotamian provinces played a role as well. Mosul in the north was Kurdish; Baghdad in the center was largely Sunni; Basra in the south was overwhelmingly Shi'a. Sunnis and Shi'as had warred with each other for centuries over their establishment and anti-establishment views of Islam. Sunnis comprised the prevailing majority within the religion. Shi'as, who followed their own traditions and interpretations of Islam, existed as schismatic minority within the global Muslim community, comprising some ten percent of the worldwide total. But in Mesopotamia, Shi'as were hardly a disaffected minority. Of the approximate 2.6 million people in Mesopotamia's three provinces, more than half were Shi'a. Sunni Kurds constituted about 20 percent. An additional 8 percent throughout Mesopotamia hailed from non-Arab and/or non-Islamic groups, such as the Jews, Christians, Armenians, Turkomans, and the secretive Yazidis, a tiny sect that abhorred lettuce and dark blue clothing. Although concentrated into a dense and commanding power base in south and central Mesopotamia, the Shi'as were still considered by the larger Arab world to be Islam's outcast 10 percent.[24]

In turn, the hatred that the alienated Mesopotamian Shi'as felt for the Sunni majority never subsided. Hence, ancient Shi'a-Sunni rivalries and ingrained disregard for infidels held fast as nationalists considered Mesopotamia's place in their precious campaign.

Just as important, who were the movers of the nationalist movement? They were not drawn from the multitudes of Bedouin and other tribal groups that constituted much of Mesopotamian life. The foot soldiers of nationalism were just that, rebellious Arab soldiers serving in the Turkish army. As 1915 began, the million-man Ottoman army included at least 100,000 Arabs, perhaps more, including many recently conscripted in the war mobilization. Mesopotamian Arabs were mainly concentrated in four divisions, the 35th through the 38th. Yet these men were stationed not in their home provinces but in Damascus and other parts of Syria.[25]

Various pan-Arab divisions hailing from lands beyond Mesopotamia, including the 12th Corps originally headquartered in Mosul, were also transferred to Syria. In fact, the 12th Corps chief of staff was a leader of al-Ahd, one of the two main nationalistic organizations. What's more, Baghdad's brightest militants, who had attended Istanbul's War College, became officers who, like the ranks they commanded, were also assigned to Syria and other regions beyond Mesopotamia. Therefore, should masses of Arab soldiers mutiny and launch a revolt, it would not be in Mesopotamia, but where they were stationed—in Syria. By virtue of the deployments to Syria, and that country's intellectual base and connections with France, Damascus had become in fact the epicenter of the Arab national movement.[26]

In truth, because of the inherent conflicts in allying with the British infidel against Muslim Turkey, Arab leaders did not care whether the facilitator of their national hopes was Istanbul or London. Arabs simultaneously offered the same fierce allegiance to both sides—the British and the Turks. For example, from the moment war broke out in August 1914, al-Fatat opposed Turkey's entanglement in a bloody Christian-European conflict. Once Istanbul officially joined Germany and Austro-Hungary, al-Fatat's administrative committee declared: "The goal of the Arabs is independence ... to guard the existence of Arab countries, and not out of hostility to the Turks. Therefore, if Arab countries will stand up to the danger of European imperialism, the Society will work alongside the Turks, together with all free Arabs to protect the Arab countries."[27] In the first flammable months of 1914, as prewar contingencies and stratagems were being brokered with Britain, one family rose to prominence: that of Hussein ibn Ali, the sharif of Mecca. Hussein, a short but striking and bearded figure, had been appointed by the Young Turks in 1908 to be the guardian of Mecca's holy sites. Hussein's Hashemite clan traced its lineage directly to the first Quraysh chieftains of Mecca, who reigned some five centuries before the Prophet Mohammed began his rise against the establishment in 610. Thereafter, the Quraysh descendants of the Prophet's wife Fatima became the honored Sunni rulers of Mecca, later known as "the Hashemites." These were the ancestors of Hussein. Through the ages, the distinguished Sunni Hashemite clan became the hereditary defenders of Mecca and superintendents of the Hajj pilgrimage to Mecca, which is mandatory for all Muslims. Therefore, Hussein's family was known throughout the entire Arab domain as a noble one. For London, despite many seething competitors and detractors, it was easy to anoint Hussein and his two sons, Abdullah and Faisal, as the chief applicants and negotiators of the Arab national movement.[28]

London's price for any Arab national reward was strategic revolt against the Turks. But could any Arab deliver? On February 5, 1914, Abdullah met with Lord Kitchener in Cairo. Kitchener was Britain's consul general in Egypt, and a leading military star who would soon become Britain's war minister. Abdullah's message: The Turks were threatening to administratively terminate his father's honorary position in Mecca. In such a case, Hussein just might lead a local revolt against the Turks. Would the British support him against Istanbul?[29]

Kitchener and the Foreign Office were cool to the whole idea. They knew that fundamentally Hussein was acting less nationalistic than protective of his financial stake in guarding the holy sites. Moreover, the English knew that a planned Turkish railway extension into the Arabian Peninsula would deci-mate Hussein's lucrative camel trade. Kitchener literally laughed at Abdullah and explained, "The Arabs of the Hejaz could expect no encouragement from us and that our only interest in Arabia was the safety and comfort of Muslim Indian pilgrims [en route to Mecca]."[30]

Several weeks later, in late March 1914, Louis Mallet, British ambas-sador in Istanbul, reported to Foreign Secretary Grey, "It is still impossible to say what real prospect there may be of any united Arab movement." But Mallet added an enticing thought. "If the Arabs are eventually successful in defeating the Ottoman armies, the loss of the Caliphate would probably fol-low, where, shorn of a further large portion of territory and of the religious leadership, Turkish rule, as it exists today, would presumably disappear." To that, he added a caution: "[But] Europe might then be faced with the question of a partition of the Turkish Empire which might easily produce complica-tions of a serious nature."[31]

Since war had not yet broken out, and commercial relations with the Ottomans remained vibrant, Britain was determined not be dragged into any localized revolt in Mecca or even in Baghdad. "If the plan of creating an insurrection in Mesopotamia should take shape," Mallet warned Grey, "one of the aims of its promoters would be to compel British intervention ... [We] have no intention of pursuing a policy of adventure, which could only com-promise serious British economic interests in Mesopotamia."[32]

But by late October, 1914, with the war in Europe fully under way and the war in the Middle East just days away from ignition, Whitehall reversed itself. Beginning some months earlier, in July 1915, the British high commis-sioner in Egypt, Sir Henry McMahon, entered a back-and-forth written cor-respondence with Hussein that included some 10 confidential letters. The full written exchange was kept secret for 15 years until revealed by the press and parliamentary investigation.[33] Those 10 letters, later to become famous as "the McMahon-Hussein correspondence," offered ambiguous British promises of national recognition within an ambiguously defined territory in exchange for ambiguous Arab offers of revolt predicated upon calculated deceptions and implied threats by both sides.

Decades later, activists on all sides of the Arab national debate would point to the McMahon-Hussein correspondence as proof—or lack of it—of broken pledges and unfulfilled national obligations. Any arguer indeed could seize upon passages within any of the several most prominent letters to vali-date any argument. But embedded within the full set of 10 letters—including some of the forgotten ones—are British demands and the Arab willingness to cede control to the British over one specified region in exchange for national rights elsewhere. The region the Arabs were willing to cede: Mesopotamia.[34]

The prelude to the historic 10-letter McMahon-Hussein correspondence was Kitchener's introductory note of October 31, 1914, which stated: "If the Sharif and Arabs in general assist Great Britain in this conflict that has been forced upon us by Turkey ... Great Britain will guarantee the independence, rights and privileges of the Sharifate against all external foreign aggressions, in particular that of the Ottomans." Referring to the notion of replacing Turkish religious supremacy with Hussein himself, Kitchener appended, "It may be that an Arab of true race will assume the Caliphate at Mecca or Medina, and so good may come by the help of God out of all the evil which is now occurring."[35]

Arab self-definition and mapping began in earnest in early 1915 in Damascus. In March and April, during a series of secret meetings, the two leading nationalist societies, al-Fatat and al-Ahd, joined forces with each other and with Emir Faisal, who was representing his father Hussein. Together, they drafted "the Damascus Protocol," which created a map for the envisioned Arab state. It resembled a dented rectangle tilted left toward eleven o'clock, encompassing and extending the Arabian Peninsula to the shores of the Mediterranean. The proposed northern border coursed east from the Mersin-Adana railway in Turkey, just beyond Syria, along the railroad tracks and across the 37th parallel to the Persian frontier; the eastern border followed the Persian frontier down to the Persian Gulf, then continued to the bottom of the Arabian Peninsula; from there the outline traveled back north to the Mersin-Adana starting point in Turkey, thus completing the geopolitical box. Both Palestine and the three Mesopotamian provinces resided completely within that approximate rectangle. The Damascus Protocol specified that if Britain granted this proposed new state, the British Empire would become the new Arab nation's sponsor and defense partner. In addition, the new Arab nation would extend "the grant of economic preference to Great Britain."[36]

Fearing Turkey's seemingly omnipresent spies, the Damascus Protocol was reduced to miniature script and then sewn into the boots of a member of Faisal's party. Faisal returned to Mecca, where he unveiled the plan to enlist his father's support for a so-called Arab Revolt. The suggested insurrection would begin during the winter of 1915 in Syria where the troops were supposedly standing by. But Ottoman commanders detected the conspiracy, and suddenly transferred most of the Arab divisions out of Syria east to the bloody Gallipoli front. That brought certain death, and Arab soldiers were promptly cut down as part of that battle's mass carnage. The Arabs in Syria did not revolt that winter.[37]

In truth, no one knows how many hundreds or thousands of Arab troops were ever really ready to turn on their commanders. But the aborted Syrian uprising was characteristic of an Arab Revolt that was always being devised and revised, located and relocated, launched and postponed. Moreover, the

Arab leaders constantly exaggerated their forces, their base of popular support, and their willingness to take action. These demerits the British understood well, which is why the British were cool and uncertain about forming reliable military alliances with Arab elements.[38]

To reassure London, Hussein on July 14, 1915, began the famous exchange with McMahon. The letter tendered the Damascus Protocol territorial outline almost word for word, asking for a straight yes or no within 30 days. "If this [30-day] period should lapse before they [the Arabs] receive an answer, they reserve to themselves complete freedom of action," the letter stated in a soon-familiar veiled threat to instead seek alliance with the Turks against Britain.[39]

Not anxious to respond to arbitrary 30-day deadlines, and disturbed over Arab contingents already fighting valiantly in Turkish units, McMahon replied a full 45 days later. Mixing overblown effusiveness with snubbing hesitation, McMahon wrote, "We rejoice ... that your Highness and your people are of one opinion—that Arab interests are English interests and English [are] Arab ... With regard to the questions of limits and boundaries," he continued, "it would appear to be premature to consume our time in discussing such details in the heat of war ... especially as we have learned, with surprise and regret, that some of the Arabs ... far from assisting us, are neglecting this, their supreme opportunity and are lending their arms to the German and the Turk, to the new despoiler and the old oppressor."[40]

A worried Hussein replied on September 9, 1915, with obsequious fawning: "To his Excellency the Most Exalted, the Most Eminent—the British High Commissioner in Egypt; may God grant him Success. With great cheerfulness and delight I received your letter dated August 30, 1915, and have given it great consideration and regard, in spite of the impression I received from it of ambiguity and its tone of coldness and hesitation with regard to our essential point ... Permit me to say clearly that the coolness and hesitation which you have displayed in the question of the limits and boundaries by saying that the discussion of these at present is of no use and a waste of time ... [and] might be taken to infer an estrangement or something of the sort."[41]

Hussein's reply continued deferentially, and at one point referred to McMahon's "perfectness." He emphasized, "In order to reassure your Excellency, I can declare that the whole [Arab] country, together with those who you say are submitting themselves to Turco-German orders, are all waiting the result of these negotiations, which are dependent only on your refusal or acceptance of the question of the limits [borders]." In the best tradition of the Turkish bazaar, Hussein's next sentence asked exactly what Great Britain wanted in return for national support. "Whatever the illustrious Government of Great Britain finds conformable to its policy on this subject, communicate it to us, and specify to us the course we should follow."[42]

McMahon's reply: Britain wanted Mesopotamia.

On October 24, 1915, McMahon wrote back that the United Kingdom would "recognize and support the independence of the Arabs in all the regions within the limits demanded by the Sharif of Mecca," but minus the Turkish portion, and minus any other area in which Britain enjoyed an obligation with other chiefs, and minus any other area, namely Syria, that would conflict with the interest of France. Plus, just one other thing: "With regard to the *vilayets* [provinces] of Baghdad and Basra, the Arabs will recognize that the established position and interests of Great Britain necessitate special administrative arrangements in order to secure these territories from foreign aggression, to promote the welfare of the local populations, and to safeguard our mutual economic interests."[43]

Hussein immediately replied on November 5, 1915 with a flurry of great defensive conviction on behalf of Mesopotamia. Using the region's historic cartographic name "Iraq," Hussein staunchly explained how inseparable and sacred Iraq was to all Arabs—and had been since time immemorial. "As the Iraqi *vilayets* [provinces] are parts of the pure Arab Kingdom," wrote Hussein, "and were in fact the seat of its Government in the time of Ali ibn Abu Talib, and in the time of all the Caliphs who succeeded him; and as in them began the civilization of the Arabs, and as their towns were the first towns built in Islam where the Arab power became so great; therefore they are greatly valued by all Arabs far and near, and their traditions cannot be forgotten by them. Consequently," he insisted, "we cannot satisfy the Arab nations or make them submit to give us such a title to nobility."[44]

The Arabs would not give up Mesopotamia—but Britain could rent it.

"In order to render an accord easy," continued Hussein, "… we might agree to leave under the British administration for a short time those districts now occupied by the British troops without the rights of either party being prejudiced thereby (especially those of the Arab nation; which interests are to it economic and vital), and against a suitable sum paid as compensation to the Arab Kingdom for the period of occupation, in order to meet the expenses which every new kingdom is bound to support; at the same time respecting your agreements with the Sheikhs of those districts, and especially those which are essential."[45]

Britain was by now persuaded by the defection of Mohammed Faruki, a key Arab officer in the Turkish army, that it was worth securing a deal with the Arabs for a revolt if the right terms could be obtained. In early November 1915, Faruki on behalf of Hussein passed a message to the British Foreign Office that the Arabs would be willing to grant Great Britain governance over Baghdad and north Mesopotamia. Faruki also assured, as a British diplomat recorded it, "Arabs would agree to Basra town and all cultivated lands to the south being British territory."[46]

But McMahon was uncertain how much financial and political consideration the Arabs would require for Mesopotamia. He was undoubtedly certain it would be complex and time-consuming. "The Government of Great Britain," he wrote on December 14, 1915 "… are ready to give all guarantees of assistance and support within their power to the Arab Kingdom, but their interests demand, as you yourself have recognized, a friendly and stable administration in the *vilayet* of Baghdad, and the adequate safeguarding of these interests calls for a much fuller and more detailed consideration than the present situation and the urgency of these negotiations permit."[47]

Hussein answered on New Year's Day 1916: "With regard to what had been stated in your honored communication concerning El Iraq, as to the matter of compensation for the period of occupation, we, in order to strengthen the confidence of Great Britain in our attitude and in our words and actions, really and veritably, and in order to give her evidence of our certainty and assurance in trusting her glorious Government, leave the determination of the amount to the perception of her wisdom and justice."[48] In other words, pay what you wish.

Of course, there was no real payment. Britain and Hussein simply agreed: Mesopotamia would be in British hands.

In fact, several opportunities for the Arabs to rise up against the Turks in Mesopotamia were never taken before or during the McMahon-Hussein correspondence. For example, when the suspicious Turks in 1915 transferred numerous Arab divisions from Syria to the gruesome Gallipoli front, they also moved two divisions, the 35th and the 36th, to Mesopotamia. There were suggestions that two leading Arab nationalists be sent in from Syria to foment the population in Baghdad and Basra. The Foreign Office shied away, since national agitation in Mesopotamia would not only inspire rebellion against the Turks, but against the new British occupiers as well. The balking Foreign Office concluded, we cannot "let loose revolutionaries whose actions may extend beyond our control." Others in the British government concurred: "Their [the two proposed agitators] political views are much too advanced to be safe pabula [baby food] for the communities of occupied territories and their presence in any of the towns of Iraq," as the three provinces were now increasingly being called, "would be, in our opinion, undesirable and inconvenient."[49]

On March 16, 1916, just after receiving a letter laying out the attack specifics against Turkish garrisons, Hussein gave the Turks yet another chance to ally with the Arabs. Turkey had declared a jihad against Britain in every mosque across the empire. Hussein offered to send desert warriors to join the jihad if Istanbul granted amnesty to Arab activists sentenced to death in Syria, granted self-rule to Arab states, and also recognized Hussein's sharifate in Mecca. Otherwise, Hussein threatened, Hejaz volunteers would sit out the war.[50]

Turkish war minister Enver Pasha's reply telegram was fierce: "Dealing with questions of war and the Arabs is none of your business. The political criminals in Syria will receive a just sentence. If you continue to concern yourself with this, the result will be no cause for you to rejoice." Then Enver added his own threat: "You will not see your son Faisal again unless you send the volunteers to the front as you promised. If you do not do this, the result for you, as we have said, will not be good."[51]

Hussein decided to cast his lot with the British. The volunteers to fight for Turkey were indeed sent to Syria on condition that Faisal lead them personally. But Faisal's forces were, in fact, mutinous, and merely awaiting instructions to rebel. On June 5, 1916, Arab fighters on camel and horse began demonstration attacks against the railways of the Hejaz. On June 9, 1916 Hussein's family sent a final telegram to the Turks offering to join the jihad against Britain if the Mecca sharifate were recognized. The Turks did not comply. The next day, June 10, 1916, the revolt began in earnest in the Arabian Peninsula and then spread elsewhere.[52]

Ironically, even as the dialogue with Hussein was fully under way, McMahon's chief advisor and director of military intelligence, Lt. Col. Gilbert Clayton, confessed to a friend: "To set up a great Arab State ... was never my idea ... The conditions throughout Arabia, Syria, and Mesopotamia did not allow of such a scheme being practical, even if anyone were so foolish as to attempt it ... the object we have to aim at is, I consider, to work to preserve all the various elements in the Arab territories very much in the same position as they were before the war, but minus the Turks. In this way we shall have an open field to work in."[53] Everyone was fooling everyone, and no one was fooling anybody.

Hussein and some of his scattered Arab forces did ultimately join the military action against Turkey in the Hejaz, Palestine, Gaza, Syria, and elsewhere. A jihad was promulgated by Hussein to justify joining infidel Christians against fellow Muslims: "The defense of the Hejaz from this evil and aggression [the Turks], the observance of the Rites of Islam that Allah has commanded, and the guarding of the Arabs and the Arab countries from the danger to which the Ottoman Empire is doomed because of the misbehavior of this wicked society—all of this will be achieved only by full independence and the cutting of all ties with the bloodthirsty conquerors and robbers."[54]

But in large part, Hussein's Bedouin fighters were "show forces." Not infrequently, they were ceremoniously marched into a town for local applause after a battle was in fact hard-won from the Turks by British units from Australia, India, or elsewhere. Britain certainly provided money and rifles for a campaign of camel riders and horsemen, led by such liaison officers as T. E. Lawrence, dubbed "Lawrence of Arabia." Lawrence's exploits were later romanticized in movies and novels. In reality, as submarine wolf packs hurled torpedoes through the waves, as airplane formations dropped bombs and strafed from the air, as tanks rumbled across the battlefield, as poison gas wafted over the trenches, and as those fighting in Europe gave their lives in a cataclysmic war that swept away 15 million, the scant Arab uprisings were considered merely cosmetic by many. Lawrence himself termed the Arab raids a "sideshow to a sideshow."[55]

The Arabs were unimportant in defeating the Turks. But more important, there was no Arab uprising in Mesopotamia when the British first entered Mesopotamia. Not when they first entered.

* * * *

The British drive for Baghdad really began in late November 1914 as the military occupied Basra and pointedly asked itself: What next? Everyone was optimistic. The Turks were oppressive masters. London believed its troops would be greeted as liberators.

"Arab element is already friendly, and notables here volunteer opinion that we should be received in Baghdad with the same cordiality as we have been here [in Basra]," reported Britain's military's chief political officer Percy Cox. He continued, "Baghdad in all probability will fall into our hands very easily."[56]

Cox, who had served as the key political resident in Persia from the first days of Anglo-Persian's oil strike, added, "I find it difficult to see how we can well avoid taking over Baghdad ... but once in occupation, we must remain." Oil advocates, such as Admiral Fisher, pressed the Prime Minister's office in a letter, "I hope you are not losing any time annexing the Tigris and the Euphrates!"[57]

The politicians misjudged everything. Often, the War Office was equally misinformed and confused. In the beginning, British military men knew that the Ottoman resistance would be formidable. True, almost all of the regular Arab-heritage brigades were absent. But the Turks had deployed other staunch fighting forces, comprised mainly of loyal Turkish-heritage soldiers. One fast-changing War Office estimate temporarily placed enemy forces in Baghdad at 15,000. But the Turks were constantly implementing draconian drafts that added more men in large numbers. Moreover, Turkish reinforcements could pour in from the Russian front en masse to defend Baghdad. "If this happened," warned one general, "... we should have to withdraw or run the risk of a considerable disaster."[58]

Another general argued against "an advance on Baghdad by land on account of the scarcity of water at camps" amid the broiling summer heat. Yet another assured that a thrust against Baghdad clearly "would be impossible to execute at present." What's more, with or without military readiness, message after message exchanged between the generals dismissed Cox's political objective of taking Baghdad as undoable and inadvisable without the local Arab population agreeing to be occupied. The locals would, by necessity, want to join the winning side for fear of reprisals after the battle. One general expressed the prevailing view held by many: "It would be unwise to decide on going to Baghdad ... till we see clearer ... the inward attitude of the Arabs."[59]

The official military history of the campaign concluded that without the friendship of the Arabs, any commander could expect "supplies and information would be cut off, and his baggage and convoys plundered."[60]

Yet the decision to take Baghdad emerged nonetheless—and for years thereafter the generals would argue about exactly who had authorized the orders. No one would take credit for the campaign. But most concluded that orders originated with British officials in Bombay, perhaps because many of the mesmerized civil administrators in colonial India considered Baghdad "the glittering prize to which all eyes turned." Certainly, Indian viceroy Hardinge energetically encouraged the campaign. In a mid-January 1915 letter to the Foreign Office, he wrote, "It is, in my opinion, a matter of cardinal importance to India that Basra should be retained and that the predominance of England in the Persian Gulf should thus be assured. We may never get the chance again." His braggadocio constantly encouraged movement north. "You will have heard of the successful attack made by our troops on the Turkish position near Basra," he wrote on April 26, 1915, adding, "We have given the Turks a real good knock."[61]

Newly installed Mesopotamian commander in chief Sir John Nixon, who led the push to Baghdad, could explain only vaguely that when he visited Bombay, "I gathered we were to advance on Baghdad." In any event, the War Office, fully apprised of the campaign once it began in September 1915, authorized its progress north.[62]

But no one was ready for what happened. The short drive up the road to Baghdad took 18 months. And it cost tens of thousands of lives.

Initial and deceptively easy victories were experienced in the first miles up the Tigris. In late September 1915, after successfully conquering the scantly defended town of Kut, suffering 4,200 dead or wounded, heat-stricken and greatly undersupplied British forces trudged farther north toward the ancient settlement of Ctesiphon. It was at Ctesiphon in 782 that the first Muslim conquerors had elected to build their new capital named Baghdad, just 16 miles north. Unbeknownst to the British, seasoned Turks were waiting in long defensive trenches. British troops were violently turned back to Kut, 100 miles south of Baghdad. Then at Kut, the British were effectively surrounded by as many as 60,000 Turks. Moreover, local hostile Arabs elements energetically joined the Ottoman jihad against the invader.[63]

By mid-January, 1916, beleaguered commanding general Charles Townshend wired, "I have twenty-two days food left, but by ... eating up the horses, we can last out much longer." Townshend ordered the immediate slaughter of 1,100 animals. By February, rations, including horsemeat and mule meat, were halved. Regardless, many Indian troops refused to eat such animals, so their hunger increased more quickly.[64]

Starvation among the troops continued. Hostile Arab merchants in Kut were loath to sell British soldiers any grain. Meanwhile, British officials in India, including Viceroy Hardinge, refused to allow commanders to describe their condition as "besieged." Indeed, reports from Kut were colored rosy, and the situation characterized as merely a momentary setback.[65]

British reinforcements were en route. But they were far off. Meanwhile, the men in Kut were falling from hunger, suffering gastroenteritis from filthy river water, and slowly dying from battle wounds. Then came rains and flood. By the end of February 1916, some 3,000 had died. Disease killed off hundreds more in the following weeks.[66]

Local Turkish commanders offered to let the starving British men retreat for a £1 million bribe, but War Minister Enver Pasha in Istanbul blocked it. London doubled the offer to £2 million. This, too, was refused. Enver Pasha did not want money—he wanted British troops to surrender. Finally, on April 29, 1916, in a humiliating defeat, 13,309 British troops and noncombatant support elements destroyed their weapons and equipment, and surrendered to the Turks.[67]

When the Turks reoccupied Kut, British officers, including the sick and dying among them, were subjected to the most savage violence. The beatings were incessant. Hostile Arabs and Turkish soldiers alike looted their few possessions, boots, and blankets, and pummeled those who resisted.[68]

Quickly, the Turks turned to any Arabs in the town of Kut who had cooperated with the British. These people, drawn from the Arab leadership, were tortured, mutilated and frequently strangled. One British translator from town was seized. The Turks broke his legs, and then hung him upside down until the pain was so unbearable he desired death. That he achieved when in an unguarded moment he hurled himself off a roof.[69]

As for the British soldiers, too emaciated from disease or starvation to walk, they were nonetheless mercilessly marched almost the entire 100 miles from Kut to Baghdad. Hundreds died of thirst, starvation, or beatings. Local Arabs along the way demanded boots or clothing for mere handfuls of dates or black bread. Uniformed Arab soldiers accompanying the march forced the feeble men forward by merciless whipping and assaults with rifle butts.[70]

"We tingled with anger and shame," recalled one key British captain, "at seeing ... a sad little column of British troops who had marched up from Kut, driven by a wild crowd of Kurdish horsemen who brandished sticks and what looked like whips. The eyes of our men stared from white faces, drawn long with the suffering of a too-tardy death .... As they dragged one foot after another, some fell, and those with the rearguard came in for blows from cudgels and sticks. I saw one Kurd strike a British soldier who was limping along; he reeled under the blows ... Some have been thrashed to death, some killed, and some robbed of their kit and left to be tortured by the Arabs. I have been told by a sergeant that he saw one ... [British naval officer] killed instantly by a blow on the head from a stirrup iron swung by a Kurdish horseman, [this] for stopping on the road for a few seconds."[71]

The captain's account continued, "Men were dying of cholera and dysentery and often fell out from sheer weakness ... A man turned green and foamed at the mouth. His eyes became sightless and the most terrible moans conceivable came from his inner being ... They died, one and all, with terrible suddenness ... One saw British soldiers in a similar state dying of enteritis with a green ooze issuing from their lips, their mouths fixed open, in and out of which flies walked ... Details of other similar cases I won't write about."[72]

The heat only worsened their desperate plight. "Seldom, if ever, have our troops been called upon to campaign in more trying heat," wrote one commander.[73]

In Baghdad, the prisoners were marched through the streets to jeering crowds. From there, they were forced farther north. At Tikrit, where some men were housed, starvation took even more souls. The men "looked ghastly," as one senior officer penned in his diary. He added, "The Arabs used to bring milk and eggs to sell and asked exorbitant prices. Consequently, they [the soldiers] would soon have no money and die of starvation or neglect ... Sometimes, when a sick man would crawl out of the hovel ... Arabs would throw stones and chase him back into the yard."[74]

When the long-marched British soldiers were finally examined by English doctors and the International Red Cross as part of a prisoner exchange, the starved British and Indian captives were reduced to corpse-like survivors, their pronounced ribcages hanging pitifully below skulls with eyes. "They were wasted to wreathes of skin hanging upon a bone frame," wrote one of the examiners.[75]

British reinforcements arrived. Kut was retaken. Then the advance to Baghdad was resumed. The British entered Baghdad triumphantly on March

11, 1917, in columns of weary Tommies and turbaned Indians, Lee-Enfield bolt-action rifles on their shoulders, a dust storm swirling around them.[76]

Baghdad was not taken for oil. It was not taken for commerce. It was taken for Kut and the memory of 13,000 captured, many of whom were propelled through a bleak nightmare gauntlet that one commander described as Dante's Inferno.[77] Baghdad was not taken for oil. Baghdad was taken because, while the British could swallow the horror of hundreds of thousands of their best and brightest dying courageously if naively in the slimed trenches and muddied fields of battle, they could not stomach the eye-searing images of their men being beaten, tortured, and slowly starved into shuffling skeletons yearning to go home or die. Baghdad was not taken for oil.

But Basra was.

CHAPTER SEVEN

PROCLAMATION

The following proclamation was read aloud in Baghdad by General Stanley Maude on March 18, 1917, one week after occupation by the British. This is the complete proclamation.

TO THE PEOPLE OF BAGHDAD

In the name of my King, and in the name of the peoples over whom he rules, I address you as follows:

Our military operations have as their object the defeat of the enemy and the driving of him from these territories. In order to complete this task, I am charged with absolute and supreme control of all regions in which British troops operate; but our armies do not come into your cities and lands as conquerors or enemies, but as liberators.

Since the days of [the Mongol warrior] Hulagu, your city and your lands have been subject to the tyranny of strangers, your palaces have fallen into ruins, your gardens have sunk in desolation, and your forefathers and your-selves have groaned in bondage. Your sons have been carried off to wars not of your seeking, your wealth has been stripped from you by unjust men, and squandered in distant places.

Since the days of Midhat, the Turks have talked of reforms, yet do not the ruins and waste of today testify to the vanity of those promises?

It is the wish not only of my King and his peoples, but it is also the wish of the great Nations with whom he is in alliance, that you should prosper even as in the past, when your lands were fertile, when your ancestors gave to the world literature, science, and art, and when Baghdad city was one of the wonders of the world.

Between your people and the dominions of my King there has been a close bond of interest. For two hundred years, have the merchants of Baghdad and Great Britain traded together in mutual profit and friendship. On the other hand, the Germans and Turks, who have despoiled you and yours, have for twenty years made Baghdad a center of power from which to assail the power of the British and the Allies of the British in Persia and Arabia. Therefore the British Government cannot remain indifferent as to what takes place in your country now or in the future, for in duty to the interests of the British people and their Allies, the British Government cannot risk that being done in Baghdad again which has been done by the Turks and Germans during the War.

But you, people of Baghdad, whose commercial prosperity and whose safety from oppression and invasion must ever be a matter of closest concern to the British Government are not to understand that it is the wish of the British Government to impose upon you alien institutions. It is the hope of the British Government that the aspirations of your philosophers and writers shall be realized and that once again the people of Baghdad shall flourish, enjoying their wealth and substance under institutions which are in consonance with their sacred laws and their racial ideals. In Hejaz, the Arabs have expelled the Turks and Germans who oppressed them, and proclaimed the Sharif Hussein as their King, and his Lordship rules in independence and freedom, and is the Ally of the Nations who are fighting against the power of Turkey and Germany; so, indeed, are the noble Arabs, the Lords of Kuwait, Nejd, and Asir.

Many noble Arabs have perished in the cause of Arab freedom at the hands of those alien rulers, the Turks, who oppressed them. It is the determination of the Government of Great Britain, and the Great Powers allied to Great Britain, that these noble Arabs shall not have suffered in vain. It is the hope of the British people and the Nations in alliance with them that the Arab race may rise once more to greatness and renown among the peoples of the Earth and that it shall bind itself together to this end in unity and concord.

O people of Baghdad, remember that for twenty-six generations you have suffered under strange tyrants who have ever endeavored to set one Arab House against another in, order that they might profit by your dissensions. This policy is abhorrent to Great Britain and her Allies, for there can be neither peace nor prosperity where there is enmity and misgovernment. Therefore I am commanded to invite you, through your nobles and elders and representatives, to participate in the management of your own civil affairs in collaboration with the political representatives of Great Britain who accompany the British Army, so that you may be united with your kinsmen in North, East, South, and West in realising the aspirations of your Race.[1]

PART II

AFTER IRAQ

CHAPTER EIGHT

INVENTING
IRAQ

C *haos* is probably too elevated a term to describe Allied wartime policy in the Mideast. As men died by the thousands each week, a glissando of contradictory public declarations, private letters, formal treaties, *sub-rosa* agreements, and governmental pledges was enunciated to allies, neutrals, strategic corporations, nationalist organizations in Turkish provinces, and international bodies. The long list of assuring and assured parties included France, England, the United States, competing nationalist Arab factions, the Zionist Organization, and petroleum companies. Nor did any government act monolithically or even cohesively. Foreign offices, war ministries, commercial bureaus, and colonial officers often issued their promises and commitments at cross-purposes, often without checking with—or even informing—their superiors.

Promises *du jour* were *de rigueur*. Some British or French official sensed a need, perceived a valuable alliance, or sniffed an opportunity, and out went a signed pledge. Nearly all of these undertakings were completely contradictory. Not a few were disingenuous. Some were simply dishonored as needed. Many spawned their own universes of international conflicts, disputes, and lasting bitterness. Indeed, for the contracting parties of World War I, chaos was a condition to aspire to—a step up from the diplomatic bedlam that ruled.

Several small libraries would be needed to explore the evolving agreements that greatly impacted the British as they occupied Baghdad and Mesopotamia, as well as the Arabs who lived there. But among the most salient was the Sykes-Picot Agreement hammered out between senior diplomats Mark Sykes of Britain, Georges Picot of France, and Russian foreign minister Sergei Sazonov. Sykes-Picot, negotiated in early 1916, was a secret tripartite collection of letters, complete with colored maps, agreeing to carve up the Mideast after the war. Baghdad and Basra were decreed British spheres of influence, while oil-rich Mosul and Syria would be French, with Russia exercising a privilege over its frontiers with Persia. France was virtually devoid of reliable oil fields. Controlling Kurdish Mosul would one day yield France the petroleum the Great War had proved was necessary in a modern world. In return for ceding Mosul, Britain would be assured that her oil and general commerce from Persia, lower Mesopotamia, and the Gulf could transit French-held Syria without encumbrance. Therefore, the control and extension of the Baghdad Railway into Syria was geographically split between Britain and France, with the French taking over from Mosul east. Sykes-Picot's terms would reward France for the immense losses she was suffering in the war, while preserving British and Russian interests.[1]

Relinquishing the still untested but much coveted oil deposits of Mosul was difficult for the British. But, "it is clear, that we shall have to make up our minds to the inclusion of Mosul in the French sphere," a diplomat in the India Office told the London Foreign Office on January 13, 1916, even as the agreement was being negotiated.[2]

Sykes-Picot was concluded just after the ambiguous McMahon promises to Hussein that would create an Arab national entity, but one that would exclude Mesopotamia. Under Sykes-Picot, that Arab entity would be a mere "confederation" under French and British economic and administrative control. More precisely, the Arab confederation was to be comprised of geographically and legally separated colonies but imbued with an amorphous Arab identity. The India Office in London expressed the thinking succinctly in a telegram to Charles Hardinge, the British viceroy of India: "What we want is not a United Arabia; but a weak and disunited Arabia, split up into little principalities so far as possible under our suzerainty—but incapable of coordinated action against us, forming a buffer against the Powers in the West."[3]

As the details unfolded, British diplomat George Buchanan in Petrograd, Russia, cabled Sykes a coded "urgent, private and secret message" warning that French desiderata in Syria and Mosul might incite "suicidal and foolish fanaticism" in the region. But French plans seemed to be moving toward acceptance. "I therefore suggest," stated Buchanan, "that in regard to Arabs, our policy should be let Arabs do what they can for themselves and ... make such concessions, declarations and arrangements in Mesopotamia with regard to Arab theory of independence and participation in administration ... [But] keep actual terms of provisional government from [the] knowledge [of] Arab leaders."[4] Indeed, during the give-and-take of the Sykes-Picot negotiations among the French, British, and Russians, neither the Arab residents of the territories nor their leaders, were ever consulted.

Sykes-Picot was formalized by the French and British foreign ministers on May 15, 1916, and almost immediately regretted by Whitehall. Its ink had literally still not dried when oil advocates within the British government initiated a campaign to scrap the agreement. Weeks before, in early April 1916, British government oil official Maurice de Bunsen was asked by the Prime Minister to establish a "Committee on Asiatic Turkey" to better assess Britain's true interests in the Middle East. The committee saw Mosul's abundance of oil as simply too precious to surrender to France. Just weeks after Sykes-Picot was framed, de Bunsen's report concluded that Turkish Mosul must remain British and that British forces ought to continue their Mesopotamian campaign northward. "Oil again makes it commercially desirable for us," de Bunsen's report concluded, "to carry our control on to Mosul, in the vicinity of which place there are valuable wells, possession of which by another power [France] would be prejudicial to our interests."[5]

The Anglo-Persian Oil Company (APOC) couldn't wait. In fact, although Anglo-Persian still possessed no petroleum concession in Mesopotamia, the company used Britain's occupation of Basra to commence oil exploration, ostensibly under the auspices of the Admiralty. In a confidential dispatch, company chairman Greenway informed the Foreign Office undersecretary, "Our geological staff has carried out extensive reconnaissance over an area 100 miles inland from the Shatt al-Arab River [in the Basra region] ... which reconnaissance shows that there are possibilities of finding oil." Greenway explained that APOC was "not putting in [a petroleum research] application for the area" in anticipation that his company would "be given the complete oil rights over any portion of the Turkish Empire which may come under British influence."[6] This presumption might have appealed to oil allies in India, but it stunned the Foreign Office, which was mindful of other commitments.

No longer was Anglo-Persian focused solely on the realm of the Tigris and Euphrates, but on any territory awarded to Britain after the war. This new approach could stretch APOC's commercial domain all the way to Istanbul and beyond into East Europe. As APOC's jurisdiction expanded, so did India's commercial subcolonization of the Mideast. Unhappy, Foreign Secretary Edward Grey himself insisted Greenway's sudden expanded view be "at once controverted" by oil official de Bunsen. Recalling the Fusion Agreement of March 1914, which granted Shell 25 percent of the new, larger Anglo-Persian entity, another Foreign Office functionary added this caution: "In case there is litigation hereafter, as I am positive there will be if we admit

Greenway's claim," Shell would certainly claim it was "unfairly treated by His Majesty's Government if ... jostled out of that 25 percent."[7]

Nonetheless, Anglo-Persian organized more pressure to keep Mosul out of French hands. The campaign intensified in the first days of April 1916, just as the Sykes-Picot bargain was becoming known to inner circles. On April 1, 1916, the India Office in London sent a letter reminding the Foreign Office, "It will be borne in mind that His Majesty's Government have supported the claim of Mr. D'Arcy to a concession of all oil deposits in the *vilayets* [provinces] of Mosul and Baghdad," and questioning whether Anglo-Persian could still exercise its claim under French control.[8]

Other lobbying continued, including APOC playing off British fears that the Germans might seize Mesopotamia's oil fields to reassert the Deutsche Bank's Anatolia Railway claim. On April 3, 1916, Greenway sent press clips to the foreign office from two German language publications, the industry journal *Petroleum* and the newspaper *Frankfurter Zeitung*. Both extolled Mesopotamian oil deposits and stressed their importance to Germany.[9]

As Anglo-Persian tried to wedge itself forward as the potentate of Mesopotamia's future oil, one insider worked behind the scenes to frustrate the company's plan. He tried to prevent any obstruction to the accord granting France primacy in Mosul. The spoiler was, of course, Gulbenkian. He had been lying in wait to reclaim what he considered rightfully his. After being expelled from the process by the British in London, Gulbenkian now sought a commercial alliance with the French in Paris.[10]

The French needed oil. Their petroleum industry was in a shambles. Gulbenkian wrote, "Having lived in France for a long time, and in view of my contacts with the French oil groups, I was fully acquainted with all the circumstances in connection with the problem ... The French oil groups ... were nothing else than a monopolistic association of grocers ... in a pitiful condition in spite of the fact that French refiners had accumulated enormous fortunes by price rigging, and dubious methods, such as bribing the press."[11]

The French government had granted refiners special economic protections and incentives to encourage development of a refinery infrastructure on French soil. But, in fact, there was no actual refining in France, according to Gulbenkian. The oil was purchased already fully refined from American firms and sometimes Royal Dutch Shell. Then, at the port, prior to shipment, French petroleum companies deliberately laced the oil tanks with "chemical dirt" that could be easily removed. This simple removal process was passed off as genuine "refining" to maintain the charade and continue the flow of French tax exemptions.[12]

But once war was declared, imported refined oil became scarce and the French government learned its refining industry was fundamentally nonexistent. Gulbenkian saw his mission as cracking "the unwholesome, self-ish and unpatriotic grip of the French refiners on their country's oil trade … [and therefore] increase the trade and influence of the Royal Dutch combine," while all along quietly bolstering Turkish Petroleum Company's fortunes. His motives? Gulbenkian claimed that, in fact, "I was prompted by a feeling of sympathy for a country where I had been residing for many years."[13]

Working with French oil industry friends he had cultivated over time, Gulbenkian convinced French officials that France must control Mosul. When it did, Turkish Petroleum would be there to grant them the bounty of Meso-potamian northern oil fields. But while Gulbenkian in Paris was promoting French hegemony over Mosul's oil, French diplomats in London were feeling Britain's immediate change of heart. Even as the main Sykes-Picot letter was being signed on May 15, 1916, Sir Edward Grey asked the French ambassa-dor in London for written assurances that France, when it took over Mosul, would recognize Britain's preexisting commercial rights. These commercial rights referred to the oil concessions gained from Turkish Petroleum Com-pany and Anglo-Persian in the March 19, 1914, Fusion Agreement. Of course, that agreement had been deemed null and void when war broke out. But if those rights had actually been acquired, even theoretically, Britain wanted to preserve them. By May 17, 1916, France provided written assurances that it was "ready to confirm, in the regions which might be attributed to it … the various British concessions bearing a date prior to the war." In other words, Britain could still control TPC rights in Mosul if it chose to somehow resur-rect the fusion deal.[14]

Gulbenkian was again circumvented, but not for long.

*   *   *   *

Occupation meant administration. Under the Hague Conventions of 1899 and 1907, an occupying military power was obligated to efficiently and prop-erly administer lands under its control and safeguard the civilian populations. Within a week of overrunning Basra, the British inaugurated a civilian admin-istration. As the British moved north, and when they eventually captured Baghdad, their occupying civil administration was extended into the new ter-ritory. Almost overnight, the occupied portion of Mesopotamia became not a national Arab state-in-waiting, not a revived version of Midhat Pasha's con-stitutional dream, and not a prelude to any pan-Arab vision. Mesopotamia became India.[15]

Turkish paper money was banned by proclamation and replaced with Indian rupees, although valuable Turkish gold liras temporarily remained in circulation, especially in the bazaars. The Eastern Bank of India opened branches in key centers of conquered provinces, sometimes in the very facilities of Deutsche Bank. So many rupees were needed, that they were boxed and shipped from Bombay, hot off the mint. When the supply of rupees was outpaced by demand, the Anglo-Persian Oil Company was asked to help through its connections at the Imperial Bank of Persia; the company was only too happy to assist. Ottoman postage stamps were retained but overprinted with Indian imprimaturs for use by the troops, and these worked their way into common use. A Revenue Department was opened at Basra to accept taxes, ordinary administrative fees, and routine payments—all in rupees of course. All government funds now wove into a local civil occupation fisc controlled from Calcutta. Financial officials in India were astonished when their efficient replacement of Turkish corruption yielded a £130,000 surplus for 1915.[16]

The former Turkish territories were now increasingly called by their regional name, "Iraq," and this identity slowly came into common usage to usher in a new governmental status. Great Britain controlled the largest Islamic population in the world, some 40 million Muslims in India. Hence, London felt comfortable in morphing Mesopotamia into what was called "an Indian appendage."[17]

The Iraq Occupied Territories Code, replicating the civil and criminal laws of India, was unveiled in August 1915, complete with courts, judges, and magistrates, all from India and under the administration of the Indian political department. Section 8 of the code explicitly declared that the Iraqi territories were the equivalent of "a district … of Bombay." Those Indian laws were not translated into either Arabic or Turkish, and it was more than a year before any court business could be conducted in Arabic.[18]

For the tribal areas not accustomed to urbanized law, Britain imported and renamed the Indian Frontier Crimes Regulations that empowered a political officer to convene a tribal *majlis*, or arbitration of elders. The political officer could veto any majlis adjudication. In many cases, Iraqi tribal customs, such as token money payments to resolve feud murders and death to women who strayed from arcane Bedouin morality codes, were set aside for British traditions of punishment. Under transplanted British Indian law, murderers were now sentenced to capital execution; women accused of violating desert mores were not.[19]

Indian policemen, headed by E. G. Gregson, a senior officer of the Indian Police Service, were imported to keep order. Several hundred men in uniform patrolled, ran the jails, and superintended night watchmen. They enforced order at government offices, the Basra docks, and at Baghdad's facilities.[20]

A huge Indian-run bureaucracy was erected. British and Indian health officials assumed the sensitive inspection of Persian and Indian Shiite corpses for burial at Najaf, and they supervised the many pilgrims who visited Shiite shrines. Prostitutes, all 180 of them, while not officially registered, were routinely inspected by the civil medical authorities to reduce venereal disease. Passenger priorities for boatmen and carriage drivers, the sale of liquor, sanitary conditions for horse stables, the treatment of sick dogs, the rental of property, carrying of arms, and all aspects of foodstuffs were regulated by Indian bureaucrats according to an English model.[21]

Reconstruction and development plans abounded to restore the golden era of Mesopotamia, and bring its long-neglected provinces into the twentieth century. British economic analysts studied all aspects of Mesopotamian commerce. Trade and traffic were to be expanded throughout the provinces and then connected to the world at large. Plans were outlined to dramatically increase the new Iraq's export of cotton and dates, as well as its imports of the manpower and machinery needed to make Iraq bloom once more.[22]

Extensive irrigation and flood control, what British trade planners called "the scientific control of the rivers," would be constructed to significantly increase food yields. Baghdad's railway, chugging north and south, would become a strategic commercial as well as military linchpin of this grand national design. Medical facilities, schools, public works, bridges, roads to reach the northern oil regions—so much was needed.[23]

To engineer the transformation, the heavy machines of progress were required: fleets of Ford and Peerless lorries, Caterpillar tractors, mechanized irrigation pumps, building materials, and spare everything. The primitive port at Basra, which often could not even handle conventional steamships, was completely in need of modernization. Within weeks of the 1914 invasion, three river steamers were requisitioned. Later, three dredgers were brought in from India to deepen the Shatt al-Arab waterway leading to Basra and improve the port area generally. Lucrative and monopolistic contracts were awarded to British steamship and transport lines. Transport itself would be a fabulous economic center.[24]

There was a nation to build. But greater Basra's entire population was estimated at just 80,000. Baghdad's was approximately 230,000, split between Arabs, Jews, Persians, Syrians, and others. Many, perhaps a majority, were still living a tribal or pastoral lifestyle. More manpower was needed to implement the rapid and sweeping infrastructure improvements experts had in mind to support both the occupying army and trade expansion. "All schemes for the agricultural development and commercial exploitation of the country," declared one key trade survey, "are, however, conditioned and limited by the capacity, temperament and character of the inhabitants. The two *vilayets* of Baghdad and Basra are thinly populated, possessing an average of nine inhabitants per square mile, which is inadequate."[25]

British eyes turned to India, which possessed an abundance of population and which could send in tens of thousands of laborers, who themselves would constitute a viable and economy-stimulating population in need of goods and service. "Stress must be laid upon the organic connection which already exists between Mesopotamia and India," the key trade survey concluded.[26]

More than a few who favored an industrial revolution for Iraq envisioned a new, revitalized nation that would be situated at the fulcrum of east-west trade and also to a large extent converted to an extension of India. Indeed, Sir William Willcocks, the man who a few years earlier designed the original Mesopotamian irrigation scheme for the Turkish government, admitted his ultimate plan was systematic repopulation. Willcocks wrote: "The Euphrates-Tigris delta will be reclaimed and settled by millions of natives of India, who will make it again the Garden of the East." Under this vision, Arabs would become a fringe minority in the provinces, subsumed by the biggest regional migration since the Arab conquest of Mesopotamian Eurasians more than 12 centuries before. These notions did not escape the local population. Indeed, during these years, the very concept of railroads and passenger shipping lines on both sides of the Atlantic was associated with mass international migration and settlement campaigns. From time to time, thousands in the provinces angrily rallied at their mosques to condemn the latest rumored British shipping and irrigation plans as "sinister intentions" to transfer in masses of Indian workers, some said 10,000 at a time, thus transmogrifying the nation.[27] Hence, as the British occupation expanded, the Arabs of Iraq, whom callous Ottoman Turkification had embittered, now wondered how they would resist British Indianization. To the Arabs, the threat to their identity was the same. Only the accents and garments differed.

* * * *

A centerpiece of the new Mesopotamian industrial dream was petroleum. As the British military maneuvered, attacked, and fortified their positions from Basra to Baghdad, so did the combative oilmen in London.

As the Great War staggered forward, with its heavy tolls and oppressive requirements for fuel, the British government tried to balance its future oil partnerships to ensure both a British character and a guaranteed supply. Anglo-Persian continually tried to shim itself into prominence as the one company for both needs.

But Anglo-Persian simply lacked the ability to supply with certainty all of the nation's needs—and the British government knew it. Moreover, quality and grade issues were coming to the fore. Persian oil was constantly being denigrated in naval reports for its viscosity, which caused it to thicken at low temperatures. British officials now eyed oil fields as far-flung as Java, Mexico,

Venezuela, and Romania. That meant once again scrutinizing Shell, the only company outside America already operating in all those realms. The answer seemed to be an elaborate effort, crafted over many months, to remake Shell as completely British in character, if not British in control, and somehow fuse it into Anglo-Persian. By this scenario, Shell would plunge into Mesopotamia under British aegis and finally overrun Anglo-Persian, again under British aegis.[28]

"The Royal Dutch Shell would probably consider no sacrifices too great to bring about this fusion," wrote a Treasury department official, and thereby "give them all that they have been aiming at for years past." Such a government-sanctioned fusion would give Shell control of nearly all major oil outside the significant American and Eastern European deposits and deliver much more of the growing British market, including the Royal Navy. Those "sacrifices" by Royal Dutch Shell would entail allowing the minority British side of the combine—that is, Shell, to predominate as the majority, assuring that British subjects would function as board directors, and agreeing to grant the United Kingdom preference over its supplies.[29]

However, when Anglo-Persian realized that British officials were favoring a move toward Royal Dutch Shell, with its well-entrenched worldwide distribution system, a network that extended right across Great Britain, APOC rushed to compete. More than being a mere driller, refiner, and supplier, APOC desperately needed to be a wellhead-to-consumer oil company like Shell or Standard Oil. Such a network would take years to construct.

So Anglo-Persian purchased an existing network. The Europaische Petroleum Union (EPU) was an amalgam of continental oil distribution arms, mainly controlled by German concerns. EPU owned an operating subsidiary in Britain. This subsidiary controlled both an international oil shipping division, the Petroleum Steamship Company, and a domestic consumer sales agency, the Homelight Oil Company. Formed in London in 1906, the EPU subsidiary was profitable, reporting a 14 percent dividend in 1914. It was ripe for a takeover. The EPU subsidiary's name was British Petroleum Company, with its first name descriptive only of its operating territory, not its true ownership, which was mainly German.[30]

When World War I erupted in 1914, the British authorities seized British Petroleum Company as "enemy property." During 1915 and 1916, APOC chairman Greenway petitioned the custodian of enemy property to purchase those seized—and hence government-controlled—oil company assets. The war was not over, the seized subsidiary's disposition was not resolved, but the petition was nonetheless granted. Anglo-Persian was still short of the funds needed for any acquisition. But in late 1917, the £2.7 million "sale" was finalized by virtue of a cashless, loanless "self-financing" miracle. Payments would be made to the custodian over five years, commencing in 1918, which could easily be generated by expected revenues. The purchasing balance sheets made clear in an explanatory note: "The Anglo-Persian Company will have no difficulty in meeting the above annual payments, without raising fresh capital, as they will be reserving [repayment funds] out of profits each year." Indeed, both the income and transferred depreciation from British Petroleum and its two divisions immediately began generating hundreds of thousands of pounds annually to Anglo-Persian. Decades later, Anglo-Persian Oil Company would change its name to that of this seized German subsidiary, British Petroleum.[31]

Anglo-Persian continued to press ahead as though it actually owned the oil rights in Mesopotamia. Even after being told by Foreign Secretary Grey that APOC did not, the company was fond of sending confidential and carefully misleading memoranda to government and financial officials, implying that it did. For example, one confidential memo circulated to the Treasury asserted, "The D'Arcy Exploration Company holds a prior claim to the concession for the petroliferous deposits in the *vilayets* of Baghdad, Mosul, and Basra." That assertion, the memo stated, was based on the defunct fusion deal of March 19, 1914. APOC felt free to honor and dishonor the March 19, 1914, agreement as the need arose—always in the name of the British government. For instance, in one case, after citing the fusion deal, an APOC official hastened to add, "Since the outbreak of hostilities we have, at the request of the Foreign Office, taken no steps to complete the arrangements ... though we have been frequently pressed to do so by Mr. Gulbenkian."[32]

In mid-1918, when the British army in Mesopotamia needed more oil faster, Anglo-Persian was temporarily authorized to drill at Hit, south of Baghdad, and other locations along the Euphrates. This was an emergency war measure. The Foreign Office concurred, but specified that APOC could function only as a subcontractor to the military, not as an independent commercial concern, this so "such action is not subsequently advanced by them as an additional ground for claiming preferential treatment of their interests in Mesopotamia."[33]

Anglo-Persian continued to pummel the Treasury with vexatious entreaties to forgo any further interest in Shell and quickly grant the company a monopoly. One such memo by Greenway, dated August 2, 1918, warned that forming a partnership with Royal Dutch Shell would mean "the government's investment [in APOC] ... will be entirely lost and the Empire [will] again be at the mercy of monopolists for its whole requirements of Petroleum products!"[34]

Continuing to type, but now in all capitals with generous use of triple exclamation marks and underlining, Greenway added: "COLLECTIVELY, THE LOSS TO THE BRITISH EXCHEQUER ... WOULD BE NOT

LESS THAN £5,000,000 PER ANNUM FROM THE CONCLUSION OF THE WAR UP TO SAY 5/6 YEARS HENCE, AND THEREAFTER ON A GRADUALLY INCREASING SCALE, NOT LESS THAN £10,000,000 PER ANNUM UP TO 10/12 YEARS HENCE—THE WHOLE OF WHICH SACRIFICE WOULD BE MADE FOR THE BENEFIT OF COMPANIES WHICH ARE EITHER WHOLLY OR LARGELY FOREIGN OWNED!!!"[35]

In the meantime, key analysts within the military and Foreign Office continued to sound the alarm throughout the summer of 1918 that abundant oil was now a must for the United Kingdom. A key paper compiled by Admiral Slade, one of the government's Anglo-Persian board members, put it bluntly: "It is no exaggeration to say that our life as an empire is largely dependent upon our ability to maintain the control of bunker fuel." After examining oil resources worldwide, from Appalachia to Galicia, Slade stated that the United States would soon consume all the oil produced in America and Mexico, and, since the world was industrializing, the options elsewhere were meager. But, he emphasized, "In Persia and Mesopotamia lie the largest undeveloped resources at present known in the world ... more than the whole of the Romanian and Galician fields put together."[36]

Slade's conclusion, backed by maps, tables, and studies: "The Power that controls the oil lands of Persia and Mesopotamia will control the source of supply of the majority of the liquid fuel of the future."[37]

Slade's conclusions were enthusiastically endorsed. One secret memo to the War Cabinet from the chief of the Air Staff echoed Slade's points "with all possible emphasis." The memo insisted, "It is essential ... to monopolize all possible supplies of petroleum" in Mesopotamia and Persia. Another secret memo, this one from the Cabinet Secretariat to the Admiralty, used Slade's memo and maps to assert, "The retention of the oil-bearing regions in Mesopotamia and Persia in British hands ... would appear to be a first-class British war aim."[38]

By the fall of 1918, the exhausted armies of Europe and the Ottoman Empire were desperate to end their seemingly senseless struggle. In early October, 1918, a broken Turkey began unraveling. The cabinet resigned, leaving the empire in the hands of caretakers eager to end the war. By mid-October, 1918, British commander Charles Townshend, previously taken prisoner at Kut, was summoned to Constantinople to arrange a cessation of hostilities. At the Sublime Porte, Townshend met privately with Field Marshal and Prime Minister Izzet Pasha in one of those solemn, dignified moments when enemy generals are weary enough to admit they have killed enough. Tears welling up in his eyes, the defeated Izzet Pasha conceded his battered country was demoralized and unable to continue. "You are willing to help us?" he asked Townshend. The former prisoner, who had been well treated during captivity, replied, "With all my heart."[39]

On October 30, 1918, the Sick Man of Europe finally died. Aboard a ship at the port of Mudros in the Aegean Sea, Turkey surrendered and agreed to an armistice. Under its terms, all hostilities were to cease at noon the next day. By dawn, October 31, 1918, a riverbank of white flags began furling across Turkish entrenchments along the Tigris. The British march north was halted in place 40 miles from Mosul. But from Baghdad, the dream of a new British Iraq, enriched by the oilfields of Mosul, was too much to resist. A note marked "Very Secret—Important," sent just weeks earlier, by a Cabinet officer to the Prime Minister's Office was typical in urging, "There may be reasons other than purely military for pushing on in Mesopotamia where the British have an enormous preponderance of force. Would it not be an advantage, before the end of the war, to secure the valuable oil wells in Mesopotamia?"[40]

Civil Administrator Arnold Wilson in Baghdad had regularly nagged Whitehall "as to the desirability of extending the scope of our war aims to the Mosul *vilayet*." Possession is nine-tenths of the law. "Whether it was ultimately to be in the French or the British 'sphere of interest' [under the Sykes-Picot Agreement]," recalled Wilson, "it was essential that it [Mosul] should be occupied by British troops before or from the moment that hostilities ceased … I contended vehemently that a bird in the military hand was worth many in the thorny thickets of diplomacy, and that in dealing with Turkey, a valid post-war title could be obtained by the Allies only by securing possession."[41]

The war with Germany continued in Europe and elsewhere, but for Turkey it was over on October 31, 1918. Clause 16 of the armistice specified the surrender of all Turkish garrisons in "Syria and Mesopotamia." Civil Administrator Wilson wrote, "From our local point of view, everything turned on the meaning of the word *Mesopotamia*, which was not in current official or diplomatic use in Turkey. Was it open to us, under the Armistice, to regard Mosul … as forming part of Mesopotamia?" Wilson preferred it both ways. Mosul was not in Mesopotamia for purposes of seizing it, but it was in Mesopotamia for purposes of Turkey's mandatory surrender.[42]

Within 48 hours of the October 31, 1918 effective date of the armistice at Mudros, Mesopotamian commander-in-chief William Marshall gave the order to take Mosul—cease fire or no cease fire. Only 1,650 outnumbered Turkish riflemen and a battery of 32 artillery pieces defended the city. General Marshall instructed the Ottoman commander to evacuate the town, and indeed the entire Mosul province, or be vanquished. The Turkish commander objected that the moving on Mosul violated the ceasefire.[43]

Marshall refused to wait for clarification from England. Quoting Clause 7 of the armistice, Marshall directed, "'Allies have the right to occupy any strategic points and War Office have ordered the occupation of Mosul." The full Clause 7 of course read: "The Allies to have the right to occupy any strategic points in the event of a situation arising which threatens the security of the Allies." It was intended for exigent circumstances. Haggard Turkish troops at Mosul were observing the cease fire and no longer threatening British troops.[44]

For several days the two sides bickered while waiting for instructions to filter back. Finally, on November 7, 1918, Marshall, willing to wait no longer, offered the local Turkish commander an ultimatum. The besieged Turks reluctantly left Mosul. The British marched in. Their occupation of Mesopotamia was now complete and included the three provinces, first Basra, then Baghdad, and now Mosul. The third province, Mosul, was home to approximately 800,000 persons, about 20 percent Arab, but more than 60 percent Kurd, with the remaining fifth split between Jews, Christians, Turks, and mystic Yazidis. An uneasy new national outline had been cobbled together that was mainly Kurdish in the north, Sunni in the midsection, and Shiite in the south.[45]

"Thanks to General Marshall," recalled Wilson, "we had established *de facto*, the principle that the Mosul *vilayet* is part of 'Iraq,' to use the geographical expression ... and whether for the woe or weal of the inhabitants, it is too soon to say." He added that had General Marshall waited just 24 hours for the restraining instructions from London to arrive, history would be otherwise. But, Wilson continued, Marshall did not wait, and so "laid the foundation stone of the future State of Iraq."[46]

A few days later, at the eleventh hour of the eleventh day of the eleventh month, all the guns fell silent. The Germans surrendered as well. The shooting stopped. The shouting would now begin.

THE PETROLEUM
OF PEACE

Like most everything else in Mesopotamia, the legality of Britain's rights to Mosul and its oil fields was fuzzy and disputed. As 1918 concluded, the land inhabited by the diverse people of Mosul, nominally under the sovereignty of the Turks, had been promised to the French by London officials, who did not own it, and occupied mainly by British India, which had only recently seized it. British forces were certainly the occupiers under international law, except they had occupied Mosul under a bruised—many said *violated*—proviso of the armistice. Not a few in the international community demanded an immediate withdrawal and reinstatement of the status quo ante of Turkish authority.[1]

Moreover, the ongoing scramble to control all three provinces of Mesopotamia continued to rivet the attention of France, England, and British India long before any international peace conference had even decided the ultimate disposition of the Turkish Middle East. "I must confess … we are rather in the position of the hunters who divided up the skin of the bear before they had killed it," quipped Brigadier General George Macdonough, even as the Sykes-Picot Agreement was being negotiated in early January 1916, nearly three years before the Turkish surrender.[2]

Non-annexation was a guiding principle of the Allies. So even though possession was nine-tenths of the law, true sovereignty over all of Mesopotamia would be decided at the 1919 Versailles Peace Conference in Paris. Strongly

103

influencing that process would be several principles from the famous Fourteen Points enunciated in 1918 by President Woodrow Wilson after America joined the war.

Point Five: "A free, open-minded, and absolutely impartial adjustment of all colonial claims, based upon a strict observance of the principle that, in determining all such questions of sovereignty, the interests of the populations concerned must have equal weight with the equitable claims of the government whose title is to be determined."[3] Translation: self-determination.

Point Twelve: "The Turkish portion of the present Ottoman Empire should be assured a secure sovereignty, but the other nationalities which are now under Turkish rule should be assured an undoubted security of life and an absolutely unmolested opportunity of autonomous development."[4] Translation: self-determination.

Self-determination. Misguided as it was, antidemocratic as it was, the reformist compulsion to grant remedial self-determination to long-exploited nationalist movements became astral among the postwar mapmakers. But who was entitled to self-determination, and how would it be implemented? Self-determination could preferentially enfranchise one identified people over another within a region along a variety of criteria: ethnicity, religion, a common language, geographic continuity, all of it, or just some of it. The result at Paris was a patchwork of impassioned, often competing, national claims: Kurds, Armenians, Jews, and Arabs among others, and not infrequently within overlapping traditional territorial boundaries.[5] In the final analysis, the anointed legitimacy of any self-determination movement was determined not in the eyes of the beholder, but in the interest of the bestower.

Nonetheless, the provinces of Mesopotamia, by any measure, were clearly a candidate for self-determination and nationhood. The Allies understood that. But not all among the Allies wanted to admit it. Britain's numerous official agencies remained sharply divided over Mesopotamia's future. Should the new Iraq be an Indian appendage, a British protectorate, or an independent Arab nation led by Faisal, son of Hussein, or perhaps some other potentate?

Many senior ranks in the Foreign Office were steeled by an overriding commitment to Woodrow Wilson's principles. However, more than a few were still hypnotized by centuries of imperialist traditions. Adding to the debate were major personalities in the Admiralty, the War Office, and the India Office, as well as a maelstrom of voices in Parliament, the Board of Trade, and the British media.

But the life-and-breath decisions and indeed the map marks that ruled British Mesopotamia on the ground were, in fact, not decided in London, Bombay, or Paris. Those decisions were made in Baghdad by one man, waiting for no one and determined to wring history between his own two hands. That man was acting Civil Commissioner Arnold Wilson, brought in from his post in Persia to manage civilian affairs in Mesopotamia. An experienced Near East technocrat and diplomat, Wilson had just finished a stint on the Turco-Persian Frontier Commission and was in large measure responsible for transferring the oil fields of Persia into Turkish Mosul in 1913. He ensured that Anglo-Persian's oil concession transferred right along with the land, thus giving the company a gray zone of exploitation in Mesopotamia. Known for his bad manners and good organizational skills, Wilson openly proclaimed himself a "rank imperialist" and freely admitted "a strong personal leaning to radicalism."[6]

In fact, no sooner had Britain taken Basra in November 1914, than Wilson fired off a memo to his political officer proposing the repopulation of Mesopotamia with Indians for the good of imperial Britain. "I should like to see it announced," Wilson wrote, "that Mesopotamia was to be annexed to India as a colony for India and Indians, that the government of India would administer it, and gradually bring under cultivation its vast unpopulated desert plains, peopling them with martial races from the Punjab."[7]

Wilson subscribed to the wisdom of his friend and fellow theorist, Arthur Hirtzel, head of the India Office political department, who at the advent of the drive to Baghdad quipped that Arabs were "no more capable of administering severally or collectively than the Red Indians [of America]." In Mesopotamia, Wilson stayed true to his self-image and his doctrine, creating a tinderbox.[8]

In theory, Britain had invaded to help the Arabs achieve national expression. In that vein, the Foreign Office regularly demanded local Arabs be employed to run their own affairs and create the infrastructure of their country's rehabilitation. For example, just days after capturing Baghdad, the War Cabinet telegraphed instructions to allow preexisting laws and customs to remain in place with subtle but *de facto* protectorate status afforded by England—not India. But Wilson launched a personal bureaucratic crusade to do the opposite, importing and imposing Indian law, Indian workers, Indian institutions, and broad strata of Indian officials.[9]

Wilson also abolished the elected municipal councils that even the Ottomans had permitted, replacing the councils with appointed Indian political officers. The provincial identities and ethnic fabrics of Mosul, Baghdad, and Basra were profoundly different, and the prevailing instruction by the Foreign Office was to administer Baghdad and Basra separately, and to maintain only a defensive military presence in Mosul. But, Wilson, on his own authority, decided to unify the three into an administrative whole. He even issued passports to cover all inhabitants in Mesopotamia who dwelled from the Persian Gulf north to the foothills of Kurdistan. By governing the three provinces—from Mosul to Basra—from Baghdad, Wilson in essence created a future Iraq by personal fiat.[10]

As an occupying power, Great Britain declared it had come to liberate Mesopotamia from the Turks. "Our armies do not come into your cities and lands as conquerors or enemies, but as liberators," proclaimed the generals upon entering Baghdad. Instead, Great Britain suddenly found itself almost at war with the local population. Once again, Wilson was the central character, wielding oppressive civil regulations. Under Wilson's direction, families were routinely evicted and their homes requisitioned by occupying forces and administrators, with the token rent often less than satisfying. Piped water was restricted to the burgeoning administrative and military sectors, depriving even the established merchants of Basra and Baghdad of their established basics. Large numbers of ordinary residents were dragooned as minimally paid compulsory laborers for British work projects, often pulling them away from fields, flocks, and shops. Freedom of movement was greatly curtailed, purportedly to preempt Turkish spies, but this practice continued long after the Ottoman threat had been purged. The local population bitterly resented these intrusive measures, which redefined their very way of daily life.[11]

In addition, Wilson controlled the movement of all food. Some foodstuffs could not be sold unless the army's needs were filled first. More important, in some cases, he decided who could eat and who would starve. Those among the nomadic tribes who cooperated with the British were fed. Those who did not were blockaded. By this selective method, Wilson declared, he "was feeding 100,000 Bedouin," while he could "prevent hostile tribes from obtaining more than a modicum of subsistence." Recalling his activities in 1918, Wilson wrote, "The shortage of foodstuffs was so great in Iraq that without our assistance most of these [tribesmen] must have died of starvation," In justification, he wrote, "If the migrants [Bedouin nomads fleeing across borders in the wake of war movements] did not give us any material military assistance, they were at least giving none to our opponents."[12]

The British found numerous sheikhs willing to be co-opted to prop up their unpopular occupation. They were empowered to collect taxes in their area and to settle disputes with the force of law, not according to tribal traditions but based on an imported Indian code, which was itself adapted from English legal precepts. During the 12 months spanning 1916 and 1917, for instance, the local British political officer in the Suq district, H. R. P. Dickson, found one sheikh willing to be elevated in each of the 22 Suq tribes. However, in many cases, the newly elevated sheikh was not the traditional ancestral chief. Hence, the tribal hierarchies themselves, developed over centuries, were rewritten by Wilson's policy.[13]

Petty abuses and high-handedness by Wilson's new strongmen were common. Both the populace and British openly considered these new boss sheikhs to be little more than stooges. One prominent reform-minded British official

of the Indian government who later joined the Baghdad administration readily explained in 1916, "Once a sheik has to rely on [the] government for support, he has lost the sympathy of his tribesmen." Refeudalizing Mesopotamia
effectively restored the corrupt ways of the Sultan that had prevailed prior to
the Young Turk reforms. But by pointing to these new faces, the occupation
could summon approbation on cue in any controversy.[14]

Only the cash influx from the British rentals, purchases, wages, and political subsidies, plus strict noninterference with religious activities, softened the
blow of the occupation. But at times, when the power of the purse retreated,
seething outrage erupted. For example, on January 28, 1918, Captain W.
M. Marshall was installed as the new governor of Najaf. During preceding
months, the city had been mutinous. British patrols had been shot at, an airplane was almost downed by gunfire, and government offices were attacked.
Intent on maintaining order, Capt. Marshall terminated all stipends and financial supports for local sheikhs, demanded all rifles be turned in at once, and
fired the entire Najaf police force, replacing them with hand-selected officers
from Kut.[15]

Local agitators, deprived of emoluments to ease the pain of occupation,
immediately decided to eliminate Capt. Marshall. On March 19, 1918, timed
with the Moslem Nawruz festivities, assassins dressed as policemen entered
Marshall's home and killed him. Punjabi guards were summoned to hunt
down the assailants, but insurgents fought them as well. When the central killers could not be found, the British blockaded Shi'a Najaf—nothing in, nothing out. Wilson and the military demanded the surrender of the murderers,
plus a fine of 50,000 rupees, plus 1,000 rifles, plus deportation to India of 100
prisoners. Until those conditions were satisfied, Wilson ruled, the residents
would suffer a total "food-and-water supply cut off." Any number of Shi'a
intermediaries from both Persia and Mesopotamia entreated Wilson's Baghdad compound offering "an amicable settlement" to help their holy city. Perhaps just the women and children could be evacuated, they pleaded.[16]

Wilson would not yield. He wanted the killers—or everyone could just
starve. With food and water dwindling, many local sheikhs and ordinary citizens joined the rebellion, or strongly considered it, out of a sheer survival
instinct. Wilson remained impervious to telegrams from London and Calcutta seeking moderation. After weeks of siege, Najafi food supplies held, but
the water was almost gone—this as the region endured a summer that would
reach 112 degrees. Finally, by May 4, 1918, quarter by quarter, the town had
been starved into submission. Najaf surrendered the culprits.[17]

A British military tribunal at Kufa speedily convicted 11 men of murder,
sentencing them to death. Nine more were sentenced to jail time for complic-
ity. Islamic notables appealed to Wilson not to execute all the ringleaders,

only the two men who actually commited the murder. Wilson refused any clemency on these—or any other—grounds. On May 25, 1918, just a few weeks after Najaf's submission, all 11 were publicly hanged in Kufa. Just hours after the execution, Wilson presumed validation when he received an invitation to a feast at the home of the caretaker of one of Najaf's shrines.[18]

In recalling the episode, Wilson wrote these words: "Najaf has never again been a source of serious anxiety to the government of the country."[19]

*   *   *   *

A chorus of hopefuls claimed Iraq's still undrilled oil. The three-way tug-of-war between Shell, Anglo-Persian, and Turkish Petroleum was itself subject to pushes and pulls by the two European Allied victors: Great Britain and France. The future oil industry of the future Iraq became the pivot among the victors competing for territorial control of the ancient Mesopotamian provinces. Once the shooting stopped, the commercial contenders and their governmental sponsors generated a long cascade of overlapping and contradictory agreements, assertions, and revocations, completely consistent with the standard of confusion that characterized everything about the promise of Mesopotamia's oil.

Within a week of the war's end on November 11, 1918, French petroleum plenipotentiary Senator Henri Bérenger arrived in London to meet with his counterpart, Walter Long, Britain's secretary of state for colonies and newly appointed head of the evolving committee that became known as "the Petroleum Executive." France wanted Mosul and its oil. Britain also wanted Mosul and its oil. On December 1, 1918, the British and French heads of state, Prime Minister David Lloyd George and President Georges Clemenceau, met in London to discuss a broad range of issues, including petroleum. In a secret exchange that even their senior ministers did not fully understand, the two leaders adopted a hazy *quid pro quo*. France would relinquish its claim on Mosul on condition it retained all of Syria as promised in the Sykes-Picot Agreement. Just one other thing, France wanted a significant share in Mosul's oil. Britain agreed.[20]

Quickly, French and British negotiators began making progress on a deal. The men turned once again to Turkish Petroleum and its 25 percent ownership by Deutsche Bank, based on the Baghdad Railway's original 1898 oil concession. Capturing Deutsche Bank's stock seemed the soundest legal tactic to securing Mesopotamian oil rights. But who owned the Deutsche Bank concession acquired by TPC? A nervous Anglo-Persian, apprised of renewed interest in TPC, claimed APOC did. On November 12, 1918, in a four-page brief, APOC argued that it had never finalized its half-ownership in TPC afforded by the 1914 fusion agreement solely because of the war and due to explicit restraining instructions from the Foreign Office. Underlining words for emphasis in its memo, as was its custom, APOC executives pleaded for a *status quo ante* wherein their 50 percent ownership of TPC would be finally consummated or, in the alternative, a full, internationally binding cancellation of any Baghdad Railway rights by a formal Allied decision at the coming Paris Peace Conference.[21]

Possession is nine-tenths of the law. British government petroleum officials, aware of the coming clash over Deutsche Bank's TPC ownership, decided to preempt. In early December 1918, they began seizing Deutsche Bank's shares as enemy property, "before the Peace Conference, not only on account of the French claims ... but in order to obviate any possibility, however remote, of the share reverting to Germany." Moreover, a Treasury official wrote on December 13, 1918, by seizing the ownership for itself, the British government ensured the shares would not "be sold to either of the rival oil groups, since this would ... complicate the [upcoming] delicate negotiations."[22]

Treasury convinced Sir Lancelot Smith to function as what officials termed "a neutral purchaser." Smith would be asked to expend only £21,000 of his own money to acquire the liquidated Deutsche Bank holding in TPC, and even that expenditure might be backed up by a parliamentary appropriation. Officials were at first hesitant about using public money for what was ostensibly a private sell-off, but they were convinced that "the rights to oil mining in Mesopotamia remains, and will undoubtedly be, a very burning one in our negotiations with the French."[23]

Indeed, the British wanted to seize control of German ownership in TPC before the French did at the Paris Peace Conference. "The existence of shares in the Turkish Petroleum Company," explained the late December 1918 Treasury memo, "which belong to an enemy, will give the French an opportunity of putting in a claim to such a share, and we shall be in a far stronger position to resist it if in fact these enemy-owned shares have been disposed of." The strategy was to dispose of the shares through the contrived sale to "neutral purchaser" Lancelot Smith. Smith, however, was in fact a Board of Trade representative sitting on one of the interministerial oil committees. Smith would own the shares in his own name as a private individual, but would in fact function as a government nominee under government control.[24]

While Treasury officials were making arrangements to sell off Deutsche Bank's 25 percent of TPC to their straw man, other British and French petroleum negotiators, by mid-December, were already agreeing to sell Deutsche Bank's ownership to a Shell subsidiary, which would then discreetly transfer the stock to the French. Indeed, shortly thereafter, a rival Anglo-French agreement to sell Deutsche Bank's ownership to Shell was confirmed in a letter by the French chargé d'affaires in London to the British foreign secretary.[25] But as 1919 opened for business, the jockeying only intensified.

Paris, in January 1919, became a monumental turning point in the modern history of the world. The Paris Peace Conference brought together President Woodrow Wilson, Prime Minister David Lloyd George, and President Georges Clemenceau, with their great delegations in tow and their lofty agendas in mind. As the peacemakers bickered, postured, and rewrote maps and ethnic destinies, righted wrongs and created new ones, some empires were dismantled and some bolstered, new nations were created and old ones reincarnated. Millions was the unit of measure: millions dead, millions wounded, millions demobilized, millions massacred, millions in war cost, millions in reparations. But just behind the proprietors of peace were the captains of commerce who spoke of their own millions.By the end of January, Clemenceau remarked, "The petroleum question seems to be one of the most important economic questions at the Peace Conference." He added, "It crucially affects the future of our national defense as well as her general prosperity."[26]

Ironically, even at the Paris Peace Conference, as the world was being reshaped with pens, the legal gateway to Iraqi oil remained the Turkish Petroleum Company and Deutsche Bank's 25 percent ownership in it. The two mutually exclusive international efforts to acquire that ownership raced ahead. While one Anglo-French team of negotiators, led by Lord Long for England and Senator Bérenger of France, planned to transfer the shares to France, either directly or through Shell, the British Treasury was creating a *fait accompli* by preemptively seizing the company through a "sale" to their "neutral purchaser."[27]

Numerous plans and permutations unfolded between Long and Bérenger at Paris. For example, on February 3, 1919, British delegates bandied about the notion of a 20 percent interest in Turkish Petroleum in exchange for a reciprocal share in French Algerian oil, as well as transit guarantees for the planned British pipeline across Syria. That was not enough. On February 12, 1919, President Clemenceau interceded, writing Prime Minister Lloyd George to insist on "strict equality in the exploitation of petroleum in Mesopotamia," adding that London and Paris must not only enjoy parity as military victors, but also as commercial victors. "An agreement must be clearly manifested," wrote Clemenceau, "in the industrial as well as in other spheres."[28]

But so many legal vagaries attached to every aspect of the Sultan's original concessions, the fusion agreement of March 19, 1914, and Turkish Petroleum Company itself. Negotiators decided that they would submit any final deal to Britain's Attorney General for review. They suggested that any legally doubtful clauses could be "righted" by a subsequent friendly treaty with whatever national or administrative national entity arose in Iraq. Moreover, an idea was floated to grant the coming Iraqi national governmental authority an unspecified interest in the oil company, perhaps as much as 20 percent. This would certainly be an incentive for any budding Iraqi national authority. Even still, there was no assertion whether this minority holding would be a mere token voting presence or whether it would include any genuine beneficial rights or decision-making power. Moreover, it was assumed Britain would control any such local government. Upping the ante, negotiators tacked on promises for France to approve not one but two British oil pipelines to the Mediterranean, one through Syria and a second via Haifa, in Palestine, which Britain also hoped to administer.[29]

Even as Long and Bérenger pondered the geographic and economic variables, the Foreign Office wondered just how real these far-reaching discussions about giving France a share of TPC were. In mid-March 1919, Mallet of the Foreign Office cautioned that talks could continue as wholly preliminary, as long as British representatives "made it clear to M. Bérenger that we were ready to admit French participation in the Turkish Petroleum Company" but that nothing could be decided "until the ultimate nature of the territorial settlement is more clearly indicated."[30]

The more detailed and advanced the conversations between Long and Bérenger became, the more they seemed to rile the Foreign Office, which had to deal with all the Allies about territorial matters. In doing so, the Foreign Office would have to embrace Woodrow Wilson's insistence on self-determined rights. This would include the local population's right to control its own national economic resources. At one point, Foreign Secretary George Curzon dismissively remarked that TPC was being traded for "a promise of facilities for two pipelines which we may never be in a position to construct through a district in which the French may never be in a position to afford us the facilities promised."[31]

But the French were tenacious. What's more, they seemed to have a complete understanding of the ins and outs of Turkish Petroleum and the value of Mesopotamian oil fields. Who was advising the French? Lead French oil representative Senator Bérenger, the minister of industrial production, key personalities in the Ministry of Finance, and the leading magnates of French oil companies all maintained a close friendship with one man. It was, of course, Gulbenkian.[32] By coaxing France into a takeover of TPC, he could reassert from Paris the 5 percent banished in London.

Working with the French during the Paris negotiations "has been very tedious work," bragged Gulbenkian, filled with "intrigues and jealousies." Not a few in the French government, including the French chargé d'affaires in London, distrusted Gulbenkian. But in the end, key French oil diplomats concluded that his involvement was merely to help France, where Gulbenkian had lived out the war. During those war years, Gulbenkian had been active in financing French oil deals to compensate for the country's petroleum deficiencies. Gulbenkian recalled that despite political alarums, one key delegate "was so convinced of my genuine collaboration that, although his hand was writing and signing the documents, it was in fact, my hand that guided his."[33]

But while Gulbenkian pushed the French forward, the British were pulling back on those confiscated Deutsche Bank shares. On February 12, 1919, the custodian of enemy property petitioned the Chancery Division of the High Court to approve selling the precious enemy property to Lancelot Smith— thus the shares would no longer exist as unclaimed enemy property. The court action set off a furious barrage of motions, arguments, and hearings from all parties, central and peripheral—including affidavits by Deterding and Gulbenkian themselves. All this occurred concomitant with the delicate negotiations in Paris.[34]

Meanwhile, Royal Dutch Shell saw its own fortunes faltering before the threats of a government takeover of TPC and from continued pressure plays by quasi-governmental Anglo-Persian. Royal Dutch Shell finally decided it was time to become a "British company" that would enjoy the benefits of official governmental favor and patronage. This corporate metamorphosis would not produce a company controlled by the British government, which was impossible due to its Dutch majority, but one "controlled" by British personalities and nominees who in turn could be controlled by British policies and preferences.[35]

On March 6 and 7, 1919, Shell and British executives finally hammered out a complex eight-point protocol referred to as "Heads of Agreement of the Royal Dutch Shell and British Government." The document focused on Royal Dutch Shell's main British subsidiary, a company known as Anglo-Saxon Petroleum. For years, Anglo-Saxon Petroleum had operated profitably within the empire and indeed was Royal Dutch Shell's official arm in its involvement with Turkish Petroleum Company. Under the agreement, "His Majesty's Government will be advised to use their best endeavors to secure, either by rearrangement of the capital in the Turkish Petroleum Company, or otherwise, that the Royal Dutch Shell by the medium of the Anglo-Saxon Persian Company … shall be admitted to equal participation [with Anglo-Persian Oil Company] in the exploitation of all oilfields in Asia Minor, including what is usually called Mesopotamia."[36]

Anglo-Saxon's operation would be completely reorganized and anglicized to ensure British oversight. "Certain shares," the protocol stated, "with a special majority voting power in the company operating in Mesopotamia, shall be controlled by His Majesty's Government and the management shall be permanently British." The government would receive 2 percent of Anglo-Saxon's shares. More important, however, the TPC voting percentages controlled by Royal Dutch's Anglo-Saxon, plus those of its rival, Anglo-Persian, as well as the government would all be replicated and twined into a special "Voting Trust," which controlled 70 percent of the voting rights of the new Mesopotamian subsidiary.[37]

Since both Royal Dutch Shell and the British government planned to lay pipelines across the Middle East to the Mediterranean, Shell also agreed "to not oppose or obstruct directly or indirectly the laying ... of a similar [pipe] line connecting the Anglo-Persian fields with that shore."[38]

The two parent companies comprising the Royal Dutch Shell conglomerate were Royal Dutch in the Netherlands, controlling 60 percent, and Shell Transport in the United Kingdom, controlling 40 percent. As a further protection, the board of directors of Shell Transport was now mandated to be 75 percent "British born British subjects ... precluded from selling or disposing of their capital assets ... outside British control." Moreover, the current approved board of directors, all British, could not change "without the consent and approval of the Governor of the Bank of England, and/or some person of similar standing nominated by His Majesty's Government."[39]

As for Henri Deterding, the Dutchman whose nationality stood at the heart of Royal Dutch's "foreign" character, he changed as well. During the war, at the beginning of these negotiations, he had become a naturalized British citizen. Shortly, he would become a knight of the British Empire, completing the transformation of his citizenship.[40]

By initialing the "Heads of Agreement" on March 7, 1919, a fiercely independent, highly competitive, unabashedly capitalist international oil combine carved out a major portion of its commercial empire to become a government-controlled enterprise, not in name but in fact—not in dollar but in deed. It was done not for love of country, but for the romance of Mesopotamia's oil fortunes.

The British now enjoyed overlapping and interlocking ownership, control, and competitive leverage in the oil of Mesopotamia, the oil that had been the subject of dreams and disputes since the previous century. Whitehall could empower or stall Shell, bury or resurrect Turkish Petroleum, favor or marginalize Anglo-Persian, govern all the oil, parcel a fraction to the French, or share a token with the local government. As the Paris negotiations proceeded, London could exercise some of those options, all of them, or none of them—as need or desire dictated.

However, regardless of what contracts or court papers were being filed in London, Anglo-Persian Oil Company was actually on the ground in Mesopotamia. With or without a concession, with or without further preferences from

London, APOC was cementing a real-world monopoly, partnering with both the invasion and the civil administration. Since 1918, the company had been actively drilling in the northwestern "transferred territories," that is, the oil-rich Naft Khana region, previously Persian but moved into Turkish Mesopotamia through the earlier frontier treaty adjustment. Most of that drilling, under the 1901 Persian concession, was proceeding under military auspices with the full endorsement of Civil Commissioner Wilson. Enthusiastically, Wilson reported, "The company takes so confident a view of the potentialities of that field, that they have dismantled a refinery in New Zealand and have had the plant shipped to Basra for the purpose of dealing with the Naft Khana output."[41]

What's more, Anglo-Persian managed and delivered all army needs through the military's Inland Water Transport, a system of pump houses and storage tank installations located in Amarah, Baghdad, Diwaniyah, Fallujah, Kut, Ur Junction, and numerous other villages, as well as "advanced bases" used by the troops. This network constituted APOC's future retail distribution arm for both kerosene and petrol after military needs were satisfied. With this in mind, APOC's chairman Greenway and Wilson worked together to change the company's relation from military vendor reporting to the army to commercial distributor authorized by the civil administration. Wilson liked the idea as long as the existing commercial middlemen were subtracted, thus moderating prices. APOC approved, as it was now ready to deal directly with consumers, and in a survey submitted to the authorities even calculated exactly how many gallons of kerosene it could store at each of 14 locations. The total was 50,401 gallons. Naturally, this would require a fleet of oil barges plying the Tigris and Euphrates. Both Wilson and APOC lobbied for these to be built and acquired.[42] The future monopoly was taking shape.

Seeing APOC's rapid entrenchment in Mesopotamia, Shell's Deterding advised his associates to enter Mesopotamia at once and get a foothold somehow. Possession is nine-tenths of the law. Recalling one frank exchange, Deterding stated, "I told [him] ... go and get all the rights he could; as there is no government in Mesopotamia, [and] the only rights anybody can secure at present would be those of possession."[43]

Back in Paris, on April 8, 1919, Anglo-French negotiators, after numerous drafts, finally signed an oil agreement, called simply the Long-Bérenger Agreement, which in some parts read very much like the agreement signed just a month earlier with Shell. As such, it could either contradict or comply with that agreement, as desired. This latest accord created yet another iteration of Turkish Petroleum, cutting the French in for 20 percent, but cognizant that everyone was indeed carving up a nation not yet acquired under the rules of victory, and certainly not yet relinquished by the native population under the precepts of self-determination.

The Long-Bérenger Agreement declared: "In the event of His Majesty's Government receiving the mandate in Mesopotamia, they undertake to make it their duty to secure from the Mesopotamian Government for the Turkish Petroleum Company, or the Company to be formed to acquire the interests of that Company, the rights acquired by the Turkish Petroleum Company in Mesopotamia, under arrangements made with the Turkish Government. The French Government [is] to have a share in the capital in the Company ... The Company shall be under permanent British control."[44]

France's payment for the shares, under Long-Bérenger, would be a mere token: "that paid by the British government to the public trustee for the shares belonging to the Deutsche Bank, plus 5 percent interest." It was now clear to the French that Whitehall was seizing those shares in court. Ironically, France was agreeing to buy those shares before the court had even ruled they would be available. Such a ruling was months away. Once the transaction was complete, however, the agreement stipulated, "The capital of the company shall be divided as follows: British interest 70 percent, French interest 20 percent, native [Mesopotamian] interest 10 percent," which would be divided between the two victorious powers if the "native interest" declined. This last feature addressed the notion of economic self-determination, although the terms of inclusion for any native interest were not set forth. For its part, the French agreed to facilitate two British pipelines, plus storage depots and wharves on Syrian territory, once again emphasizing that the parties were not "implying that any territorial rights are in existence."[45]

Ten days later, the form and shape of the future Iraq and other liberated or occupied territories were becoming more apparent. In place of colonialism emerged a new concept, the "mandate." Those populations identified for self-determination but not deemed capable of forming their own government or national expression were to be mandated by the international community to "advanced nations" for "tutelage."

On April 28, 1919, the newly formed League of Nations finalized its noble covenant. Article 22 proclaimed: "To those colonies and territories which as a consequence of the late war have ceased to be under the sovereignty of the States which formerly governed them, and which are inhabited by peoples not yet able to stand by themselves under the strenuous conditions of the modern world, there should be applied the principle that the well-being and development of such peoples form a sacred trust of civilization and that securities for the performance of this trust should be embodied in this Covenant."[46]

The Covenant continued, "The tutelage of such peoples should be entrusted to advanced nations who by reason of their resources, their experience, or their geographical position can best undertake this responsibility ... as Mandatories on behalf of the League." Article 22 specifically referenced "certain communities formerly belonging to the Turkish Empire [which] have reached a stage of development where their existence as independent nations can be provisionally recognized subject to the rendering of administrative advice and assistance by a Mandatory until such time as they are able to stand alone."[47]

Hence, more than 7,000 years after Mesopotamia gave the world the gift of civilization, a concept of commercial fair play, and the written word itself, the great powers were convinced the battered, exploited region could not stand with the civilized nations and peoples of the world.

*   *   *   *

It was becoming crystal clear that Britain would receive the mandate for the new Iraq, including oil-rich Mosul, which Britain and Wilson occupied. France began to fear that perhaps it had conceded the greatest known oil field in the world too easily, for a mere percentage of a British-controlled commercial company. The Long-Bérenger Agreement was signed by the two men April 8, 1919, and sent on to Paris and London for formal adoption by their governments. The British, seeing the accord as the final and much-desired demise of Sykes-Picot, notified the French ambassador in London on May 16, 1919, that they had accepted. The French, however, refused to reciprocate. After continued delays, diplomatic nerves became frayed. In the midst of a fractious dispute regarding Syria, Prime Minister Lloyd George angrily denounced the entire arrangement.[48]

On June 17, 1919, the French government introduced a bill to establish a state oil monopoly to import refined oil. About a month later, with no progress on its reinstatement, Foreign Secretary Curzon of Britain formally annulled the Long-Bérenger Agreement. In the wake of this rescission, both the French and the British exchanged notes that acknowledged the protracted and bitter end of Sykes-Picot.[49]

By the end of July 1919, the High Court ruled in favor of the British government's petition to liquidate Deutsche Bank's one-quarter holding in Turkish Petroleum, thereby enabling its sale to Lancelot Smith.[50] The British government now controlled Turkish Petroleum directly through its acquisition of Deutsche Bank's 1898 oil concession and, even more substantially, albeit indirectly, through its March 1919 Heads of Agreement accord with Shell, which itself was an original 25 percent owner of TPC.

However, there was just one other thing about the High Court's order. While the High Court did confirm the government's right to liquidate the enemy property, it refused to rule on Gulbenkian's passionate objections regarding the serpentine March 1914 fusion agreement. The judge ruled:

"And it is ordered that this order is not ... a confirmation by any party of the convention dated 4th March, 1914 ... or as a recognition that such convention is still [in force] ... or to prejudice any question ... in regard to the said convention or to any rights or interests ... in regard to the shares hereinbefore mentioned."[51] Translation: It didn't matter who liquidated or acquired Deutsche Bank's stock; the true ownership and validity of Turkish Petroleum was anyone's guess.

Gulbenkian had them all guessing. The more elaborate the competing interest in Turkish Petroleum, the more the world industrialized and needed what Iraq possessed, the more valuable were his unresolved claims to the undrilled oil in the undeclared Iraqi state.

In mid-November 1919, Lancelot Smith, as chairman, imperially called a board meeting of Turkish Petroleum to undertake some "clerical matters." At about this time, mindful of the court order and the legalities, Gulbenkian's name was finally added to the roster of shareholders.[52] From the day the company was registered on January 31, 1911, until that November 1919, Gulbenkian had actually preferred to keep his stock ownership verbal, unrecorded, and arguable. At least now there was a physical piece of paper to point to—not that it would help.

Efforts to revive the Anglo-French oil negotiations continued until the end of 1919. Long-Bérenger was reformulated and revised.[53] Other ideas were floated. But all discussions about just who owned the land and the oil of the still undeclared country of Iraq would soon be subordinated to events.

The jihad was coming.

CHAPTER TEN

OIL AND THE
1920 JIHAD

I n Paris, the Peace Conference began dismantling the Ottoman Empire in the Middle East. Nothing would be easier than to brand it all as a grand ploy for oil. But what empowered their avarice? What made it palatable and more than justifiable for the distinguished peace conferees to deprive Turkey of her provinces? The West's ingrained hatred of the Ottoman Empire and despotic Turkish rule played a major role.

For centuries, despite its value as the commercial nexus between East and West, the Ottomans had earned a dark place in the hearts of Europeans and Americans. The Ottomans were known to many Western minds as the "Terrible Turk" and the "Lustful Turk," caricatured as sexually perverted and bloodthirsty. Images of mass fratricides, palace murders, punishment by impalement, and severed heads presented to the sultan on silver platters all created cyclonic disgust within polite modern society. Going over the top, Turkish royalty was commonly depicted in Western illustrations as dripping in blood, consorting with skulls, or otherwise engaged in ghastly acts.[1]

Beyond personal misconduct, the Ottoman Empire was reviled by many twentieth-century Western leaders for creating the Eastern Question in the first place, thus inspiring wars throughout the Continent. Typical was the combined opinion of three distinguished American envoys to the Sublime Porte, Ambassadors Henry Morgenthau, Oscar Straus, and Abram Elkis. In a major *Washington Post* essay, published March 21, 1920, and headlined "Former

Envoys' Remedies for Evil of Turkish Rule," the three raised the question: "What is to become of those countries which constitute the Near East is a problem, which has always been of great interest to the whole world, and now of great and immediate interest to the American people. Today the great European powers are discussing what is to become of one of the great prizes of the war—the dominion of the Ottoman Empire ... During the last two centuries ... every European war has had its origin or its cause in the Ottoman Empire."[2]

Beyond blame for the wars that were endured by nations, the Turk was particularly accursed for the wholesale slaughter of innocent civilians. "They had held in bondage many races, some of them Christian," exclaimed one April 1920 *Washington Post* editorial, "and had abominably mistreated them, so atrociously, in fact, that the very word 'Turk' conjured up in the minds of scores of millions the personification of all that was evil."[3] Indeed, decades before the word *genocide* was invented, the Turks systematically murdered whole populations, not once, not twice, but repeatedly. Frequently, these onslaughts were perpetrated against defenseless Christians, further inflaming Westerners.

Abdulhamid II, the Sultan who reigned just before the Young Turks' revolution, became synonymous with the mass murder of Christians. For example, in the spring of 1876, a series of massacres collectively termed the "Bulgarian Horrors" or "Bulgarian Atrocities" was graphically reported by numerous eyewitnesses in the newspapers of the world, from New York and Washington to London, Paris, and St. Petersburg. In an attempt to suppress a Christian rebellion in the Balkans, Turkish troops and their militias raped the women and young girls in some 65 Bulgarian villages. In Kalifer, the women were herded into barns that were then set ablaze. In Karlovo, most of the homes were pillaged and then burned and many of the women ravished. In many cases, young girls were sold to other Muslims as sex slaves for five francs.[4]

In the wake of the Bulgarian outrages, former British liberal Prime Minister William Gladstone published his caustic pamphlet, "Bulgarian Horrors and the Question of the East," stigmatizing the Ottomans as bloodthirsty murderers. His tract became an immediate bestseller in London, selling 40,000 copies in a single week. A Russian-language version set a record, selling 10,000 copies in a month. In fact, it was Gladstone who coined the derogatory moniker "Abdul the Damned," which gained worldwide acceptance.[5]

Abdul the Damned, undeterred, went on to commit more atrocities against Christians. U.S. Ambassador to Turkey Henry Morgenthau recorded in his diary that among the Ottomans, Christians were commonly referred to as "dogs" and ranked less valuable than a camel or a horse. Ottoman hatred of infidels played out most brutally against Armenians, who were highly nationalistic and arguably the oldest Christian community in Europe. In the mid-1890s, a series of heinous raids against Armenian villages by Ottoman Kurds led to an uprising by Armenian militias in which they took their revenge on Kurdish towns and villages. In retaliation, Abdulhamid sent in shock troops to murder, maim, and rape masses of Armenians in the Sasun highlands. For example, in the village of Semel, the local priest was encouraged by Turkish commanders to surrender the populace, which he did. But once in captivity, the priest's eyes were gouged out, he was bayoneted to death, and then all the women were raped as their husbands screamed nearby from their own tortures and execution. British and American diplomats gave ample documentation of these horrors in regular dispatches to their foreign ministries. Such organized atrocities against Armenians continued throughout the realm, not only in the far-off districts, but also on the streets of Istanbul before the eyes of ambassadors who pleaded in vain for a pause. Ghastly pictures of mass graves published in British magazines revolted London.[6]

The Young Turks deposed Abdul the Damned in 1908. With their noble ideas about human rights and a lofty constitution resurrected from the pen of Midhat Pasha, many hoped for a new Ottoman era. But as the entrenched Young Turks turned ultra-nationalist, demanding to turkify all the empire, the Ottomans returned to old habits. In 1909, bloody massacres were again inflicted upon the Armenian population, this time in Adana. Provocative photographs published in Western capitals showed brutalized children, their skin flayed off with cotton-chopping tools.[7]

Beginning in 1915, in the midst of the war, systematic extermination on a monumental scale horrified the twentieth-century world. First, the Armenians were commercially boycotted, then identified and rounded up for destruction. They were "deported" from all over Turkey to numerous killing centers, including several in and around the Mosul province, where Kurds joined in the process. Railroad boxcars, concentration camps, and death marches through numerous Arab towns became the gruesome hallmarks of the process. Along the way, stragglers were shot, hacked to death, or hung from bridges. Newborns were ripped from their mothers' clutches and smashed to a bloody death against trees. Hundreds of thousands were sadistically murdered in a systematic state effort to exterminate once and for all the entire Armenian people.[8]

This merciless extermination continued into 1916 in full view of the world, regularly reported by diplomats and protested in Congress and Parliament. For example, on July 15, 1916, at 1:00 p.m., Ambassador Morgenthau sent a dispatch from the embassy in Istanbul: "Deportation of and excesses against peaceful Armenians is increasing; and from harrowing reports of eyewitnesses, it appears that a campaign of race extermination is in progress under a pretext of reprisal against rebellion." In England, Lord Bryce submitted an official government white paper and denunciation in October 1915, again using the term "extermination."[9]

The leading newspapers of the world headlined the inhuman campaign. In 1915 alone, the *New York Times* published approximately 145 articles detailing what was openly called "extermination." October 4, 1915: TELL OF HORRORS DONE IN ARMENIA; Report of Eminent Americans Says They Are Unequaled in a Thousand Years; TURKISH RECORD OUTDONE; A Policy of Extermination Put in Effect Against a Helpless People; ENTIRE VILLAGES SCATTERED; Men and Boys Massacred, Women and Girls Sold As Slaves and Distributed Among Muslims ... October 7, 1915: 800,000 ARMENIANS COUNTED DESTROYED; 10,000 DROWNED AT ONCE; Peers Are Told How Entire Christian Population of Trebizond Was Wiped Out; December 15, 1915: MILLION ARMENIANS KILLED OR IN EXILE; American Committee on Relief Says Victims of Turks Are Steadily Increasing; POLICY OF EXTERMINATION; More Atrocities Detailed In Support of Charge That Turkey Is Acting Deliberately.[10]

In the United States, the Armenian extermination became a cause célèbre. Families were jingoistically exhorted to remember the starving Armenian children dying in camps and on death marches. One day at the height of the killing, Talaat Pasha, one of the architects of the extermination, was so sure all Armenians would perish, that he summoned Ambassador Morgenthau to discuss their insurance policies. New York Life Insurance and Equitable Life of New York were both leading life insurers of the Armenian middle class. He bragged that 75 percent of the million or more Armenians were already dead and the Turkish government would leave none living to take revenge. "I wish," Talaat then asked Morgenthau, "that you would get the American life insurance companies to send us a complete list of their Armenian policy holders. They are practically all dead now and have left no heirs to collect the money. It, of course, all escheats [legally defaults] to the State. The Government is the beneficiary now. Will you do so?" Morgenthau angrily refused.[11]

Talaat had previously challenged Morgenthau's protests over the Armenian extermination. "You are a Jew, these people are Christians ... Why can't you let us do with these Christians as we please?" Morgenthau replied that he was speaking as an American, not a Jew, and that made his protests "97 percent Christian." Adamant, he assured Talaat that Americans "will always resent the wholesale destruction of Christians in Turkey." He also warned, "After this war is over you shall face a new situation ... You will have to meet public opinion everywhere, especially in the United States. Our people will never forget."[12]

In the Paris of 1919, all memories on all topics were still fresh. In fact, Armenia was one of the national groups identified for self-determination and nationhood, to be administered in mandate by the United States. The Armenian mandate, however, was not pursued because the U.S. Congress never ratified America's entry into the League of Nations.[13]

Certainly, as the political vivisection of the Sick Man proceeded, the commercial captains circled, rubbing their hands and shifting into better positions. But the Allied leaders that tore the Ottoman Empire limb from limb thought of far more than oil. Allied leaders also thought of 8 million soldiers dead, 21 million wounded, 2 million missing in action, whole populations uprooted, millions of civilians east and west massacred, $180 billion spent, war reparations demanded of Germany, and an equivalent levy against Turkey in the form of oil resources. That's why Allied leaders felt completely justified in all they did in Mesopotamia. They even held the written consent of Hussein of Mecca. They just never asked the Arabs who actually lived there.

*   *   *   *

Conflicting Allied declarations in the Middle East parted the sea for some fleeing persecution, and drowned the hopes and aspirations of others chasing independence.

On November 2, 1917, the British foreign secretary had issued a declaration to Zionist organizations worldwide that Britain had identified the displaced and long-persecuted Jews as one of the many groups qualified for self-determination. Specifically, it committed Britain to facilitate "the establishment in Palestine of a national home for the Jewish people ... it being clearly understood that nothing shall be done which may prejudice the civil and religious rights of existing non-Jewish communities in Palestine, or the rights and political status enjoyed by Jews in any other country."[14]

Modern Zionism had been born two decades earlier when Jewish activist Theodor Herzl proposed an ingathering of the exiled Jews back to their ancestral home as the only solution to the centuries of unstoppable civil and violent persecution. From 1903 to 1907 alone, some 284 heinous state-encouraged pogroms in czarist Russia resulted in 50,000 Jews being killed or wounded. During World War I, anti-Jewish laws throughout Europe continued to proscribe Jewish citizenship, land ownership, many professions, and even freedom of movement for millions of Jews. For example, some 4.8 million Jews in Russia were restricted to a "Pale of Settlement" and subjected to scurrilous anti-Semitic decrees.[15]

Jews had dwelled in Palestine, the seat of Judaism, for millennia. They survived the Babylonians who exiled them, the Romans who crucified them, the Crusaders who slaughtered them, and the Ottoman Turks who hanged them in the square as infidels. Throughout modern history, Jewish communities flourished in Jerusalem, where they constituted a majority—in 1864, out of 15,000 residents, some 8,000 were Jews, 4,500 Muslims, and 2,500 Christians. By the time of the Balfour Declaration in 1917, some 45,000 of Jerusalem's 65,000 inhabitants were Jewish. Additionally, Jews had always lived throughout the nearly barren land of Palestine in such cities as Gaza, Ashkelon, Jaffa, Caesarea, and Tsfat. Indeed, Jews lived in great numbers throughout the Ottoman Empire's Middle East, from Syria to the Persian Gulf.[16]

The intention of the Balfour Declaration and its French equivalent was to create two homelands, Arab and Jewish, living harmoniously side by side in the same fashion as other national groups.[17] The Jews would receive a homeland carved out of the larger Palestine territory. But the Arabs despised the very idea of Zionism. Of course, Jews and many other religions groups had dwelled among the Arabs for centuries. But these Zionist Jews were seeking autonomy and self-determination. The Christians and Jews, could live under Muslim authority as *dhimmis*, that is, protected second-class citizens who acknowledged the sovereignty of Islam, paid special taxes, and observed special restrictive laws. The idea of Jews establishing their own autonomous communities with international recognition was anathema.

Certainly, any number of other citizens of the Ottoman Empire, or indeed from anywhere in the Eurasian region, migrated into barren and sparsely settled Palestine during the preceding decades. Local Arabs, who constituted the majority in overall Palestine, welcomed Muslim newcomers—but not the Jews. Official protests and demands by Arab committees that the Sultan expel Jews trace back to the earliest Russian pre-Zionist Jewish immigrants in the late 1880s. Long before Herzl's 1896 promulgation of Zionism, Turkish anti-Jewish laws were a fact of life in Palestine.[18]

When news of the Balfour Declaration reached the Arab masses, along with the explosive details of the Sykes-Picot Agreement, the Allies sought to reassure the restive and resentful Arabs that their national aspirations would not be supplanted. On November 7, 1918, just as the war was rapidly coming to a close, Paris and London issued the Anglo-French Declaration to the Arabs. The promulgation stressed one goal: "the complete and definite emancipation of the peoples so long oppressed by the Turks and the establishment of national governments and administrations deriving their authority from the initiative and free choice of the indigenous populations."[19]

The joint November 7 declaration guaranteed "France and Great Britain are at one in encouraging and assisting the establishment of indigenous Governments and administrations in Syria and Mesopotamia ... and recognizing these as soon as they are actually established." The declaration averred that these "Governments and administrations [should be] freely chosen by the populations themselves."[20]

But as the Paris Peace Conference opened in January 1919, the Arabs, represented by Sharif Faisal, were snubbed by the French. Regardless of prior representations by the British, the French were uninterested in relinquishing their designs on greater Syria, especially since the Lebanon region was overwhelmingly Maronite Christian. Many French officials simply considered the Arabs a threat. Typical was a memo from the Quai D'Orsay that stated, "Damascus is a Muslim center which is very hostile to France, to tell the truth, the most hostile in all Islam. It is there that the fanatical Arabs of North Africa go who want to elude our control. It is there where all the plots against our authority in the Muslim countries are hatched, and it is there where the agitators come and preach rebellion ... Damascus [must] be placed under our control."[21]

Faisal, who now became the face of Arab nationalism to the Peace Conference, busily engaged in his own declaring and maneuvering. On January 1, 1919, he submitted a formal memorandum to the Supreme Council of the Peace Conference outlining his vision for Arab nationalism throughout the Mideast. It was not monolithic or pan-Arab. The Arab national movement was headquartered in Damascus and, plainly put, they wanted Syria, along with the region of the holy cities of Medina and Mecca.[22]

"The various provinces of Arab Asia—Syria, Iraq, Jezireh, Hijaz, Nejd, Yemen—are very different economically and socially," asserted Faisal's petition, "and it is impossible to constrain them into one frame of government." Certainly, Faisal's petition was unyielding on Syria and the Hijaz, that is, the Arabian Peninsula encompassing Mecca. "Syria ... thickly peopled with sedentary [settled] classes, is sufficiently advanced politically to manage her own internal affairs." He added proudly that while Syria would accept foreign advisors, it would do so only without paternalism. "We are willing to pay for this help in cash; [but] we cannot sacrifice for it any part of the freedom we have just won for ourselves."[23]

It was totally different for Mesopotamia. In keeping with his earlier promises in the McMahon-Hussein correspondence, Faisal reiterated that he was willing to relinquish Iraq to the British. Faisal readily acknowledged: "Jezireh [encompassing northeastern Syria and the Mosul provincial region] and Iraq are ... made up of three civilized towns, divided by large wastes, thinly peopled by semi-nomadic tribes." He readily acknowledged Western commercial designs, continuing, "The world wishes to exploit Mesopotamia rapidly, and we therefore believe that the system of government there will have to be buttressed by the men and material resources of a great foreign Power."[24]

Rather than seeking elections in Iraq, Faisal suggested a custodial government handpicked by London and patient British tutelage to bring the population into modern times. "We ask, however, that [while] the Government be Arab, in principle and spirit, the selective rather than the elective principle being necessarily followed in the neglected districts, until time makes the broader basis possible. The main duty of the Arab Government there would be to oversee the educational processes, which are to advance the tribes to the moral level of the towns."[25]

An Arab national state in Syria was of such major importance that Faisal was even willing to endorse both an Arab and a Zionist state in Palestine, existing side by side, under a British mandate, if that would smooth the way. Therefore, while Faisal's petition stipulated that, "In Palestine, the enormous majority of the people are Arabs." He added in the next sentence, "The Jews are very close to the Arabs in blood, and there is no conflict of character between the races. In principles, we are absolutely at one." That said, he acknowledged that Palestine was important to many faiths and therefore the Arab national movement "would wish for the effective super-position of a great trustee, so long as a representative local administration commended itself by actively promoting the material prosperity of the country." That promulgation welcomed a British mandate over the envisioned two-canton Palestinian entity. Continuing his own cascade of political zigs and zags, Faisal then met in Paris with Zionist Organization president Chaim Weizmann. Following up on meetings the two leaders had held the previous year in Aqaba, Faisal signed an enlightened and tolerant nine-point agreement, endorsing the Balfour Declaration and inviting the Zionists to coexist in Palestine. "Article II: Immediately following the completion of the deliberations of the Peace Conference, the definite boundaries between the Arab State and Palestine shall be determined by a Commission to be agreed upon by the parties hereto. Article III: In the establishment of the Constitution and Administration of Palestine, all such measures shall be adopted as will afford the fullest guarantees for carrying into effect the British Government's [Balfour] Declaration of the 2nd of November 1917 ... Article IV: All necessary measures shall be taken to encourage and stimulate immigration of Jews into Palestine on a large scale, and as quickly as possible to settle Jewish immigrants upon the land through closer settlement and intensive cultivation of the soil. In taking such measures, the Arab peasant and tenant farmers shall be protected in their rights and shall be assisted in forwarding their economic development."[27]

The entire agreement was typed in English in January 1919. But at the bottom, Faisal hand-penned in Arabic this stern warning: "Provided the Arabs obtain their independence as demanded in my [forthcoming] Memorandum dated the 4th of January, 1919, to the Foreign Office of the Government of Great Britain, I shall concur in the above articles. But if the slightest modification or departure were to be made [regarding our demands], I shall not be then bound by a single word of the present Agreement which shall be deemed void and of no account or validity, and I shall not be answerable in any way whatsoever." Directly beneath that inscription were the signatures of Weizmann and Faisal duly affixed.[28]

The Allies could have Palestine and Iraq, but Faisal and the Arab national movement demanded Syria.

In mid-April 1919, Faisal met with President Georges Clemenceau and was promised total Arab independence for Syria. A declaration was typed up on April 17. But the French offer involved just one other thing: As part of that independence, the French army would occupy Damascus, and the new Arab nation would actually be a mere federation of local autonomous states in which all the government advisors, including the governors and heads of major government bureaus, as well as the judiciary, would be French, and under Paris's control as they currently were in Lebanon, plus Faisal would be compelled to publicly declare the importance of France's historic relationship with the Maronite Christians.[29] Other than that, Syria would be completely independent.

Faisal quickly refused, encouraged by Lawrence of Arabia who advised him to demand total independence "without conditions or reservations." Clemenceau, however, would not tolerate what he considered Arab impudence. Faisal summarily left Paris for Syria to claim his nation.[30]

Throughout later 1919, the multilateral negotiations dragged on with the usual permutations, frustrations, reversals, and "by the ways." Eventually, a disenchanted Faisal admitted he preferred that the mandate be given to any nation other than France. He even suggested United States or Britain.[31] But France would not yield.

From the French point of view, it could not retreat from dominating Greater Syria, especially from Lebanon. French troops, religious groups, and civilian organizations had undertaken an impressive economic and administrative reconstruction of the neglected Turkish Lebanese provinces. Courts were overhauled, new banks were installed with generous loans extended, emergency food was distributed, sewers laid, streets paved, and dozens of schools opened. One leading French columnist and government advisor warned that if forced out of Syria and Lebanon, "World opinion would consider France 'a finished people.'" Using blunt language, an adamant Clemenceau made it clear if Faisal and the Arab nationalists did not have "absolute respect ... [and] satisfy me," the entire region would be taken "through force."[32]

Finally, on January 6, 1920, Faisal and Clemenceau reached a provisional agreement. Syria, under a Faisal regime, would include Lebanon and would be permitted a parliament that could enact laws and taxes; the national language would be Arabic, not French or Turkish; and the French army would not massively occupy the country. To help ensure that Faisal adhered to the

January 6 accord, Clemenceau had already installed in Beirut a new high commissioner for Lebanon, General Henri Gouraud. Fiercely chauvinistic, pro-Christian, and anti-Arab, Gouraud had been the intrepid commander at the Second Battle of the Marne and was still prepared to fight any enemy of France. Soon, Faisal found himself teetering atop a tightrope between two constituencies. Some virulently branded him a traitor to the infidel. Others praised Faisal as the national hero who had negotiated Syria's independence.[33]

Muslim rejectionists had already been attacking the existing French troops in the region. Arab soldiers in the defeated Turkish army were now repatriated to Syria and ready to again take up arms. Rapidly, the situation deteriorated. Faisal now had to choose between the French and the possibility that their ingenuous promises might be kept, and the fervid and distrusting Arab nationalists who everywhere demanded instant independence. By late February 1920, Faisal had transformed himself once again, insisting on not only total independence for Syria, but now demanding the British do the same for Palestine and Iraq.[34]

Nobody was keeping any promises. Pacts and promulgations were solemnly propounded, only to be breached, padded, and then reconstituted by all sides. Like the Great War that had just finished, political preemption led to political provocation, which led to further preemption. The vicious downward spiral was gaining velocity.

On March 7 and 8, 1920, the Second General Syrian Congress, a representative assembly of Arab nationalists from many countries, raced ahead of any League of Nations decision. It vehemently declared independence for a Greater Syria, to extend both into Lebanon and south into Palestine. The Congress elected Faisal as King of Syria. Iraq was likewise declared independent and Faisal's brother, Abdullah, elected its king.[35]

The Allies were outraged. On March 11, the French premier insisted to Prime Minister Lloyd George that the Second General Syrian Congress was an illegitimate enterprise and its decisions of no value or import. The French were supporting the United Kingdom territorial desiderata on Iraq and Palestine. Now, in return, Paris demanded Britain support French claims to Syria. Otherwise the hard-fought rights gained in the Middle East would be lost to all the Allies. Lord Curzon, the British foreign secretary, angrily scolded the French ambassador in London, "The future of France and Great Britain in [the seized Turkish Mideast] was imperiled because of the way in which the French Government, in pursuance of traditional or historical aspirations, had insisted on forcing themselves into areas where the French were not welcomed by the inhabitants."[36]

The British, now also on the defensive, demanded that Faisal engineer the nullification of the Second General Syrian Congress's declaration of Iraqi independence. "The right of anybody at Damascus to decide the future of Mesopotamia or Mosul," insisted Lord Curzon in a letter to Faisal, "is one that cannot be admitted in any circumstances."[37]

At stake was more than geography, more than prestige. There was oil in Iraq, and it had to be transported across Syria and Palestine, as well as south through Basra. The Allies needed the Mideast.

About a month later, on April 19, 1920, the Allies, working through their League of Nations, gathered at San Remo, Italy, for a several-day conference to carve up Turkey. *Carving* was the word of the hour. Indeed, the night before the conference, the *Washington Post* article about the conference was even headlined, "The Carving of Turkey." The *Post* presaged the conference's "far reaching importance" as "the Allies try to arrange for satisfactory government of many races, some of them warlike and all of them backward" who had emerged from centuries of Turkish neglect. These included national groups in the Balkans, Azerbaijan, Greece, Hungary, Georgia, and across the many provinces of the Mideast. The delegates convened against the background of numerous bloody European conflicts still flaring. The Bolshevik revolution and its consequences were burning throughout Eastern Europe and Eurasia, including such countries as Latvia, Poland, and Bessarabia. Postwar Germany was in civil upheaval. Innocent civilians were being massacred regularly, as national groups contended for primacy.[38]

With the last dusk of the San Remo Conference, the conferees granted France the mandate for both Syria and Lebanon—two new nations-in-waiting were created. The British received the mandate for Iraq—one new nation-in-waiting was created. Britain also received the mandate for Palestine, under a provision to create a Jewish homeland, therefore writing the Jewish nation's establishment into international law—one nation-in-waiting was re-created.[39]

The Zionists had cooperated with the British during the war and the peace negotiations to follow. Indeed the Jewish nation's major incubating governmental institutions were almost all British corporations based in London. Zionists understood that only desperate and persecuted Jews would relocate to Palestine's inhospitable terrain, and in so doing, bring it to life for later generations of middle-class Jews. Palestine would become a commercial engine in the region. Moreover, once established, a Jewish state in Palestine was sure to be a reliable Western ally and British foothold in the heart of the Middle East. All land gained was to be legally purchased under international law. The Jews were among several peoples selected for transfer under international auspices. A million Greek Muslims were slated for transfer into Turkey, and a half million Turkish Christians were to migrate into Greece. All Jews going to Palestine were to transfer in under international law, just as decided for other national groups.[40]

Many establishment Jews in the major cities of Europe and America, especially Jews of German origin, denounced the Zionist ethic as a threat to their precarious assimilated existence. But even as San Remo delegates met, helpless Jewish villagers were being murdered by the thousands in Poland as a mere sidelight to a Polish-Russian conflict. Masses of impoverished Jews, persecuted by European regimes, as well as Jews already dwelling throughout the Ottoman Empire, now waited to enter Palestine and escape persecution into a national homeland of their own.[41]

At San Remo, America did not receive the much-vaunted mandate for Armenia because Congress blocked U.S. admission into the League of Nations. America was not even a participant in the discussions. Consequently, France and Britain were both the grantors and the grantees of the mandates and the oil wealth that attached.[42]

On April 24, 1920, away from the main diplomacy of the San Remo Conference, Anglo-French petroleum negotiators concluded their own agreement. It was initialed by Frenchman M. Philippe Berthelot, director-general of the commercial affairs section of the Foreign Ministry, and by John Cadman, Britain's latest oil czar. In many ways, the so-called Berthelot-Cadman agreement resembled many of the previous accords negotiated and renegotiated by Anglo-French interlocutors. But Berthelot-Cadman was hardly an international treaty sanctioned by the League of Nations and subject to the elaborate peace process. This was a secret deal between France and Great Britain to divide up the oil of Europe, Asia Minor, North Africa, and Mesopotamia. The language made clear that this latest, and seemingly final, agreement, was essentially a resurrection of previous oil contracts going back to prewar times.[43]

"By order of the two Governments of France and Great Britain," the document began, "the undersigned representatives have resumed, by mutual consent, the consideration of an agreement regarding petroleum. This agreement is based on the principles of cordial co-operation and reciprocity in those countries where the oil interest of the two nations can be usefully united." The memorandum listed Romania, Asia Minor, the former czarist territories and Galicia, as well as the French and British colonies.

Clause 7 specified the previously acceptable language about the Turkish Petroleum Company: "Mesopotamia—The British Government undertake to grant to the French Government, or its nominee, 25 per cent of the net output of crude oil at current market rates which His Majesty's Government may secure from the Mesopotamian oilfields, in the event of their being developed by Government action; or in the event of a private petroleum company being used to develop the Mesopotamian oilfields, the British Government will place at the disposal of the French Government a share of 25 per cent in such company ... It is also understood that the said petroleum company shall be under permanent British control."[44]

Clause 8 committed both France and England to each offer a 10 percent participation of the private company to a Mesopotamian government if such a government emerged—this as a token nod to American concepts of self-determination. Nothing more about local participation was specified. Clause 9 assured that "the British Government agree to support arrangements by which the French Government may procure from the Anglo-Persian Company supplies of oil, which may be piped from Persia to the Mediterranean through any pipeline which may have been constructed within the French mandated territory and in regard to which France has given special facilities, up to the extent of 25 per cent of the oil so piped, on such terms and conditions as may be mutually agreed between the French Government and the Anglo-Persian Company."[45]

The next day, April 25, 1920, the initialed Berthelot-Cadman agreement was confirmed, and then signed by the two heads of state, British Prime Minister David Lloyd George and newly elected French president Alexandre Millerand. While the oil covenant remained secret, the League of Nations mandates soon became public.[46] News of the mandates, denying Arab sovereignty in Syria while establishing a Jewish national home, quickly burned throughout the Arab world.

On May 8, 1920, an irked Faisal sent a formal protest to the Supreme Council of the Peace Conference that he "was much surprised to learn, through public channels, the decision taken at the Conference of San Remo on the Arab countries detached from Turkey ... The wishes of the inhabitants have not been taken into account in the assignment of these mandates." He cautioned grimly, "The Arabs, fully conscious of their rights and their duties, did not hesitate to take up arms against their co-religionists, and to sacrifice their noblest blood in defense of the Right, thereby rendering abortive the threatened Holy War [declared by the Ottoman Empire], which the Turks and Germans wished to exploit in their struggle with the Entente [the Allies]."[47]

Faisal reminded the League of Nations that the stated intent during the Arab uprisings against Turkey was "nothing less than their complete deliverance from a foreign yoke, and the establishment of a free and independent government, which would allow them [the Arabs] to resume their place in the concert of civilized nations." Ominously, Faisal added, "The decision of San Remo puts an end to this hope. The moderate elements in the young nation, who have endeavored, and are still endeavoring, to guide it towards a policy of sincere collaboration with the Allies, are now discouraged and rendered powerless by this decision."[48]

For more than a year, Arab and Kurdish resentment of the occupation, inflamed by Bolshevik agitation in the region and resurgent Turkish postwar nationalism everywhere, had yielded Christian massacres, assassinations of political officers, ambushes of British and Indian officers, and attacks on convoys throughout the three Iraqi provinces. As the fuse of San Remo burned, Arab militancy and violence across the occupied Mideast—in Palestine, Mesopotamia, and Syria—already a problem, now ratcheted up.[49]

On May 18, 1920, Britain's foreign secretary, fed up with the violence, washed his hands of Syrian Arabs, cabling Paris, "The French authorities must be the best judges of the military measures necessary to control the local situation, and ... they have complete authority in taking such measures." Quickly, French president Millerand confirmed to General Gourand, "Action against Faisal is indispensable and urgent." General Gourand immediately prepared to invade Syria with several divisions backed by tanks, airplanes, and heavy artillery.[50]

General Gourand issued a 48-hour ultimatum to Faisal to desist and facilitate French efforts to restore order—or else. This ultimatum was calculated to be unanswerable because of the sheer difficulties of rapid communication across the region. Nonetheless, Faisal instantly agreed to General Gourand's demands, but his reply came one day late. Therefore, General Gourand's march on Damascus began in full force. But then British and French diplomatic sources debated whether they could move against Syrian Arabs in view of Faisal's actual acceptance of the ultimatum—even though his reply had been one day late. An irate French president Millerand saw Faisal's promises as empty, a mere ploy for time. "So as not to fall back into the previous situation," demanded Millerand, "it is now necessary to continue to take—without lending yourself to the Sherifian's [Faisal's] game to gain time—all steps necessary for your safety and for the total execution of the mandate."[51]

On July 24, 1920, French forces continued their invasion toward Damascus. The Arabs rallied to meet them at Maysalun, just west of the city. Charging with swords and bolt-action rifles, they were said to have displayed "strong resistance." But they were no match for the modern warfare that had emerged over the recent years. French tanks, airplanes, machine guns, and overwhelming infantry force slaughtered the Arabs within eight hours. The French now occupied Damascus and successfully established their mandate.[52]

That same day, July 24, 1920, after persistent fragmentary leaks, the secret San Remo oil agreement became public after being submitted to the House of Commons.[53] Clearly, the French and British had divided up the Middle East for its oil.

That same day, July 24, 1920, the Zionist Conference concluded in London with a flourish for the future. Gathering in a large hall, bedecked with Jewish-star-emblazoned flags hanging vertically from the balconies and across the stained glass windows at the front, inspired before a great Union Jack with a Jewish star inset with a portrait of Herzl, the Jewish delegates were determined to end the tragic wandering, persecution, and decimation of their people. Their solution: a legal, internationally sanctioned return to the homeland from whence they had been exiled a millennium earlier. In many ways, the Zionist Conference functioned as a counterpart to the international Arab conclave at the Second General Syrian Congress in Damascus that voted to establish an Arab nation. The Zionist Conference did the same for Jewish Palestine. Its crowning resolution created Karen Hayesod organization to support the Jewish National Fund with cash donations from Jews worldwide to legally purchase lands for kibbutzim and to finance the formation of new Jewish villages in Palestine. Just days earlier, Whitehall had appointed Sir Herbert Samuel as High Commissioner of Palestine, empowered to oversee the orderly immigration of Jews into Palestine. The Jewish homeland was being sanctioned, being purchased, being peopled, being slowly brought to life.[54]

On that same day, July 24, 1920, for the Arabs, it was over. The Jews had gained Palestine. The West had gained oil. The Arabs had lost Syria. For the Arab world, this was to be *Am al-Nakba*.

To the Arabs, it did not matter that during the war, Britain had deployed some 900,000 men against Turkey while only token platoons of Arabs had fought behind the lines; from the Arab perspective, Arabs did in fact fight, and fight valiantly. They upheld their end of the bargain. It did not matter that the Arabs had cruelly battled against the British in Mesopotamia alongside the Turks at Kut, at Baghdad, and elsewhere; from the Arab perspective, Mesopotamia was not part of the bargain anyway. It did not matter that within the pages of the serpentine McMahon-Hussein correspondence, nothing was firmly promised; from the Arab perspective, they sanctified the sentences most precious to them. What mattered most was that the West and the Jews had triumphed, and the domination of the Arabs would continue, but this time under a Christian mandate and now with autonomous Jews in their midst.

Three intertwined evils—the infidel European Allies, the infidel Zionists, and the black substance the West craved—became conflated in the Arab mind to create one great Satan. Indeed, these three evils would galvanize the Arab consciousness for virtually the next century. For the first time in centuries, the Arabs stopped fighting each other. Sunni and Shi'a, tribal enemies, those of the desert and those of the city, the intellectual and the peasant—all could unite under one Islamic banner, because this was *Am al-Nakba*. Forevermore, 1920 would be a black year in the collective Arabic consciousness. In Arabic, *Am al-Nakba* means "The Year of the Catastrophe."[55]

Now, across the Arab rectangle, a great jihad would be unleashed. Faisal had earlier warned the peace conference: "The unity of the Arabs in Asia has been made more easy of late years, since the development of railways, telegraphs, and air-roads. In old days, the area was too huge, and in parts necessarily too thinly peopled, to communicate common ideas readily." Arab anger could now move quickly and with coordination. The Arabs would strike most fiercely where it would hurt most. They would strike in Mesopotamia, where Britain and France dreamed of the oil that had not yet been drilled and that had not yet flowed, but that the Allies could already taste. The Arabs wanted that taste to be bitter and bloody.

*   *   *   *

Ten perfect circles were drawn vertically on the paper along with the notations: "Speed = 75 MPH. Interval of Release = 2 Secs. Area: 2,000 feet long, half-mile wide, varying with wind."[56] The British had been preparing for more than a year.

War-weary and undermanned in Mesopotamia, poorly supplied and thinly deployed across the three provinces, Britain had concluded by early April 1919 that it could not police and control a roiling Iraqi insurgency with mere ground troops. Air bombardment was the only answer. A November Air Ministry survey of air squadrons in the Middle East and India revealed that less than two squadrons were available to bomb positions or provide reconnaissance in Iraq.[57]

But the insurgents in Iraq were too dispersed for concentrated bombardment, air service officers believed. Moreover, in the mountainous Mosul region, Kurdish rebels often hid in caves and hard-to-identify mountain passes. A different weapon would be needed: gas bombs.

On April 29, 1919, the Royal Air Force in Cairo advised the Air Ministry in London, "Gas bombs are required by 31st Wing for use against recalcitrant Arabs as experiment, the suggestion being concurred in by the General Staff, Baghdad."[58]

Poison gas had been a staple of the Great War. The French were the first to use nonlethal irritant gas projectiles in August 1914, the first month of the war. The Germans responded with lethal gas. Although the German use of toxic gases was roundly condemned, eventually all the Allies joined in. In the last months of the War, President Woodrow Wilson also adopted the principle of poison gas warfare. On July 18, 1918, Wilson signed General Order #62, establishing the Chemical Warfare Service. The combatants deployed chlorine, phosgene, and mustard gases, generally in artillery shells, as the preferred killing agents. When the air had cleared, more than a million casualties had fallen, some 86,000 fatally. Russia sustained the most killed, some 56,000.[59]

But gas bombs had never been successfully deployed from the air. On May 2, a handwritten note was sent to the Flying Operations Directorate at the Air Board Office in London wondering about innocent casualties and the dangers posed to the troops: "1. Could you please give the War Office view concerning the employment of gas in any form against uncivilized tribes? 2. It should be pointed out that gas is dangerous both to those who employ it and, naturally, to those against whom it may be quite unwittingly used. The great difficulty of differentiation between innocent and guilty once more presents itself and is merely accentuated by this form of warfare. 3. Gas bombs are not available at present. The question of their being produced subsequently is under discussion. 4. [Air Vice Marshal] General [Geoffrey] Salmond is against the employment of gas in any form, [and] is of the opinion that the necessary effect is quite satisfactorily obtained with bombs of the ordinary nature."[60]

A debate ensued about the morality of gas bombs. The matter was decided several days later on May 12, 1919, when Winston Churchill, then secretary of state for War and Air, ruled in favor of tear gas and perhaps more. "I do not understand this squeamishness about the use of gas," he wrote. "We have definitely adopted the position at the Peace Conference of arguing in favor of the retention of gas as a permanent method of warfare. It is sheer affectation to lacerate a man with the poisonous fragment of a bursting shell and to boggle at making his eyes water by means of lachrymatory [tear] gas."[61]

He added with reservation, "I am [also] strongly in favor of using poisoned gas against uncivilized tribes. The moral effect should be so good that the loss of life should be reduced to a minimum. It is not necessary to use only the most deadly gasses: gasses can be used which cause great inconvenience and would spread a lively terror, and yet would leave no serious permanent effects on most of those affected."[62]

On May 19, deputy chief of the Air Staff R. M. Groves confirmed in a note, "S of S [Secretary of State for War and Air Churchill] approves the policy of utilizing gas bombs – please see enclosure 5A. Will you therefore please take the necessary steps with DGSR [Director General of Science and Research] to obtain supplies?" Several days later, he also advised the Flying Operations Directorate, "I understand that the S of S ... has approved the general policy of using poisonous gas against uncivilized tribes. So far, although considerable time and trouble was expended on research during the war, we have not yet evolved suitable and practicable gas bombs for use from aircraft."[63]

Shortly thereafter, the Air Ministry's director of research Henry Robert Brooke-Popham dashed off a handwritten note, "I think the first thing is to obtain from the gas experts of the late trench warfare department an opinion of the best gas to use. A: For incapacitating the enemy without permanently injuring him. B: For killing or permanently incapacitating him. Also, an opinion on the weight of gas or gas-producing material necessary to produce an effective concentration in a given area in average atmospheric conditions."[64]

On June 16, 1919, director of research Brigadier General Brooke-Popham circulated a memo. "I sent Col. Ranken over to see the Chemical Warfare Department at the War Office to get accurate information regarding the position of gas bombs. The position is as follows – (a) the 9.45" Trench Mortar Shell has been converted into an aerial bomb. The design of this is completed and the shell has actually been tried in the air and found satisfactory. There are shells converted for use as aerial bombs available now and only require filling and exploders provided for them. I do not know the number. They could be filled with any of the following types of gas: (1) Lachrymatory; (2) Mustard Gas; (3) Chlorine; (4) Phosgene. It is estimated that it would take at least six weeks before any filled shells complete with all their exploders would be provided ... The Chemical Warfare Department have made up two sample 520 lb. bombs with a modified case, but these have never been tried or put up for approval. These cannot be considered a practical proposition at the present time, and it would probably be months before this type could be issued as suitable."[65]

By the end of June, 1919, Brooke-Popham concluded, "The best gas to use appears to be as follows: A) Lachrymatory; B) Phosgene." He explained, "Mustard gas is likely to make a casualty of an affected person for some six months and will foul the ground for a long period so that people stepping on rocks or stone on which the bomb has burst will become casualties. I also understand that natives of India or Africa would be liable to be killed off by mustard gas more than Europeans would be. I attach a chart showing the approximate area affected by ten 9.45 gas bombs dropped at 2 seconds intervals ... The chart assumes that the first bomb is dropped in approximately the correct position with reference to the objective and that the machine keeps on a straight course for 20 seconds during which the bombs are dropped in succession. I am having a calculation made ... The accuracy of bombing varies so enormously with the conditions on the ground and in the air."[66]

Attached was a chart. Ten perfect circles were drawn vertically on the paper, along with explanatory notations: "Speed = 75 MPH. Interval of Release = 2 Secs. Area: 2,000 feet long, half-mile wide, varying with wind."[67] Yes, it was possible. But could it be done in time?

*   *   *   *

The jihad against Britain in Iraq did not have a precise starting date because insurgent violence, from simple sniper fire to massacres of Christians, had been ongoing in Mesopotamia since the end of World War I. But a major precursor to the full-fledged revolt erupted at 3 A.M. on December 11, 1919. Hundreds, perhaps thousands, of tribesmen stormed Dair al-Zur, a town in the no-man's-land between Syria and Mosul. Invaders, joined by local residents, set fire to the Political Office, forced open the safe and stole the money, and then attacked the hospital, a church, and even a mosque. Then, they broke into the prison, freeing all prisoners. Two hours later, the marauders raided the fuel depot, setting off explosions in the process which killed some 30 insurgents and injured dozens more. At first light, a British armored car sent out for patrol was repulsed by hostile gunfire. British machine guns, mounted on rooftops, took aim, but were also put out of commission by the rebels.[68]

British soldiers and police retreated to the barracks on the outskirts of Dair al-Zur. But by midmorning, the barracks was also under siege. Late in the morning, a momentary truce was declared, allowing the British commander to talk to the frenzied group. Just then, at 11:30 A.M., two airplanes from Mosul came into view. They carried no gas bombs, as such weapons were still months from completion. But the airborne machine guns let loose on the town, throwing the village into panic. A frantic second truce was called as the British bargained for the safe return of their hostages and the Arabs demanded a cessation of the air strike.[69]

On December 14, 1919, three days after the assault began, Churchill announced a greatly expanded air force. Since the war, the British air fleet had dwindled from 22,000 aircraft to a mere 200 planes in 28 squadrons. Churchill asked for the equivalent of $75 million annually to fund new aircraft. This included three squadrons for Iraq. However, those planes were months away. British forces could not hold Dair al-Zur on the ground. They were forced to withdraw, and the territory was later ceded to Syria.[70] Dair al-Zur, the British thought, would now be France's problem.

But Dair al-Zur remained a British problem as well. Dair al-Zur was the closest contact point in Iraq to Damascus, and it became a new launch site for insurrection. The revolt soon spread south. On March 31, 1920, some 4,000 tribal warriors met at Kaimakamjazir to plan a general uprising. Its first glimmer occurred within 48 hours, on April 2, 1920, as a British convoy was attacked 50 miles northeast of Mosul. Ten Indian soldiers were killed.[71]

On May 1, 1920, acting Commissioner Wilson received official confirmation of the San Remo decision. Several days later, he was instructed to publish news of the mandate over Iraq bestowed by the League of Nations. The gist of London's proclamation declared, "Iraq has now been rescued from Turkey by military conquests, and armies of the British Empire are in military occupation of the country." Using visionary language and uplifting justifications, Britain promised to establish an interim civilian authority to "prepare the way for the creation of an independent Arab State of Iraq." To that end, London also pledged to form "representative divisional and municipal councils in different parts of the country." Therefore, the British mandate, the announcement declared, was "in fulfillment of promises that have been made to Arab peoples" and to Faisal.[72]

Wilson was both resentful of the "independence" being promised and extremely nervous about the restive Iraqis. He urgently requested permission to announce within the coming days—certainly before the onset of Ramadan—that he planned to immediately implement a constitutional process. "Once this is done," he wrote," we shall be in a position to deal with extremists." In a separate memo, Wilson explained that in his view there were two types of extremists: "1) the sane extremists, who desire Arab independence under British control; and 2) the ultra-extremists, who desire to see the abolition of European control of all sorts throughout the East."[73]

Wilson's notion of Iraqi independence was colonial independence, or perhaps colonial control but self-management. The notion of representative government for Mesopotamia's masses distressed him. The people of Iraq should be told, not asked. "I submit," he protested to London, "that it is for His Majesty's Government as Mandatory Power to prescribe what form of Government shall be set up in the immediate future. To refer the question afresh to divisional councils and to 'local opinion' can have but one result. The extremists who, following the example of their colleagues in Syria, are demanding absolute independence for Iraq—with or without [King] Abdullah [as their monarch]—will by threats and by appeals during the coming month of Ramadan to religious fanaticism, win over moderate men who have hitherto looked to the Government for a scheme offering a reasonable chance of success … The moderates cannot afford to oppose extremists unless they know that Government is prepared to give them active support."[74]

On May 19, 1920, the Ramadan observances that so worried Wilson began at Sunni and Shi'a mosques throughout the land. Apprehension became reality. After the religious services, combined audiences of Shi'a and Sunni gathered at the mosques to hear fiery nationalist rhetoric. In Baghdad, highly agitated throngs would emerge from the mosques, rolling through the streets, chanting and demanding independence. Moreover, some mosques featured aspects of both Sunni and Shi'a traditions. By inviting their co-religionists as special guests, it projected an open show of Islamic unity.[75]

It was what Wilson feared. He recalled, "The first symptom of a rapprochement had occurred in the summer of 1919, when on two occasions Sunnis attended religious meetings which were held in memory of … [a revered and recently] deceased Shi'a *mujtahid* [revivalist]." Wilson continued that it was not until Ramadan in May of 1920 "that the political significance of the reconciliation became apparent. We were well aware of the danger ... in March and April... before the great fast began."[76]

Periodically, Arab deputations would try to communicate with Wilson. It was in vain. For example, when 15 delegates of the Baghdad community requested a meeting with Wilson to present their demands, he brusquely rebuffed them and denied they were genuine representatives of anyone. He instead chose to invite his own assembly of 40 handpicked representatives, all of whom he expected to support his agenda. The fact that one of these 40 was a Baghdadi Jew and two were local Christians further inflamed the Muslim populace, which only wanted a majority Islamic government.[77]

Secret meetings multiplied. A surreptitious network was established to help coordinate the coming revolt. Newly stitched national flags were quietly circulated. Leaflets printed in Najaf and Karbala rallied tribe and townsman alike for a concerted uprising. Then Imam Shirazi, a spiritual leader of Najaf, issued a pivotal fatwa that declared, "None but Muslims have any right to rule over Muslims." Day and night, printing presses churned out copies of Shirazi's fatwa as activists stealthily disseminated them throughout the cities, villages, and tribal areas.[78]

Quickly, the situation deteriorated. It the early hours of June 4, 1920, in the village of Tel Afar, near Mosul, the commander of the gendarmes, Captain B. Stuart, was suddenly murdered in the street by his own Arab subordinate. Captain Stuart's two assistants tried to help, but a bomb killed them in their bullet-riddled bunker. Another officer was taken captive; he managed to escape, but was chased down and murdered on the outskirts of town. Convoys on the nearby road were raided. Two armored cars were dispatched, but they were surrounded and overturned; their crews, totaling 14 men, were also killed.[79]

The British retaliated. The next day, June 5, 1920, troops marched out from Mosul to Tel Afar. En route, they burned crops needed to feed the vicinity. Once at the scene of the outrages, Wilson recounts, the troops "chased the entire population of Tel Afar, innocent and guilty alike, into the desert." They destroyed suspect houses, but did not apprehend the killers.[80]

To reason with the most moderate militants, London tried to employ a more acceptable lexicon, parsing such concepts as *self-rule, autonomy, emerging democracy,* and other less-than-sovereign conditions—but all nonetheless subject to the British "tutelage" prescribed by Article 22 of the League of Nations Covenant. Words were worthless in this war. One rebellious newspaper from time to time typically verbalized the embittered feeling of the Arabs, belittling the Allied vocabulary: "We do not reject the mandate because of its name but because [of] its very meaning, which is destructive of independence ... [Many] words... are used by the colonizers. But they all translate to 'mandate,' and are intended to deceive weak nations. Only the name is changed, just as when they talk of liberating humanity, [and] healing the weak."[81]

On June 6, 1920, nationalist pamphlets bearing the five-pointed emblem of resistance circulated everywhere, demanding the expulsion of the British. Ten days later, the new call to arms rallied defiance against the mandate decision at San Remo. Everywhere the movement proclaimed Faisal's brother, Abdullah, to be Iraq's king, as decided at the Second Syrian General Congress at Damascus several months earlier.[82]

On June 30, 1920, the revolt intensified dramatically. In the lower Euphrates river town of Rumaitha, an activist sheikh was gruffly rebuked for not paying his estimated agricultural tax and then arrested by the assistant political officer. Within hours, his followers descended on the local terra-cotta prison, freeing him. Emboldened, the rebels rampaged through the area, burning all the local bridges and cutting the railroad lines. Despite hard fighting and several attempts at reinforcement, the beleaguered garrison at Rumaitha was not relieved until July 20, 1920, at a cost of 35 British soldiers killed and 150 wounded. A third of the garrison they came to rescue was dead. Their surviving comrades in hand, the British civil and military authorities promptly evacuated.[83]

Even as Rumaitha was overtaken, insurgents overran the village of Samawa. By mid-July 1920, tribesmen had asserted themselves in Abu Sukhair, Kufa was blockaded, and the Bani Hasan tribe rose up defiant. Revolutionary governments were set up in Najaf, Samawa, and in additional village after village as the undermanned British evacuated. Three companies of the Third Manchesters, plus cavalry and artillery, augmented by Sikh fighters, were deployed from Hilla to restore order, but only half survived the 118-degree heat and the onslaught of some 500 attackers who suddenly appeared on their flank. The British fought at close range with bayonets, but were overwhelmed: 180 killed, 60 wounded, 160 taken captive.[84]

Following the multiple events of July 24, 1920, crowned by the French victory over Damascus, nationalist Arabs concentrated their defiance in Iraq. Insurrection became all-out jihad once formal declarations from religious leaders were promulgated during the first week of August. National zeal escalated into religious fanaticism, as everywhere the Arabs attacked everything Western.[85]

Immediately, the whole country ignited. On August 9, 1920, the village of Baquba was ransacked, the rail line cut, and the nearby Armenian refugee camp attacked. On August 10, 1920, the British vessel *Greenfly* went aground on the lower Euphrates just outside Khizr; hostile Arabs surrounded the ship, prevented it from being towed, starved the crew into surrender, and then murdered them all. On August 11, 1920, extremists tried to assassinate a political officer in the midst of a truce negotiation; the tribesmen suddenly opened fire on his military escort. On August 12, 1920, a similar ambush occurred when a political officer tried to meet with an Arab leader at Arbil.[86]

Shortly thereafter, the supply ship "S9" ran aground in the low Euphrates water; it was captured, set afire, and the crew massacred. Trains fared little better. It did not matter whether the trains were armored. Once the track was blown, belligerents attacked and killed all the passengers. So much railroad line was blown up that the British were forced to erect a series of protective blockhouses mile-by-mile along the track. Even constructing these was often a fatal exercise, as work crews were constantly attacked. In the Hilla area alone, six waves of attacks were repulsed, with an estimated 200 dead among the rebels and 40 British casualties.[87]

Nor it did not matter whether the victim was a soldier involved in combat or reconstruction. Colonel G. E. Leachman had spent much of his time dispensing liberal subsidies to Iraqis to win their hearts and minds. He spoke fluent Arabic and was popular among local farmers. On August 12, 1920, Leachman was summoned to a meeting with Sheikh Dhari at Fallujah to discuss crops and revenue. After arriving with a military escort, Leachman was abruptly informed of a highway robbery outside of town. Intuitively, the colonel dispatched his armed escorts to assist. That left him unprotected. Sheikh Dhari then approached with two followers. Leachman knew Sheikh Dhari well, had assisted him in the past, and welcomed him. That's when Sheikh Dhari's followers shot Leachman at close range. Sheikh Dhari approached the dying man. Leachman looked up and asked why, as he had never offended anyone in Iraq. Without hesitation, Sheikh Dhari drew his sword, and mercilessly finished the job.[88]

Monstrous treatment at the hands of Arab captors was common. On occasion, British prisoners were marched from town to town in the summer heat, barefoot and nearly naked. Two captured pilots were set upon by angry crowds who murdered them, cut off their ears to deliver them as prizes to the local mullah, knocked out all their teeth and sold these as trophies, and finally further mutilated the bodies for all to see.[89]

Nor it did matter if the British were Muslim Indians or Christian. Some 85 percent of the civilian and military men were Indians—many of them Muslim. Yet, they were killed with equal fervor. Fallen Muslims were frequently denied an Islamic burial by the embittered religious authorities. Not infrequently, their wives were sought out and violated, and their children viciously beaten in the streets for being from treasonous families.[90]

When jihadists who had been taken prisoner were interrogated, they were sometimes asked why they fought so fiercely. One report from Wilson gave this answer: "they tell me that ... life or death is a matter of indifference."[91]

Britain was outnumbered and poorly situated. The new Mesopotamian commander, General Aylmer Haldane, semi-retired and physically unfit, had arrived just a few months earlier with Victorian flourish. Haldane himself recalled that he "disliked the idea of remaining in Baghdad throughout the hot weather" because he could only exercise "an hour or two in the late afternoon." What's more, he freely admitted, "I had no conception of the system on which we governed Mesopotamia, for it had not been possible to obtain much information regarding it."[92]

How many troops could Haldane deploy? Subtracting the sick and heat-stricken, as well as artillerymen, only 29,500 cavalry and infantry, 90 percent Indian, were available to restore civil order, guard 14,000 Turkish prisoners still unrepatriated from the war, and protect the substantial civil administration.[93]

Against Haldane's 29,500 poorly supported British soldiers were multitudes of Arab tribal warriors. From Basra to Baghdad along the Euphrates: 43,000 Muntafik, 11,500 Khazail, and 17,500 from smaller clans; and along the Tigris: 18,500 Bani Malich, 8,000 Albu Muhammad, plus 17,800 from lesser clans. From Fallujah to Ashur, some 27,000 Dulaim fighters were raiding. One military report estimated the total fighting strength in the Baghdad and Basra provinces as 160,000 warriors, plus 481,000 Kurdish fighters.[94] Everywhere and every day, the rebels sniped, murdered, pillaged, burned, kidnapped, robbed, laid siege, sabotaged, and unwove the very fabric of Britain's presence.

Only air power could save the British now, a reality that Churchill had accepted months earlier in late March 1920, when he announced to the House of Commons that the disturbances in Mesopotamia were too costly and challenging to control with ground troops. Air power would be used. Gas bombs were being rushed, but not yet ready. Trials and training were still under way.[95]

Throughout August and September 1920, the Royal Air Force strafed and bombed enemy concentrations and sympathetic towns. August 21 at Baquba, the scene of numerous outrages: "today intense bombing raid carried out on rebel villages in neighborhood." August 23 at Baquba: "bombing raiders inflicted severe casualties on rebels—86 known killed in Baquba and [nearby] Shiftah." Kufa was bombed heavily, especially its mosque, which had become a center for political activities. On one day alone: At Samawa, "air bombing had good effect"; outside Baghdad, "aeroplanes retaliated by bombing"; seven miles northeast of Hilla at the village Munaihillalmarjan, "aeroplane today attacked."[96]

It was never enough, and Haldane and Wilson continually asked for more airplanes to subdue the seemingly irrepressible insurrection. Additional planes did not exist. Once more, on September 28, 1920 gas was requested. London replied again they were not ready: "We have requested Air Ministry who are now carrying on trials to push on their experiments."[97]

The purpose of the airplanes was not just military, but to shock and awe the population, what the Air Ministry called "Morale Bombing." The chief advocate and developer of Morale Bombing was Chief of Staff Hugh Trenchard, who reported directly to Churchill. One Trenchard memo to Wilson, in June 1920, set forth the new philosophy of warfare. "Aircraft depend," the memo explained, "to a great extent on the moral effect that they create; this is at present considerably owing to ignorance in the native mind. If they are constantly used for petty operations which cause no great material damage and cannot, owing to the smallness of the unit, be long sustained, *respect will change to annoyance and contempt*. If this should ever come about, the re-inspiring of the natives with proper respect for the air arm will be a long and expensive task. It follows, therefore, that when air operations are resorted to, they should be carried out in a strength sufficient to inflict severe punishment and in numbers adequate to sustain the attack for as long a period as may be necessary. It will be realized then that aircraft ... by their mere presence will often induce the natives to return to peaceful ways."[98]

A keen disciple of Trenchard's philosophy was Squadron Leader Arthur Harris, who relentlessly bombed Iraqi civilian areas. Harris would go on to earn the nickname "Bomber Harris." During the next major war with Germany, it would be Bomber Harris who advocated and oversaw the carpet bombing of the city of Dresden.[99]

What was not achieved in Iraq by bombing from the air was accomplished by torch on the ground as Britain intensified its retaliation. Village after village was set on fire. Gertrude Bell, a staunch Arabist ally of both T. E. Lawrence and Faisal, expressed the agonizing hopelessness of the campaign as the British found themselves in the schizophrenic position of reconstructing and democratizing the country while bombing and burning it into passivity. "We are hampered by the tribal uprising ... I think rightly ... the tribes must be made to submit to force. In no other way was it possible to make them surrender their arms, or teach them that you mustn't engage lightly in revolution, even when your holy men tell you to do so ... Nevertheless, it's difficult to be burning villages at one end of the country by means of a British Army, and assuring people at the other end that we really have handed over responsibility to native ministers."[100]

By late October, 1920, outside funding for the fighters had dwindled to a trickle, their ammunition depleted. Karbala, a spiritual epicenter of the insurrection, was totally blockaded, and the canals cut to shut down the water supply; the village finally surrendered. Najaf notables were instructed to lay down their arms or the city would be bombed; to avoid plague and devastation to thousands of refugees, the elders complied. The submission of Karbala and Najaf was the beginning of the end of the revolution. Most of the fighters elsewhere simply retreated to their homes. Most—but not all—of the cities became quiet.[101]

Wilson was removed as acting civil commissioner. His replacement, Percy

Cox, was brought in from Persia to oversee an immediate transition to a provisional government, which would include a general elective assembly and a constitutional process. Cox announced the provisional government on November 11, 1920. With that, two years after the Great War ended, the lingering conflict in Mesopotamia finally began to wind down. By spring 1921, the country was calm enough to bring in its new leader. It was not Abdullah, but Faisal. The British felt they could do business with him. The sharif of Mecca, who fought alongside Lawrence, who became the elected leader of Damascus for just a few months, was now finally anointed by the British as the "King of Iraq." Faisal officially arrived in Iraq on June 23, 1921, with all pomp and circumstance, and acceded to the throne August 23. The nation of Iraq was born.[102]

The Iraq revolt of 1920 was costly: 426 British killed, 1,228 wounded, 615 missing or captured. Among the Arabs: some 8,450 casualties. British taxpayers spent some £40 million pounds. Iraq in many places was in cinders. The British public became dispirited over its losses in Mesopotamia. London's media regularly excoriated the government. One article in the *Daily Mail*, titled "The War Mongers," railed that "there is nothing in all our history to compare with our folly in Mesopotamia."[103]

Cox's replacement as high commissioner was Sir Henry Dobbs. Looking back, Cox wrote, "So now to raise up this Iraq we have squandered blood, treasure, and high ability. We have bound debts and taxes on the necks of generations of our descendants ... We have suffered the imputation that on the scene of their agony we living have betrayed the hopes of our dead. You ask: for all this, shall we have our reward? I answer that I cannot say."[104]

George Buchanan, who had administered the waterways and dredging of Iraq in the Wilson administration, published his own retrospective years later. "And so the tragedy of Mesopotamia remains," Buchanan wrote, "a tragedy of heroism, suffering, wasted lives, and wasted effort, which began in 1914 when the Indian Expeditionary Force entered the Shatt al-Arab River and which had not ended when military control ceased in 1921. The soldiers did their work, and by force of arms wrested the country from the Turks. The civilian administrators did their work and established law and order, peace and prosperity, throughout the land. The statesmen did their work and successfully annulled all that had been accomplished by the soldiers and administrators. Mesopotamia has been called the cradle of the human race, and was at one time the granary of the world. Will its former glories ever be revived and the enormous sacrifices made by Great Britain ultimately be justified by the evolution of a happy, prosperous, and free nation?"[105] Buchanan did not answer his question.

As for Wilson, the lifelong bureaucrat left government service for a new career. He went into industry. Wilson was immediately hired by Anglo-Persian Oil Company.[106]

CHAPTER ELEVEN

THE RED LINE

Iraq was not quite a nation and Faisal was not quite a king when he and
Great Britain signed a formal treaty of alliance on October 10, 1922. While
it was labeled a "treaty" as if between two governments and bore regal
seals on its cover, the treaty was actually not with the nation of Iraq, but with
the king as an individual. That's because the new Iraq was nominally an independent kingdom; yet, under international law, it was still a mandated territory
under the control and tutelage of the British. Moreover, King Faisal, although
proclaimed a monarch, was required to take counsel and instructions from
Britain's appointed resident, High Commissioner Sir Percy Cox.[1]

The 1922 treaty in many ways read like the earlier protectorate contract
with the Sheikh of Kuwait. Except in this case, it was not the nation being protected. After all, recalcitrant villages were still regularly being bombed by the
Royal Air Force.[2] The real protectorates were British commercial interests—
shipping, railroading, oil exploitation, and pipelines, and they were being protected against Iraq itself.

Article VIII guaranteed that no Iraqi land would be ceded or leased to
any power other than Britain. Article IV assured that Faisal "agrees to be
guided by the advice of His Britannic Majesty tendered through the High
Commissioner on all important matters affecting the international and financial obligations of His Britannic Majesty for the whole period of the treaty."
Article XI included an all-important nondiscrimination clause with a vital

145

parenthetical: "There shall be no discrimination in Iraq against the nationals of any State" with whom England maintained diplomatic relations. The parenthetical added: "(including companies incorporated under the law of such State.)"[3] This last was in effect the key to the "Open Door."

What was the Open Door? It had manifested some three years earlier when Iraq's oil was handily split between England and France. The San Remo petroleum agreement granted Paris the 25 percent of the Turkish Petroleum Company once owned by Deutsche Bank. The French government then transferred that 25 percent to what later evolved into the Compagnie Française des Petroles, a combine of some scores of smaller oil concerns that created a new government-controlled oil monopoly.[4] By the authority invested in San Remo, and subject to a more stabilized Iraq, France and her petroplex now gained a reliable source of crude oil. At the same time, Great Britain would be able to drill deep into Iraq, continue its exploitation of Persian oil, and transport the black treasure across Syria to the Mediterranean. But, there was just one other thing. France and Britain left out one power, the newest of the great powers: the United States of America. "An Open Door policy" with respect to Iraq's oil was demanded by President Woodrow Wilson, the State Department, and even more importantly, Standard Oil of New Jersey.

By way of background, the first years of the twentieth century's oil development were completely different in America than in Europe. Rockefeller's Standard Oil had accrued too much commercial power too quickly and was stopped by the U.S. government with antitrust prosecutions. But in Great Britain and Germany, the oil baronies were tools and extensions of the government itself—to a degree, even owned by the government. By the time the Great War ended in 1918, America's military-industrial self-conception had evolved. It no longer felt the pangs of containment. True, the Senate had refused to ratify Wilson's League of Nations treaty; and therefore, America was the only victor excluded from the spoils. But who supplied 80 percent of Britain's oil? America. Who fielded great armies on land, sea, and air, shoulder-to-shoulder with the Allies? America. Who was now being left out of the oil riches of Mesopotamia? Once again, America.

President Woodrow Wilson demanded equality in the great new world order sketched by his Fourteen Points, specifically Point III: "The removal, so far as possible, of all economic barriers and the establishment of an equality of trade conditions among all the nations consenting to the peace." This point was buttressed by the League's own principle on mandates that the Mesopotamian territory was to be administered "to assure equal treatment to the commerce and to the citizens of all nations." What's more, Britain had secured international support for its mandate by pledging "that the natural resources of

Mesopotamia are to be secured to the people of Mesopotamia and to the future Arab State to be established."[5]

Activism began in earnest at the September 27, 1919, meeting of the American Petroleum Institute in Colorado Springs, where the organization's Committee on Foreign Relations launched its campaign for access to Iraqi oil. The committee, headed by Standard Oil president Walter C. Teagle, resolved to use "diplomatic channels" to press the crusade. A formal approach was made to United States Secretary of State Robert Lansing.[6]

The American oil industry produced a series of white papers and memoranda castigating the British and French oil monopolies as anti-democratic, anti-American, and, of course, ungrateful. Inflammatory rhetoric was borrowed from the day's preoccupation with the Red Scare and anti-Bolshevik fears of world domination. Couching the protection of American oil interests in the same phrasing as protecting the American heartland spurred the government and informed circles. One such paper titled "The Menace of Foreign State Monopolies to the American Petroleum Industry" asserted, "During the war, the conduct of commerce and industry throughout the world was largely placed under governmental control. This was the result of the necessity under which governments labored, of devoting all their resources and all their energies to the work of the destruction then going on ... But it was understood to be purely temporary and was expected to come to an end with the close of the war. The fulfillment of this expectation is now gravely threatened."[7]

Another industry memo warned in early October 1919, "For a number of years, Great Britain has been slowly maturing plans ... [for] the domination of the world's oil supplies. Great Britain needs oil for her navy, for her mercantile marine, for her industries, and the demand is that the sources of supply should be under British control." The memo recited the list of governmental oil monopolies Britain was establishing in the West Indies, Asia, and Latin America, but was especially apprehensive about Mesopotamia. "It would seem," the industry memo insisted, "that the British and the European conception of a mandate is nothing short of annexation."[8]

One policy statement, headlined "Imperative Need for Aggressive Foreign Policy as Regards the Oil Industry," bluntly proclaimed: "America produces and consumes two-thirds of the petroleum in the world, and to this extent has greater interests involved than all the rest of the world combined." Asserting that domestic use was now outpacing domestic production, the oil industry démarche again pressed the government to move decisively on Mesopotamia.[9]

Presaging a long-term struggle—twice as long as the Great War itself—the first memo prophetically concluded: "American capital, American technical knowledge, American brains and push, properly organized, can defeat the far-reaching plans of the British. It will be a strenuous fight for a decade, but there is no reason short of sheer stupidity on the part of America, why the greater part of the oil resources of the world should not be controlled by American capital."[10]

Yet another position paper decried, "The door has already been closed to American enterprise in Persia, where the Anglo-Persian Oil Company has an exclusive concession, granted on May 28, 1901, for a term of sixty years." Hence, the name "Open Door" was affixed to America's insistence that Iraq not go the way of Persia.[11]

It was all terribly awkward. True, the United States had been a principal ally in the Great War and a full-fledged party to the Paris Peace Conference, helping to establish the course of the mandate system over Mesopotamia. But the United States had never ratified the treaty creating the League of Nations and was therefore not entitled to act the role of a member. Moreover, America had only declared war against Germany, which had attacked U.S. vessels sailing for European ports. Hence, America had never been at war with the Ottoman Empire, which formerly controlled the three provinces of Mesopotamia. Still, America expected its voice to be heeded, and the European Allies indeed expected to heed it.

America's voice, of course, loudly insisted on compliance with the lofty ideals of equal treatment for all the companies of all nations and avoidance of monopolistic behavior. But these demands were in fact mere verbal levers, jingoes, and rationales coating the true driving principle: No monopoly in Iraq could be created without America. Once Standard Oil was allowed in, America could butt out of Britain's business.

Agitation against the unshared monopoly quickly became public. It included resolutions led by Henry Cabot Lodge in the Senate, stern congressional inquiries, official surveys and studies of Middle East oil, as well as newspaper editorials, plus a strategic letter-writing campaign to all the right people, from Woodrow Wilson to local legislators.[12]

When in December 1919 the Civil Administration in Iraq stopped two American geologists in Baghdad from attempting to survey the land, it was nothing short of a diplomatic affront. The Civil Administration had earlier speciously assured the State Department: "No concessions in Mesopotamia for the acquisition of oil lands or oil have been granted nor has the acquisition of such concessions been permitted, and ... no change in this policy will be effected until the future administration of this country is settled."[13]

Worried British officials from several agencies huddled at the India Office on January 2, 1920, trying to get their stories straight about what the Turkish Petroleum Company was and what it was not. "If the American Government should protest against the company being allowed to monopolize the exploitation of these wells as contrary to the principles of the Peace Conference," the officials agreed, they would simply answer that the British accepted those principles, but "were bound to recognize an agreement which had made with the company before the war." This referred to the Foreign Office-engineered Fusion Agreement of March 19, 1914. As the January 2, 1920 strategy session progressed, the British bureaucrats parsed words and diced the semantics of control. One Foreign Office oil expert thought they could distract Washington's scrutiny of the commercial operation if everyone would "just emphasize the military nature of the operations."[14]

Once the secret San Remo agreement dividing up Iraq's oil was initialed on April 24, 1920, the tension escalated. On May 7, 1920, a Standard Oil executive in Paris finally obtained a copy of the secret protocol. The U.S. Embassy forwarded it to recently sworn in Secretary of State Bainbridge Colby, himself a former antitrust prosecutor. Colby was furious. Within a few days, on May 12, 1920, without revealing that Washington had access to the San Remo agreement, American ambassador to Britain John Davis delivered to British foreign secretary Lord Curzon an unusually stern epistle of America's new policy. "During the Peace negotiations at Paris," the cable reminded, "leading up to the Treaty of Versailles ... [the United States] consistently took the position that the future peace of the world required that as a general principle" any territory secured from Turkey, "must be held and governed in such a way as to assure equal treatment in law and in fact to the commerce of all nations."[15]

Blunt and incisive, the cable asserted that in the minds of most Americans, the mandate for Iraq "had given advantage to British oil interests which were not accorded to American companies and further that Great Britain had been preparing quietly for exclusive control of the oil resources in this region." Ambassador Davis demanded, "That no exclusive economic concessions covering the whole of any mandated region, or sufficiently large to be virtually exclusive, shall be granted, and that no monopolistic concessions relating to ... such commodity [oil] shall be granted."[16]

Outrage in American official and industrial circles over the San Remo accord intensified with each day. On May 13, 1920, M. L. Requa, a former director of the U.S. Fuel Administration, vigorously warned an assistant undersecretary of state that America owned 90 percent of the automobiles in the world. Moreover, America was the most rapidly industrializing nation on earth. The country was already forced to import more than 60 million barrels annually from Mexico. But Mexican exports were declining due to political conditions. No matter how domestic reserves and growth were extrapolated, argued Requa, the U.S. would run out of oil in less than two decades unless it secured equal access to Iraq.[17]

In such a case, Requa predicted, "the United States will practically pay the British war debt in the purchase of [Iraqi] petroleum, which, if things go on as they are, will within ten years amount to the purchase of 500 million barrels a year ... [amounting to] $1.5 billion per annum." Requa ended his screed, "Pardon this outburst; but, as an American citizen, whose ancestors came here in 1680, and as an authority on petroleum, I cannot refrain from raving at the utter indifference and incapacity of our Government toward this critical situation."[18]

On May 12, 1920, Ambassador Davis in London confronted British petroleum czar John Cadman in person. "No reference was made to the San Remo agreement ... of which they, no doubt, believe us to be ignorant," reported Davis. First making clear that all of America would be deeply offended by any hint of monopoly, Davis demanded to know whether any oil concessions in fact had been granted in Iraq. Cadman replied that he well understood "the folly" of antagonizing America. He admitted there was some sort of company called Turkish Petroleum, which possessed some sort of concession dating back to Ottoman times. A clearly nervous Cadman lied, claiming he knew nothing of the details. Davis knew he was lying.[19]

America's petroleum industry and its friends in high places continued to foment the waters of public and governmental opinion. Newspaper articles railed against British attempts to dominate America. Restrictive legislation was proposed against British firms operating in America. Senator J. D. Phelan was prepared to draft a retaliatory bill against Shell's several subsidiaries in the United States. Washington caustically accused London of abusing its mandate in Iraq and the secretary of state issued a long condemnation in November 1920. But at about that time, President Wilson had become an invalid whose failed cross-country effort to rally public support for the League of Nations had broken his spirit and his health. London dispatched British Petroleum official Cadman to America to begin negotiations with the American Petroleum Institute and perhaps buy time. Lord Curzon himself waited until February 1921, after newly elected American president Warren Harding assumed office, before filing a formal protest to what he called America's unfair allegations of British commercial misconduct. In a long report, Lord Curzon traced the tortuous origins of Deutsche Bank's Baghdad Railway concession from the Sultan in 1898, its formalization into a treaty in 1903, its transfer to the Turkish Petroleum Company in 1912, its British-inspired fusion with Anglo-Persian just before the outbreak of war in 1914, its seizure as enemy property after the war, its route through a succession of Anglo-French postwar oil agreements, and finally its deliverance to the French as a war spoil at San Remo in April 1920. All of it was perfectly legitimate, argued Lord Curzon. With that, Lord Curzon rebuked America for promoting exclusionary monopolies in Haiti and the Philippines while decrying Britain for the same purported actions in Iraq.[20]

None of that mattered to American policymakers. The door in Iraq must open.

Negotiations moved to England in early 1922. On April 9, Cadman, along with Anglo-Persian president Charles Greenway and Standard Oil chairman A. C. Bedford, conferred at the stately Stanbridge Earls Boarding School—Greenway's old boarding school—in southeast England. Bedford suggested that the entire question of Iraqi oil had become too politicized, with diplomats, legislators, and regulators leading the charge. Of course, that was the American Petroleum Institute's original strategy, to use governmental and diplomatic sources to pressure Britain. Perhaps, said Bedford, it was time to convert the crisis into a purely commercial transaction.[21]

The impasse could disappear if America were simply allowed to join England's Anglo-Persian, Shell's Anglo-Saxon, and France's incubating cartel as a coequal member of Turkish Petroleum. Bedford revealed that a consortium of American companies were ready to join Standard to create an American oil bloc in Mesopotamia. Greenway welcomed the opportunity. Both men agreed to lobby their respective governments for a formula of inclusion that would dissolve all American complaints about monopoly.[22]

In other words, the door to Iraq's oil wealth would be created and remain open just long enough for American oil to enter. That door would then shut behind them. But how?

Nothing could be more complex. Three governments and numerous commercial concerns, all government-controlled or regulated, were required to compromise on their portion of the billions lying beneath the Iraqi soil. Every percent was sanctified as an indispensable national imperative. In these brittle negotiations, all who won did so at the other's expense. But none could win unless all agreed.

In mid-July 1922, American Petroleum Institute representatives, led by Standard Oil president Teagle, worked the government offices and corporate boardrooms of London and Paris. The first several meetings established the lofty Wilsonian principles of transparency, equal trade, and a share of the wealth dedicated to the local population—this to comply with State Department expressions. The artifice to achieve equality among all nationals was an elaborate subleasing scheme in which numbered plots of oil-rich Iraqi fields would be periodically advertised in certain oil publications in Holland, the United States, England, and France—all of which were already participating with their controlled or regulated cartels. A year after the advertising, these plots would be auctioned off to the highest bidder, fundamentally among themselves, as decided in a special process by TPC, which they themselves would own. The "native population"—Faisal's government—would receive a royalty.[23]

Since several American petroleum companies, led by Standard Oil, were joined together in the American syndicate, the scheme did not violate U.S. antimonopoly statutes. The various oil companies, seven at first—Standard Oil of New Jersey, Standard Oil of New York, Gulf Corporation, Atlantic Refining, Sinclair Oil, and two smaller firms—would ultimately create what they called the Near East Development Company to represent their participation in the emerging captive, multinational TPC enterprise. On August 22, 1922, the State Department endorsed the principles as conforming to the equal commerce tenets of the Open Door. The State made clear it would continue to object to the validity and legality of the Turkish Petroleum Company and its San Remo formula until the U.S. companies joined in.[24] Not quite three weeks later, on October 10, 1922, the treaty of alliance between Great Britain and King Faisal was signed. It carefully incorporated the Open Door policy, ensconced between parentheses wedged into Article XI. The treaty covered the three provinces of Mesopotamia.[25] But no one knew whether Mosul province—questionably seized—would remain within the sovereign limits of the new Iraq. They barely knew where Mosul began and ended, since its approximate realm lay within hazy Ottoman frontiers with Syria, Persia, traditional Armenia, traditional Kurdistan, and even the new state of Turkey.

Indeed, with the war four years behind them, and riding a surge of nationalism, the Turks were demanding the return of the Mosul province—and its untapped oil billions. Yet another international conference was called, this one at Lausanne, Switzerland, in November 1923 to finally settle the numerous conflicting treaty and peace provisions between the Allies and Turkey. America could not participate because it was not a member of the League of Nations and had never been at war with the Ottoman Empire.

But America's presence was felt as an official observer. Washington's nine conditions for U.S. passivity at Lausanne required adherence to such Wilsonian goals as the protection of minorities, freedom of international navigation, and preservation of American archaeological research. Point 3, titled "Protection of American Commercial Interests," demanded that all conferees "maintain the principle of the Open Door and equal opportunity."[26]

During the tempestuous conference, which lasted several months, the British refused to relinquish Mosul. The Turks refused to cede it, insisting the province had been illegally conquered days after the armistice of 1918. A worried American establishment wondered if the region might go back to Turkey, thus neutralizing the San Remo agreement it sought to join. Secretary of State Charles Hughes, on November 27, 1922, cabled the American Lausanne mission: "The position of the Department is, in brief: 1) That the

American companies would receive Department's support in their efforts to obtain adequate participation in the development of Mesopotamia, if Mesopotamia, including the Mosul *vilayet*, remains under British mandate. 2) That a new situation would be presented if the Mosul area reverts to Turkey. But it may be stated in general that the Department would refuse acquiescence in any monopolistic concession in the Mosul area resulting from a political trade ... In view of American contribution to the common victory over the Central Powers, no discrimination can rightfully be made against us in any territory won by that victory. The United States claims equality in economic rights in territories under mandate."[27]

Secretary of State Hughes carefully added, "The United States has nothing to conceal. It is not seeking any secret arrangements for itself and does not expect any on the part of other governments."[28] That said, if Mosul were restored to Turkey, America would lose mandate oil.

Britain and the Allies who controlled the League of Nations would not allow Mosul to revert to Turkey. British foreign secretary Lord Curzon himself chaired the conference. Sidestepping the issue of the illegal territorial seizure, he staunchly proclaimed that his nation entertained no oil interests in the area. In one typical defensive speech, Curzon thundered, "It is supposed and alleged that the attitude of the British Government to the *vilayet* of Mosul is affected by the question of oil. The question of the oil of the Mosul *vilayet* has nothing to do with my argument. I have presented the case on its own merits and quite independently of any natural resources that may be in the country. I do not know how much oil there may be in the neighborhood of Mosul, or whether it can be worked at a profit, or whether it may turn out after all to have been a fraud."[29]

Curzon explained away the Turkish Petroleum Company by insisting, "Both the British government and the T.P.C. itself recognize that oil is a commodity in which the world is interested and ... a great mistake to claim or exercise [as] a monopoly. Accordingly, the Company, with the full knowledge and support of the British Government, took steps ... to associate the interests of other countries and other parties in this concern so that all those who are equally interested may have a share. If the enterprise is successful, Iraq will be the main gainer ... That is the substance of the oil affair which I have explained to the Conference in order that they may know the exact amount of influence, and that is *nil* ... of oil on ... the question of Mosul."[30]

Right through the Lausanne conference, petroleum executives and government officials continued to huddle in various capitals. The French and Shell were reluctant to reduce their participation or accept a new partner. But finally, on December 12, 1922, in London, the British and Americans both gave a little to acquire a monumental gain. Anglo-Persian, which controlled roughly half of Turkish Petroleum, agreed to transfer about half of its holdings to the American consortium. Once transferred, British Anglo-Persian, the still-evolving French corporation, British-Dutch Shell's Anglo-Saxon, and the new American consortium would each own a quarter of TPC. To compensate Anglo-Persian for cutting its ownership in half, Anglo-Persian would receive 10 percent of TPC's oil free of charge.[31] Everyone would be happy.

Not everyone. There was just one other thing: Gulbenkian. Mr. Five Percent still owned his original fraction of Turkish Petroleum. So the plan was tweaked. Each of the four giant oil combines would reduce their one-quarter holding by a single percent, to 24 percent. That totaled 96 percent. Each of the four coequal partners would then proffer 1 percent of their quarter share, to create a 4 percent nonvoting beneficial holding for Gulbenkian—yes, down from 5 percent, but then everyone had reduced their shares for the common good.[32] That seemed fair.

Standard Oil's representative in London wired a note of success to Standard Oil president Teagle, who, in turn, passed the information to the secretary of state in Washington. His message included the note that TPC "does not anticipate difficulty in getting acceptance of French and Gulbenkian."[33] They were quite wrong.

TPC general manager Herbert Nichols seemed to be the only person who could communicate with the irascible Gulbenkian. Nichols began talks with Gulbenkian at once. After several meetings in Paris, Gulbenkian hemmed and hawed but finally agreed not to 4 percent of the company, which would have obligated him to contribute 4 percent of the massive capitalization, but simply 4 percent of the profits. This way Gulbenkian suffered no ongoing cash obligation and merely collected 4 percent of the profits, free and clear. Nichols and the group believed this to be an extravagant concession, but agreed. With the French nearly in concert, the deal seemed on its way.[34]

But the Saturday after agreeing, Gulbenkian unexpectedly phoned Nichols and woke him from a sound sleep. There was just one other thing. Nichols was still half asleep when Gulbenkian began railing. Maybe profits were not a good thing. Gulbenkian knew, after all, that oil companies regularly manipulated their net profits to avoid taxes. Hence, 4 percent of the simple "profits" could equal simply nothing. Gulbenkian insisted on net profit, accenting *net*.[35]

A few days later, Nichols tried to reason with him in a letter filled with complex numbers, proportions, and calculations. "Let us suppose that £8,000,000 goes into the Company—if you had shares, as we propose, you would have to provide £320,000 which at 6% (a moderate figure this) is equal to £19,200 per annum. This latter sum I maintain must fall to be deducted from your suggested alternative, [that is,] 4% of the net profits. Am I not right? ... This is a far more attractive way of dealing with the matter than the one you suggest, inasmuch as there is the risk that there will always be differences of opinion as to what constitutes 'net profits.'... Why not agree to shares, and the matter is settled? ... I shall await your writing with much interest, and can only impress upon you the urgency of getting this question cleared up quickly."[36]

No. Gulbenkian held firm, he wanted 4 percent *net* profits. Fine, Nichols agreed. Plus, Gulbenkian insisted on a careful definition of exactly what constituted net profits. Fine, Nichols agreed. Plus, Gulbenkian insisted on a £10,000 reimbursement for any expenses thus far. Fine, Nichols agreed to that as well. With all points agreed upon, Nichols immediately organized a three-page agreement itemizing everything.[37]

But at the last minute, Gulbenkian just did not feel right about the arrangement. He did not sign. With billions in the balance, the oilmen and their governments were astonished. By any measure, he would be greatly enriched. But Gulbenkian just didn't like the deal. No signature.

*   *   *   *

Western oil powers held their collective breath as the Lausanne Conference dragged into early 1923, with Mosul's fate undecided. Lord Curzon continued to deny Britain was in Iraq for the petroleum. "Oil has not the remotest connection," Lord Curzon disingenuously protested, "with my attitude, or with that of his Majesty's Government on the Mosul question, or the Iraq question."[38]

Since Britain would not yield to argument, demanded Turkey, would it yield to a plebiscite? If the local populations—some 800,000 over a 35,000-square-mile region—were to be consulted in their own national destiny according to Wilsonian doctrine, why not let them vote: Remain with Britain under mandate or return to Turkey. Curzon ridiculed the very notion. "Why shall a plebiscite be invoked in the province? Ankara [Turkey] demands a plebiscite. Kurds have never demanded it. This poor nation even does not know what it means. Arabs and Turks in the province have also never demanded plebiscite. The only people demanding it are the Turks of Ankara."[39]

Finally, on February 4, 1923, Lord Curzon barked at the Turkish delegate: "War may break out anew. I wish you to accept this. You have ... half an hour in which to save your country." But the Turks did not yield. Turkey had already reconstituted its own borders with a National Pact, which included Mosul.[40]

In July 1923, after drama, oratory, and not a few corridor exchanges, Britain and Turkey finalized their peace through the Treaty of Lausanne. Final except for one item: the Mosul question. Under the rules, the Mosul dispute would be negotiated further, and then, if still unresolved, referred to the League of Nations Council for formal international arbitration. Turkey, of course, was not a member of the League of Nations. Britain was.

While oil circles nervously awaited a decision, Gulbenkian continued his campaign of obstruction. One long-winded disputation after another flew into Nichols hands, cleverly alternating charm and sincerity with hostility or hurt feelings. As important as the details was Gulbenkian's penchant for abstruse logomachies and endless ifs, ands, buts, and maybes. Each time Nichols sent over a revision to satisfy Gulbenkian's sticking point, a new one emerged.

For example, on January 11, 1923, Gulbenkian protested, this time to obtain the expenses not paid when he had refused to sign the December 18, 1922 document and then was asked to contribute his share of TPC's normal minor operating costs. "You must agree," he carped, "that it is most unfair that the other two parties ... should vote themselves their expenses and entirely ignore my own." In a postscript he appended, "What is still more stupendous is that by the action you have taken, not only I am not repaid, but you ask me, in effect to refund some of your expenses to my detriment, as I shall have to contribute a part of what you have got the company to repay you. Then you say that the other claims are 'years old' but you miss the point that mine is *the origin of it all*."[41]

His whole idea was not to negotiate in good faith to resolve the fine points, but to wear everyone else down. Gulbenkian constantly suggested that a final agreement might yet be just one or two more exchanges away, and then he would abruptly dash hopes. Meetings were a good method of wasting time and draining strength. "Sir Henry [Deterding] suggests that it will be better that we all meet together [in October]," Gulbenkian wrote Nichols from Paris on September 19, 1923. "Kindly let me know the date that would be convenient to you." Invariably the anxious oilmen seized the opportunity to make progress. Nichols eagerly replied that he and Deterding would meet, "as soon as we can arrange a date."[42]

Gulbenkian continually kept negotiators off guard. Occasionally, he would refer to a promissory letter that no one could locate. For example, as he cajoled the oil companies to increase their offer from 4 percent back to his original 5 percent, he claimed Deterding and TPC had jointly promised in writing that his 5 percent would never be reduced. A letter? What letter? Nichols and staff scrambled to find such a letter, and finally wrote to him, "As neither he nor we can trace any such letter, will you be good enough to send me a copy?"[43] Did Gulbenkian have such a letter, written as long as a decade earlier? No one knew.

Gulbenkian's five percent was based on an almost undocumentable marginal investment in Turkish Petroleum Company in 1912, when the entity was nothing more than a sheaf of correspondence. Yet a decade later, he played the victim with skill, and often as though the big companies that would spend millions drilling, erecting refineries, and constructing pipelines and shipping facilities were on an equal footing with his paper percentage. Gulbenkian understood completely that while the majority can rule, the minority can obstruct.

While Nichols fenced with Gulbenkian, oil circles in Washington, New York, Paris, and London felt certain the man would come to his senses. They forged ahead, keeping the American Secretary of State informed of every step with long reports every few days. By late September 1923, Teagle and colleagues had drafted a new concession document for Faisal to grant to Turkish Petroleum. TPC, as now envisioned, would be a jointly held nonprofit entity that merely drilled for oil and sold the crude to its owners, Anglo-Persian, Anglo-Saxon, plus the French and American syndicates. It was just as Gulbenkian had suspected. TPC would be run without profits as a corporate conduit for the oil.[44]

"I see that during my absence, the matter has again been twisted," he complained to Nichols in an October 26, 1923 missive about the latest plan. In his best accusatorial tone, Gulbenkian added, "It is no use twisting the real facts … I do not want you to be under any misapprehension … that by coercion of one kind or another, I am going to allow myself to be imposed upon with unfair and unjust conditions."[45]

For good measure he added a dollop of thinly veiled blackmail. "The document now proposed [converting TPC into a nonprofit entity] deprives His Majesty's Government of a considerable amount of income tax; it deprives the Government of Iraq of legitimate rights in the exploitation, and, above all, it is an unfair and grasping document in regard to my own rights as a private shareholder. The first two points are no concern of mine if the interested parties care to acquiesce; but as regards myself, I ask you to read this letter in a most friendly spirit, but with the deep conviction that I shall not submit to injustice."[46]

Gulbenkian's tirades were always emboldened by his adversaries' kid-gloved responses. Nichols immediately replied with caution to the October 26, 1923 harangue: "Read your letter in the most friendly spirit. You are quite wrong in assuming that things have been twisted round. You will agree with me that we can hardly hope to arrive at a speedy and amicable understanding by the constant exchange of long, argumentative letters, and that consequently it is in every way preferable that we should have an early talk between the three of us in order to make a determined effort to arrive at a settlement. I should like such a meeting to take place at an early date—the sooner the better—and shall be glad to learn whether it is likely that you will be in London in the near future."[47]

Every time the oilmen rewarded Gulbenkian's abuse by continuing to chase him for a settlement, Gulbenkian was reassured that the stakes were surely worth billions and that they needed him more than he needed them. The longer Gulbenkian held out, the more intransigent he acted, the better for the deal. The men of Standard Oil, Turkish Petroleum, Shell, and the French companies had never encountered anyone like Gulbenkian. They were great men of business. But he was a master of the bazaar. All good things come to those who wait. What's more, Gulbenkian enjoyed the game, making the powerful squirm and seeing his slim fraction aggrandize, all at the same time.[48]

*   *   *   *

The Open Door remained open, but no one could pass through because everything was still so uncertain. In the first weeks of 1924, Turkish Petroleum officials wondered if they should change the name of the corporation to "Iraqi Petroleum" in anticipation of Mosul remaining in mandatory Iraq. They elected to register the new name, but to continue under the old Turkish Petroleum identity in the event Mosul reverted to Turkey and they needed to work anew with officials in Istanbul.[49]

Gulbenkian's intransigence remained a fixture of the stalled Iraq oil plans. In fact, the stalemate dragged on so long, and concomitantly the stakes became so much more greatly valued, that the dispute itself became a family enterprise. Calouste Sarkis Gulbenkian's son, Nubar Sarkis Gulbenkian, joined his father as co-negotiator in the year-to-year bickering. The long-bearded Nubar acted just as vain, conceited, and pejorative as his father. Nubar once quipped: "The best number for a dinner party is two—myself and a damn good head waiter." In his negotiations, Nubar was pushy and condescending. He could treat his well-heeled adversaries as mere servants, inasmuch as he held a card that all the players wanted, his father's card, that is, the virtual Five of Points.[50]

Once, Nubar even snarled at one of the oil executives, "Hold your tongue!" Nonetheless, he was deferred to as the ever-important go-between to his father, much as during a bygone decade when the Sultan reigned and proximity meant power. Typical was a January 25, 1924, letter from Nichols to Nubar reviewing the latest propositions from Standard Oil president Teagle: "The enclosures are sent to you in duplicate, as you will probably wish to send copies to your Father. I am not clear whether he is yet ready to take an active part in these discussions, although I believe he is back in Paris. You might let me know?"[51]

At times, some of the chief executives thought they could improve upon Nichols' tireless efforts. In late July 1924, Teagle and others traveled to London for three days of face-to-face discourse. Teagle wrested numerous concessions and compromises from Gulbenkian and agreed to some himself—progress, but nothing decisive. Nichols wistfully wrote Teagle, "Had you come to terms, you would have achieved in three days what I have failed to do in eighteen months." Of course, Gulbenkian used these meetings to launch a hitherto unvoiced claim against TPC. When Teagle asked Nichols for any information about this new claim, Nichols frankly replied, "It has only recently been put forward, and for all practical purposes it does not exist."[52]

With or without Gulbenkian, the chief executives were determined to move forward, and they used their late July meeting to develop a so-called Working Agreement, or self-denying covenant, which very much resembled the original self-denial agreements crafted by Gulbenkian when TPC was first organized in 1912, and repeated in the Fusion Agreement of 1914. Under this latest version, the four combines agreed not to engage in any oil business within a defined area except through Turkish Petroleum, which they would all jointly own and operate. This Working Agreement would enshrine TPC in perpetuity as the fulcrum of the entire oil industry in Iraq: drilling, refining, shipping, pipelining, and retailing—everything would be funneled through this one concentrated commercial entity.[53]

Seeing clear advancement without him, Gulbenkian's attorneys quickly fired the first shot. The prestigious firm of Freshfields, Leese and Munns, on August 12, 1924, delivered a threat: "Such an agreement," their letter warned TPC, "would be a fraud on the rights of the minority shareholders, of whom we believe Mr. Gulbenkian is the sole representative." Freshfields demanded written assurance within seven days that the Working Agreement would not be implemented. Failing that, the law firm would obtain a restraining order.[54]

Nichols sent a letter, marked "Strictly Private," to the French partner, Compagnie Française des Petroles, "Since both Mr. Teagle and I have failed to settle with Mr. Gulbenkian, and he has seen fit to threaten legal proceedings, I have considered it best that no further meetings of principals should take place at present. No fresh proposals have therefore been made on either side, but our respective lawyers are discussing the position. My own opinion is that Mr. Gulbenkian's lawyer also considers that he is 'looking for the moon,' and that we shall in consequence shortly receive some more reasonable proposal from that quarter."[55]

Meanwhile, the outside oil syndicates deployed their own law firms, headed by attorney Harold Brown, who drafted a highly detailed, historically researched, eight-page rebuttal to Freshfields. After numerous minor changes, Brown's brief was messengered September 26, 1924. As for the Working Agreement, Brown wrote, "We have gone into this explanation of the genesis of the 'Working Agreement' as we think, although your client has been kept closely informed of the negotiations at every stage, he is inclined to lose sight of some of these facts and, without the smallest justification, to treat the document as a plan hatched with the main object of depriving him of his full rights as the holder of five percent of the shares in the Turkish Petroleum Company."[56]

Every effort had been made to find an accommodation, to no avail, according to Brown. "Up to date," he argued resolutely, "your client's reply to these proposals, which seem to us very fair, has been to offer obstruction … [and] demand a position of preference and privilege out of all proportion to his rights … [How can these demands] be justified unless he thinks that his consent must be bought by our clients at any cost."[57]

Revving up the rhetoric, Brown warned, "In a last and final effort to secure your client's adhesion and thus avoid litigation and possible disaster for the whole enterprise, our clients have instructed us to make the offers set out below." Several advantageous formulae were propounded.[58] Gulbenkian did not flinch.

Teagle dispatched a memorandum to the State Department stressing that "the American Group" did not want a percentage of a foreign company, Turkish Petroleum, but reliable access to crude oil to sell in America or anywhere in the world. Gulbenkian was now demanding an equal place on the board of directors, a deciding vote on every decision, and an exorbitant royalty on any oil produced anywhere by TPC, even outside of Iraq. "All of the partners in the Turkish Petroleum Company," Teagle informed Washington, "including the American Group, considered Mr. Gulbenkian's proposal so unreasonable and burdensome as to preclude their acceptance."[59]

Secretary of State Hughes delivered a long report to America's ambassador in London. "Gulbenkian's position is considered unreasonable by the American Group." Hughes's report itemized the minutiae of their complaints against Gulbenkian and instructed the ambassador: "You should at once bring to the attention of the Foreign Office the view set forth in the three preceding paragraphs." The gist was that this obstruction was so pronounced it was construed as "an attempt to exclude American interests from a proper participation in developing Mesopotamia resources." In other words, Gulbenkian was by himself slamming shut the Open Door that America demanded remain wide enough for it to enter. Gulbenkian was a naturalized British national, and Washington expected the British government to do something about him. Hughes directed his ambassador to promptly telegraph the results of his protest to the Foreign Office.[60]

Gulbenkian knew the protest had reached diplomatic channels. He wrote to the Foreign Office on September 27, 1924, asking for help and a meeting to explain his side. He had resorted to such appeals in the past during the rocky days of the fusion negotiation. But on October 10, 1924, his best contact at the Foreign Office, William Tyrrell, wrote back that the British government simply "could not usefully intervene."[61]

Delegates of the four cartels then met in London on November 11, 1924, "to consider the impasse which has arisen owing to the impossibility of coming to terms with Gulbenkian." The next day, Nichols informed the partners in Paris, "It was decided that an entirely new line of action would have to be adopted."[62]

In early 1925, the four syndicates moved swiftly to create a *fait accompli*, that is, to secure a new concession from Faisal in favor of the Turkish Petroleum Company. With or without Gulbenkian, and even before the Americans had joined the company, this new concession would be along the lines envisioned in the Working Agreement. Hence the Working Agreement would be, to a degree, written into law.

The oil oligarchy knew that the longer the Gulbenkian crisis continued, the more additional claimants would creep onto the stage. By early 1925, Deutsche Bank was insisting its original 1912 transfer of the Anatolia Railway concession was improper. The many heirs of Sultan Abdulhamid II had hired high-powered lawyers in New York and London to press their claim that the Young Turks in 1908 and 1909 had improperly seized the oil concessions from the Sultan's *Civile Liste* and that they were the rightful heirs. Plus the French were now wondering why they should relinquish even 1 percent, let alone slightly more, to create a 4 to 5 percent beneficial interest for Gulbenkian when they had received Deutsche Bank's original 25 percent share in TPC; that share had been properly seized in London and duly transferred at San Remo. When plural billions are at stake, the values of single percents add up, and France became reluctant to part with any fractions thereof. All these emerging claimants, and several others, only added to the corporate angst. Gulbenkian demanded in a February 2, 1925, note to Nichols: "Kindly let me know how we now stand with regard to the concessions and why these are dragging so; the longer they drag, the more of these mushroom growths we shall find."[63]

On March 14, 1925, after an intense back-and-forth, Faisal issued a new 75-year oil concession covering all of Iraq. It was a problematic concession for sure. This new convention guaranteed royalties to the government based on a profit formula linked to market prices against the cost of production and transportation. But the document did not address the TPC's ability to manipulate market prices. Nor did Faisal write in any safeguards against the company threading expenses through a vast fleet of its own subsidiaries and captives to inflate the cost of drilling, refining, transporting, and pipelining. In addition, while the concession identified the territory as "the defined area of Iraq," it did not actually define what areas lay within corporate Iraq. Still, no one knew whether international arbitration would parcel Mosul to Iraq or back to Turkey. Finally, important performance benchmarks were written in to speed the pace of royalties. The concession required no less than 12,000 feet drilled before any pipelines could be laid to transport Persian oil and, in any event, 36,000 feet within three years.[64]

The clock was now ticking. Backed by the new concession, in March 1924, the four syndicates and TPC assembled an intricate and tenuous provisional agreement, termed the "Heads of Agreement," for Gulbenkian to consider anew. While the Americans believed it imperative to coax Gulbenkian to sign anything, whether the Heads of Agreement or any other instrument, Teagle and his circle were opposed to affixing their own signatures. The idea of "provisional agreements" was unbusinesslike, in their opinion. Moreover, they were rapidly approaching the point of complete fatigue over Gulbenkian's escalating demands.[65]

Nonetheless, Nichols and company pressed on. No sooner did their patience collapse than Gulbenkian renewed it with a hopeful signal. The new Heads of Agreement offered to buy out Gulbenkian at a very favorable rate yet to be established. Once more, Gulbenkian teased and annoyed the anxious oilmen with waves of seeming acceptance and then the ever-present reluctance. This latest chapter in the saga continued for months, consuming many reams of paper and causing many sleepless nights among the executives. Finally, frustrated TPC officials in London prepared a disconsolate cable for Teagle in New York. "Hopeless to expect final agreement acceptable to Gulbenkian and ourselves under several more months tedious negotiation." With a production now governed by the clock, Nichols added, "Three groups feel that if they are not to risk forfeiture of [Faisal's] Convention they must at all costs proceed with operations in Iraq." One TPC executive fretted about telling Teagle too much worrisome news, and scribbled underneath those words, "Suggest leaving this out. Don't threaten, but act—without necessarily giving Americans notice."[66]

Just as hope was to dissipate, Gulbenkian sounded hopeful. He asked to make a few modifications to the buyout agreement—just a few. But by the time he was done in September 1925, one embittered oil syndicate attorney called the revisions "a travesty."[67] Still, as the demand for oil in the world surged, syndicate negotiators could only again steel themselves to the onerous task of drilling until they struck a deal.

Finally, on October 6, 1925, the American Group gathered in New York to approve Gulbenkian's latest demands for royalties, payments, rights, and prerogatives. They even agreed to convert Gulbenkian's beneficial interest into an almost regal position, wherein he could appoint in his place his son or son-in-law, just as the sultans used to do. That was an improvement—but not enough. Gulbenkian would not sign.[68]

On October 29, 1925, the top executives, including Shell's Deterding, Nichols, and Anglo-Persian chairman Greenway, as well as attorneys, huddled. They debated one approach after another, one contractual variance after another. Exasperated, Deterding snapped, "If Gulbenkian dislikes that position, let him come to the TPC with a proposition to be bought out."[69]

Matters worsened when the passage of time prompted Faisal to balk at allowing the Americans to participate, since they had not been part of the TPC group at the time of the March 1925 concession. Why admit more foreigners? The Americans acted as though they were valid partners, but in fact they were not legally in TPC and would not formally join until the Working Agreement and Gulbenkian's crisis was finalized. The King's reluctance only trebled the oil syndicate's worries about arranging American participation. In a December 2, 1925, review, one TPC executive, completely incensed at the whole situation, offhandedly opined: "Has not the time come, to use such pressure (e.g. a hint of withdrawal of military protection) as may be necessary to bring home to the Iraq government that the British Government, who brought them into existence, and without whose aid they could not survive for a month, cannot allow them to obstruct indefinitely the fulfillment of promises made to the French and American Governments, and the exercise by a British Company of pre-war rights on terms pronounced by British Government experts to be eminently reasonable and fair?"[70]

If matters could not become more intense, on December 5, 1925, newly installed U.S. secretary of state Frank Kellogg sent the Foreign Office a blunt message. "The Department has been informed, by the American Group," Kellogg cabled, "that there is serious danger that their negotiations with the Turkish Petroleum Company will reach an impasse due to failure up to now of the other groups in the Turkish Petroleum Company to come to an agreement with Mr. C. S. Gulbenkian ... The American Group informs the Department that they would be sincerely sorry to have to withdraw from further attempts to obtain participation in the Turkish Petroleum Company on a fair basis and that they are still hopeful that an agreement will be reached which will make participation possible ... The Department is aware that neither our Government nor the British Government would wish to intervene in negotiations which are of a purely business nature. The British Government, however, in view of its [ownership] connection with the Anglo-Persian Oil Company, which is one of the chief parties to these business negotiations, may be able to persuade British subjects or companies not to assume an attitude which would make it impossible for American interests to participate in the Turkish Petroleum Company."[71]

Then came the threat: "Should the American Group withdraw because of failure to obtain participation in the Turkish Petroleum Company on a fair basis, the Department would reserve its entire freedom of action ... to secure the right to a fair share in the development of the oil resources of Mesopotamia through other means than the Turkish Petroleum Company."[72]

Finally, through unending ups and downs and following the cautious intervention of Deterding, British government officials, and Gulbenkian's various contacts at TPC, a breakthrough appeared at the very end of December 1925. A new formula was finally acceptable whereby Gulbenkian would transfer his shares to Anglo-Saxon and Anglo-Persian in exchange for a diverse package of ample compensation. There was hope, and a 24-page contract between the four syndicates was drawn up finally creating a Working Agreement that could be signed. By now the TPC was operating under two names, Turkish Petroleum Company and Iraq Petroleum Company; hence the firm was ready to function with either regime once the Mosul question was decided. The intricate December 1925 agreement specified all the percentages and procedures the partners would observe, and even recited Gulbenkian's intransigence as the foundation for the accord. But it was all completely dependent upon a so-called "Gulbenkian Agreement," referred to on page 5. This was the agreement for Gulbenkian to transfer his shares.[73]

The oilmen held their breath and hoped years of contractual anguish would finally come to an end that Christmas. But Christmas day, Gulbenkian sent off a note to John Cadman, one of the latest British government go-betweens. "I must say that I am disappointed," sniped Gulbenkian, "... chopping gradually away [at] certain rights." Gulbenkian would not sign the stock transfer agreement, but he did conclude the letter to Cadman with warm felicitations: "I send you and Lady Cadman my sincerest greetings for a happy New Year."[74]

*　　*　　*　　*

When, on January 2, 1926, Deterding learned of Gulbenkian's latest escapade, he issued a blunt letter on behalf of Royal Dutch Shell to the entire Anglo-Persian Oil Company staff. "Dear Sirs: We have to inform you that our relations with Mr. Gulbenkian are ended," declared Deterding, "and we want to sever all connections with him ... Mr. Gulbenkian has ... [been] rather successful in befogging the issue, and making it appear as if he were on the verge of being made a poor victim of the other four groups ... Mr. Gulbenkian is trying to exploit the other shareholders of the Turkish Petroleum Company, and has been trying to make out a pitiful tale of being squeezed by the 95%, whereas [in reality] his 5% has been trying to squeeze the 95% ... Finally we beg to place on record that we will have no more conversations with Mr. Gulbenkian, and that all proceedings must take place in writing through our Solicitor, Mr. Harold Brown."[75]

Deterding had been Gulbenkian's closest business ally since the earliest days of the century when Gulbenkian was financing overseas deals for Shell, and Gulbenkian was relying on Deterding to vote with him as a bloc in Turkish Petroleum. Once Deterding's support crumbled, Gulbenkian stood alone, truly alone, against all the governments and the oil companies arrayed against him.

At about that time, the League of Nations Council in Geneva had ruled and all appeals had been exhausted on the Mosul question. Citing Turkey's record of genocide, mass rape, and neglect of the Mosul province, as well as strong messages of independence from the Kurds, Mosul was to remain within the British Mandate. As of March 11, 1926, the decision was final.[76]

No delay could now be justified. Mosul was open for drilling. Its oil fields were ready. Negotiations between Nichols and Gulbenkian resumed with new vigor and velocity. The Heads of Agreement—negotiated in March 1925 and almost ready in December 1925—were revisited. Finally, a year later, they were approved in principle, with some changes. On April 1, 1926, Nichols was able to notify the British government, "It gives me great pleasure to inform you that at long last we have come to a settlement with Mr. Gulbenkian." The paperwork was being readied, and with it the long-postponed entry of the American oil firms through the Open Door and into TPC. Nichols assured the government, "You may conclude that the Americans are now within the bosom of the Turkish Petroleum Company."[77]

Gulbenkian was traveling while the papers were being drawn up. But on April 12, 1926, he reassured Nichols in a warm note: "Believe me, I highly appreciate your friendly feelings, and you are aware that all along I have been animated with but one desire—to see the T.P.C. a united entity … Nothing will give me more pleasure than to work cordially with all my colleagues for the end we must all have in view."[78]

On May 7, 1926, oil syndicate lawyers produced a revised version of the Heads of Agreement that incorporated Gulbenkian's demands. In a 10-page opinion, dissecting every clause, they warned TPC that there were still many vagaries and problems. But it "would be wise to accept the draft as it stands," as Gulbenkian's attorney, who had helped draft the compromise "feels fairly confident that he can get Mr. Gulbenkian to accept it." The new agreement was printed and presented to Gulbenkian.[79]

But then Gulbenkian wanted "a few changes." A month later, on June 7, 1926, syndicate attorneys found those changes to be totally astonishing. Their nine-page clause-by-clause analysis was filled with rejections: Clause 3: "The suggestion is … of course, utterly untenable." Clause 7: "This is an additional obligation and … we see no reason to agree to it." Clause 12: "The last three lines must be deleted." Clause 16: "The phraseology is utterly unacceptable … The second paragraph of the clause must be deleted altogether."[80]

In the meantime, the industrialization taking place in America and Europe increased the demand for oil on an exponential basis. The Roaring Twenties gave birth to the new consumer economy. America's population center had shifted from the farm to the city. The have-nots began having. Henry Ford's new Model A, almost ready to sputter off the assembly lines, was expected to revolutionize automobile production. Movies. Dance clubs. Household appliances. Personal convenience. Gadgets. Factory mass production. Factory mass employment. The Bolshevik revolution and mass industrialization. A renewed arms race. Transatlantic shipping. Air travel. The velocity of the world had become supercharged. It all required fuel, lubricants, illuminants, petrochemicals—the stuff beneath the ground in Iraq.

After arduous weeks of agonizing over the smallest points, progress with Gulbenkian was revived during later 1926, but several salient stumbling blocks remained. The most important was how Gulbenkian was going to be paid for his 5 percent by a company ordained to never record a profit. Solution: He would be paid in oil. But at what price? The market price. But that could be manipulated; the oil monopolies were famous for manipulating market prices. Solution: global averages, calculated on separate months of the year, pegged to January, the coldest month, when prices were highest. But Gulbenkian did not want to sell oil; he possessed no retail arm. He just wanted the money. So the four cartels would purchase his oil allotment—then he would have money. But the American Group did not want to make a 75-year commitment to purchase oil from Gulbenkian. Well, then the French could step in. They needed oil, Gulbenkian was known to them, and they could buy all his oil in a special side agreement.[81]

A second major question was just what territory the Working Agreement would cover. Under the self-denying principle, none of the oil companies could function within "the defined area" except through TPC. But oil deposits know no borders. It would be easy for the oil companies to drill into the same subterranean layers on the Turkish side of the border or to discover oil in the Arabian Peninsula or along the Gulf. Then make it broad: Designate the whole of the Ottoman Empire. Which Ottoman Empire? The Ottoman Empire of the nineteenth century, before the Balkans War in 1912, before the onset of World War I in 1914, before the armistice of 1918, before the League of Nations adjudication of 1926?[82]

In February 1927, the British government suggested yet another face-to-face conference. This time, Gulbenkian demurred. "Many of the members who would attend such a conference," Gulbenkian wrote the Petroleum Board, "are full of suspicion and have had bitter experiences in the past."[83] Once more, negotiations for a Working Agreement and buyout underwent more iterations of burial, exhumation, reanimation, and slow death.

Then in October 1927 everything changed. Once Mosul had been adjudged Iraqi territory, TPC geologists quickly scampered all over the region to find the most likely point to sink a gusher. It did not take long. Early in the morning of October 14, 1927, at the tract known as "the fiery furnace" for its noxious gasses and seepages, in the high foothills near the northern town of Kirkuk, the realm of Iraq finally opened its spigot. It was an utter blowout. At an estimated flow of 90,000 barrels per day, the fabulous Baba Gurgur Well #1 strike saturated everything with black gold. So fierce was the pressure, when diverted through the drilling arbor head, it created a massive horizontal jet of oil. Two American workers were overcome by deadly fumes. The effluent formed a flammable river of oil as wide as the Jordan. The seemingly unstoppable gusher did not catch fire, but continuously spewed flammable gases. It was no longer a vision. The air itself was thick with the wealth of oil.[84]

The Baba Gurgur gate valve could not be capped for three days.[85] Once capped, it stood inactive. No one could ignore the reality anymore. It was now or never. Yet another new agreement was negotiated among all the parties.

On the morning of July 31, 1928, an Imperial Airways 14-seater Handley Page charter plane flew from London to Ostend. The long-fuselaged biplane, powered by four engines and sporting a distinctive triple tail, carried Nubar Gulbenkian, an attorney for the Freshfields firm, as well as other members of the Gulbenkian family and clerical staff. Their destination was the Royal Palace Hotel. Once there, they ordered a sumptuous lunch of turbot along with a bottle of fine champagne. While the meal was being prepared, Nubar and his group stepped into one of the private rooms. There a group of oil company presidents awaited them, along with Nubar's father, Calouste Sarkis Gulbenkian himself.[86]

A 54-page document with numerous attachments, annexes, and supplements was ready. Every issue had been resolved. Each of the four partner cartels would own exactly 23.75 percent of Turkish Petroleum; each had yielded 1.25 percent to create Gulbenkian's everlasting 5 percent. A newly created family company, registered in Canada, called the Participations and Investments Company, or Partex for short, would hold the 5 percent. America's Near East Development Corporation was composed of Standard Oil of New Jersey, Standard Oil of New York, Atlantic Refining, Pan American Oil, and Gulf Petroleum. France's Companie Française des Petroles would buy Gulbenkian's oil; the complex price and procedure were arranged.[87]

Emblazoned with red foil signets, green and purple witness stamps, corporate embossments, and notary seals, the massive convention had been years in the making. Page 49 was filled with the signatures of the six major corporate participants. First, the director and secretary of D'Arcy Exploration signed for the original entity creating Anglo-Persian Oil Company, with a red foil stamp fixed to the right. Beneath that were two signatures for Shell's Anglo-Saxon Petroleum, marked to the right by an embossment. Then the two executives of Companie Francaise des Petroles signed beside the company's oval embossment. Beneath that, Teagle and another executive signed for the five companies that comprised the Near East Development Company, with the corporate seal embossed just to the right. Beneath that was affixed the seal of Partex, Nubar Gulbenkian signing for the firm. At the bottom, Turkish Petroleum's director and secretary signed with their firm's serrated red foil seal to the right. Page 51: Anglo-Persian signed for itself and all its associated companies, and a red foil seal was affixed. Page 52: Royal Dutch and Shell Transport signed for the Shell combine, and a red foil seal was affixed. Page 53: The presidents and secretaries of Standard Oil of New Jersey, Standard Oil of New York, Pan-American Petroleum, Atlantic Refining, and Gulf Oil signed, in that order, each penning his name as corporate seals were pressed over their signatures for surety.[88]

Page 54, the last page, read as follows: "I, the undersigned, hereby recognize that the parties to the above written agreement have only agreed to execute the same conditionally on my entering into the underwritten Agreement, and I accordingly agree, as well on my own behalf, and on behalf of my executors administrators and estate, and on behalf of any Company which I now or may hereafter in any matter whatsoever control, to be bound by the definitions, obligations, and restrictions contained in the above written Agreement, including particularly the waiver of claims contained in clause 26 in like manner as if I had been a party thereto jointly with or in place of the Participations Company." Beneath that oath were the words: "Signed Sealed and Delivered by Calouste Sarkis Gulbenkian in the presence of" the British proconsul.[89] It was now up to Gulbenkian to place his pen upon the paper. His would be the last and most important signature. The British proconsul had flown in from Paris to witness the ratification. Billions hung upon his pen stroke, and none really knew if Gulbenkian would actually sign the agreement.

It all depended on the red line. A red line?

Gulbenkian checked the map. During negotiations, to break the stalemate over the true borders of the Ottoman Empire, Gulbenkian had insisted not on country names and internationally set borders, which could change from time to time and war to war, but a simple red line drawn on the map. There it was on pages 21 and 22 of the agreement, faithfully reproduced per his instructions, complete with alphabetical points and a map legend. The red line circumscribed the Ottoman Empire as it existed during his lifetime, beginning with the Treaty of Berlin in 1878. Gulbenkian's line began near Baku, where an *A* was printed, and proceeded down the adjusted Turco-Persian frontier, coursing over precise zigs and zags to map points marked *B* and *C*, including all of Mesopotamia, and then down to Basra, where the red line took a pronounced detour around Kuwait, and then encircled the entire Arabian Peninsula. From the tip of Yemen, it proceeded north up to the Gulf of Aqaba, where it reached Palestine at map mark E, approximately at Eilat. The red line then skirted the Egyptian Sinai Desert north to Port Said on the Mediterranean coast. From there, the line encompassed all of Turkey, and then ended back at Baku.[90]

Names, sovereignties, nationalities, colonies, and mandates, self-determined or undetermined—none of it mattered. Within the bounds of that red line, none of the companies could engage in any oil business except through their common monopoly, the Turkish Petroleum Company, thus creating the most spectacular monopoly of all time. Finally, a full generation after the Sultan granted the Anatolia Railway an oil concession, 18 years after Turkish Petroleum was created from paper, 16 years after the fusion deal that merged TPC with Anglo-Persian, eight years after San Remo divided the wealth, nearly a decade after America demanded equal standing, Gulbenkian finally signed, not with his usual elegant penmanship but with an almost illegible scrawl. All eyes in the room nervously followed his pen strokes. The British consul formally witnessed the signature and quickly affixed his stamp. Two green certification stamps were pasted down and then rubber-stamped, as six additional seals and embossments were added. Forevermore, that document would be known as the "Redline Agreement."[91]

The ceremony was brief. The Gulbenkian party returned to the restaurant before their meal was served. After three decades of struggle, the matter was finished in the time in takes to cook turbot.

It was finally over. By the power of a trillion-dollar pen stroke and the authority vested by the almighty red line, Iraq's oil would finally flow. The country now belonged not just to Britain, but to all the great powers.

It was finally over, but in truth it was just beginning.

CHAPTER TWELVE

NAZI OIL

D uring World War II, a confusing web of complex and contradictory political and economic relationships coursed from London to Berlin to Jerusalem and back, all involving oil, the Jews, and the Mideast. In 1941, the locus shifted to Iraq, as the forces of Arab nationalism joined Nazi aggression to confront the arch-importance of oil and the question of Jewish existence. The threads of this drama came together at the height of World War II, but they had been building for years.

After the Iraq Petroleum Company's oil began flowing, the royalties—deflated or not—greatly enriched King Faisal's throne and the national treasury of Iraq. England, in 1930, renegotiated its treaty with what was now the sovereign nation of Iraq. The revised treaty guaranteed the British two air bases, along with military transit and basing rights in the event of war. By pre-agreement, the League of Nations ended Britain's mandate in 1932, and London sponsored Iraq's admission into the league itself as a full member.[1]

Two pipelines, as originally envisioned years earlier, were constructed to carry Iraqi and Persian oil to the Mediterranean. One, completed in mid-July 1934, passed through Syria to meet the sea at Tripoli, Lebanon. The second, completed January 14, 1935, traveled from Kirkuk south to the Haifa coast in Palestine. The Kirkuk-Haifa line was opened to great fanfare. The King of Iraq presided in the presence of many government officials, Redline consortium executives, and some 250 invited VIPs. That year, 1935, Persia was renamed "Iran" when the Shah resurrected the country's ancient name, in a show of solidarity with the Nazis. Anglo-Persian Oil Company changed its name to Anglo-Iranian Oil Company. By this time, the Redline consortium of the Iraq Petroleum Company had formed hundreds of wholly-owned and interlocking subsidiaries throughout the Mideast and the world to drill for, refine, transport, and sell its petroleum.[2]

Throughout the 1920s, the Zionist movement in Palestine—still under British Mandate—struggled to purchase land, found kibbutzim, drain swamps, and create new Jewish towns. Immigration was unrestricted and even promoted by the British, but results were meager. Most well-established Jews were too comfortably assimilated in postwar Europe and America to emigrate to the barren and inhospitable Jewish homeland in Palestine. It was common for establishment Jews to support Zionism for others but not for themselves. They preferred to donate funds and make speeches about helping their disadvantaged coreligionists in Eastern Europe. Hence, Jewish Palestine in the twenties was still mainly a movement of Jewish idealists helping their Eastern European brethren.[3]

The Jewish presence in Palestine grew slowly in the 1920s, but was strongly resisted at every juncture and expansion by the local Arab population. The leader of Palestine's Arabs was Haj Muhammad Amin al-Husseini. He incessantly organized fiery political resistance to the Jewish presence and his followers frequently broke into riots and committed acts of violence and vandalism. Hardly a local rabble-rouser, Husseini would rise from an obscure figure to become the preeminent nationalist in the Arab world. His voice would not only be heard in the mosques and casbahs of Palestine, but also in the stately halls of the League of Nations and the mandatory powers, where he regularly represented the Arab cause with charisma and aplomb. Husseini had access to Hitler personally. For the Third Reich, Husseini was the key to a calculated strategy to restage the Lawrence of Arabia saga, but in reverse—using the Arabs to help eliminate the Jews and to help seize the oil Germany needed to dominate the world.

Who was Husseini? Muhammad Amin al-Husseini was born in 1895 in Jerusalem. The Husseini clan was one of Palestine's wealthiest and most honored. As early as the seventeenth century, members of the Husseini family had served as the muftis of Jerusalem. In Islamic tradition, a mufti was the respected interpreter of Koranic law, but, in many ways, also revered as the titular head of the community.[4]

As a young man, Amin Husseini was self-conscious, short, and frail. He spoke with a lisp. But he impressed others as highly intelligent and seemed mature for his age. His father, Tamir, held the title of mufti until his death in 1908. Amin was too young to fill his father's shoes. Instead, the eldest brother,

Kamil, assumed the important post. Kamil sent 16-year-old Amin to Cairo to study at al-Azhar University. In Cairo, Husseini met prominent Islamic reformers and the earliest champions of Arab nationalism. Soon, the teen-aged Husseini became his own self-styled activist, recruiting other Palestinian students to agitate against Zionism. Husseini held Zionism as the greatest threat to Arab nationalism—years before the Balfour Declaration was ever even framed.[5]

Once back in Jerusalem, Amin began writing mordant articles attacking Zionism. To sharpen his leadership skills, he went off to Istanbul to become an officer in the Turkish army. Harsh army training and deprivation toughened Husseini, both physically and emotionally. But the fervent Arab found he could not turkify himself into a true Ottoman. He abandoned the Turkish army, returning to Jerusalem and his beloved campaign for Arab nationalism. Quickly, he was elected president of Jerusalem's Arab Club, whereupon he assumed the leadership of the anti-Zionist movement.[6]

Husseini specialized in riling up the rumor-infused "Arab Street" with wild, often hysterical warnings of pending Jewish destruction of Islamic holy sites, Zionist conspiracy, and blood libel. He and his closest associates were instrumental in orchestrating the violence that broke out between Jews and Arabs in the April 1920 riots. Husseini escaped arrest by fleeing across the Jordan River, but was sentenced in absentia to 10 years in prison. Ironically, Palestine high commissioner Herbert Samuel, himself a Zionist, pardoned Husseini as a gesture to the seething Arab community. That brought Husseini back to Jerusalem.[7]

From that point, Husseini donned the classic rounded white-topped *imama,* or religious turban, grew a cleric's beard, and immediately launched a campaign to become the next mufti. Husseini's brother was near death, and Husseini wanted to succeed him. The position was technically not hereditary, and candidates from several rival Jerusalem families actively vied for the post. But Amin, showing his organizational prowess, began a petition drive to prove he was the choice of the Arab masses. When the votes were counted in council, Husseini ranked only fourth. But the Husseini clan attacked the legitimacy of the council itself.[8]

More petitions were presented to High Commissioner Samuel, who under British rules would make the final selection. Posters mysteriously appeared in the Old City accusing the Jews of conspiring to place a stooge in the mufti's office, someone who would then "sell" the Temple Mount to Zionists so they could rebuild the Jewish Temple. Such wild accusations became Husseini's hallmark. To keep peace on the excited Arab Street, and after Husseini declared that he and his family would be "devoted to maintaining tranquility in Jerusalem, Samuel relented and appointed the 26-year-old Husseini.

Thereafter, Husseini was known as the Grand Mufti of Jerusalem. He spent the next decade battling every increase in Jewish presence, no matter how incremental.[9]

Everything changed in Palestine when Adolf Hitler shocked the world on January 30, 1933, suddenly rising to power in Germany at the dénouement of an election crisis.

Germany's relationship with Palestine was complex. The Nazis wanted to oust the Jews of Germany, and indeed of all Europe, seizing their assets in the process. While the violently anti-Semitic Nazis hated the Jews, they reluctantly promoted the Jewish national movement for the sole purpose of kicking Jews out of Germany and into another region—far-off Palestine. The idea was to pen Jews up into a "reservation" where they could be dealt with at a later time. In that ironic fashion, Nazi anti-Semitism actively supported a Jewish homeland.[10]

Upon gaining power, Hitler organized Jewish expulsions from the professions, deprived German Jews of their assets, subjected them to humiliating street rampages, and began their systematic ouster. Concentration camps were opened across the Reich, their atrocities bannered in the newsreels, radio broadcasts, and headlines of the day. Nazi surrogates in Poland, Lithuania, Hungary, and elsewhere around Europe joined the fascist movement to dismantle their Jewish communities and force their Jewish neighbors out of Europe.

Suddenly, hundreds of thousands of middle-class Jewish refugees, pitiful and penniless, flooded the capitals of the world, balancing children on their hips and a few overstuffed suitcases under their arms. Many appeared with little more than books stuffed into satchels or tied with twine. Clamoring for anywhere safe—maybe New York, London, Paris, Amsterdam, or a dozen other potential sanctuaries—the refugees escaped with their lives but were now homeless.

Quickly, the fleeing multitudes became too great for a Depression-wracked world to absorb. The doors of relief were shut. One nation after another blocked the Jewish throngs at the borders they had dashed to—or been dumped at. Country after country enacted restrictive entry legislation, denied visas on flimsy grounds, and, in unison, declared that somehow another solution to the Jewish problem was needed. That solution was, of course, to be found somewhere beyond everybody's borders. But where? Zionist Organization president Chaim Weizmann lamented that for Europe's Jews, the world was divided into two realms: "places where Jews cannot live, and where Jews cannot enter."[11]

As thousands of Jews were thrown into poverty, concentration camps, or ghettos, and brutalized every day in the expanded Third Reich and elsewhere in Europe, the threat soon lurched into a race against time. The remaining destination was their ancestral home in Palestine. Palestine was then still a British Mandate under the auspices of the League of Nations. Jews entered Palestine via elaborate financial transfer and trade agreements designed to bring in the middle class, via Zionist youth programs intended to save the young, and via illegal smuggling operations determined to rescue those snatched from the very jaws of the Holocaust. All these newcomers, whether from Germany, Czechoslovakia, Poland, or elsewhere, brought into Palestine their desperation and energy, but also their European ways—from Mozart to motorcars to Linzer tortes. They also brought money, and quickly established their own European-style economy in Palestine.[12]

Between 1933 and 1941, various emergency transfer plans and corollary commercial agreements with the Third Reich enabled some $100 million in direct transfers, along with some 60,000 Jews from Germany and elsewhere in Europe, to flow into Palestine. Many ousted Germans were able to transfer into Palestine virtual replicas of their German existence—homes, shops, and factories. The heartfelt donations of anguished Jews and Christians through religious and secular relief operations everywhere added to the effort to transplant displaced Jews of all classes into Palestine. By the outbreak of war in 1939, Jews represented roughly half of Palestine's overall population.[13]

Many Jews worked in the oil industry, processing Iraq Oil Company crude through a newly built refinery, bunkering it in towering oil tanks planted on the landscape, and loading it onto tankers for shipment overseas. Haifa, with its new, well-dredged harbor and thriving oil and shipping center, became a Jewish metropolis. So did Tel Aviv, as did a newly expanded western Jerusalem. Moreover, poor working class Jews displaced cheap Arab workers in the kibbutzim. Fruits and vegetables from Jewish agriculture supplanted Arab produce in the market stalls.[14]

The Arabs saw ancient Palestine transform before their very eyes. For years, the Mufti of Jerusalem had led the local jihad against the Jews and everything Zionist. A demographic race of sorts sprang up as Arabs did all they could to encourage Muslim immigration and an Islamic renaissance to counterbalance what they called "the Jewish menace." But the Arabs could not compete with the pace of Jewish expulsions from Europe and the concomitant immigration and financial transfers into Palestine.

In April 1936, Arab agitation, led by the Mufti through his Arab Higher Committee, exploded into another prolonged campaign of anti-Jewish violence. This uprising, known as the Arab Revolt, called for all Palestinian Arabs to stop paying British taxes and to close their shops and major institutions, thus bringing their economy and British mandatory oversight to a halt. Then in May, 1936, the murders started. Jews were shot at point-blank range in the Old City, in the Edison film theater, and in other places where they tradi-tionally felt safe. Arab extremists also killed fellow Muslims who were simply working with Jews: an Arab vegetable vendor selling his goods in the Jewish market, an Arab watchman at a Jewish company. The terror campaign touched everyone. Riots against Jews ignited all over Palestine. In Haifa, 2,000 Arabs marched until they broke into rock throwing. At Nablus, an unruly throng assembled after midday prayers and promised a fight to the end. In Jaffa, pro-testors ran wild through the streets. Jewish buses were stoned everywhere. Bombs exploded with regularity across the country, including Jerusalem. On May 17, 1936, Jerusalem was besieged with riots. The results were disastrous. Due to the general strike, the Arab economy was almost exhausted.[15]

In 1936, yet another British fact-finding body, the Peel Commission, investigated—as had so many previous panels after surges in Arab violence. But this time, the commission's conclusions were dramatic. The next year, Peel's commission concluded, "An irrepressible conflict has arisen between two national communities within the narrow bounds of one small country. There is no common ground between them. Their national aspirations are incompatible. The Arabs desire to revive the traditions of the Arab golden age. The Jews desire to show what they can achieve when restored to the land in which the Jewish nation was born. Neither of the two national ideals permits combination in the service of a single State."[16]

Peel's white paper added, "The Arab Higher Committee was, to a large extent, responsible for maintaining and protecting the strike last year. The Mufti of Jerusalem, as President, must bear his due share of responsibility … The functions, which the Mufti has collected in his person, and his use of them, have led to the development of an Arab *imperium in imperio* [an empire within an empire]."[17]

Finally, the white paper called for partition in Palestine, that is, separat-ing the two peoples in the same fashion that had been done for the Greeks and Turks when 1.5 million Muslims and Christians were transferred across bor-ders. In Palestine, two sovereign cantons were to be created, one Arab and one Jewish. Rather than create the first Arab state to rule in Palestine, the Mufti decreed a "no" to all plans and propositions—not with autonomous Jews in their midst. His followers intensified the campaign of incendiary language, random violence, political assassination and the broad incitement of inter-reli-gious strife.[18] Those who felt it possible that the two peoples in Palestine could separate peaceably were now being bullied, stabbed, shot, and dynamited by the followers of the Mufti, who always stayed aloof from the actual terror.

The elusive Mufti had always known how to evade capture. Once in 1936, he and his large traveling party slipped out of the country, driving to Damascus where, on June 22, 1936, he checked into the Orient Palace Hotel.

There he participated in numerous conferences with Palestinian agitators about merging the Syrian national bloc with the Palestinian Istiqlal resistance group. These meetings were attended not only by Syrians, but also by representatives from Saudi Arabia and Iraq.[19]

On July 3, 1937, the Mufti departed for the mountain village of Sofar in Lebanon, and then continued on to Beirut. Driving all day from Beirut, he suddenly reappeared in Palestine on July 4, 1937. Back in Jerusalem, the Mufti hid within the protective grounds of the Dome of the Rock, where no Christian could enter. As Mufti and chairman of the local Waqf religious trust, Husseini was custodian of the precious mosque complex. In fact, it was Husseini who had begun the restoration and the famous gold leafing of the Dome, which only magnified his prestige within the Arab population. Nonetheless, the British were determined and prepared to dispatch Muslim officers from the Indian army to arrest him.[20]

London had long wanted to exile Husseini in a distant internment camp on the tiny Seychelles islands in the Indian Ocean. But indecision had delayed any move. Finally, at the end of September 1937, British authorities shut down all the agitation committees in Palestine. They issued arrest warrants for some 200 members of the Arab Higher Committee, with the Mufti at the top of the list. The first group apprehended was immediately deported to the Seychelles.[21]

But Husseini was one step ahead. On October 14, 1937, the Mufti lowered himself down the outer wall of the Temple Mount complex to a waiting car, which drove him to the Jaffa port. There he boarded a boat for Lebanon, making good his escape. Once in Beirut, the French supposedly placed the Mufti under house arrest. But his "house arrest" was a pleasure. Husseini regularly regaled fellow nationalists and other leading Syrian personalities at festive dinner parties with his talk of a pan-Arab state stretching from Damascus to Jerusalem—all to the constant chagrin of the British. For two years, the Mufti was less a prisoner in Beirut than a *bon vivant.*[22]

At 6:00 A.M., September 1, 1939, Hitler launched his blitzkrieg against Poland, thus beginning World War II. This was the Mufti's moment. He seized it.

The French, eager to curry favor with Palestinian Arabs during the forthcoming struggle with Germany, continued to kowtow to the Mufti. When, just after war broke out, Husseini openly thanked various luminaries in the French government for gracious treatment during his visit, the highest authorities were quick to respond. For example, General Maxime Weygand, commander in chief of French forces in the eastern Mediterranean, effusively replied: "The letter in which Your Eminence has expressed to me his personal thanks, and that of the members of the Arab Higher Committee, for the hospitality extended to them by the French authorities ... has touched me deeply.

I have been particularly moved," General Weygand added, "by the allusion which Your Eminence has made to the humanitarian spirit of France, which is one of the most noble traditions of my country. Your Eminence has been good enough also to assure me of the loyalty of the Arabs in Palestine; for this, I express to you all my gratitude. I beg your Eminence to accept the assurance of my highest consideration."[23]

But Husseini needed to say good-bye to his hosts in Lebanon. Hitler was fighting the two greatest nemeses of the Palestinian Arabs: the Jews and the British. The Mufti bribed the French chief of police with £500 to make sure gendarmes outside his house looked the other way. The morning of either October 13 or 14, 1939, Husseini and his assistants donned the coverings of devout Muslim women, and drove off unmolested. Only after Husseini failed to appear for his regular morning walk the next two days, did guards admit that they saw the car depart, but presumed all within were women.[24] The next day, the Mufti appeared in Baghdad, the epicenter of Britain's Mideast strategy and the font of its oil.[25]

*   *   *   *

Hitler's plans were fueled by hate. But Hitler's tanks, trucks, automobiles, warships, submarines, and airplanes were fueled by octane. Moving parts in machinery, from locomotives to Lugers, required lubricants. Economic recovery was dependent upon great factories, Military campaigns deployed great armies and defenses. Foreign domination hinged upon intrusive, far-flung administrative machinery. All of that required petroleum. Hitler needed oil. The more territory Hitler took, the more oil he needed to sustain his conquests.

In 1938, Reich consumption of petroleum products, from kerosene to aviation fuel, was estimated by some British experts at more than 6.5 million tons per year and growing exponentially as the Reich continued to mechanize, industrialize, rearm, and make ready for the war that everyone expected. Indeed, 1938 consumption grew by 1.2 million tons over the preceding year. Through synthetic means and some local deposits, Germany produced only a few million tons of its overall usage. The rest was imported. One typical top-secret analysis, titled "The Oil Supply Problem in Germany," concluded, "In spite of her efforts, Germany was still dependent on imports for over 50 percent of her requirements." An almost weekly cascade of such British estimates varied in tons and percentages. But, despite Nazi industrial secrecy that fudged the numbers, British intelligence consistently concluded that Germany was overwhelmingly dependent on foreign oil. Moreover, the expanding Reich was counting every barrel, because its shortfalls were several million tons per year.[26]

In 1939, Germany's oil industry was a maze of more than 70 refiners and distributors, most of them small, dominated by a half dozen or so giant firms. Several of these dominating companies were in the forefront of importation. Chief among them was a firm named Olex.[27]

Olex had long been a household name in Germany, with thousands of convenient gas stations across the country. The company's name derived from its original 1904 telegraphic address, PETROLEXPORT; the middle four letters formed OLEX. In addition to its consumer profile, Olex was also a key importer of oil. Its number one source was Romania. In 1937, Olex stocks in hand included some 6,100 metric tons of Romanian light benzine, 5,800 metric tons of Romanian middle benzine, 1,150 metric tons of Romanian heavy benzine, and 387 metric tons of Romanian white spirit, plus Romanian tractor vapor oil and kerosene, all imported through Hamburg and Regensburg. A September 3, 1936, company memo examining imports spotlighted "the Romanian market, the chief source of Olex supplies."[28]

At the end of 1937, Olex's total on hand of all petroleum products, from motor fuel to diesel oil to lubricants, equaled 88,800 metric tons valued at approximately 14 million reichsmarks. Its total 1938 sales of all products topped 475,300 metric tons.[29]

But Olex also imported gas oil, diesel oil, and kerosene from Amsterdam. The Dutch oil was brought in through a subsidiary registered in the Netherlands, the stock certificates of which were held in two locations: 995 shares in the Olex company safe in Berlin and 5 shares in its attorney's office.[30]

Iran was also an important source for Olex because the company and Nazi Germany needed foreign currency. Much of the world would not accept any of the numerous species of reichsmarks, almost all unusable outside Germany, and many based on fraudulent values. Moreover, the international anti-Nazi boycott had dramatically reduced all Nazi exports. So Germany was earning precious little foreign currency and was rationing its reserves. But through complicated barters, Olex could earn the foreign currency it needed to purchase oil, bolster Reich reserves, and earn a profit. Boycott-breaking barters were terribly complicated, generally disguised, and involved several companies in different parts of the world swapping products at a discount in exchange for some foreign currency.[31]

In a typical Olex barter, the company would import Iranian oil and sell it to the German steel company Ferrostahl, which would pay Olex in Germany with worthless reichsmarks spendable only in Germany. But how would Olex find the British pounds to pay Iran? Ferrostahl purchased 15,000 tons of inferior Iranian champa rice at an inflated price in exchange for first-class construction and railroad steel that Iran paid for in British pounds. The steel company would then turn over its British pounds to the Reichsbank, which would use it for general Nazi rearmament and other state purposes. Olex could then receive a portion of those British pounds to pay for the oil it purchased from Iran. An Olex review of the serpentine Ferrostahl barter concluded it was necessary for the Reich "because in this way Germany earns the right to some Iranian [foreign] currency." Indeed, without a cornucopia of intricate, multi-transactional barters, Germany could not import the tons of British-controlled Iranian oil it craved.[32]

Iranian barter deals like the Ferrostahl swap were common for Olex. A 1938 company balance sheet included separate entries for "barter transactions," which in that reporting period totaled 150,000 reichsmarks (RM), yielding £12,000 in one category, and RM 171,000, fetching £12,457 in a second. So entrenched was Iran as a source of Olex's imports that when a German highway publication asked Olex for a pictorial, company advertising managers wrote, "Although we shall discuss in our article mainly our distribution facilities in Germany, we shall have to mention the Iranian origin of our motor fuel and give a short description of your production and refining activities in Iran and submit a few photos."[33]

Olex was a loyal vendor with the Third Reich, and highly visible. At first, Olex managers were worried about the ascent of Hitler. Depression-era sales had stagnated when they should have grown. But no sooner had *der Führer* assumed power than sales volume soared from slightly more than 200,000 long tons in 1932 to double that amount by the end of 1938. By 1939, Olex operated 7,000 gas stations throughout the country, sometimes adding as many as 1,000 per year as Hitler's forced economic recovery proliferated throughout the nation. During three months of 1938, Olex ran seven advertisements at one-week intervals in more than 300 German newspapers, including Nazi party newspapers. Moreover, Olex printed the newest road maps of Germany, which immediately incorporated the latest Nazified street names, such as Adolf Hitlerplatz and Adolf Hitlerstrasse. In this way, Olex became an important cog in the cultural apparatus of National Socialism.[34]

Who owned Olex? Olex was a wholly owned subsidiary of Britain's Anglo-Iranian Oil Company, also known as Anglo-Persian Oil Company. In 1926, Anglo-Persian had acquired 40 percent of the old-line Olex, increased its ownership to 75 percent in 1929, and then in 1931 bought out the remaining 25 percent from minority owner Deutsche Petroleum. Anglo-Persian called the new entity *Deutsche Benzin- und Petroleum*, or BP. Throughout Great Britain, Anglo-Persian's green BP three-pointed shield logo stood for British Petrol. Throughout the Reich, the identical shield stood for Benzin-und Petroleum. As a wholly owned subsidiary of Anglo-Persian, all of Olex's affairs were tightly controlled out of London.[35]

Other Redline partners were also leading purveyors of Nazi oil. Standard

Oil of New Jersey operated Deustche Amerikanische Petroleum Gesellschaft or DAPG. As one of Germany's top six firms, DAPG operated 17,500 gas stations in Germany. Shell operated 16,500. In fact, of Germany's approximate 64,000 gas stations in 1939, Shell, Standard, and BP operated 41,000. Olex also became a key supplier of German's growing aircraft industry.[36]

When Olex purchased Iranian oil, it was dealing with another subsidiary of the same company, its parent Anglo-Iranian—also called Anglo-Persian. The so-called Iranian oil it purchased was often Iranian in name only, since the twin oil fields of Naft Khana and Naft i Shah straddled either side of the Iraq-Iran border; and, in fact, the Iraqi side was considered "transferred territory." British military planners at the time declared they could consider "the two sections of Naft Khana/Naft i Shah of the northern field as one unit." The "transferred territories" were, after all, Iraqi land under the original 1901 Persian concession. But Iraqi oil processed through the Iranian refinery at Abadan, across from Basra, now bore the stamp of Iran.[37] Oil deposits, and the companies that tap them, do not recognize national borders because their precious commodity runs underground.

Hence, with a clenched fist, England staunchly resisted the rise and rearmament of Hitler, while with its own imperial enterprise, Anglo-Iranian Oil Company, partially government-owned and fully government controlled when it came to international matters, contributed mightily to the recovery of the Third Reich and Hitler's preparations to wage war against nations and ethnic groups. So did the other Redline partners, Shell, Standard, and CFP. Indeed, the massive consumption of the Third Reich allowed Redline companies to compensate for Depression days when demand and profits stagnated.

Once war began, Anglo-Iranian Oil Company and Olex followed Nazi Germany across Europe. "It should be noted," recounted an Anglo-Iranian internal review just after the war, "that Olex took advantage of the expansion of Germany to extend their distributing network in Austria and into Poland and Czechoslovakia." For example, in Yugoslavia, the company was known as Olex Proizvodi, headquartered in Zagreb in Croatia. After Britain declared war on the Reich and its Axis partners, German "custodians" in Berlin designated Olex as enemy property, but Reich economic officials did with Olex as they did with IBM, Ford, and General Motors. The companies were seized in name only, meaning that the funds were merely sequestered in protected blocked accounts for collection later by the corporations. Such companies were left independent, and "in the case of Olex," Anglo-Iranian's internal review recounts, "the directors and managers were reappointed by the Custodian as his advisors."[38] There was no change from one day to the next at Olex. Anglo-Iranian's executives continued to run the company—only the profits were temporarily frozen.

Ironically, the British also deemed Olex and its foreign operations as enemy activity. The Trading with the Enemy office in London sequestered what few accounts of Olex it could find in random bank accounts. For example, Olex Yugoslavia's minor assets in London were sequestered in Trading with the Enemy account Y 40720.[39]

Two other Redline partners were also declared enemies. The first was the Compagnie Française des Petroles (CFP), because France had surrendered and transformed itself into a bifurcated national entity, half Nazi-occupied in the north, half Nazi collaborationist with a capital at Vichy in the south. However, by a special high-level British government decision, CFP was permitted to conduct its normal business, making investments in Iraq Petroleum Company oil ventures as called for under the Redline Agreement. CFP would merely contribute through the British custodian, who would forward the cash to the Redline partners of Iraq Petroleum.[40] Thus France's CFP was able to expand its Iraq-based oil empire during the war years.

The other declared enemy was C. S. Gulbenkian, because he was living in France. The Redline Agreement called for Gulbenkian's 5 percent allotment to be purchased by Compagnie Française des Petroles. Naturally, Gulbenkian fiercely protested his enemy status and threatened to retaliate by rescinding a huge endowment to build a new domicile for the National Gallery and canceling what officials called "a fabulous offer of pictures [art treasures gifted to the National Gallery] ... because he was declared an enemy." The whole idea of being declared an enemy did not please Gulbenkian. He promised to call his attorneys. He promised to sue his Redline partners in the Iraq Petroleum Company because he held them responsible. He reminded everyone, he had rights.[41]

*   *   *   *

As the war progressed in late 1940, Hitler needed more and more oil. Reich purchases from Romania were not keeping up with the needs arising from German aggression. The Allies wanted to deny Hitler the all-important fields in Romania by any means possible. Some even suggested defensively purchasing all Romania's output, just to keep petroleum out of Reich hands. Every other day, another British intelligence estimate forecast an ever-increasing Nazi shortfall, sometimes 1 million tons, sometimes more. No one knew the exact figures, but they knew that oil was powering the Nazi onslaught. Many analysts predicted Germany would invade Romania by spring 1940 to seize the Ploesti oil fields. As expected, in October 7, 1940, a division of Nazi troops were sent in to "guard" the Romanian oil fields.[42]

But even Romanian production was not enough to fuel what Hitler had in mind. At the end of 1940, der Führer issued secret Directive 21, authorizing Operation Barbarossa, the full-scale invasion of Russia, to commence in late spring 1941. The unprecedented offensive would require thousands of long-range bombers, 3 million soldiers, thousands of tanks and artillery pieces, and 600,000 motor vehicles—all in a coordinated three-pronged attack.[43] Barbarossa would drink a lot of petroleum.

The Allies were expecting the thrust into Russia because of decoded messages during the long run-up to the invasion. Given the Nazi rape of Poland, the conquest of much of Western Europe, the establishment of heinous concentration camps, and horrid civilian ghettos across the Continent, the Allied leadership was convinced that only a titanic effort could stop Hitler. Debate after debate yielded a common conclusion: Only by drying up the Reich's oil supply could the Nazi war machine be halted.[44]

Typical was a mid-1940 British report by Lord Weir to Prime Minister Neville Chamberlain, which asked, "Has this formidable enemy [the Third Reich] any real weakness on which we can concentrate?" Lord Weir then answered his own question: "I believe it has such a real weakness. Germany cannot deploy her great hitting strength for any sustained effort unless she can produce, take from storage or import vast quantities of petrol, diesel oil, and lubricating oil. She is so committed to the internal combustion engine in every one of its applications—military and civil—that any dislocation of supply must limit and control her effort. No transport vehicle, no tank, no aeroplane, no submarine can function without fuel and lubricating oil. No great Army, Air Force or Navy, no amount of hard work or unity can find its effective expression without immense supplies of fuel. Germany lost the last war through lack of human fuel. This time, she should be made to lose it through lack of the fuel which goes into the fuel tanks."[45]

All attention now focused on where Hitler could find the extra fuel he needed. Answer: the gargantuan oil fields of Iraq and Iran. A 1941 War Cabinet strategy report concluded, "Oil is, of course, Germany's main economic objective both in Iraq and Iran (Persia). The oil production of Iraq (4 million tons a year) would be sufficient to solve Germany's oil problem, but there are many difficulties in the way of transporting it to Germany. The pipelines to Haifa and Tripoli must be under her control, and the sea routes in the Eastern Mediterranean must be open to her shipping."[46]

At the same time, British war planners understood that if Germany somehow did seize Iraq's oil fields, it would be cataclysmic. "The denial to us of the Iraq oil [and its pipelines]," the War Cabinet strategy report continued, "would be serious, as alternative sources of supply would involve the extra use of tankers, of which there is already a shortage." A Foreign Office report summarized the threat, "But for British control of oil production, Germany could buy all the oil which Iran could produce." Nazi Germany was already Iran's leading trading partner, with Reich advisors installed throughout the country and virtually controlling the nation's infrastructure.[47]

Even more blunt was a focused report titled, "Note on Iraq as a Possible Source of Oil Supply to the Enemy." The report made clear that if Romanian oil was insufficient, the Nazis "must turn to the nearest source: Iraq." Focusing on the estimated billion-ton Kirkuk oil field, the report asserted that Iraq possessed enough petroleum "to supply the [British] Empire's oil requirements for half a century." Fortunately, the report explained, for 15 years "relations between the concessionaire [the Redline group] and the Government have been smoother than the relations of any other oil concessionaire with any other Government." The report continued, "Proof ... can be cited [by] the fact that Iraq has leased to one set of interests [the Redline group] the whole of its oil resources, a monopoly that no other country has emulated."[48]

Despite the smooth relations, the report emphasized that if the Third Reich somehow achieved a political foothold in Iraq—now an independent country—everything would change. The Mideast, the Gulf, and then the connection to India itself would come under Nazi domination. Germany would be unstoppable west to east. The report ended, "Conclusion: The Enemy could not be denied Iraq oil if he got there ... Once there, the game is up, not only with Iraq oil, but with the whole of the Near East—and perhaps beyond."[49]

Enter the Mufti of Jerusalem.

Within weeks of the war's beginning, Husseini escaped his "house arrest" and dashed back to Baghdad. The Iraq he found in October 1939 had changed dramatically over recent years. In 1933, King Faisal had become ill. After tending to an outbreak of mass murder, rape, and looting by Kurdish tribesmen and Iraqi soldiers against Assyrian separatist villages, he returned to Switzerland in September for medical treatment and died within days. Faisal had, however, lived long enough to see Iraq gain its independence and enter the League of Nations as a full member.[50]

Faisal's 21-year-old son, Ghazi, succeeded him. Under King Ghazi, the nation quickly descended into a cavalcade of military coups, assassinations, tribal uprisings, military show trials, and political upheaval. New political parties and power bases emerged from communists, reformers, pan-Arabists, and ultra-nationalists. So volatile was the country that the London-based general manager of Iraq Petroleum concluded in a November 11, 1937, meeting that he was unable to visit Baghdad to negotiate for additional oil development. Meeting minutes recorded: "It was considered that the political situation in Iraq at the moment was unsuitable for negotiations."[51]

Seven Sunni military men, all of them conspirators in previous coups and political murders, emerged as the strongmen of Iraq. The most powerful of these seven formed their own quadrumvirate, known as the "Golden Square" for the four corners of authority they possessed. Civilians governed only with their approval—tacit or explicit.[52]

In April 1939, King Ghazi died in a car crash. The nation went into mourning as great crowds lined up to see his funeral procession. Rumors that the British were responsible burned across Iraq, fanned by anti-British elements. Ghazi was succeeded by his son, Faisal II, a three-year-old toddler. A regent was needed to act for the boy king, so yet another Hashemite scion from the Arabian Peninsula, Prince Abd al-Ilah, was recruited to fill the post. Prince Abd al-Ilah was selected as regent precisely because he was pro-British. He, in turn with London's approbation, established a new government led by Prime Minister Nuri al-Said, generally viewed as tolerant of the British presence in Iraq and accepting of the Peel white paper calling for partition of Palestine. In fact, Nuri, years earlier, while serving as foreign minister, had been brought in by the British in Palestine to negotiate with the Mufti and the Arab Higher Committee to end the paralyzing Arab revolt of 1936.[53]

The new pro-British rule of Prime Minister Nuri al-Said and Regent Abd al-Ilah ran afoul of the fiercely nationalist and militantly anti-British Golden Square. At the outbreak of World War II, Nuri publicly proclaimed Iraq would honor its alliance with Great Britain. The Prime Minister went further and severed diplomatic relations with Germany, expelling its diplomats and interning German nationals. Against this fertile background of power imbalance and fast-moving events, the Mufti, in mid-October 1939, arrived in Baghdad. His entry was especially welcomed by the Golden Square because three of the four generals had served with Husseini years earlier in the Turkish army. They had long ago become fast friends and comrades in the cause of Arab nationalism.[54]

The ground had been seeded for the Mufti's mission during his so-called house arrest in Beirut. In 1938, Husseini met secretly with Wilhelm Canaris, chief of Germany's *Abwehr*, or military intelligence. The *Abwehr* had sought to smuggle weapons into Palestine through Saudi Arabia to assist the Arab revolt, but plans were aborted because Berlin feared the British would discover the source. In another meeting, this one in Damascus, Nazi diplomat and Arabist Fritz Grobba gave the Mufti's secretary £800 just to keep the financial connection with Berlin alive. Grobba had been watching Iraq and had earlier reported to Berlin that Baghdad was now the most vociferous center of defiance against Peel's white paper. By 1939, Germany had finally concluded three minor arms sales with Baghdad, providing Iraq with numerous machine guns, 18 anti-aircraft pieces, and other equipment. Germany was known for pre-positioning military necessities in other countries through seemingly routine commercial transactions. Grobba and the *Abwehr* believed, as an intelligence colleague noted in his diary; "The Arab movement should be activated immediately."[55]

Ironically, just as the Nazis detested the Jews and yet promoted a Jewish homeland, they also considered the Arabs merely another exemplar of a reviled subhuman species: the Semites. Nazi Germany organized its ethnic relations along a pseudoscientific race science, called *eugenics*, which created an inescapable genetic hierarchy of worthy human life, with Aryan Nazis at the top. All other racial or national groups were to be dominated, or even destroyed. As Semites, Arabs were just a second branch of the same eugenic line that created the Jews Hitler hated. In fact, Hitler had personally named Operation Barbarossa for King Frederick Barbarossa, who in 1190 led the German Crusade against Islam in Palestine. However, for the sake of its goals for world domination, the Reich was willing to promote the diametrically opposed national aspirations of both the Jews and the Arabs in Palestine. After all, even as the Nazis bolstered their condemnation of Jewish settlement in Palestine, Berlin had fostered prewar trade and transfer agreements with the Zionist Organization that brought to Palestine some 60,000 Jews, along with $100 million in goods, thus dramatically expanding the viability of the Jewish State. This rapid expansion of Jewish Palestine was, in fact, the very cause of the Arabs' protest.[56]

But the Mufti did not care about the motivations of the Nazis, only how the Reich could advance the aspirations of Arab Palestine. Upon entering Iraq, Husseini immediately set about establishing a power base. The collaborationist Vichy police in Syria made things comfortable by hand-delivering the Mufti's motorcar and household goods from Beirut. In March 1940, two police inspectors traveled to Baghdad with Husseini's personal property as a sort of moving service. Their travel expense report totaled 23,350 piastres for the 17 tins of automobile gasoline hauled along, plus food and lodging for two days in Baghdad, plus an additional 100 piastres for the gasoline funnel they used to refill their vehicle from time to time.[57]

The Mufti began activating his campaign. Husseini wrote passionately to the powerful All-India Moslem League in Bombay, seeking support for Palestine. He hoped to open yet another political front against Britain, this time in India. The Mufti also organized the Arab National Party to agitate for a Palestine without Jews. The new group included the foursome of the Golden Square, as well as leading government official Rashid Ali. Golden Square officers were only too eager to join. Their bitterness with Britain was aggravated because London, short of equipment and fearing the very agitation that was then under way, had refused to sell the Iraqi military any quantity of arms. Months earlier, when the Iraq military had requested new equipment, London replied it could only spare only four small howitzers and a few radio sets.

Under the close hand of the Mufti, this new Arab National Party met in secret, its members used assumed names, and they swore allegiance on the Koran. At the same time, many in Iraq's new power structure were doctrinaire swastika-wearing Arab Nazis.[58]

As his first major plan of upheaval, the Mufti tried to spark a Palestine-style violent outbreak against Britons in Iraq. Everywhere, he and his follow-ers sowed rumors about such an uprising in the spring or summer of 1940. Nuri's government called for postal censorship. Plainclothes security police began arresting troublemakers in cafés. But the population grew more restive. Soon, with pressure mounting, Nuri resigned as prime minister, to be replaced by Rashid Ali, the Mufti's comrade in the fight against Zionism. Nuri stayed on as foreign minister, but the power had suddenly shifted demonstratively toward the Mufti and his cohorts in the Golden Square.[59]

Throughout May 1940, some local newspapers tried to calm the popu-lace. One typical story in *Al Istiqlal*, on May 22, excoriated a "gang of the biased and wicked ... engaged in the promotion of false rumors."[60]

Newly installed Prime Minister Rashid Ali informed British representa-tive C. J. Edmonds in Baghdad that the entire Anglo-Iraqi relationship was now completely tied to the events in Palestine. If London solved the Jewish question in Palestine, England would not need to divert resources from the global war to defend Iraq and its oil fields against a German invasion. The men debated Palestine back and forth, but it was as though they were not speaking the same language. Edmonds used political syllogisms and diplomatic ver-biage. Rashid Ali insisted that no matter what rationales were invoked, every-thing in Iraq now was being driven by events in Palestine.[61]

Edmonds wrote that Rashid Ali then craftily declared, "This country would easily raise 100,000 men to take its part in the common defense. But as things were, he [Rashid Ali] could not be sure that the Iraq Army would [even] march to its appointed positions." In fact, if the army did deploy, said Rashid Ali, no one could guarantee they would not fall apart due to "internal trouble." Edmonds reported that Rashid Ali was explicit: "The situation could only be rendered sound by the solution of the Palestinian problem."[62] In others words, the Iraqis would let the Germans walk in unopposed and seize the oil wells unless Zionism was promptly thwarted in Palestine.

Startled, Edmonds retorted that he was profoundly shocked "that the Iraqi Army might not cooperate in the defense of their own country." Rashid Ali replied vaguely, but returned the discussion to negotiations with the Palestin-ians to undo the white paper. When the meeting ended, Rashid Ali sharply reminded Edmonds, "that the time was the present, and Baghdad the place; the Palestinian leaders were here and the Iraqi government, the honest broker, was willing and anxious."[63]

Soon, British diplomats in Iraq were sending home report after report warning that the Mufti was orchestrating a range of anti-British plots in Iraq, and the local situation was rapidly deteriorating. Typical was one diplomatic summary that belittled the new Iraqi "instinct to indulge in blackmail over Palestine." In July 1940, Rashid Ali's justice minister met secretly in Turkey with the Reich ambassador, Franz von Papen. The Mufti then sent his own secretary to talk to German foreign minister Joachim von Ribbentrop in Berlin. The Mufti's condition for an Arab rebellion in Iraq: a German declaration against the Zionist homeland and in favor of a pan-Arab state.[64]

The outlines of the demanded declaration were embodied in the Mufti's personal eight-point draft. It covered all the Islamic nations of the Arab realm: Syria, Lebanon, Kuwait, Egypt, Saudi Arabia, Sudan, Dubai, and Oman. All these countries were to be liberated from British protectorates, reservations, and mandates. Key to the Mufti's draft declaration was point 7: "Germany and Italy recognize the illegality of the 'Jewish Home in Palestine.' They accord to Palestine and other Arab countries the right to resolve the problem of the Jewish elements in Palestine and other Arab countries in accordance with the interests of the Arabs, and by the same method that the question is now being settled in the Axis countries."[65]

To Nazi eyes, the phrase was perfect: "resolve the problem of the Jewish elements in Palestine and other Arab countries ... by the same method that the question is now being settled in the Axis countries." How was the Jewish problem being settled in the Axis countries of Greater Germany, Hungary, Romania, occupied Poland, and elsewhere? Identification, expulsion from the economy, confiscation of assets, enforced starvation, ghettoization, concentration in camps, and mass murder. The Mufti's offer was to extend Hitler's merciless international campaign of Jewish destruction into the Middle East.

The Mufti was not the only extremist courting the Third Reich. Other opportunist-minded Arabs beckoned as well, including Rashid Ali. Each saw Berlin replacing London as the stage manager for nationalist aspirations in Palestine and across the Arab crescent. Just as 15 years earlier, the promises and enticements only escalated as the oil and strategic location of Iraq became the prize. The new Arab-Nazi alliance was not the efforts of a single mufti; it was a mass movement of tens of thousands ordinary Arabs as the angry tip of an immensely popular sentiment within the Arab world.

The converse of the Lawrence of Arabia drama was now unfolding. The Arabs would once again rise up for nationalism, but this time for German sponsors, not the British. In fact, Fritz Grobba, the central Nazi figure in rallying the Arab revolt, was openly nicknamed the "German Lawrence." Grobba was actually born Arthur Borg. For affectation, he took his name, A. Borg, reversed the letters to read "groba" and added a second B for style to create

"Grobba." His mysterious exploits and evolving alliances were covered in the newspapers. One *New York Times* article, headlined "'German Lawrence' Stirs Revolt," carried his photograph with the caption: "Dr. Fritz Grobba, whose exploits in the Arab world rival those of Britain's famous Lawrence."[66]

The *New York Times* article opened: "Behind the scenes of the war in Iraq, a German agent called Dr. Grobba has been playing an active part. Occasionally, his name has been mentioned in the dispatches, but it has never been disclosed who this man is, what he has done in the past, and what he is still doing. Officially, Dr. Grobba is the German envoy at the court of Ibn Saud, the ruler of Saudi Arabia. Previously, he was for many years German envoy to Iran. But behind this official mission something altogether different is concealed. In informed circles, in Berlin, London, Cairo, Baghdad and Mecca, this man is called 'the German Lawrence.' It is true that he does not bear the slightest outward resemblance to his famous British predecessor of the [first] World War ... but so far as success is concerned, Grobba is not far behind the prototype."[67]

Nonetheless, *der Führer* still viewed Arab nationalism as a mere means to an end, as a stepping-stone to the Nazi conquest and domination of the entire Middle East. Grobba talked to Hitler about Iraq, and recalled, "When the deep split [rivalry] emerged in Berlin between Haj Amin [Husseini] and Rashid Ali, I found myself facing a serious dilemma. Both sought from Hitler recognition as leader of the Arab world, and both put pressure on me to influence the Fuhrer in this respect. Although Rashid Ali was the most prominent Arab politician who joined us against the democracies, we were aware that Haj Amin [Husseini] enjoyed tremendous prestige in the Arab and Muslim world, as being fearless in the revolt against the British. When I tried to raise the issue of recognition in my talks with Hitler, *der Führer* put me off, arguing that the time had not yet come to install an Arab leader, and that the subject would be discussed when we conquered the Arab region."[68]

The Arabs carried no illusions about their status in Western eyes. Europe cared about them only as the people who walked the ground above the oil deposits. Beginning in July, the Iraqi catchphrase of the day became "absolute neutrality," which was in fact an open codeword for disavowal of the Anglo-Iraq Treaty of Alliance, which called for mutual military assistance in times of war. But more than that, the term "absolute neutrality" advertised an Arab allegiance purchasable by either side—British or Nazi—for satisfaction of national desires.[69] Iraqis, and indeed Arabs everywhere, called this moment a "golden opportunity."

Al Istiqlal, July 4, 1940: "Iraq's attitude of neutrality only safeguards her future and her integrity and the maintenance of her sovereignty." *Al Nasr*, August 6, 1940: "[Germany and Britain] each proclaim itself to be the sole champion of the Arabs and Arab ideals. But we may wonderingly ask whether any nation has ever served any cause but its own interests." *Al Yaum*, August 8, 1940: "The imperialistic powers are trying to make Iraq take sides, but such poisonous propaganda cannot grow in the soil of Iraq." *Al Istiqlal*, August 13, 1940: "Two peoples are fighting for world domination, each pretending to be fighting for the cause of civilization and the deliverance of small nations." *Basra Al Sijil*, September 2, 1940: "The real intentions of both sides are well-known by weak peoples, who realize that the present struggle is inspired by greed and the desire to subjugate peoples and rob them of their wealth."[70]

Often quoted by worried British officials was *Al Istiqlal*'s August 12, 1940 editorial: "The reason for this insistence [absolute neutrality] lies in the desire on the one hand to avoid the danger of war, and on the other to exploit all opportunities which occur." The Mufti's forces in Iraq constantly preached solidarity. *Al Rai al Am*, September 28, 1940: "The Arabs cannot turn this golden opportunity to profit, nor remove the yoke of imperialism, unless they organize themselves."[71]

By early October 1940, reports from Baghdad triggered serious alarms in Whitehall. Telegraph service between Iraq and Germany had been restored. Prime Minister Rashid Ali was openly cultivating diplomatic support from the Reich. Just a few months earlier, London had believed it could safely transport Indian regiments north through Iraq, per its treaty rights, to confront an expected Nazi advance in Syria or to secure the oil fields. This was now in doubt. Their conclusions: "A) Active hostility on the part of the Iraqis might make it impossible to use the overland route for the passage of troops from Basra to Haifa or for the maintenance of our forces in the Middle East; B) Difficulties might be expected in the use of the Empire air route from Egypt to India, the Far East and Australia, which passes through Iraq; C) The Iraqis might cut off at [the] source the oil which was piped across the desert to Haifa. The hostility of Iraq might influence Iran, and so reduce the reliance to be placed on [the] Abadan [refinery] as a source of oil; D) If Iraq and Iran become subservient to the Axis powers, our enemies would be at the gates of India."[72]

Many in Whitehall now decided to either kidnap the Mufti and deport him to Cyprus or simply kill him—they weren't sure which. As for Rashid Ali, they wanted him "eliminated" as well. In a November 1, 1940, War Office review of the German push through the Balkans and into Syria, with the help of thousands of Muslim and Arab fighters, military planners wrote under Iraq "A) Removal of present Iraqi Prime Minister: *We agree.* B) The elimination of the Mufti: *We do not agree that the assassination of the Mufti is unlikely to have ill effects. We agree, however, that it is essential to put an end to his current activities.*" Fully appreciating that thinly-stretched British forces could not be diverted to Iraq, other planners wondered if the Iraqis could be bought off as in prior crises. "C) Financial and Economic Aid: *Since we are unable to spare troops for Iraq, or such war materiel as anti-aircraft guns, practically the only inducement for the Iraqis to behave in accordance with our wishes lies in the financial and economic sphere.*" But militant Iraqis weren't interested in stopping Nazism—just in furthering Palestine and Arab nationalism.[73]

Nuri, now waiting in the wings as foreign minister, agreed that drastic action was needed, and "evolved scheme after scheme for his [Rashid Ali's] elimination," as one British diplomat wrote, "but none progressed beyond its initial stages." In the end, London decided to ask the regent to exercise the powers of the King and simply fire Rashid Ali.[74]

Meanwhile, the Arab link to the Axis was growing closer. On January 20, 1941, the Mufti sent a long appeal to Adolf Hitler, using all the well-known anti-Semitic and trigger phrases of Nazi hate doctrine. "Your Excellence: England, that bitter and cunning enemy to the true freedom of the Arab nation, has never ceased to forge fetters to enslave and subjugate the Arab people, either in the name of a deceitful League of Nations, or by the expression of perfidious and hypocritical humanitarian feelings but with the actual aim of effecting her imperialist machinations, which are camouflaged by principles of democracy and of deceitful internationalism." The Mufti detailed the Arab plight: "By geographical coincidence, the Arab people find themselves at the center of a land and sea crossroads which, according to the English, is the major intersection of the English Empire's 'transport lines'… the 'holy' British transport lines!"[75]

The Mufti condemned Arab monarchs for giving England oil pipelines. "King Faisal the First," he wrote, "agreed to a *modus vivendi*, and signed a treaty with England, and, despite the opposition of the majority of the Iraqi people, sold the relative independence of Iraq in return for oil concessions." Husseini's missive reviewed decades of international transgressions by the French in Syria and British in Palestine and Iraq, punctuating it with the resonant words, "This was done with the agreement of the Jews."[76]

Turning to Palestine, the Mufti made his point: "His Excellence is well aware of the problem faced by this country," he wrote, "which has also suffered from the deceitful actions of the English. They attempted to place an additional obstacle before the unity and independence of the Arab states by abandoning it to world Jewry, this dangerous enemy whose secret weapons— finance, corruption and intrigue—were aligned with British daggers … The Palestinian problem united all of the Arab states in a mutual hatred of the English and Jews. If mutual hatred is a prerequisite for national unity, it can be said that the problem of Palestine hastened this unity."[77]

Then came the Mufti's casbah-like offer of allegiance: "Freed from certain material impediments, the Arab peoples will be ready to serve the common enemy his just deserts, and to take their place enthusiastically alongside the Axis in order to fulfill their part in bringing about the well-deserved defeat of the Anglo-Jewish coalition ... Allow me to add that the Arabs are willing to put all their weight behind the campaign, and to shed their blood in the holy war for their national rights and aspirations—on condition that certain interests of a moral and material order are assured." Husseini specifically focused on the Arab ability to disrupt "the transport lines of the [British] Empire and sever the contact between India and the Mediterranean region ... through the Persian Gulf, and thus end the exploitation of the flow of oil for the benefit of England.[78]

"I close with wishes for long life and happiness for His Excellence and for a shining victory and prosperity for the great German people and for the Axis in the near future."[79]

In March 1941, Hitler replied through State Secretary Ernst von Weizacker. "Der Führer received your letter dated January 20," Weizacker's response began. "He took great interest in what you wrote him about the national struggle of the Arabs. He was pleased with the friendly words addressed to him in the name of Arab Nationalism." Now Hitler, through Weizacker, conveyed the words the Arabs wanted to hear. "Germany has never occupied any Arab countries and has no ambitions whatsoever in Arab lands. Our view is that Arabs, who possess an ancient culture and have proved their administrative, judiciary, and military maturity, are capable of self-government. Germany recognizes the full independence of the Arab countries, or where this has not yet been attained, their right to it.[80]

"The Germans and the Arabs have common enemies in England and the Jews," the letter continued, "and are united in the fight against them. Germany, traditionally friendly to the Arabs ... is ready to cooperate with you and to give you all possible military and financial help required by your preparations to fight against the British for the realization of your people's aspirations. In order to enable the Arabs to begin the necessary preparations for their future war against the British, Germany is prepared to deliver to you immediately military material, if the means for transporting this material can be found." He added, "I request you keep the contents of this communication secret."[81]

Hitler's reply, however, fell short of the unequivocal statement of national recognition the Mufti was seeking, the type der Führer had extended to other ethnic groups in Europe to cement their support.

Although the language was still evolving, the Arab-Nazi axis was moving ahead. The Mufti's intrigues were not unknown to London intelligence. Whitehall most feared that Vichy Syria would allow the Germans to occupy and invade the Iraq oil fields as part of a complete push past Russia and on to the east. Britain moved quickly now. London insisted that the regent dismiss Prime Minister Rashid Ali, and in doing so stymie the Golden Square, the Mufti and the Nazi threat. The compliant regent was prepared to arrest Rashid Ali and his accomplices, but the Golden Square learned of his plans. On April 1, 1941, troops loyal to the Golden Square surrounded the palace, preparing to arrest him. The nervous Regent donned a disguise, quietly slipped out to his aunt's house, and then stealthily made his way in a motorboat down the Tigris to Basra, where he rendezvoused with a British gunboat. From Basra, the gunboat steamed to safety outside of Iraq.[82]

On April 3, 1941, with the Regent gone, the Golden Square launched yet another coup d'etat, forming a new government under Rashid Ali and appointing trusted cronies to all the key positions, including the regency. Almost simultaneously, neighboring Syria, the anticipated gateway for the Nazi invasion, exploded with Reich propaganda, supported by Gestapo agents and specially trained Arab Nazis. The Arab Club, the National Youth Organization, and the Group of National Action all went into action. Their members all spoke fluent German. They distributed additional copies of the Arabic version of the Nazi Party's rabid newspaper, *Völkischer Beobachter*, and ensured that "the whole country is a hotbed of Nazi propaganda," as the *New York Times* reported. Soon posters were popping up in the market. One featured a large swastika surrounded by the words "In Heaven, Allah is thy ruler. On Earth, Adolf Hitler will rule us."[83]

An anxious War Office sent a general to Baghdad to analyze the British mission's defensive position. If the Iraqis moved against British interests, then diplomats, staff, and civilians in the oil industry across the country, along with their wives and children, would need evacuation from Baghdad and military protection. Code words were established: *sapphire* or *emerald* meant evacuate immediately to the British base at Habbaniya by any means possible. But the small contingent of British soldiers at Habbaniya would be hopelessly outnumbered. Sending additional weapons would not help, they concluded. The situation was dire; there were no armaments to spare. Nonetheless, 25 rifles and a few other small arms were dispatched.[84]

When calls for relief troops circulated, military commanders in the region confessed they were unable to assist. The commanding general cabled, "My forces are stretched to limit everywhere and I simply cannot afford to risk part of forces … at Basra."[85] With the British outmanned, with German troops preparing to enter via Vichy Syria to occupy the oil fields, and with the Iraqis willing to facilitate the Nazis, there seemed to be only one option remaining.

Destroy the oil. Destroy it all.

*   *   *   *

No one was quite sure how to destroy an oil field. But the contingency had been considered as much as a year earlier. Some experts thought the fields could simply be dynamited. But they quickly concluded that an explosion would only bring more oil to the surface. Perhaps the field could be set ablaze, the fire might burn for years, they thought. But a new drill site into the vast oil layer of Kirkuk would reestablish the supply within months, even as another well burned. The wells could be plugged, but again, new borings would remedy that.[86]

Then the infrastructure would have to be blown, that is, the storage tanks, pumping stations, pipelines, and refineries—everything from Kirkuk to Tripoli to Haifa. That was the only way to deny Iraq's oil to the Reich just as Barbarossa was about to launch.

A memo was circulated to a trusted manager of the Iraq Petroleum Company. "It is now advisable," the memo explained, "to consider what action the IPC should take in the way of preparations for demolition or putting plant[s] out of action, and/or prevent[ing] the possibility of supplies getting into enemy hands. It is suggested ... in the following order: 1) The destruction and elimination of stocks of Crude Oil from Tripoli [Lebanon]. These stocks of crude oil today are approximately 113,300 tons. It is suggested that arrangements should now be made for the disposal of these stocks: by burning, or by opening the lines to allow the oil to discharge into the sea ... Consideration should be given to the immobilization of the field as a whole ... The IPC Management should now ... draw up a line of attack ... if, and when, it is necessary ... In the meantime, the IPC should give consideration to immediate action in the way of plugging up wells which are not required ... to keep Haifa Refinery going on a one million tons per annum basis; that is, only those wells that are in production should be left open and all others plugged off and even disconnected from the pipeline system. [In addition] stocks of crude oil at K1 and K3 [pumping facilities] should now be reduced to an absolute minimum."[87]

Some in the Ministry of Economic Warfare in London began to worry about just how many oil executives would be privy to the secret plans. On June 26, 1940, one planner wrote, "To this oil committee go quite a large number of persons, several of whom are in almost continual touch with representatives of the oil companies, many of which are international in character, and some of which must at the present time have in mind the future interest of their companies."[88]

By mid-July 1940, the War Cabinet concluded that pipelines running through Syria to Tripoli, Lebanon must be blown as well. "If the German war effort were to be turned eastwards," they decided, "it would be of the highest importance that the northern branch of the Iraq Pipeline should not remain intact. Even if the Kirkuk Oilfield in Iraq were put out of action, it would only be a few months before it could be brought back to production; only a relatively short part of the northern line runs through Iraq and this could be repaired by the time the field was able to produce. Destruction of the pumping stations and pipeline throughout Syria could cause a much greater delay before transport could be resumed."[89]

By November 1940, as the situation worsened, the generals wanted the demolition sequence solidified. "Plans already in preparation for the destruction of the Iraqi oil wells and the pipelines in Iraq, Syria and Palestine should be perfected," instructed one memo, "and brought to a state in which they could be operated without interference on a very short notice." The memo added, "It is important to keep these plans secret from the Iraqi Government."[90]

IPC general manager J. Skliros corrected the planners. During a December 18, 1940 conference on the question, Skliros explained that destroying Iraqi oil facilities would not be easy. In Palestine and Trans-Jordan, he said, where British authorities reigned, the facilities could be junked at will, with troops overseeing the explosives. But in Iraq, Britain maintained a mere shadow military presence. "The Iraqi government probably suspected that such schemes were in mind," cautioned Skliros, "and, if occasion to put them into practice rose, the Iraqi Government would probably take measures to prevent the entry of British Military personnel into Iraq for the purpose, and the movements of Company personnel would probably be subject to surveillance."[91]

In the first days of April 1941, just after the Golden Square coup forced the regent to flee and then installed a tougher Rashid Ali government, Iraqi police units took up positions at Kirkuk and various pumping stations, as expected. Moreover, oil company personnel were now under suspicion and scrutiny.[92]

On April 18, 1941, Britain finally found a small contingent of troops to assist. They were suddenly airlifted and sealifted into Basra, ostensibly to transit through the country pursuant to treaty rights, but, in fact, were to protect the oil fields and British civilians. As the naval ships approached, senior Iraqi officials were undecided whether they should challenge the landing or honor the treaty. Formal permission was granted just two hours before the seaborne troops actually arrived. The men were permitted to proceed to the British base at Habbaniya. But in view of the rapidly deteriorating position, more men would need to be mustered from Britain's overstretched forces.[93]

Ten days later, on April 28, 1941, the British Embassy advised the Iraqis that three more ships would be landing, this time carrying 2,000 men, only 400 of whom were actual combat troops. Within a few hours, the Golden Square issued a swift reply: They could not enter. The British, however, were determined, especially since an uprising against British civilians was rumored to erupt within a few days.[94]

The next day, April 29, 1941, evacuation orders were broadcast by the embassy. British women and children from all over Iraq were bused to the large base at Habbaniya. On April 30, 1941, Iraqi officials confronted the IPC's oil fields manager, demanding "a written guarantee that no wells or installations would be sabotaged." The statement was signed, and the installations were promptly taken over by Iraqi troops for good measure. In the meantime, a column of Iraqi troops was ordered to proceed to the British base.[95]

The Habbaniya base, located almost midway between Fallujah and Ramadi, sprawled across an eight-mile square. Within its cantonment, it housed several thousand troops, 8,000 civilians, churches, shops, and barracks. Habbaniya was extremely habitable, but quite poorly defended. One British commander fondly remarked, "It is notorious that when the Germans occupy a new station, their first task is to build defenses around it, whereas the British in similar circumstances lay out cricket and football fields." Out front, a quaint crossroads sign sported arrows with two air distances: London 3,287 miles to the west, Baghdad 55 miles to the east. The base, mainly the home of a military flying school, was hardly ready for combat.[96]

On April 30, 1941, an English-speaking Iraqi messenger delivered a demand to the base commandant that all British aircraft remain grounded and all troops remain confined to base. British commanders considered the note an "impertinent gesture." Planes were demonstratively sent aloft to photograph the enemy encampments. This revealed that Iraqis and several dozen howitzers were dug in just a half mile outside the perimeter and all across the high escarpments overlooking Habbaniya. Moreover, Golden Square forces had evacuated local tribesmen in surrounding hamlets to make way for a military action against the base. One British soldier who ventured out to collect mail was arrested.[97]

During the night of May 2, 1941, Iraqi advance troops penetrated to the perimeter. At 5 A.M., the British commander opened fire. Iraqi mortar shells began raining in on the base. The flight students scrambled to become instant combat pilots to strafe and bomb Iraqi positions.[98]

One student, with only a few hours flying experience, jumped into an Airspeed Oxford trainer to ride as navigator for a sortie over Ramadi. At 2,000 feet, ground fire hit the plane, killing the pilot with a shot to the heart. The young lad pulled the pilot off the controls and attempted to land on his own. After three or four approaches, the student was finally able to put down safely.[99]

The students flew as many as 9 or 10 sorties each, round the clock, hitting every encampment and concentration of Iraqi troops. When the Iraqis tried to bring up a column from Fallujah, it became bottlenecked three miles from a bridge at a narrow bend in the road. At that choke point, the lane squeezed between palm groves elevated above irrigation ditches on either side. Hence,

there was no possible way to turn around. British aircraft spotted the crawl-
ing line and attacked. First, they destroyed the lead vehicles, and then they
hammered them over and over again with strafing runs and dive-bombing.
Ammunition trucks exploded, a convoy of troops in an assortment of vehicles
caught fire, and a battery of mobile artillery and every other type of mechanized vehicle was turned into twisted, smoldering wreckage.[100]

The German high command acted. Its chief of air staff sent one of his top
aviators, Major Axel von Blomberg, along with two others, to survey available
landing strips so that the Luftwaffe could fly in and assist Rashid Ali. Blomberg flew in circuitously by way of Athens and Damascus, landing in Mosul
on May 11, 1941. There, he found two disused German Heinkel 111 bombers
from the Iraqi air force. The next morning Blomberg flew one of the Heinkels
to Baghdad to meet with Rashid Ali. Flying low, the clearly marked German
craft aroused celebratory fire from tribesmen. But several bullets pierced the
cockpit, killing Blomberg. He was buried the next day, with Rashid Ali offering special condolences at the funeral.[101]

Now, the Germans launched missions in earnest. A heavy-fighter unit
and a bomber unit dispatched 16 more Heinkels and 10 Messerschmitt heavy
fighters to aid in the attack on Habbaniya. Meanwhile, some two dozen German mechanics and airmen filtered into the country, along with Grobba and
other Reich diplomats. The Luftwaffe began running strafing and bombing
missions of their own against Habbaniya, as well as commando formations
crossing the desert to aide the besieged camp. As feared, the Germans pri-
marily used the massive Rayak airbase in Vichy Syria. In addition, several
trainloads of French arms were packed and dispatched to Mosul, where the
Germans set up their local airbase.[102]

With Germans running bombing missions and Habbaniya under continu-
ous attack, the British turned off the oil spigot at Basra. The commander-in-
chief in India sent a coded telegram to the War Office: "Iraqi troops have also
occupied pumping station K1 and K2. Iraqi police have arrested engineer in
charge of plant at H3." The telegram added. "All refineries and oil installations are in Iraqi hands and demolition now [only] possible by air action."[103]

But the students and instructors at Habbaniya were heroically flying day
and night against the small Iraqi air force. Most enemy craft were destroyed
on the ground, sometimes a dozen at a time. Churchill had already sent a fore-
boding cable to U.S. president Franklin D. Roosevelt, stating that if the Mideast fell to the Germans, victory against the Nazis would be a "hard, long and
bleak proposition." [104] All understood that if Germany would secure Iraq's oil,
she might proceed all the way to the East.

By May 15, 1941, urgent messages burned the telegraph wires as British
commanders in the area informed London that land operations were now out

of the question. One typical note declared: "In view changed situation Iraq, consider it will be impossible to destroy Kirkuk wells at short notice."[105]

Besieged and out of options, the British called in the Irgun from Palestine. The Irgun was an extremist Jewish defense organization in Palestine formed to defend kibbutzim and villages and retaliate for the constant Arab attacks. Irgun commander David Raziel, at that moment, was in a British prison in Palestine. Raziel was approached by British intelligence and asked if he would undertake a dangerous mission to destroy the oil refineries in Iraq, thereby denying the fuel to the Germans. The answer was yes, on one condition: Raziel wanted to kidnap the Mufti of Jerusalem and bring him back. Agreed.[106]

The next morning, May 17, 1941, Raziel and three comrades, along with a British officer, quietly entered the Tel Nof air base which was located south of Tel Aviv. There they climbed into an RAF plane, which flew them to Habbaniya. While in flight, however, the British high command in London decided that the destruction of Iraq's refineries should be delayed until the very last moment in the hope it would not be necessary. Rebuilding the pipelines would take years and place an enormous strain on British fuel needs for the rest of the war. Perhaps the Germans could be stopped after all. When Raziel landed in Iraq, he was given new orders: Undertake an intelligence mission preparatory to a British sweep into Fullajah as part of the final drive to retake Baghdad from Rashid Ali and the Golden Square.[107]

As Raziel was landing, a new Zionist military organization was being formed, again with the consent of the British. They would be known as the *Palmach*, or strike forces. Even before the units were properly assembled, their first mission would be an elite commando raid, made up of 23 volunteers and commanded by Zvi Spectre. British Major Anthony Palmer accompanied them. Their objective: Blow up the refineries in Tripoli that were providing fuel to the German airplanes bombing Iraq. Very late on the evening of May 18, 1941, a small British vessel, the *Sea Lion*, equipped with three oar-driven landing boats, departed Haifa for Vichy Lebanon. By this time the British were bombing Tripoli, which placed Vichy defense forces around the Tripoli refinery on high alert. In the hours to come, the *Sea Lion* and all its men disappeared. *Palmach* commanders believed they were killed while approaching the refinery.[108]

Meanwhile back in Iraq, on May 17, 1941, Raziel, his three comrades, along with a British officer, set out by car from the Habbaniya base toward Fallujah. At the first river, they found a boat, only big enough for two. Raziel ordered his comrades to proceed, while he went back to the car with his fellow Irgunist and the British officer. Just then, from nowhere, a plane—no one knows if it is British or German—dived from on high, dropping a bomb. The car was destroyed and Raziel with it.[109]

That same day, RAF commanders notified the Air Ministry that the situation was becoming more precarious each day. Once German airpower had advanced from Syria into Iraq, it would constitute a major threat to the refinery at Abadan and to the Suez Canal. By May 22, 1941, the RAF cabled back to London, "I submit that the time has come for taking action against the oil refinery at Alwand (about 100 miles northeast of Baghdad)" as well as four pumping stations. "Thus, we remove his [the enemy's] main attraction in that part of the world. The cable pleaded with the high command to remember that "the history of [such] demolitions is a history of 'too late.'"[110]

A few days later, May 25, 1941, Hitler issued Order 30, redoubling support for Iraq. "The Arabian Freedom Movement in the Middle East," he wrote, "is our natural ally against England. In this connection special importance is attached to the liberation of Iraq. It strengthens beyond the Iraq borders the forces in the Middle East hostile to England, disturbs English communications, and ties down English troops as well as English shipping space, at the cost of other theaters of war. I have therefore decided to move forward in the Middle East by support of Iraq. Whether and how the English position between the Mediterranean and the Persian Gulf—in connection with an offensive against the Suez Canal—is to be later finally solved, is not up for decision until after Barbarossa."[111]

The Admiralty in London now gave the final order to destroy the refineries and pumping stations in Iraq at will. "If Germans occupy Iraq and Syria," the message read, "they cannot profit by the oil resources there for at least some time." But suddenly, the forces at Habbaniya were gaining the upper hand. Persistent bombing, Arabs abandoning their positions and equipment en masse to disappear into the populace, plus the sheer exhaustion of supplies had delivered what seemed like a victory to British forces. On May 30, 1941, the British-organized Arab Legion, led by legendary Major Henry Glubb of Britain, pushed past fatigued ground resistance and a steady barrage of German air attacks. Major Glubb reached Baghdad at about 4:00 A.M. to meet two Iraqi truce officers waving a white flag hanging from a pole. By now, Rashid Ali, the Golden Square, and Grobba had fled to Iran. The mayor of Baghdad was the only one left to come out and sign the cease-fire document.[112]

After the main players fled, the coup and the threat were over, at least for now. The regent returned to Iraq. Reich bomber crews flew from Mosul back to Germany. Only two of the Heinkels had escaped destruction. Grobba and his staff departed Mosul by car.[113]

London rushed new superseding instructions about destroying the oil installations. "Scheme for the denial of the Iraq oil to the enemy ... is quite clearly out of date. If we regain control in Iraq, one of our first steps must be to secure the key points on the oil system with a view to their demolition [only] if we are compelled to withdraw subsequently." The instruction added, "Dangerous as it is to delay, I think we should not take immediate action against the Haifa pipe lines or the installations which feed it until the success or failure of 'Exporter' becomes apparent." However, the note continued, local commanders must be prepared "to ensure the destruction of the Iraq-Haifa pipeline system in the event of the failure of 'Exporter.'"[114]

The threat to Iraqi oil was not over. The Germans were still threatening a major new advance into Vichy Syria and Lebanon. Operation Exporter, conceived almost overnight, was the only Allied hope of denying the Reich an open door in Vichy Syria. An Australian strike force, augmented by Free French Forces, assembled to launch a sneak attack.[115]

Again, the British called upon the *Palmach*, this time to cross into Syria and pave the way for Exporter. *Palmach* commanders Moshe Dayan and Yitzhak Rabin were among the men who would lead the commando missions. Dayan assembled a force of 30. The British required all of them to know Syrian territory intimately and speak perfect Arabic so they could enter disguised as Arabs. Dayan's commandos lied. None of them spoke Arabic. They didn't even have a map of Syria. But Dayan did hire a trusted Arabic guide. On the night of June 6, 1941, the *Palmach* commandos set off with a team of Australians to disrupt telegraph and telephone communications, eliminate key potential installations, and secure bridges and other strategic points. By preemptively capturing or neutralizing resistance at the major crossing points, Exporter forces could race through Vichy Syria and Lebanon to secure the oil installations and airfields.[116]

Dayan's group was operating successfully at the Litani River. Suddenly, on the morning of June 8, 1941, having secured most of their objectives, Dayan's group came under French heavy machine-gun fire. He picked up a pair of binoculars to scout out the firing positions. An incoming bullet hit the binoculars, driving steel and glass deep into Dayan's left eye. The eye could not be saved, and Dayan would later don the eyepatch that, for decades, identified the icon of defense for the Jewish people. Rabin, the youngest member of the squad, spent most of his time cutting phone lines atop telephone poles and did not sustain any injuries.[117] Both Rabin and Dayan went on to become commanders of the Jewish State's defense forces. Rabin would go on to become the state's prime minister.

The next day, the three-pronged Exporter assault was launched from Iraq, from Palestine, and from the sea to seize Vichy Syria and Lebanon, thereby denying Germany the operating base it needed to dominate the Middle East. A British reporter, embedded with the first troops punching in from Palestine, sent back an eyewitness dispatch. Using just paper and pencil, he wrote, "I crossed from Palestine into Syria just before dawn this morning with Australian troops and am now speeding northward with our forces along the white cliffs toward Lebanon. Our advance into the French-mandated territories began under cover of darkness. Long lines of transports filled with grinning Diggers [Australians] ... are now pushing forward at several points, accompanied by Bren gun carriers, guns and tanks. British troops, the Royal Air Force and the navy are cooperating. From dusk until midnight Sunday night our column had moved toward the frontier. While scouts crossed No-Man's Land, we waited under cover for the signal to advance ... French positions knew nothing."[118]

Within a matter of days, the Allied surprise attack, made up of Free French, Australian, and British forces, supported by *Palmach* scouts and commandos, overwhelmed tough Vichy forces in Syria and Lebanon.[119] The Allies became entrenched in Lebanon and Syria, stopping the Nazi advance in the Middle East. Hitler's Operation Barbarossa was launched against Russia on June 22, 1941, but without Iraqi petroleum.

All eyes now turned to the Anglo-Iranian Oil Company source in Iran. Like Iraq, Iran had become a hotbed of Nazi influence.

In 1939, when war broke out, the Shah Reza Pahlavi did what other Nazi-leaning British allies did. Tehran declared "neutrality." This, in essence, was a green light for Germany. Some 2,000 German advisors were swarming all over Iran's commercial, military, and governmental establishments. The Reich was diverting some 30 percent of all Iranian ore production. A terminal had been established at Semnan to transport 60 percent-pure iron ore, as well as high-quality nickel, copper, lead, and sulfur—all military necessities. By the time the war was in full swing, 103 of 109 Iranian locomotives were German or Austrian. Reich construction crews worked at a frantic pace on rail lines crisscrossing the vital routes of Iran. Those rail tracks were compatible only with the Reich railroad system.[120]

On June 22, 1941, some three weeks after the British regained control of Iraqi oil, Operation Barbarossa was launched. The Nazis invaded Russia. Now the military value of Iran's vital supply lines and oil was clear. The Mufti of Jerusalem, the Golden Square, and German Gestapo agents had all congregated and stayed active in Iran since fleeing neighboring Iraq weeks earlier. Allied leaders now feared the Iranian army would go the way of Iraq's and join the Axis outright, especially with the Mufti exerting his leadership. If the Iranian military ousted the tenuous Shah and joined hands with Germany, Hitler would have unlimited oil for his blitzing army, the very oil that the Axis had wanted all along to deny to Britain and Russia.[121]

After Germany's June 1941 Russian invasion, Churchill and Stalin demanded the Shah immediately expel those 2,000 Nazi advisors and administrators from Iranian territory. Every one of them was suspected of being a spy or a Wehrmacht advance man. A major wartime intelligence operation had been established in Tabriz and in areas near Baku to report on Russian industrial operations that could be taken over. The Nazi media openly suggested creating German colonies in Iran. The joint Allied demand for expulsion of its German advisors made on July 19, 1941, was ignored by Tehran.[122]

By August 16, 1941, Britain and Russia again jointly demanded that the Shah expel all German advisors. Hitler sent the Shah a note demanding he hold firm while the Reich army proceeded against southern Russia. Intelligence suggested that a Golden Square-style coup was scheduled to oust the Shah sometime between August 22 and August 28. The clock was now ticking down to a new Islamic alliance with the Reich. This one would deliver Reich forces across the Caucasus Mountains and place them on a direct path to Palestine.[123]

The Mufti, long part of the Nazi intelligence apparatus, saw the war coming and to avoid capture by the British, made plans to move from Tehran to Turkey. But with Husseini a wanted man, the Turks denied him a visa. He asked Saudi Arabia, but the British presence there was still too great, and it was unclear how he could travel there in view of wartime conditions. He turned to Afghanistan and nervously awaited some word.[124]

The British columns that had rescued Habbaniya were now combined with other forces and cobbled together with British Indian units into a special rapid strike force. The Russians also assembled a rapid-deployment phalanx. At dawn on August 25, 1941, rushing at top speed in hopes of preventing another Axis coup, British and Russian forces invaded Iran. Oil facilities at Abadan operated by Anglo-Iranian Oil Company were seized by British Indian forces. Soviet bombers and ground forces attacked from the north. The Iranian military instantly collapsed. Allied units grabbed the key facilities of the Trans-Iranian Railway. By September 17, 1941, the Russian and British armies met up in Tehran. The Shah was arrested and exiled to South Africa. Thousands of Germans, Italians, Hungarians, and agents of other Axis members were quickly rounded up by the British and expelled. The Shah's son, also named Reza, was installed on the Peacock Throne on his promise to cooperate with Britain and Russia.[125]

Mideast oil was kept secure for the Allies. Fuel, urgently needed by the Nazis, was denied to them. The oil installations of the Mideast were not destroyed, not in Iraq, not in Iran, not anywhere.

CHAPTER THIRTEEN

BRITISH
PETROLEUM

T he drums of war. The drums of oil. In Iraq and the Middle East, all the drums played together. The deafening tumult was heard worldwide throughout the post-World War II era.

Three themes—bitter resentment over foreign interference, anti-Zionism, and Arab nationalism—fused into a rage against the West that pulsed through the last half of Iraq's turbulent twentieth century. Those agitated decades in Iraq were punctuated by a cascade of coups, sometimes dressed up as revolutions, sometimes encased within a so-called parliamentary process. In Iraq's thin political lexicon, the words *coup* and *revolution* often functioned as synonyms. Competing with the coups were insurrections from the north and south, putsches within putsches, religious strife between Shi'as and Sunnis and a permanently seething population that never drank from the fountain of the nation's unlimited potential.

Yet throughout those decades of upheaval, the world continued to focus its political and military attention on Iraq. Why? The world did not crave the sand of Iraq. It was the substance beneath the sand. It was never about the people, it was never about their quests and aspirations. It was always about the oil.

*   *   *   *

As far back as the 1930s, Iraq's incessant political drumbeat had driven the Redline consortium of the Iraq Petroleum Company to seek new dunes to exploit. Gulbenkian's red line, circumscribing the Arabian Peninsula and the bulk of the Ottoman Empire, offered plenty of other opportunities. First, the IPC turned to the newly sovereign Saudi Arabia, but its traditional commercial formulae of pittance royalties quickly became unacceptable to the savvy Saudi mind. The Saudis demanded remittances in gold, rather than any printed paper equivalent, and required annual payments whether oil was struck or not. Thus, the concessionaire had ample incentive to quickly drill, pump, and ship, thereby justifying payments. Moreover, the Saudis refused to be pawns for any company involved in Iraq. They understood that if included in the portfolio of the Iraqi Petroleum Company, the Saudi oil concession could be used as a strategic counterweight to Iraqi national instability. Instead, King ibn Saud turned to an American firm, Socal—Standard Oil of California—which met ibn Saud's terms and, in July 1933, secured the bountiful, strictly American concession with liberal Saudi participation. Texaco later joined Socal and its Saudi partners, and the combined venture became known as Aramco (Arabian American Oil Company).[1]

The Redline group fared better with the rest of the Gulf. The IPC signed lucrative concessions with a palette of British protectorates and client states. These included Oman, Qatar, Abu Dhabi, and a series of other sparsely populated Bedouin emirates. The smaller sheikhdoms were lumped together into "the Trucial Coast States," and later, the United Arab Emirates. In addition, the Iraq Petroleum Company secured exploratory concessions in mandatory Palestine, Syria, and Lebanon. These IPC concessions resembled the company's traditional royalty-based bargains, albeit more generous than the ones it had negotiated decades earlier in Iraq and Iran.[2] Hence, with the major exception of Saudi Arabia, the Iraq Petroleum Company fulfilled the dream of Gulbenkian's thick red line, creating a fabulous oil empire within its confines.

Ironically, the red line's demonstrative detour around Kuwait was a fateful cartographic boon for the United States. It opened the door for a member of the Redline group's American contingent to seek concessions both in Kuwait and in neighboring Bahrain. America's Gulf Oil, working with an Anglo-Persian-dominated group, secured those concessions in the 1930s, although it required extensive negotiations with the British to waive the protections of the nineteenth-century "nationality clauses," which granted British citizens exclusive rights in those protectorates. Once these were waived, however, American companies and citizens could participate.[3]

As the postwar world reassembled itself, Iraq remained at the apex of oil promise. But now there were many other countries with promises to keep and pipeline miles to sweep, up and down the Arabian Peninsula, including

Kuwait next-door. These new sources of Mideast supply played a mighty role in Iraq's own oil quandary, since its next-door neighbors were able to capitalize on their petroleum while Iraq remained mired in frustrated output and self-inflicted economic woes.

From the corporate side, the postwar IPC was also in disarray. After World War II, a liberated France deeply resented its enemy status, as did Gulbenkian. Both Compagnie Française des Petroles and Gulbenkian resumed their full participation in IPC. But both demanded compensation for the oil allotments suspended during France's Nazi collaboration and occupation years. At the same time, Standard Oil of New Jersey acquired Standard Oil of California, which enjoyed the Saudi Arabian concession. That violated the Redline Agreement, which obligated its signatories to never compete within the encircled area. Standard, fresh from America's triumphant victory in Europe, decided that the Redline Agreement was no longer in force because of the enemy status assigned to CFP and Gulbenkian.[4]

It took several years of grueling negotiations, but the four oil groups and Gulbenkian eventually came to terms in a final signed document of post-war resolution.[5]

Even if the Redline partners briefly stopped feuding, however, it became increasingly difficult for the IPC and Britain, for that matter, to function in Iraq. Britain was more than reviled for its intervention against the pro-Hitler Rashid Ali coup and the Mufti in 1941 as well as its seeming sponsorship of Israel. In fact, in January 1948, just after London and Baghdad renegotiated their so-called Portsmouth Treaty of military alliance, which extended the 1930 pact another 20 years, Baghdad broke out into bloody street riots. That day 11 people were killed; in all 70 died before calm returned. To pacify their anger, the Regent denied that the agreement had actually been signed. During a funeral procession for slain protesting students, demonstrators demanded the government reclaim the British base at Habbaniya and cancel all foreign military rights. Placards urged the mob to "execute the Iraqi negotiators." Understandably, the premier who had negotiated the agreement in London fled the country on the earliest available aircraft.[6]

The antagonism only deepened in 1950 as a result of Iraq's severe economic dislocation. Iraq had expelled or pauperized virtually all its Jewish citizens and in the process subtracted their commercial vitality. After the State of Israel was born, the Kirkuk-Haifa oil pipeline was permanently destroyed. What's more, Iraq's massive military expenditures in the failed pan-Arab invasion of Palestine during Israel's War for Independence had all but wrecked Iraq's national treasury. The only way the country could keep functioning was with an advance on future IPC royalties—in other words, a multimillion-pound loan. This only further salted the wounded Iraqi sense of dependence on a foreign European nation and an export industry it despised. Then on December 30, 1950, shock waves rumbled through the Mideast oil industry after the American concessionaires agreed to a fifty-fifty split of profits with Saudi Arabia. Now the IPC's negotiations with each oil-rich realm acquired a tense new dimension.[7]

In Iran, an imperialist's nightmare was being acted out. During the prior half-century, Anglo-Iranian Oil Company, which also owned about a quarter of Iraq Petroleum, had established a prodigious presence in Iran. AIOC's complex at Abadan was a sight for Middle Eastern eyes. The British enclave boasted art deco office buildings and movie theaters, Olympic-size swimming pools with triple-decked diving boards, elaborate banquet halls, large schools, vast rows of neatly arranged housing for the company's mostly British workforce, and delightful bungalows for the corporation's managers. The company's medical system, with four hospitals and 35 clinics, was deemed "a general practitioner's dream" by a British Medical Association review. AIOC's operation in Iran, once the linchpin of Britain's naval oil supply, was worth billions. But now, all that was coming to an end in the face of Iran's national purge of foreign oil domination.[8]

Within days of the Saudi Arabian fifty-fifty agreement becoming known, Iran reacted. Quickly, Anglo-Iranian's problems became insurmountable. All the company's men could not negotiate or renegotiate their way back into a concession. Newly empowered Iranian strongman, Prime Minister Muhammad Mossadegh, who never stopped making new demands, now headed the Teheran government. Mossadegh was partially deaf and, therefore, spoke to company officials at a six-inch distance. He was not interested in any elaborate explanations of international law, commercial custom, or contractual rights and obligations. He just wanted to know how soon officials could vacate. Frantic, the company begged for the chance to arbitrate and promised a £10 million advance and £3 million per month payment even as arbitration progressed. The more AIOC offered in hopes of delaying the inevitable, the more Mossadegh was convinced the intensely valuable concession must be nationalized.[9]

On June 10, 1951, Iranian officials arrived in force at the company's facility in Khurramshahr for an official takeover ceremony. First, they slaughtered a sheep. The Iranian flag was hoisted up the flagpole atop the building, and then the Navy played the national anthem. A thousand company employees stood, closely packed on every surface high and low, straining to hear the historic proclamation: The newly established state-run National Iranian Oil Company had now seized the facilities. AIOC's general manager, Eric Drake, suddenly found a soldier sporting a bayonet-fixed rifle in his office. Policemen guarded all the doors. Drake was informed that he was now an employee of

National Iranian Oil Company. The new supervisors demanded he turn over organizational charts and all recent financial statements. Drake refused without written authorization from London.[10]

Days later, back in Teheran, celebratory mobs stormed AIOC's office, pulled down its illuminated sign, and marched through the streets, carrying it above their heads as an exalted trophy. A few days later, Drake, who had refused to comply with Iranian orders, was accused of industrial sabotage. He fled to Basra before he could be arrested.[11]

Teheran laughed at efforts by the AIOC to submit the matter to the International Court of Justice at The Hague. Iranian officials declined to answer a summons, refused to recognize the concession clause calling for such adjudication, and rejected the court's supposed jurisdiction, since the takeover of AIOC was an exercise of national sovereignty. Shortly thereafter, all British personnel were evicted from their corporate premises. The families were evacuated from Abadan, where the "atmosphere had become one of siege." Everything was taken over by the state: refineries, pipelines, ships, repair shops, the company printing press, office furniture, paper, and pencils. With the whole world watching, Arab and European alike, Anglo-Iranian Oil Company, the company that had invented the Mideast's oil industry a half-century before as Anglo-Persian, was expelled from whence it began it all.[12]

Two years later, in mid-August 1953, Mossadegh was overthrown in Operation Ajax, a joint CIA-MI6 engineered coup. The Shah of Iran assumed the reins of leadership. By that time, Anglo-Iranian Oil Company's position as an international oil conglomerate, tethered to an oil supply it did not control, had become more and more untenable. In December 1954, two workmen in coveralls at Anglo-Iranian's curved and stately Britannic House headquarters in Finsbury Circus in London climbed up the two steps at the entrance. They carefully removed the large brass plaque next to the door. It read ANGLO-IRANIAN OIL COMPANY LIMITED. In its place, they installed a new plaque. It read: THE BRITISH PETROLEUM COMPANY LIMITED. Through patient negotiation with the Shah, a fifty-fifty arrangement was finalized. The company was again permitted access to its oil. Compensation for its nationalized assets was set at £25 million, payable in 10 installments, plus several hundred million dollars in oil and other emoluments. A British tanker resumed oil shipments out of Abadan on October 29, 1957.[13]

*   *   *   *

The summer of 1951 was not good for British oil in the Middle East. Just as the Saudis' fifty-fifty deal had sparked outrage in Iran, Iraq also demanded its rightful share of the petroleum industry—and more. In March 1951, deputies in Iraq's parliament lined up support for nationalizing its oil indus-try—pipe, tank, and barrel. More drastic action would have been taken, but, simply put, Iraq still needed the IPC. The country's oil infrastructure was still a generation behind most of its neighbors, a situation exacerbated by the Haifa pipeline closure. Diminished throughput meant depressed royalties. Baghdad called upon the IPC to lay more pipeline to the Mediterranean, circumventing Israel. The IPC complied, quickly finishing the northern branch of a 16-inch pipeline as well as additional links to Syria.[14]

The tension between the company and the government was palpable. Iraq needed the IPC for oil infrastructure improvements. At the same time, the company fully understood that every inch of pipeline laid and every pound sterling invested could be nationalized with the next breath.

During prolonged give-and-take sessions throughout 1951, the IPC finally agreed to fifty-fifty profit sharing; and, in January 1952, the company signed a new agreement with Iraq. The fifty-fifty arrangement was made retroactive to January 1, 1951. This incremental financial upgrade only bought time for the company. The firm had, however, built in its own safety valve. Those profits promised to Baghdad were pegged to the "posted price," that is, the officially posted world price for petroleum. Hence, the Iraqi treasury was once again at the mercy of international oil manipulations. The IPC, and its associated company, Anglo-Iranian, could create a glut or a scarcity at will by leaning or tugging on the supply and production throttle anywhere in the world. What's worse, that world oil supply now included the vast new supplies from nearby Gulf States.

In frustration, Baghdad watched Kuwait, its tiny neighbor to the south, quickly outpace the output of all three Iraqi provinces combined. Kuwait had only begun producing oil in 1946 with an 800,000-ton year. By 1948, that number had increased nearly sevenfold, to 6.3 million tons. In 1950, Iraq's shackled production totaled approximately 650 million tons, while Kuwait's had zoomed to nearly triple that number. Iran, now a nationalized independent that set its own production levels, was still a market giant. Bahrain and Qatar added significantly to the world supply. So, in 1950, while fractious Baghdad was forced to seek an IPC loan just to make ends meet, a smooth-running Saudi operation added approximately $2 million to the Saudi treasury each week.[15] Iraq's culture of resentment continued to roil, especially over the issue of the foreign oil exploitation.

In many ways, the anger rose from the bottom up. The masses remained largely destitute, significantly unemployed, and detached en masse from their nation's oil wealth, none of which even trickled past their doors. Instead, the riches seemed to be divided among an irrelevant government establishment, the wealthy elite, and European executives. It never took much to unleash the bitter alienation of the common man who had nothing to win and little to lose.

With the rise of Cold War communism in the 1950s, Britain remained as eager as ever to maintain a strong military presence in Iraq and thereby protect its oil fields. London summoned its best friends into yet another international military alliance, and this included calls to Nuri Said, who had once again assumed the role of Prime Minister. As concerned about the advance of communism as any capital in the West, in February 1955, Pakistan, Turkey, Iran, and Iraq joined Great Britain in creating a northern bulwark against the Soviet Union. The West saw the Baghdad Pact alliance as a reaction to the new Cold War military reality, but the citizens of Iraq saw the compact as yet another surrender to Britain and Western oil interests. All this came at a time when Nuri was disbanding political parties and trying to quell the further fires of pan-Arabism. The plotting began.[16]

This time, the ignition switch for Iraq's unrest did not reside in Baghdad, London, or Damascus; this time, it was Cairo. Egypt's president, ultranationalist Gamal Abdel Nasser, who had given postwar refuge to Rashid Ali and the Mufti, was now energizing the Arab world with his pan-Islamic, anti-Western bravado. Indeed, in February 1958, Syria and Egypt had already formed a two-state union, called the United Arab Republic (UAR). Even though the two countries were on different continents and separated by Palestine and Israel, they had merged into a single, albeit politically cumbersome, entity.[17]

To achieve his goals, Nasser courted Moscow as a counterweight to the capitalist West, just as the Mufti had courted Hitler as the alternative to the Allies. Hence, the West and some oil-rich Arab states saw the UAR in the context of a destabilizing communist move. Nuri and his Baghdad government had refused to recognize the Syrian-Egyptian UAR; and, in response, the Baghdad regime promptly announced its own federation, a new Hashemite binary with Jordan to be called the Arab Union. Clearly, the Arab Union competed with Nasser's UAR for pan-Arab primacy, and he was infuriated.[18]

During the next several months, Nasser viciously denounced the Baghdad regime and its Arabian Peninsula Hashemite monarchy. Nasser's vituperations were more than mere words. July 14, 1958 would mark the end for the Hashemites in Iraq. At 5:00 A.M., the 19th Brigade of the Free Officers, followed by a frenzied mob, suddenly attacked the King's sprawling tree-lined palace with volleys from machineguns and anti-tank weapons. The royal family hastily mustered outside. In an exchange of gunfire, 23-year-old King Faisal II was shot. Abd al-Ilah, the former regent, was also shot. Later, his hands and feet were chopped off, jammed onto pikes, and paraded through the streets like treasured icons. More protesters poured into the streets of Baghdad, as though on cue, now carrying oversized photographs of Nasser and holding dogs aloft as representations of their executed Hashemite rulers. The mutilated body of the Regent was gleefully dragged through the city. Eventually, his dismembered body was ignominiously hung from a balcony.[19]

Now where was Nuri Said? The wild crowd converged on his home, chanting "Long live Nasser." Nuri could not be found. A reward of 10,000 dinars was broadcast for his capture. Nuri had escaped through an emergency tunnel beneath his home. However, he was soon discovered walking on a street, dressed in a woman's garb. The mob pounced and strung him up. But that was not enough. They dragged his dead body through the streets, along with those of other officials, flaying them with shoes in a traditional show of disrespect. As a further expression of the mob's rage, a vehicle repeatedly ran over Nuri's body—back and forth.[20]

The new strongman was Abdel Karim Kassem. Immediately, he announced recognition of Nasser's UAR. Simultaneously, Cairo radio stations celebrated the revolution in Iraq. Hashemite rule in Iraq was dead. The planned Arab Union was dead. The Baghdad Pact was dead. An effort to thrust Syrian-Egyptian pan-Arabism into Hashemite Iraq and Jordan was very much alive. Syrian forces massed on the Jordanian border, and Lebanon's leaders were told they were next. The Mideast was about to explode again.[21]

Officials in Beirut, itself nearly in a state of civil war, and Amman, which was threatened by UAR neighbors, sent out calls for help from the West. Immediately, President Dwight Eisenhower dispatched the Sixth Fleet in the Mediterranean toward Lebanon. On July 15, 1958, the day after the Iraqi coup, 1,700 amphibious Marines landed on the beach at Beirut, with more troops airlifting into the airport. Two days later, July 17, 1858, a British airborne force of 2,000 commandoes landed in Amman, responding to King Hussein in Jordan.[22] The Nasserite advance was blunted.

For the moment, Mideast oil was stable. Not safe, but stable.

*   *   *   *

Mindful of the CIA-MI6 coup that had overthrown Iran's Mossadegh in 1953 and the Anglo-American forces that had instantly reacted after the July 14, 1958 revolution in Iraq, the IPC and Kassem's Baghdad government resumed negotiations over what was tantamount to nationalization. In 1959, strongman Kassem made it clear that he wanted to rescind nearly all of IPC's concessioned lands. The company eventually agreed to a large giveback of the concession territory, so long as it could keep the 25 percent containing the most petroliferous fields in the north. That was unacceptable to Kassem. Frustrated IPC officials in London, tiring of the whole process of serial creeping nationalization, concluded that they "must call a halt to the current process of bazaar bargaining." One wrote, "The time has come when the company must dig in their toes."[23]

At the same time, the very same northern oil regions under discussion were in deep turmoil. Kurdish nationalists had stepped up their campaign of insurrection in the Mosul province. Official Baghdad was certain that the Mosul revolt bore the earmarks of oil company sponsorship. Whoever was to blame, Kassem's forces exacted horrific punishment on the region, hanging and mutilating villagers in a broad reign of terror.[24]

Throughout 1959, Kassem continued his brutal repression of the Kurds and consolidation of power in Iraq. At the same time, he became solipsistic about his role in Iraq, seeing himself as something more than regal and perhaps something closer to "a deliverer." Moreover, Kassem conducted himself in such an aloof fashion, disassociating himself from the political parties, that he earned the moniker, "the Sole Leader."[25]

By now, Kassem had survived several coup attempts, including one by the dissident Ba'ath Party. The Ba'athists had dispatched two junior officers for the attempt. One was an obscure street enforcer named Saddam Hussein. But Saddam and his teammate botched the job. Saddam was wounded by one of Kassem's bodyguards and fled to Syria to convalesce. Kassem remained in power and continued to press the Redline group to relinquish its concession. The company, at some point, agreed to a full 70 percent return, but they insisted on keeping the most productive tracts.[26]

Kassem would probably have taken action, but, once again, the Baghdad treasury went anemic. The country was still dependent on the very foreign hand it hated: the IPC. At the end of March 1961, IPC officials in London were urgently summoned back to Baghdad for consultation. Kassem's government needed an advance of IPC's quarterly tax and royalty payment, due later in April. The company agreed, accelerating a £20 million payment by several weeks and thereby saving the treasury.[27]

The £20 million favor paused but did not halt the Iraqi demand to reclaim its concession. On December 12, 1959, the Iraqi Parliament passed Law 80, which rescinded 99.5 percent of IPC's concession. The Redline group would be left with only those operating wells that were actually producing revenues. The reclaimed lands included the prized but still undeveloped North Rumaila fields.[28]

After Law 80 was passed, IPC officials messengered letters of objection. These were ignored. Several days later, formal letters of protest were sent to the Iraqi Oil Ministry, and they were not even accepted. A year of fruitless dialogue followed. In 1962, a weary IPC submitted the matter to arbitration. Baghdad ignored the arbitration request as well.[29]

Company hopes now rested on the very nature of Baghdad politics. Executives were confident that the proven Iraqi cycle of coup and countercoup would cure their problem with Kassem. At that very time, Kassem's monstrous repression of the Kurds was still under way. The plotting Iraqi military saw him as detached. In February 1963, a band of army officers rose up and killed "the Sole Leader." His bullet-riddled corpse was displayed on Iraqi TV.[30]

Iraq's new oil minister was a skillful petroleum engineer, Abdul Aziz al-Wattari. He had graduated from the University of Texas and spoke the same language as IPC officials. During the next two years, as government revenues dropped again, al-Wattari and Redline negotiators hammered out an agreement. The most precious lands, seized by Law 80, were returned, including the Rumaila fields. The Redline companies, except for Standard Oil of New Jersey, agreed to create a partnership with a new, state-owned Iraqi National Oil Company (INOC), which would own a third of the enterprise.[31]

Redline oil kept pumping.

*   *   *   *

An enduring legacy of "the Sole Leader," Kassem, was his facilitation of a new international organization that would soon prove more potent than all the armies and all the mob violence of the Middle East.

It began in 1959, when Cold War petropolitics resulted in a post-Stalin Soviet attempt to reinvigorate its oil industry and recapture the market they once dominated. The communist tactic was to regain old customers with cheaper prices. Ironically, although the CIA characterized the crisis as a destabilizing "Soviet economic offensive," the communist tactic merely employed the time-honored, free-market traditions of price competitiveness—something the controlled-market Western consortiums feared. The major oil companies responded by slashing their own prices, thus inaugurating a price war. In April 1959, BP sliced 18 cents off its price per barrel, a 10 percent reduction. Four months later, Standard followed with a 14-penny drop, a 7 percent reduction. Whether political push or price war, the oil states suddenly found their royalties choked by Cold War economic tactics. [32]

For some time, two Texas-trained oil experts, one from Saudi Arabia and one from Venezuela, had been secretly planning a consortium of oil-exporting nations. A group of oil ministers and representatives had, in fact, already signed what they called a "Gentleman's Agreement" at a secret meeting held during the 1959 Arab Petroleum Conference in Cairo. In the face of the latest oil company price cuts, they were determined to create their own controlling association. Cairo was the logical choice for the next meeting because Nasser had been the chief patron of the export organizers. However, to check Nasser's further pan-Arab ascendancy and to elevate his own importance in the Arab world, Kassem, despite concerns over further coup attempts, had preemptively dispatched invitations to the oil ministers to convene in Baghdad. Kassem, with his iron military grip, made certain the inter-ministerial conclave was protected.[33]

On September 10, 1960, Baghdad streets filled with tanks and troops which took up positions as oil ministers from Saudi Arabia, Venezuela, Kuwait, Iraq, and Iran huddled. During the tense proceedings, an armed bodyguard stood behind each delegate. When the ministers finally emerged, they had founded a new international body, the Organization of Petroleum Exporting Countries. Henceforth, those whose lands held the oil would control production and pricing.[34]

OPEC first flexed its muscles in 1967 after the Six Day War. Israel had preemptively devastated the combined armies and air forces of Egypt, Syria, and Jordan just before those countries could launch their loudly announced war to finally push the Jewish State into the sea. In humiliation, OPEC's Arab countries tried to coordinate an oil blockade against those countries that supported Israel. It did not work. But for its part, Iraq tore up al-Wattari's accommodation agreement that had restored lands to the Redline group. Law 97, passed in August 1967, once again revoked the old IPC concessions, except for those wells already operating and producing revenue. A month later, Law 123 completely reorganized the Iraqi National Oil Company, purging its ranks of pro-Western executives and technocrats.[35] This set the stage for not just a wounded, bandaged, and rehabilitated Iraqi oil industry, but a reinvented one.

New contracts to new countries were let, with an accent on those that had not supported Israel. In November 1967, the first such contract was announced: a 20-year concession to a French state-owned oil exploration entity. This was followed in December by a technical assistance pact with the Soviet Union.[36]

The next year, 1968, in July, yet another coup brought a new group into power. The Ba'athists now controlled Iraq. Newly empowered Ahmad Hassan al-Bakr ruled with brutality, purging his enemies, real and potential. Any thoughts that the new Ba'athist regime under al-Bakr could improve on the Iraqi human rights record were quickly dispelled.

The nation continued to define itself by deep-seated rage against the West, Jews, and Zionism, and hostility toward its minorities, as well as carefully cultivated resentment over perceived injustices perpetrated by its oil-rich neighbors.

* * * *

Modern nations never existed in the tribal Middle East until they were created by, for, and with the corporation that began as Anglo-Persian Oil Company and which ultimately changed its name to British Petroleum. But for the governmental-mandated, military-empowered primacy of British Petroleum and the oil it sought to control, the political and military landscape of the last century would be vastly different. How many would live? Where would they live? How would they live?

During the turbulent sixties and seventies, the West's colonial and imperial influence in the Middle East began its tall topple. Like all cataclysmic orogeny, the upheaval and impact was tectonic. The dust never settled and the mountains are still moving.

In a post-colonial and post-imperial latter twentieth century, the transformation of British Petroleum began in earnest. Shut out from its former realms of extended Middle Eastern monopolies, the company turned to other petroliferous zones of the Earth. Its exploration of the oil-rich North Sea, the Alaskan North Slope, and other unpoliticized and insurrection-free regions returned many millions of barrels of oil and many billions of petrodollars. During these years, the company earned great money without great military. Traveling far from the original aims of British imperialism, the company was now reinventing itself as a true globalized enterprise, devoid of political allegiance— beholden to no one other than itself and its tempestuous history.

Soon, the "British" would be separated altogether from the "Petroleum" in a long process of further geopolitical distillation in the high-pressure refinery that constituted the last years of the last century. The company's activities, now deeply dug into the strata beneath the North Sea and Alaska, as well as numerous other regions beyond roiling Middle East petropolitics, eventually convinced the British government and public that this company should exist as a purely commercial enterprise, devoid of government control or ownership. British Petroleum's role as a beast of oil imperialism and foreign policy was now archaic. In 1979, this dusk of oil imperialism met the dawn of British privatization.

Conservative Britain's push for free markets was substantially boosted after two Mideast oil crises that echoed up from British Petroleum's past. During the so-called "1973 oil shock," Arab oil flexed its powerful muscles on the West as it did during its first Arab Oil Embargo. The first Arab Oil Embargo was sparked 48 hours into the Six Day war with Israel. Long lines of automobiles waiting for fuel and gas station flare-ups swept across the West. In 1973, OPEC again punished the West for supporting Israel, this time during the Yom Kippur War. This time, OPEC clamped down another selective oil embargo that triggered fresh waves of unemployment and inflation, and also prolonged the pain of the pre-existing stock market crash of 1973–74. These economic consequences hit especially hard in the United Kingdom. Then, the so-called "1979 energy crisis" gripped an even more oil-dependent world. The Ayatollah Khomeini ousted the Shah and installed the Iranian Revolution and a brutal theocracy. The Iraq-Iran War ensued. For many months, vital Iranian oil supplies were either cut or sharply reduced, made up only by Saudi Arabia, which increased production to make up some of the shortfall.

On March 28, 1979, amid increased inflation and unemployment in Britain, along with the rise of the term "economic stagflation," the Labour Government suffered a vote of no confidence. This triggered a general election which brought the Conservative Party to power in Great Britain and, with them, the concept of free markets was unleashed from government domination.

From the moment in 1979 that conservative titan and free market apostle Margaret Thatcher became Prime Minister, the British government began a systematic divesture of control and ownership of its great state-embraced enterprises. Enormous companies such as British Airways and British Telecom were suddenly freed. British Petroleum was among the corporations suddenly privatized. Soon, the oil conglomerate would belong to the highest bidder, share by share. The world bought into British Petroleum. Ultimately, about forty percent of the total investment would be British and about 39 percent American, with the remainder dispersed among investors worldwide. Henceforth, stockholders the world over would own fractions of the company that had once intrepidly plumbed the ruddy depths of war and the pitch-dark cisterns of oil during a fiery century. The company that helped make our world now belonged to the world.

As the last century closed, the globally-powered British Petroleum became a composite giant. Through merger and acquisition, the behemoth that was British Petroleum would inhale other gargantuan creatures of the petroleum age. Standard Oil of Indiana, a spawn of the Rockefeller empire, was re-spun into Amoco, and in 1998, this purely American oil company merged with British Petroleum under the trans-Atlantic moniker "BP Amoco." Aggressive acquisitions continued as the new, larger giant breathed in Atlantic Richfield, also known as ARCO, Burmah-Castrol, and many other oil enterprises.

May 1, 2001, a general shareholder vote by a 98 percent margin approved a name change to the company's new globalized identity. From that date, the detachment was complete. The new name going forward was simply *BP*. Moving swiftly into many other realms of energy, such as solar and hydrogen, the new logo's tag line was still anchored to the letters B and P, but now those two initials stood for "Beyond Petroleum."

When the Deepwater Horizon exploded in an inferno, and an entire gulf shore was shocked, the economic ruination of a coastline and its ecosystem was but another milepost in the company's tradition of coping with monumental calamity. In comparison to the world wars, the coups, and the mass bloodshed, the gulf coast catastrophe must have indeed seemed small. Hence, when after a White House meeting with President Barack Obama, BP Chairman

Carl-Henric Svanberg quipped to reporters that the company "cares about the small people" living along the Gulf coast, that is because people have always been smaller than oil. Nations have been smaller than oil.

When humankind steps in oil, the residue tenaciously clings for generations. BP is determined to move beyond its imperialist and war-infused history. Yet, its omnipresent legacy still rules the twenty-first century world. All oil exists as the dense accretion of dead organisms. This is more than petrochemical. This is petropolitical.

One company has moved beyond petroleum. It is unknown when the rest of the world will.

TOP: Anglo-Persian Oil Company's original 1901 oil concession.

MIDDLE: Native workman carrying cans of Anglo-Persian kerosene via mule, circa 1905-1910.

BOTTOM: Tribal horsemen hired to protect Anglo-Persian oil wells in Persia, circa 1905.

All photos: BP Archive/BP plc

TOP: Iraq's first oil gusher, Baba Gurgur, October 14, 1927. *BP Archive/BP plc*

INSET: River of oil from first oil gusher, Baba Gurgur, October 14, 1927. *BP Archive/BP plc*

BOTTOM: British Indian troops shell the Turks during Mesopotamia Campaign, circa 1916. *Imperial War Museum*

INSET: C. S. Gulbenkian's passport
picture, circa 1933.

BELOW: C. S. Gulbenkian relaxing with
kitten.

C. S. Gulbenkian Foundation

TOP: Detail of a Standard Oil highway map in Nazi Germany featuring a gas station attendant giving a Hitler salute. *Author's Acquisition*

BELOW: Mufti of Jerusalem Haj Muhammed Amin al-Husseini reviews Moslem Waffen-SS troops in Bosnia, as shown on a Nazi magazine cover, 1944. *Author's Private Collection*

NOTES

Chapter 1: Flaming Waters

1. US Coast Guard and Bureau of Ocean Energy Management, *Transcript of the Testimony of the Joint United States Coast Guard/Bureau of Ocean Energy Management Investigation*, Oct 5, 2010. Douglas A. Blackmon, Vanessa O'Connell, et al., "There Was 'Nobody in Charge,'" *Wall Street Journal* (*WSJ*), May 27, 2010. Simon Rogers, "BP Oil Spill: The Official Deepwater Horizon Disaster Timeline," *The Guardian* (*TG*), Sep 9, 2010, www.guardian.co.uk/news/datablog/2010/sep/09/bp-oil-spill-deepwater-horizon-timeline. See generally "Oil Spill Gulf of Mexico," *nola.com*, ca. Apr 2010, www.nola.com/news/gulf-oil-spill/.

2. *USCG/BOEM Testimony Transcript*. Rogers, "BP Oil Spill Timeline." Blackmon, O'Connell, et al., "'Nobody in Charge.'"

3. *USCG/BOEM Testimony Transcript*. Rogers, "BP Oil Spill Timeline." Blackmon, O'Connell, et al., "'Nobody in Charge.'" David Hammer, "Oil Spill Hearings: Dramatic Testimony of the Rig's Final Moments," *nola.com*, May 28, 2010, www.nola.com/news/gulf-oil-spill/index.ssf/2010/05/oil_spill_hearings_dramatic_te.html.

4. *USCG/BOEM Testimony Transcript*. Rogers, "BP Oil Spill Timeline." Blackmon, O'Connell, et al., "'Nobody in Charge.'"

5. USCG/*BOEM Testimony Transcript*. David Hammer, "Flashing Warning Lights on Deepwater Horizon Were 'A Lot to Take In,'" *nola.com*, Oct 7, 2010, www.nola.com/news/gulf-oil-spill/index.ssf/2010/10/flashing_warning_lights_on_dee.html. Rogers, "BP Oil Spill Timeline." Blackmon, O'Connell, et al., "'Nobody in Charge.'" "Engineer: Deepwater Horizon Alarm 'Inhibited,'" *Washington Post* (*WP*), Jul 23, 2010, www.washingtonpost.com/wp-dyn/content/video/2010/07/23/VI2010072302554.html?sid=ST2010072305432.

6. Rogers, "BP Oil Spill Timeline." "Video of Deepwater Horizon Fire," CNN, Jul 15, 2010, www.cnn.com/video/data/2.0/video/us/2010/07/15/ac.fisherman.video.cnn.html

7. Joseph Shapiro, "Rig Blast Survivor: 'I Thought I Was Going to Die,'" *Morning Edition*, May 10, 2010, www.npr.org/templates/story/story.php?storyId=126650691.

8. Shapiro, "Rig Blast Survivor." Blackmon, O'Connell, et al., "'Nobody in Charge.'"

9. Shapiro, "Rig Blast Survivor."

10. Hammer, "Flashing Warning Lights 'A Lot.'" "Extra: Capturing the Disaster," *60 Minutes*, May 16, 2010, www.cbsnews.com/video/watch/?id=6490138n. "Chris Choy CNN Interview," ca. May 2010, author's collection. "BP Oil Rig Explosion," ca. May 2010, author's collection. Shapiro, "Rig Blast Survivor."

11. "Extra: Capturing the Disaster." "Chris Choy CNN Interview," video, ca. May 2010, author's collection. "BP Oil Rig Explosion," video, ca. May 2010, author's collection. Shapiro, "Rig Blast Survivor." Hammer, "Flashing Warning Lights 'A Lot.'" Hammer, "Oil Spill Hearings." Blackmon, O'Connell, et al., "'Nobody in Charge.'"

12. "Exclusive Photos of Deepwater Horizon," WKRG, Apr 23, 2010, www.wkrg.com/gulf_oil_spill/article/exclusive-photos-of-deepwater-horizon/879596/Apr-23-2010_5-37-pm/. "Burning Oil Rig Sinks into Gulf of Mexico, Coast Guard Says," *nola.com*, Apr 22, 2010, www.nola.com/news/index.ssf/2010/04/burning_oil_rig_sinks.html.

13. Jenny Marder, "New Gulf Oil Spill Flow Rate Estimate Released," *PBS NewsHour*, Sep 23, 2010, www.pbs.org/newshour/rundown/2010/09/latest-oil-flow-estimate-tops-government-numbers.html. "Gulf Coast Oil Leak Widget," *PBS NewsHour*, www.pbs.org/newshour/rundown/horizon-oil-spill.html. "BP Oil Spill Timeline," *TG*, Jul 22, 2010, www.guardian.co.uk/environment/2010/jun/29/bp-oil-spill-timeline-deepwater-horizon.

14. "BP CEO Tony Hayward: 'I'd Like My Life Back,'" video, May 30, 2010, author's collection. Patrik Jonsson, "America's 'Small People' and BP's Gaffe-prone Gulf Oil Spill Response," *Christian Science Monitor*, Jun 17, 2010, www.csmonitor.com/USA/2010/0617/America-s-small-people-and-BP-s-gaffe-prone-Gulf-oil-spill-response. "BP Chief Apologizes for Small People Remark," *Reuters*, Jun 17, 2010, www.reuters.com/article/idUSTRE65G06X20100617.

CHAPTER 2: BIRTH OF THE OIL AGE

1. d'Errico, Francesco, "The Invisible Frontier: A Multiple Species Model for the Origin of Behavioral Modernity," *Evolutionary Anthropology*, vol. 12 (2003), 193. Longrigg, Stephen H., *Oil in the Middle East: Its Discovery and Development* (London: Oxford University Press, 1968), 10–11. Giddens, Paul H., *The Birth of the Oil Industry* (New York: Macmillan, 1938), 11. Rister, Carl Coke, "The Oilman's Frontier," *Mississippi Valley Historical Review*, vol. 37, no. 1. (Jun 1950), 4–5.

2. Roux, George, *Ancient Iraq* (New York: Penguin Books, 1992), 151–152, 163. Exodus 2:2–3, NIV Study Bible. Ellis, Edward S., and Charles F. Horne, "Biography of King Sargon of Akkad," *The Story of The Greatest Nations and the World's Famous Events*, vol. 1 (New York: Auxiliary Educational League, 1921).

3. See Longrigg, *Oil*, 10.

4. Xenophon, *Cyropaedia*, Henry G. Dakyns, trans., F. M. Stawell, ed. (Champaign, IL: The Gutenberg Project, 2002), bk 7, chap. 5. Hitti, Philip K., *History of the Arabs* (New York: Palgrave Macmillan, 2002), 202. Longrigg, *Oil*, 11.

5. Miller, E. Willard, "The Industrial Development of the Allegheny Valley of Western Pennsylvania," *Economic Geography*, vol. 19 (1943), 401. See Scoville, Warren C., "Growth of the American Glass Industry to 1880–Continued," *Journal of Political Economy*, vol. 52 (1944), 345. Giddens, 19–20.

6. Giddens, 2–3, 14. Longrigg, *Oil*, 11.

7. Rezneck, Samuel, "Energy: Coal and Oil in the American Economy," *Journal of Economic History*, vol. 7 supp. (1947), 63. See Darrah, William Culp, *Pithole: The Vanished City* (Gettysburg, PA: William C. Darrah, 1972), 2. See Tarbell, Ida M., *The History of the Standard Oil Company*, vol. 1 (Gloucester, MA: Peter Smith, 1963), 5. See Giddens, 14, 58–59. Miller, 402.

8. See Darrah, 2–3. Miller, 394. Tarbell, vol. 1, 10, 12. See photo, "The Drake Oil Well in 1859—The First Oil Well," Tarbell, vol. 1, 10f.

9. Tarbell, vol. 1, 12–20, 30–34. Rezneck, 64, 65. Giddens, 30. Miller, 394–395.

10. See Tarbell, vol. 1, 30–33. Miller, 391.

11. Darrah, 3. Giddens, 83, 86, 87, 114. See "Table of Yearly and Monthly Average Price of Refined," Tarbell, vol. 1, 384–385.

12. Lloyd, H. D., "Story of a Great Monopoly," *Atlantic Monthly*, vol. 47 (Mar 1881), 317–334. Giddens, 100. Rezneck, 64. Tarbell, vol. 2, 395. See Giddens, 101–113. See report, "Yearly Production of Crude Petroleum of the Principal Oil Producing Countries Since 1900," ca. Jan 1918: PRO CAB21/119.

13. Montague, Gilbert Holland, "The Rise and Supremacy of the Standard Oil Company," *Quarterly Journal of Economics*, vol. 16 (1902), 267. Rezneck, 65. See Giddens, 101–113.

14. Darrah, 32, 38, 40–42, 60–61, 77, 231, 232. See Montague, 266. See Tarbell, vol. 1, 24–25. See photo, "Holmden Street, Pithole, August, 1895," Giddens, 136f. See Giddens, 139–140.

15. Tarbell, vol. 1, 43–44. See Montague, 265–292.

16. McKay, John P., "Baku Oil and Transcaucasian Pipelines 1883–1891: A Study in Tsarist Economic Policy," *Slavic Review*, vol. 43 (1984), 606. "Petroleum Developments in Foreign Countries," *Science*, New Series, vol. 41, no. 1050 (Feb 12, 1915), 250–251. "The Oil Wells of Baku," *Science*, vol. 7, no. 158 (Feb 12, 1886), 149–150.

17. "The Oil Wells," 149–150. McKay, 606, 609. See Hewins, Ralph, *Mr. Five per cent: The Biography of Calouste Gulbenkian* (London: Hutchinson & Co. Ltd., 1957), 23–24. See Hitti, 292. See Maunsell, F. R., "The Mesopotamian Petroleum Field," *Geographical Journal*, vol. 9 (1897), 531–532.

18. "The Oil Wells," 149. Hewins, 23–24. McKay, 607. Gulbenkian, Calouste Sarkis, *La Transcaucasie et la Peninsule D'Apcheron: Souvenirs de Voyage, 1890* (Lisbon, Portugal: Calouste Gulbenkian Foundation, 1989), 274.

19. Ferrier, R. W., *The History of the British Petroleum Company*, vol. 1: *The Developing Years, 1901–1932* (Cambridge, UK: Cambridge University Press, 1982), 4. Gulbenkian, *Transcaucasie*, 186, 199, 202, 203, 218. McKay, 607. Hewins, 23.

20. Gulbenkian, *Transcaucasie*, 186, 246. Hewins, 20–21, 22.

21. Gulbenkian, *Transcaucasie*, 219.

22. Gulbenkian Foundation, *Calouste Sarkis Gulbenkian: The Man and his Achievements* (Lisbon, Portugal: Calouste Gulbenkian Foundation, 1999), 5. See Hewins, xiv, 12.

23. Gulbenkian, C. S., "Memoirs of Calouste Sarkis Gulbenkian with Particular Relation to the Origins and Foundation of the Iraq Petroleum Company Limited," Sep 16, 1945: NA RG 59 890.G.6363/3-148, 3. Hewins, 7, 8.

24. Gulbenkian Foundation, 5–6. Hewins, 12.

25. Hewins, 4–5, 13.

26. Hewins, 14–15. Gulbenkian, "Memoirs," 3. Gulbenkian Foundation, 9.

27. Gulbenkian, "Memoirs," 3. Gulbenkian, *Transcaucasie*, 186, 218–219, 225, 226, 229. Hewins, 23–25.

28. Gulbenkian, *Transcaucasie*, 226.

29. Gulbenkian, *Transcaucasie*, xxxi. Hewins, 27. Gulbenkian, "Memoirs," 3.

30. Gulbenkian, "Memoirs," 3. Hewins, 29–30. Longrigg, Stephen H., *The Origins and Early History of the Iraq Petroleum Company, Known from 1912 to 1929 as the Turkish Petroleum Company*(BP Archive, 1968), 13.

31. Telegram, Ambassador Davis to Charles E. Hughes, Mar 1, 1921: NA RG 59 800.6363/229, *FRUS* 1921, vol. 2, 81. Sultan Abdulhamid II, Decree of Transfer, Apr 8, 1889 (5 Chaban 1306): BP IPC 174-530A. Longrigg, Stephen H., *Four Centuries of Modern Iraq* (Oxford: Clarendon Press, 1925), 355. Gulbenkian, "Memoirs," 3. Longrigg, *Oil*, 12–13. Hewins, 29–30.

32. See Letter, John D. Archbold to John D. Rockefeller, Jul 6, 1886: RF 1, box 51, fol. 378. See Pugach, Noel H., "Standard Oil and Petroleum Development in Early Republican China," *Business History Review*, vol. 45 (1971), 452–453. See Ferrier, 1, 259–260, 548. Generally see Tarbell, vols. 1 and 2.

33. Ferrier, 1. Longrigg, *Oil*, 12. Bishop, Michele G., "History of Exploration," *Petroleum Systems of the Northwest Java Province, Java and Offshore Southeast Sumatra, Indonesia*, U. S. Geological Survey Open-File Report 99-50R, 2000, www.usgs.gov.

34. See Jones, G. Gareth, "The British Government and the Oil Companies 1912–1924: The Search for an Oil Policy," *Historical Journal*, vol. 20 (1973), 647–648. Fielden, Ralph, "The Romance of Shell," *Great Britain and the East*, Nov 1958, cxxxvii. Miles, Lebron, "A Shell's Tale," *Insight*, vol. 4, no. 2 (Q2 2003), 19–20. "History of Shell," www.shell.com. See Moody-Stuart, Mark, "A Lasting Commitment—the Royal Dutch/Shell Group in Asia," Apr 1998, and "Protect Our Marine Environment—Globally," Jan 2001, www.shell.com. Ferrier, 4–5. Longrigg, *Oil*, 16–17.

35. Jacobs, Stefan, and Mirik Kania, "The Lubricants Industry in Poland," presentation, Union Indépendante de l'Industrie Européennne des Lubrifants, European Meeting, Budapest, Oct 25, 2002, www.ueil.org. "Tale of the Family Tree," ca. 1950: BP 90030, 1. "Drohobycz: The Petroleum Industry," www.jewishgen.org.

36. Youngquist, Walter, "Survey of Energy Resources, 2001: Country Notes—Australia," World Energy Council, www.worldenergy.org. See "Petroleum Resources Exploration," www.geoscience. gov.au. Lishmund, S. R., ed., "Report No. 30: Oil Shale," Department of Mines, Geological Survey of New South Wales, 1971, 5. Stanley, David, "Oil Springs and Petrolia," www.authorsden.com. See "Drohobycz: The Petroleum Industry."

37. Bright, Arthur A., Jr., *The Electric-Lamp Industry: Technological Change and Economic Development from 1800 to 1947* (New York: Macmillan, 1949), 70–71, 71n3. Rezneck, 64.

38. Longrigg, *Origins*, 9. Ferrier, 18–19.

39. Ferrier, 24. Longrigg, *Oil*, 14, 17. See Tarbell, vol. 2, 210, 211.

40. Thornton, A. P., "British Policy in Persia, 1858–1890 Part I," *English Historical Review*, vol. 69 (1954), 560, 561. See Farmayan, Hafez, "Portrait of a Nineteenth-Century Iranian Statesman: The Life and Times of Grand Vizier Amin ud-Dawlah, 1844–1904," *International Journal of Middle Eastern Studies*, vol. 15 (1983), 338. Longrigg, *Oil*, 14. Ferrier, 24.

41. Letter, Lepel Griffin to Earl of Rosebery, Dec 6, 1893: PRO FO60/576, as cited by Ferrier, 26. Ferrier, 26. See Thornton, "British Policy," 561n1.

42. Palmer, Alan, *The Decline and Fall of the Ottoman Empire* (New York: M. Evans & Co., 1992), 128. Lord Kinross, *The Ottoman Centuries: The Rise and Fall of the Turkish Empire* (New York: William Morrow & Co., 1977), 509. Quataert, Donald, *The Ottoman Empire, 1700–1922* (Cambridge, UK: Cambridge University Press, 2000), 71–72. See Anderson, Olive, "II: Great Britain and the Beginnings of the Ottoman Public Debt, 1854–55," *Historical Journal*, vol. 7 (1964), 47–51. See Longrigg, *Four Centuries*, 277–278.

43. "The Life of Midhat Pasha: An Illustrious Chief of Young Turkey", *New York Times* (*NYT*), Aug 31, 1877, 2. "Death of Midhat Pasha: The Career of the Great Reformer in Turkey," *NYT*, May 12, 1884, 5. Shaw, Stanford J., and Ezel Kural Shaw, *The History of the Ottoman Empire and Modern Turkey*, vol. 2: *Reform, Revolution, and Republic: The Rise of Modern Turkey, 1808–1975* (Cambridge, UK: Cambridge University Press, 1977), 67. Saliba, Najib E., "The Achievements of Midhat Pasha as Governor of the Province of Syria, 1878–1880," *International Journal of Middle East Studies*, vol. 9, no. 3 (Oct 1978), 307, 307n3. Hitti, 738.

44. Nakash, Yitzhak, *The Shi'is of Iraq* (Princeton, NJ: Princeton University Press, 1994), 32–34.

Tripp, Charles, *A History of Iraq* (Cambridge, UK: Cambridge University Press, 2000), 16–17, 18. Farouk-Sluglett, Marion and Peter Sluglett, "The Transformation of Land Tenure and Rural Social Structure in Central and Southern Iraq, c. 1870–1958," *International Journal of Middle East Studies*, vol. 15 (1983), 492–495. Longrigg, *Four Centuries*, 298–300, 306–307.

    45. Longrigg, *Four Centuries*, 299, 316. Nakash, 198. See Nakash, 184–186. See Shaw and Shaw, 68.

    46. Palmer, 139, 147. Hitti, 738. Kinross, 515–516. See Longrigg, *Four Centuries*, 300.

    47. "The Ottoman Constitution, Promulgated the 7th Zilbridje 1923 (December 11/23, 1876)", included in Dispatch No. 113, Dec 26, 1876, MS Records, Department of State, as reproduced in *American Journal of International Law*, vol. 2, no. 4, supplement: Official Documents (Oct 1908), 367–387. See Shaw and Shaw, 166, 174–175.

    48. Saliba, 317–318.

    49. "The Murder of Abdul Aziz; An Attempt to Arrest Midhat Pasha—Taking Refuge at a Consulate," *NYT*, May 18, 1881, 2. Saliba, 317–318. Shaw and Shaw, 180. Kinross, 529. "Death of Midhat Pasha."

    50. Shaw and Shaw, 216. "He Tells of a Murder: Former Sergeant in the Turkish Army Says that Midhat Pasha Was Strangled to Death," *NYT*, Feb 14, 1897, 15.

    51. "He Tells of a Murder."

    52. "He Tells of a Murder." Shaw & Shaw, 216.

    53. Sultan Abdulhamid II, Decree of Transfer, Apr 8, 1889 (5 Chaban 1306): BP IPC 174-530A. Sultan Abdulhamid II, Decree of Transfer, Sep 24, 1898 (5 Diamazi-ul-Ewell 1316): BP IPC 174-530A. Earle, Edward Meade, "The Turkish Petroleum Company—A Study in Oleaginous Diplomacy," *Political Science Quarterly*, vol. 39 (1924), 266. See Longrigg, *Oil*, 27, 28.

CHAPTER 3: DUELING MONOPOLIES

    1. Jon Tetsuro Sumida, "British Naval Administration and Policy in the Age of Fisher," *The Journal of Military History*, vol. 54, no. 1 (Jan 1990), 3–4. See Archer Jones and Andrew J. Keogh, "The Dreadnought Revolution: Another Look," *Military Affairs*, vol. 49 (1985), 124–131. Ferrier, R. W., *The History of the British Petroleum Company*, vol. 1: *The Developing Years, 1901–1932* (Cambridge, UK: Cambridge University Press, 1982), 10. See photo, "Coaling Ship, 1910," Berry Ritchie, *Portrait in Oil: An Illustrated History of BP* (London: James & James Publishers Ltd., 1995), 28. Geoffrey Miller, *Straits: British Policy towards the Ottoman Empire and the Origins of the Dardanelles Campaign* (Hull, UK: University of Hull, 1997), 424.

    2. See report, "Yearly Production of Crude Petroleum of the Principal Oil Producing Countries Since 1900," ca. Jan 1918: BNA CAB21/119. See letter, Francis Hopwood to W. S. Churchill, ca. Mar 1912: BNA CAB1/33. See Ida M. Tarbell, *The History of the Standard Oil Company*, vol. 2 (Gloucester, MA: Peter Smith, 1963), 270–274. Stephen H. Longrigg, *The Origins and Early History of the Iraq Petroleum Company, Known from 1912 to 1929 as the Turkish Petroleum Company* (BP Archives, 1968), 18. Ferrier, 1–3. See Miller, 424, 426. See table, "World Crude Oil Production 1900–1932," Ferrier, 638.

    3. Letter, Sir H. Drummond Wolff to Lord Salisbury, Jun 30, 1890: BNA FO60/511. Ferrier, 24, 25, 27.

    4. See confidential letter, Sir Arthur Hardinge to Lord Lansdowne, Feb 1, 1902: BNA FO60/660. See letter, Sir Arthur Hardinge to Lord Lansdowne, Feb 16, 1902: BNA FO60/660. See Ferrier, 28–29.

    5. "Petroleum Concession Granted by the Persian Government to William Knox D'Arcy, May 28, 1901," as reproduced in NA RG59 891.6363/16, *FRUS* 1920, vol. 3, 347–351. Stephen H. Longrigg,, *Oil in the Middle East: Its Discovery and Development* (London: Oxford University Press, 1968), 17. Ferrier, 29. 35.

    6. "Petroleum Concession," 348. See photo, "Concession Agreement," Ritchie, 10. Letter, William Knox D'Arcy to Lord Lansdowne, Jun 27, 1901: BNA FO248/733. See letter, Foreign Office to W. K. D'Arcy, Jul 9, 1901: BNA FO284/733.

    7. Longrigg, *Oil*, 18. Longrigg, *Origins*, 27. Report, Boverton Redwood, Jul 30, 1901: BP H17/96, as cited by Ferrier, 55. See Ferrier, 3–4, 33, 57.

    8. See photo, "Bakhtiari Guards," Ritchie, 15. Longrigg, *Oil*, 18. Ferrier, 56–58, 74.

    9. Paul Ghrostopnine, "Report on Oil-Wells in Mesopotamia," attachment to letter, Rear Adm. Mark Bristol, U. S. High Commissioner, to Secretary of State, Apr 27, 1920: NA RG59 800.6363/135. See Letter, Murrietta and Company to Capt. E. Atkin, Dec 4, 1911: PRO FO371/1263. Longrigg, *Origins*, 14. See Longrigg, *Oil*, 14.

    10. Lord Kinross, *The Ottoman Centuries: The Rise and Fall of the Turkish Empire* (New York:

William Morrow & Co., 1977), 565–566. Longrigg, *Origins*, 17. Letter, Arminius Vambery to Thomas Sanderson, Nov 28, 1898: BNA FO800/33, as cited by Miller, 8. See photo, "State Visit to Jerusalem of Wilhelm II of Germany in 1898," Matson Collection, LC-DIG-matpc-04610, www.loc.gov. See photo, "The Jaffa Gate," *Encyclopedia Judaica*, 1,427.

11. "The Baghdad Railroad Convention, 5 March 1903," Cd. 5635 (1911), 37–48 as reproduced in J. C. Hurewitz, ed., *Diplomacy in the Near And Middle East*, vol. 1, *1535–1914* (Gerrards Cross, UK: Archive Editions, 1987), 252–263. Longrigg, *Oil*, 27. Longrigg, *Origins*, 35. Marian Kent, *Oil and Empire: British Policy and Mesopotamian Oil, 1900–1920* (London: Macmillan Press Ltd., 1976), 16.

12. Rohrbach, Paul, *Bagdadbahn* (Berlin: Wiegandt & Grieben, 1911) quoted by Schonfield, Hugh, *The Suez Canal in Peace and War, 1869–1969* (Coral Gables, FL: University of Miami Press, 1969), 62–63.

13. Rohrbach, 43–44 quoted by Kent, *Oil*, 16.

14. "Agreement by the Shaikh of Kuwait Regarding the Non-reception of Foreign Representatives and the Non-cession of Territory to Foreign Powers or Subjects, 23rd January 1899," *The Road to Independence*, Al-Diwan Al-Amiri, www.da.gov.kw/eng/. "Exclusive Agreement: The Kuwayti Shaykh and Britain, 23 January 1899," reproduced in Hurewitz, vol. 1, 218–219. Mary Ann Tetreault, "Autonomy, Necessity, and the Small State: Ruling Kuwait in the Twentieth Century," *International Organization*, vol. 45 (1991), 570–575. See Alan deLacy Rush, ed., *Records of Kuwait, 1899–1961*, vol. 1 (London: Archive International, 1989), 149, as cited by Tetreault, 575. See Longrigg, *Oil*, 26.

15. "The Baghdad Railroad Convention, 5 March 1903." See Longrigg, *Oil*, 27. See generally Edward Mead Earle, *Turkey, the Great Powers, and the Baghdad Railway: A Study in Imperialism* (New York: Macmillan Company, 1923).

16. "Contrat Entre le Ministère Impérial de la Liste Civile et la Société du Chemin de Fer Ottoman D'Anatolie Concernant les Oisments Pétrolifièrers en Mesopotamie," Jul 4/17, 1904: BNA FO371/344 no. 36290. See Longrigg, *Oil*, 27–28. See Kent, *Oil*, 161–162. See Longrigg, *Origins*, 240–241.

17. Marian Jack, "The Purchase of the British Government's Shares in the British Petroleum Company 1912–1914," *Past and Present*, no. 39 (Apr 1968), 140, 140n1, 141. "Summary of Investigations of the Committee Dealing with the Supply of Oil Fuel for His Majesty's Ships with Notes on Subsequent Action," Contract Department, Admiralty, Sep 1907: May Ms, NMM MAY 6, as cited by Miller, 424. Miller, 424.

18. Ferrier, 59, 68, 70–72. See Ferrier, 42–73.

19. Gulbenkian, C. S., "Memoirs of Calouste Sarkis Gulbenkian with Particular Relation to the Origins and Foundation of the Iraq Petroleum Company Limited," Sep 16, 1945: NA RG59 890.G.6363/3-148, 3–4. Longrigg, *Oil*, 28. "Statement of D'Arcy Exploration Company's Claim to Mesopotamian Oil Concession," Nov 12, 1918: BP 100687.

20. H. E. Nichols, "Demand to the Sultan, 21st July, 1904," trans., quoted by Longrigg, *Origins*, 242–243.

21. Nichols, quoted in Longrigg, *Origins*, 242–243.

22. Letter, Ohannès Effendi Sakisian (Minister of the Civile List) to Ottoman Railway Company of Anatolia, Jul 26/Aug 8, 1905, no. 320 (letter 1), reproduced in Kent, *Oil*, 163. "Contrat."

23. Sakisian to Ottoman Railway Company, Jul 26/Aug 8, 1905.

24. Letter, M. Huguenin to Ohannès Effendi Sakisian, Sep 4, 1905, no. 2114 (letter 2), reproduced in Kent, *Oil*, 163–164. Earle, *Turkey*, 63.

25. Huguenin to Sakisian, Sep 4, 1905.

26. Letter, Ohannès Effendi Sakisian to Ottoman Railway Company of Anatolia, Oct 9/22, 1905, no. 442 (letter 3), reproduced in Kent, *Oil*, 164.

27. See letter, Edward Atkin to Secretary of State, Jan 5, 1912: BNA FO371/1487. See minutes, Jan 12, 1912: BNA FO371/1487 no. 911. See Ferrier, 72–73. Miller, 425.

28. Donald Quataert, *The Ottoman Empire, 1700–1922* (Cambridge, UK: Cambridge University Press, 2000), 76–78. Stephen H. Longrigg, *Four Centuries of Modern Iraq* (Oxford: Clarendon Press, 1925), 108, 279–280. Earle, *Turkey*, 10–11, 24n3, 25n4. See Earle, *Turkey*, 95–96. See letter, Bey to Hamilton Fish, no. 314, Sep 29, 1875: *FRUS* 1876, 591–592.

29. Gulbenkian, "Memoirs," 4.

30. Letter, Ohannès Effendi Sakisian to Ottoman Railway Company of Anatolia, Jul 13/26, 1906, no. 233 (letter 4), reproduced in Kent, *Oil*, 164.

31. Letter, Ohannès Effendi Sakisian to Ottoman Railway Company of Anatolia, Jul 27/Aug 9, 1906, no. 355 (letter 5), reproduced in Kent, *Oil*, 165. Letter, M. Huguenin to Ohannès Effendi Sakisian, Aug 22, 1906, no. 2162 (letter 6), reproduced in Kent, *Oil*, 165.

32. Letter, Ohannès Effendi Sakisian to Ottoman Railway Company of Anatolia, Oct 11/24, 1906,

no. 556 (letter 7), reproduced in Kent, *Oil*, 166. "Draft of Contract," ca. Nov 1906, reproduced in Longrigg, *Origins*, 244–248.

33. Letter, M. Huguenin to Ohannès Effendi Sakisian, Feb 9, 1907, no. 354 (letter 10), reproduced in Kent, *Oil*, 167–168. Letter, Ohannès Effendi Sakisian to Board of Ottoman Railway Company of Anatolia, Feb 19/Mar 4, 1907, no. 753 (letter 11), reproduced in Kent, *Oil*, 168–169.

34. Huguenin to Sakisian, Feb 9, 1907. Sakisian to Board of Ottoman Railway Company of Anatolia, Feb 19/Mar 4, 1907.

35. Letter, N. R. O'Conor to Arthur Hardinge, Oct 16, 1907: BNA FO371/343 no. 12713.

36. Longrigg, *Origins*, 22–23, 39. "Agreement between S. E. Hubib Effendi Melhamé and Col. Thomas English," Nov 9/27, 1901, reproduced in Longrigg, *Origins*, 235–238.

37. Gulbenkian, "Memoirs," 6. Ralph Hewins, *Mr. Five per cent: The Biography of Calouste Gulbenkian* (London: Hutchinson & Co. Ltd., 1957), 71. See Kent, *Oil*, 22.

38. Gulbenkian, "Memoirs," 7.

39. Letter, Gilchrist Walker & Co. to H. E. Nichols, Aug 27, 1907, reproduced in Longrigg, *Origins*, 249–250.

40. Longrigg, *Origins*, 44.

41. "Memorandum of Association of the Anglo-Persian Oil Company, Limited" Apr 14, 1909: BP 90423. Ferrier, 67, 86–88. Miller, 425. Ritchie, 19.

42. See "The Ottoman Constitution, Promulgated the 7ᵗʰ Zilbridje 1293 (December 11/23, 1876)," included in dispatch no. 113, Dec 26, 1876, MS Records, Department of State, reproduced in *American Journal of International Law*, vol. 2, suppl.: Official Documents (1908), 367–387. Stanford J. Shaw and Ezel Kural Shaw, *The History of the Ottoman Empire and Modern Turkey*, vol. 2: *Reform, Revolution, and Republic: The Rise of Modern Turkey, 1808–1975* (Cambridge, UK: Cambridge University Press, 1977), 255–256, 257.

43. "The Turkish Transformation," *Washington Post* (*WP*), Aug 3, 1908, 6. "New Turkish Cabinet," *New York Times* (*NYT*), Aug 6, 1908, 3. "Young Turks in Control," *NYT*, Aug 7, 1908, 4. "Turkey in New Guise," Aug 9, 1908, *WP*, 6. "The Turkish Situation," Aug 9, 1908. *WP*, E4. Shaw and Shaw, 266–267. See Longrigg, *Origins*, 44.

44. Miller, 28–29.

45. See Bent Hansen, "Interest Rates and Foreign Capital in Egypt under Foreign Occupation," *Journal of Economic History*, vol. 43 (1983), 867–868. Albert Baster, "The Origins of British Banking Expansion in the Near East," *Economic History Review*, vol. 5 (1943), 76–86. See Longrigg, *Oil*, 14–15.

46. Marian Kent, "Agent of Empire? The National Bank of Turkey and British Foreign Policy," *Historical Journal*, vol. 18, (1975), 367–389. See Edward Meade Earle, "The Turkish Petroleum Company—A Study in Oleaginous Diplomacy," *Political Science Quarterly*, vol. 39 (1924), 265–279. Longrigg, *Origins*, 28, 52. Gulbenkian, "Memoirs," 8–9.

47. See Gulbenkian Foundation, *Calouste Sarkis Gulbenkian: The Man and His Achievements* (Lisbon, Portugal: Calouste Gulbenkian Foundation, 1999), 10. See C. S. Gulbenkian's British passport, June 1902, reproduced in Gulbenkian Foundation, 11. Gulbenkian, "Memoirs," 6, 8–9. See Kent, "Agent of Empire."

48. Correspondence, Marcus Samuel and Robert Waley-Cohen, ca. 1909: BNA FO371/777 nos. 28640, 28858, 31930, 32301, as cited by Kent, *Oil*, 24. Correspondence, Louis Mallet and William D'Arcy, Aug–Sep 1909: BNA FO371/77 no. 32838, as cited by Kent, *Oil*, 24. See Kent, *Oil*, 24. See Kent, "Agent of Empire," 379–380, 384–385.

49. Letter to Charles Marling, Sep 30, 1912, BNA FO800/358, 393–395. Note, Hardinge to Grey, Nov 20, 1908: BNA FO371/549 no. 45717. Correspondence, Samuel and Waley-Cohen. Kent, "Agent of Empire." Kent, *Oil*, 24.

50. Longrigg, *Origins*, 44–46. See "The Baghdad-Basra Concessions Limited," private and confidential memo, ca. 1908: BNA FO371/1263.

51. Longrigg, *Origins*, 44–46. See "The Baghdad Railroad Convention."

52. Longrigg, *Origins*, 45–46.

53. Longrigg, *Origins*, 45–46.

54. Longrigg, *Origins*, 46–47.

55. Marquise de Fontenoy, "Guns Trained on Sultan's Palace," *WP*, Apr 3, 1909, 6. "Sultan Has Earned Name of Assassin," *NYT*, Apr 20, 1909, 2. "Young Turks Decree Death to the Sultan," *NYT*, Apr 20, 1909, 1. Stephen Bonsal, "The Red Sultan," *NYT*, Apr 25, 1909, SM2. Miller, 65–66. See Shaw and Shaw, 280–282.

56. "Dispatch Escapes Censors," *NYT*, Apr 17, 1909, 1. Longrigg, *Origins*, 47. Shaw and Shaw, 280, 281–282.

57. "Sultan Must Quit," *NYT*, Apr 20, 1909, 1. "Abdul Awaits Fate; Young Turks Have Not Told What They Will Do," *NYT*, Apr 21, 1909, 1. Frances McCullagh, "Sultan Beaten; Capital Falls; 6,000 Are Slain," *NYT*, Apr 25, 1909. Shaw and Shaw, 279–280. See Longrigg, *Origins*, 47.

58. See Longrigg, *Origins*, 47.

59. "Abdul Hamid Deposed," *NYT*, Apr 28, 1909, 8. Frances McCullagh, "Abdul Hamid is Deposed; Mehmed V Rules," *NYT*, Apr 28, 1909, 1. "Deposition of Sultan Abdul Hamid and Accession to the Throne of Mohammed V," paraphrase of telegram, Ambassador Leishman to Secretary of State, Apr 27 1909: File no. 10044/167, *FRUS* 1909, 581. Letter, Ambassador H. Kiazim to Secretary of State, Apr 27, 1909: File no. 10044/174, *FRUS* 1909, 581.

60. "Sultan to Pay Young Turks' Bills," *NYT*, Apr 27, 1909, 2. "Abdul Not to Be Tried," *NYT*, Apr 29, 1909, 1. "250 Mutiny Leaders Executed in Turkey," *NYT*, Apr 30, 1909, 1. "Young Turks Suspend Siege in Honor of New Sultan," *NYT*, Apr 29, 1909, 2. Longrigg, *Oil*, 28–29.

61. "The Baghdad-Basrah Concessions Limited," confidential memo, ca. Nov 1911: BNA FO371/1263 no. 48964. Longrigg, *Oil*, 29. Longrigg, *Origins*, 47.

62. Longrigg, *Oil*, 29–30. Longrigg, *Origins*, 47–48.

63. Longrigg, *Origins*, 48. Kent, *Oil*, 22–23.

64. "Oilfields in Mesopotamia," confidential summary of correspondence, Dec 1911–Jan 1912, Jan 26, 1926: BNA FO371/1487 no. 911. Memo, Apr 6, 1912: BNA FO371/1487 no. 911. Letter, Gerard Lowther to Edward Grey, Oct 13, 1912: BNA FO371/1487 no. 911. Kent, *Oil*, 22–23. See Longrigg, *Origins*, 66–67, 68–75.

65. Kent, *Oil*, 23, 24, 218n45.

66. Winston Churchill, "Oil Fuel Supply for His Majesty's Navy," report, Jun 16, 1913: BNA CAB/115/39. Adm. Fisher to Winston Churchill, Dec 10, 1911, *WSC Comp.*, vol. 2, pt. iii, 1926–1927, as cited by Miller, 425. Ferrier, 13, 163. See letter, W. S. Churchill to Lord Fisher, Jun 11, 1912, quoted by Randolph S. Churchill, *Winston S. Churchill*, vol. 2, *1904–1914: Young Statesman* (Boston: Houghton Mifflin, 1967), 590.

67. Ferrier, 132–134, 135, 139–140, 148–149, 162–163. See photos, "*SS Anatolia*, First Vessel alongside Abadan, 1909," "Laying the Pipeline, 1910," Ferrier, 131, 133. Ritchie, 22–24, 25. See photo, "A Group of Bakhtiari," Ritchie, 22.

68. W. Churchill, "Oil Fuel Supply for His Majesty's Navy." Ferrier, 163.

69. Letter, Winston Churchill to John Fisher, Jun 11, 1912, reproduced in R. Churchill, 590–591.

70. Ferrier, 150. Ritchie, 25. Admiralty memo on adequacy of supplies of oil, Mar 18, 1913: BNA ADM116/1209, vol. 3, 44–45.

71. Questions to Marcus Samuel, "First Report of the Royal Commission on Fuel and Engines," Adm. Fisher, Chairman, Sep 1912–Jan 1913: BNA ADM116/1208. Questions to Charles Greenway, "First Report."

72. Louis Mallet, memo, Nov 15, 1912: BNA FO371/1486 no. 48688. Questions to Greenway, "First Report."

73. Louis Mallet, minute sheet, Nov 1912: BNA FO371/1486 no. 55654, quoted by Jack, 147.

74. Confidential letter, Louis Mallet to Charles Greenway, Feb 5, 1913: BNA FO371/1760 no. 2463. See confidential letter, Foreign Office to India Office, Feb 5, 1913: BNA FO371/1760 no. 2463.

75. Louis Mallet, memo, Nov 6, 1912: BNA FO371/1486 no. 47846. Jack, 142n9.

76. Questions to Greenway, "First Report."

77. Admiralty memo on adequacy of supplies of oil, Mar 18, 1913. See "For British Navy's Oil," *NYT*, Jun 17, 1914, 4.

78. Winston Churchill, secret Admiralty memo, Jun 16, 1913: BNA CAB37/115.

79. Confidential letter, Charles Marling to Edward Grey, Jul 27, 1912: BNA FO371/1486 no. 637. Confidential letter, Louis Mallet to Henry Babington-Smith, Aug 12, 1912: BNA FO371/1486 no. 637.

CHAPTER 4: MR. FIVE PERCENT

1. Lodwick, John, with D. H. Young, *Gulbenkian: An Interpretation of "The Richest Man in the World"* (Garden City, NY: Doubleday & Company, 1958), 41–42.

2. Gulbenkian, Nubar, *Portrait in Oil: The Autobiography of Nubar Gulbenkian* (New York: Simon & Schuster, 1965), 17–19, 22.

3. Gulbenkian Foundation, *Calouste Sarkis Gulbenkian: The Man and his Achievements* (Lisbon, Portugal: Calouste Gulbenkian Foundation, 1999), 13–14, 17–18.

4. Gulbenkian, Nubar, 38–39.

5. Gulbenkian, Nubar, 96. Gulbenkian, C. S., "Memoirs of Calouste Sarkis Gulbenkian with Particular Relation to the Origins and Foundation of the Iraq Petroleum Company Limited," Sep 16, 1945: NA RG59 890.G.6363/3-148, 11.

6. Gulbenkian, C. S., 15. Also see letter, N. Gulbenkian to Under Secretary of State, Feb 3 1938: PRO WO371/21855 no. 19238. Also see Williams, "Claim of Mr. N. Gulbenkian against the Iraqi Government," memorandum, Feb 4, 1938: PRO WO371/21855 no. 19238. Also see letter, Baggallay to N. Gulbenkian , Feb 10, 1938: PRO WO371/21855 no. 19238. Also see letter, N. Gulbenkian to Under Secretary of State, Feb 15, 1938: PRO WO371/21855 no. 19238. Also see "Gulbenkian case," memorandum, Feb 15, 1938: PRO WO371/21855 no. 19238. Also see letter, Hugh Montgomery to Baggallay, Feb 23, 1938: PRO WO371/21855 no. 19238.

7. Longrigg, Stephen H., *The Origins and Early History of the Iraq Petroleum Company, Known From 1912 to 1929 as the Turkish Petroleum Company* (BP Archives, 1968), 55, 71–72. "History of the IPC and Mr. Gulbenkian's Part in its Foundation," Apr 1944: BP 27508, 1–2. Gulbenkian, C. S., 7–11.

8. Longrigg, *Origins*, 28. Gulbenkian, C. S., 7–12.

9. "History of the IPC," 2. Gulbenkian, C. S., 9. See Longrigg, *Origins*, 252–256.

10. Gulbenkian, C. S., 8–12. Kent, Marian, *Oil and Empire: British Policy and Mesopotamian Oil, 1900–1920,* London: Macmillan Press Ltd., 1976, 36. Note from Mallet to Grey, Sep 10, 1912: Grey mss, PRO FO800/93, as cited by Kent, *Oil*, 36.

11. Nicolson to Marling (charge), private, Sep 30, 1912: Nicolson mss, PRO FO800/358, as cited by Miller, Geoffrey, *Straits: British Policy Towards the Ottoman Empire and the Origins of the Dardanelles Campaign* (Hull, UK: University of Hull, 1997), 428.

12. Longrigg, *Origins*, 59–60, 253–256.

13. Longrigg, *Origins*, 59–60, 257.

14. Longrigg, *Origins*, 60, 257–259.

15. Longrigg, *Origins*, 60. Gulbenkian, C. S., 10.

16. Kent, *Oil*, 37.

17. See Johnson, David, "Balkan Wars," essay.

18. Jack, Marian, "The Purchase of the British Government's Shares in the British Petroleum Company 1912–1914," *Past and Present*, no. 39 (Apr 1968), 149.

19. Gulbenkian, C. S., 10.

20. Longrigg, *Origins*, 60, 260.

21. Longrigg, *Origins*, 61–62.

22. Letter, Foreign Office (FO) to the Admiralty, Nov 15, 1912: PRO FO371/1486 no. 40516.

23. Immediate and confidential letter, Mallet to India Office (IO), Dec 9, 1912: FO371/1486 no. 51935.

24. Immediate and confidential letter, Admiralty to FO, Dec 28, 1912: FO371/1486 no. 55654.

25. Telegram, Sir Edward Grey to Sir G. Lowther, no. 1092R, Dec 6, 1912: FO371/1486 no. 51845.

26. Private letter from Lowther to Maxwell, Dec 11, 1912: FO371/1486 no. 53729.

27. Lowther to Maxwell.

28. Dumas, diary entry, Jan 7, 1913: IWM PP/MCR/96, as cited by Miller, 428.

29. "Royal Commission on Oil Fuel, Second Report, Evidence of Mr. H. W. A. Deterding," Feb 26, 1913: PRO ADM116/1209.

30. "Admiralty memorandum as to the adequacy of supplies of oil," Mar 18, 1913: PRO ADM116/1209, vol. 3.

31. Kent, *Oil*, 50–53.

32. Shell files, MEP 102, as cited by Kent, *Oil*, 53. "Extracts from Documents Bearing on Claims by, and the Position of, the Turkish Petroleum Company": Shell files, MEP 20, as cited by Kent, *Oil*, 53.

33. Kent, *Oil*, 51, 54–57. Gulbenkian, C. S., 13. See "Extract from the Frankfurter Zeitung," memo, Mar 5, 1914: PRO FO371/2120 no. 10028. See letter, Mallet to Grey, Mar 10, 1914: PRO FO371/2120 no. 10784. See letter, C. Greenway to FO, Mar 10, 1914: PRO FO371/2120 no. 10880. Also see "An Agreement made the 24th day of June 1914," memorandum: BP 100687.

34. Sir G. Lowther to Sir Edward Grey, dispatch 349, Apr 25, 1913: FO371/1760 no. 19792.

35. Longrigg, *Origins*, 71–73.

36. Longrigg, *Origins*, 73. Kent, Marian, "Agent of Empire? The National Bank of Turkey and British Foreign Policy," *Historical Journal,* vol. 18, no. 2 (Jun 1975), 385.

37. Admiralty memo, June 16 1913: PRO CAB37/115. Churchill, Winston, "Oil Fuel Supply for His Majesty's Navy," Jun 16, 1913: PRO CAB37/115/39.

38. Asquith mss: Bodleian Library, Oxford vol. 7 (Cabinet Letters to the King, 1913–1914), as cited by Jack, 157.

39. Asquith mss: P.D., 5, 1913, lv, 1474–1475, as cited by Jack, 157.

40. Kent, *Oil*, 48–49.

41. Ferrier, R. W., *The History of the British Petroleum Company*, vol. 1: *The Developing Years, 1901–1932* (Cambridge, UK: Cambridge University Press, 1982), 183. See photo, "Members of the Admiralty Commission in Persia, 1913," Ferrier, 194. Kent, *Oil*, 48. Slade to Churchill, Nov 8 1913, excerpt in Admiralty memorandum for the Cabinet, Anglo-Persian Oil Company, Proposed Agreement, December 1913: PRO ADM 116/3486, as cited by Ferrier, 195. Admiralty Commission Second Interim Report, Jan 26, 1914: PRO ADM 116/3806, as cited by Ferrier, 196. See Slade, Sir J. W., et al., "Admiralty Commission on the Persian Oilfields," Jan 1914: PRO T1/11952/20174.

42. Longrigg, *Origins*, 74, 76. Mallet to Istanbul as cited by Longrigg, *Origins*, 74.

43. "Protocol Relating to the Delimitation of the Turco-Persian Boundary Signed at Constantinople on November 4th (17th), 1913." See Barstow, "Points Discussed at the Conference," Apr 9, 1919: PRO T1/12544/18025 no. 1920.

44. Gulbenkian, C. S., 12–13. Longrigg, *Origins*, 74–75. Letter, C. Greenway to Foreign Office, Jan 31, 1914: PRO FO371/2120 no. 4452. Written minutes, "Asiatic Turkey and Arabia—Confidential," Dec 13, 1913: PRO FO321/1761 no. 54400.

45. "Asiatic Turkey and Arabia—Confidential." Ashley, minutes, "Enclosure 7 in No. 1," Nov 28, 1913: PRO FO371/1761 no. 54729.

46. Gulbenkian, C. S., 12.

47.. "Asiatic Turkey and Arabia—Confidential." Parker, Alwyn, "Mesopotamian Oil Concession: Interview with Hakki Pasha respecting Mr. Gulbenkian's Attitude in This Question," confidential minutes, Dec 10, 1913: PRO FO371/1761 no. 55859. See confidential letter and enclosure, H. Babington-Smith to Sir E. Crowe, Dec 9, 1913: PRO FO371/1761 no. 5551. Kent, *Oil*, 81–82, 85

48. Gulbenkian, Nubar, 20.

49. "Asiatic Turkey and Arabia—Confidential."

50. "Asiatic Turkey and Arabia—Confidential."

51. "Asiatic Turkey and Arabia—Confidential."

52. Minutes from Sir L. Mallet to the Foreign Office, Jan 15, 1914: PRO FO371/2120 no. 2096. Confidential telegram, Sir L. Mallet to Sir Edward Grey, Jan 15, 1914: PRO FO371/2120 no. 2096.

53. Confidential letter, W. Langley to C. Greenway, Jan 16, 1914: PRO FO371/2120 no. 3468.

54. Confidential letter, C. Greenway to W. Langley, Jan 31, 1914: PRO FO371/2120 no. 4452.

55. Minutes, "Turkey—Confidential" Jan 27 1914: PRO FO371/2120 no. 3592.

56. "Turkey—Confidential." Gulbenkian, C. S., 14.

57. Sir H. Llewellyn Smith, "Mesopotamian Oil," Feb 16, 1914: PRO FO371/2120 no. 7067.

58. Alwyn Parker, memorandum, Feb 16 1914: PRO FO371/2120 no. 7068.

59. Parker, memo, Feb 16, 1914.

60. Admiralty memo, Churchill to Cabinet, Feb 10 1914: PRO CAB37/119.

61. Private letter, Alwyn Parker to Percy Ashley, Mar 2, 1914: PRO FO371/2120 no. 9311.

62. Urgent and confidential letter, Alwyn Parker to Percy Ashley, Mar 5, 1914: PRO FO371/2120 no. 9869.

63. Official letter, Percy Ashley to Alwyn Parker, Mar 6, 1914: PRO FO371/2120 no. 10010. Confidential letter, FO to Sir H. Babington-Smith, Mar 6, 1914: PRO FO 371/2120 no. 10010.

64. FO to Babington-Smith.

65. Gulbenkian, C. S., 13–14.

66. "Mesopotamian Oilfields," memo, March 10 1914: PRO FO195/2456. Letter, C. Greenway to Foreign Office, March 10 1914: PRO FO371/2120 no. 10880.

67. Letter, Grey to Mallet, March 11 1914: PRO FO195/2456 no. 64.

68. Jack, 160–161.

69. Churchill, Winston, *The World Crisis* (New York: Scribner, 1963), 91, as cited by Miller, 462.

70. "History of the IPC," 7.

71. Gulbenkian, C. S., 14. Foreign Office, "Turkish Petroleum Concession," Mar 19 1914: PRO FO195/2456. See Earle, Edward Mead, "The Turkish Petroleum Company—A Study in Oleaginous Diplomacy," *Political Science Quarterly*, vol. 39, no. 2 (Jun 1924), 269.

72. "Turkish Petroleum Concession."

73. "Turkish Petroleum Concession."

74. "Turkish Petroleum Concession."

CHAPTER 5: THE FUSE IGNITES

1. "Turkish Petroleum Concessions: Arrangements for Fusion of the Interests in Turkish Petroleum Concessions of the D'Arcy Group and of the Turkish Petroleum Company," Mar 19, 1914: PRO T1/11953 no. 119238, and BP 174-T16A: Treaties & Agreements, pt 1, 1917–37. Gulbenkian, C. S., "Memoirs of Calouste Sarkis Gulbenkian with Particular Relation to the Origins and Foundation of the Iraq Petroleum Company Limited," Sep 16, 1945: NA RG59 890.G.6363/3-148, 15. See Kent, Marian, *Oil and Empire: British Policy and Mesopotamian Oil, 1900–1920* (London: Macmillan Press Ltd., 1976), 59–94.
2. Gulbenkian, "Memoirs," 15.
3. Gulbenkian, "Memoirs," 14.
4. Telegram, Anglo-Persian to F. W. Stock (decrypted), Mar 20, 1914: PRO FO195/2456 no. 64. Telegram, Henry Babington-Smith to F. E. Whittall, Mar 20, 1914: PRO FO195/2456 no. 64. Ernest Weakley, memo of telephone call, Mar 21, 1914: PRO FO195/2456 no. 64. Telegram, H. Babington-Smith to F. E. Whittall, Mar 23, 1914: PRO FO195/2456 no. 64. "History of the IPC and Mr. Gulbenkian's Part In Its Foundation," Apr 1944: BP 27508, 8. Longrigg, Stephen H., *The Origins and Early History of the Iraq Petroleum Company, Known from 1912 to 1929 as the Turkish Petroleum Company* (BP Archive, 1968), 78–79. Telegram, Edward Grey to Louis Mallet, Mar 19, 1914: PRO FO 195/2456 no. 64.
5. Longrigg, *Origins*, 79, 81, 82, 83. Kent, *Oil*, 103–107. See "Minute re—Civil List Firmans," May 27, 1914: PRO FO195/2456 no. 64, 454. Kent, Marian, "Agent of Empire? The National Bank of Turkey and British Foreign Policy," *The Historical Journal*, vol. 18, no. 2 (Jun 1975), 379–385.
6. Edward Grey, "Turkish Petroleum Concessions," memo, Apr 20, 1914: PRO FO195/2456 no. 64, 368. See "Minute re—Civil List Firmans," May 27, 1914.
7. "An Agreement, Made the Twentieth Day of May 1914," May 20, 1914: BP 99693. Winston Churchill, confidential Cabinet memo, May 11, 1914: PRO CAB37/119 1914 no. 61.
8. Letter, Anglo-Persian Oil Company to the Treasury, May 20, 1914 as reproduced in Ferrier, R. W., *The History of the British Petroleum Company, Volume 1: The Developing Years, 1901–1932* (Cambridge, UK: Cambridge University Press, 1982), app. 6.1, 644–645. "An Agreement," May 20, 1914. Jack, Marian, "The Purchase of the British Government's Shares in the British Petroleum Company 1912–1914," *Past and Present*, no. 39 (Apr 1968), 161–162.
9. See telegram, Eyre Crowe to Gerard Lowther, enclosure no. 1, Feb 24, 1913: PRO FO424/237 no. 237, 119, as cited by Haddad, Mahmoud, "Iraq Before World War I: A Case of Anti-European Arab Ottomanism," Rashid Khalid et al., eds., *The Origins of Arab Nationalism* (New York: Columbia University Press, 1991), 134. Longrigg, *Origins*, 82, 83. Kent, *Oil*, 109. Grey, "Turkish Petroleum Concessions."
10. Churchill, minute sheet, Jun 9, 1914: PRO CAB 37/120 1914 no. 68. Miller, Geoffrey, *Straits: British Policy Towards the Ottoman Empire and the Origins of the Dardanelles Campaign* (Hull, UK: The University of Hull, 1997), 460–461. "The Naval Oil Agreement; Protest by Traders," *Times*, Jun 10, 1914: PRO T1/11953 no. 119238. See "Orders of the Day: Anglo-Persian Oil Company (APOC), Acquisition of Capital," Jun 17, 1914: PRO T1/11953 no. 119238, cols. 1123–1124.
11. Churchill, "Parliamentary debate on APOC's acquisition of capital," Jun 17, 1914, *Parliamentary Debates*, vol. 63 (1914), cols. 1138, 1139.
12. Watson Rutherford, "Parliamentary debate," Jun 17, 1914, cols. 1138–1139, 1228–1229, 1232.
13. Churchill, "Parliamentary debate," Jun 17, 1914, cols. 1140, 1146.
14. Churchill, "Parliamentary debate," Jun 17, 1914, col. 1137.
15. Churchill, "Parliamentary debate," Jun 17, 1914, cols. 1152–1153.
16. George Lloyd, "Parliamentary debate," Jun 17, 1914, cols. 1156, 1159.
17. George Lloyd, "Parliamentary debate," Jun 17, 1914, col. 1155.
18. Arthur Ponsonby, "Parliamentary debate," Jun 17, 1914, col. 1174.
19. Ponsonby, "Parliamentary debate," Jun 17, 1914, col. 1178.
20. "Parliamentary debate," Jun 17, 1914, col. 1250.Letter, Charles Greenway to John Cargill, Jun 19, 1914: BP 78/63/4, as cited by Ferrier, 199.
21. "The Navy and Persian Oil," editorial, *Times*, Jun 18, 1914, 9. "Oil for British Navy; Admiralty to Contract With a Persian Company for Supply," *New York Times* (*NYT*), May 23, 1914, C3. "For British Navy's Oil," *NYT*, Jun 17, 1914, 4. See "Producers Attack British Oil Deal," *NYT*, Jun 11, 1914. "Great Britain's Interest in Persian Oil Fields," *Wall Street Journal* (*WSJ*), Jun 10, 1914, 5. See also "What Fuel Oil Means to the Petroleum Industry," *WSJ*, Jun 6, 1914.

22. "The Navy and Persian Oil."

23. See Earle, Edward Meade, "The Turkish Petroleum Company—A Study in Oleaginous Diplomacy," *Political Science Quarterly*, vol. 39 (1924), 270. See Kent, 238n57.

24. Letter, Grand Vizier of Turkey to British Ambassador, Jun 28, 1914, as quoted in "History of the IPC," 8–9.

25. Grand Vizier to Ambassador, "History of the IPC," 8–9.

26. Jevtic, Borijove, "Assassination of Archduke Franz Ferdinand," ca. Jun 1914, World War I Document Archive, www.lib.byu.edu.

27. "Memoir of Count Franz von Harrach," ca. Jun 1914, Primary Documents, First World War Online, Michael Duffy, ed., www.firstworldwar.com. Jevtic, "Assassination."

28. "Archduke Ignored Warning," Jun 28, 1914, *NYT*, 1. "Bravery of Archduke," Jun 28, 1914, *NYT*, 1. "Exchanged Dying Words," *NYT*, Jun 29, 1914, 2. Shackelford, Michael, "Assassination of Archduke Franz Ferdinand," essay, ca. Dec 2003, World War I Document Archive.

CHAPTER 6: BLOOD FOR OIL

1. "Casualty Record of Belligerents," *NYT*, Jan 19, 1919, 39. "Military Casualties of World War One," Michael Duffy, ed., *firstworldwar.com*, www.firstworldwar.com. BBC News, "The War to End All Wars," news.bbc.co.uk. "Timeline: 1914–1918—Casualty Figures," *Trenches on the Web: An Internet History of the Great War*, The Great War Society, eds., www.worldwar1.com. See "The Cost of War," *WP*, Nov 27, 1916, 4. See "Primary Documents: D. F. Houston on U. S. War Readiness, 1917," *firstworldwar.com*.

2. "The Battle of the Somme, 1916," Aug 2001, *firstworldwar.com*. "The Battle of Verdun, 1916," *firstworldwar.com*. "The Gallipoli Front—An Overview," Aug 2002, *firstworldwar.com*. BBC History, "Battle of the Somme: 1 July–13 November 1916," Mar 2002, www.bbc.co.uk. BBC History, "Daily Mirror Headlines, Published 31 July 1916," Jan 2002, www.bbc.co.uk. "At Verdun," *NYT*, May 3, 1916, 12. See "Allied Efforts on the Somme Called 'Gallipoli on the Continent,'" *WP*, Dec 10, 1916, 5. See "How the Battle Was Won," *NYT*, Dec 17, 1916, 2. "Timeline: 1914–1918—Casualty Figures." "Military Casualties of World War One."

3. Sir George Buchanan, *The Tragedy of Mesopotamia* (London: William Blackwood & Sons, 1938), 4–5. See map, Buchanan, 287ff. Brigadier General F.J. Moberly, *History of the Great War: The Campaign in Mesopotamia, 1914–1918*, vols. 1–3. (London: H. M. Stationery Office, 1925), 78–81. Letter, Anglo-Persian Oil Company to Sir John Bradbury, Jul 30, 1914: BNA T1/11952/20174/1916 pt 1 no. 119238. Letter, John Bradbury, Nov 27, 1914: BNA T1/11952/20174/1916 pt 1 no. 119238. H. M. Treasury resolution, Nov 27, 1914: BNA T1/11952/20174/1916 pt 1 no. 119238.

4. Moberly, vol. 1, 104. See Buchanan, 4.

5. Moberly, vol. 1, 127–128, 130–131. Buchanan, 4–5. Sir Arnold T. Wilson, *Loyalties: Mesopotamia, 1914–1917: A Personal Record* (London: Oxford University Press, 1930), 10–11.

6. "Parliamentary Debate on Anglo-Persian Oil Company's Acquisition of Capital," Jun 17, 1914, *Parliamentary Debates*, vol. 63 (1914), cols. 1131–1252. Marian Jack, "The Purchase of the British Government's Shares in the British Petroleum Company 1912–1914," *Past and Present*, no. 39 (Apr 1968), 163. R.W. Ferrier, *The History of the British Petroleum Company*, vol. 1: *The Developing Years, 1901–1932* (Cambridge, UK: Cambridge University Press, 1982), 202.

7. See George R. I., "By the King: A Proclamation Relating to Trading with the Enemy," Jan 7, 1915: BNA T1/11730.

8. Letter, Charles Greenway to Under Secretary of State, Nov 2, 1914: BNA T1/11952/20174/1916 pt. 1 no. 119238.

9. Letter, Maurice de Bunsen to Charles Greenway, Nov 23, 1915: BP IPC 168-F4-FO Agreement Correspondence, Oct 1912-Oct 1927.

10. Letter, H. Babington-Smith to Undersecretary of State, Oct 21, 1914: BNA T1/11952/20174/1916 pt. 1 no. 119238. Letter, E. Blackwell to the Secretary of the Treasury, Dec 2, 1914: BNA T1/11730. B. McKenna, letter of permission, Nov 30, 1914: BNA T1/11730.

11. C.S. Gulbenkian, "Memoirs of Calouste Sarkis Gulbenkian with Particular Relation to the Origins and Foundation of the Iraq Petroleum Company Limited," Sep 16, 1945: NA RG59 890.G.6363/3-148, 16–17. Stephen H. Longrigg, *The Origins and Early History of the Iraq Petroleum Company, Known From 1912 to 1929 as the Turkish Petroleum Company* (BP Archive, 1968), 90.

12. Sir Edmund Barrow, "Military Situation in the Middle East," Jan 25, 1915: BNA CAB37/123/5. Geoffrey Miller, *Straits: British Policy towards the Ottoman Empire and the Origins*

of the Dardanelles Campaign (Hull, UK: University of Hull, 1997), 463. See table, "World Produc-tion of Petroleum, 1913–1920," Marian Kent, *Oil and Empire: British Policy and Mesopotamian Oil, 1900–1920* (London: Macmillan Press Ltd., 1976), 202–203.

13. Letter, Hardinge to Chirol, Apr 21, 1915: Asquith ms, vol. 93, pt. 2 no. 325, as cited by Kent, 119.

14. Hardinge to Nicholson, Feb 4, 1915: BNA FO800/377. "Establishment of the British Protec-torate Over Egypt," December 18, 1914, as reproduced in J. C. Hurewitz, ed., *Diplomacy in the Near and Middle East*, vol. 2 (Gerrards Cross, UK: Archive Editions, 1987), 4–5. Letter, Foreign Office to Hardinge, Mar 31, 1915: BNA FO800/377. Telegram, Chargé Blake to the Secretary of State, no. 881.00/592, Dec 20, 1914, *FRUS* 1914, 923. See "Secret Notes and Private Telegram from the Viceroy regarding the Future Settlement of Eastern Turkey in Asia and Arabia," Mar 1915: FO800/377. See "Soon to Make Egypt Part of the British Empire," *NYT*, Jun 14, 1914, SM5.

15. FO to Hardinge, Mar 31, 1915.

16. Letter, Hardinge to H. M. the King-Emperor, Oct 8, 1915: Hardinge ms, vol. 105, pt 2, as cited by Kent, 119.

17. See C. Ernest Dawn, "The Origins of Arab Nationalism," in Rashid Khalidi et al., eds., *The Origins of Arab Nationalism* (New York: Columbia University Press, 1991), 3–23.

18. Eliezer Tauber, *The Arab Movements in World War I* (London: Frank Cass, 1993), 1–9, 57. See Rashid Khalidi, "Ottomanism and Arabism in Syria Before 1914: A Reassessment," in Khalidi et al, eds., 50–65. See George Antonius, *The Arab Awakening: The Story of the Arab National Movement* (New York: Capricorn Books, 1965), 35–40, 68–70. See Ernest, 8–9, 10–13, 15–16, 21–23.

19. See Tauber, 1–10, 57.

20. See Stanford J. Shaw and Ezel Kural Shaw, *The History of the Ottoman Empire and Modern Turkey*, vol. 2: *Reform, Revolution, and Republic: The Rise of Modern Turkey, 1808–1975* (Cam-bridge, UK: Cambridge University Press, 1977), 302–303, 304, 309–310. Antonius, 102. 104–105, 106–107. See Tauber, 2–3.

21. Elie Kedourie, "The End of the Ottoman Empire," *Journal of Contemporary History*, vol. 3, (1968), 20. Wilson, *1914–1917*, 22.

22. See Tauber, 2–3, 4, 5, 7, 8–9. See "British Imperial Connexions to the Arab National Move-ment, 1912–1914; Lord Kitchener, the Emir Abdullah, Sir Louis Mallet—the Case of Aziz Ali, 1914," based on G.P. Gooch and Harold Temperly, eds., *British Documents on the Origins of the War, 1898–1914*, vol. 10, pt 2: *The Last Years of Peace* (London: H. M. Stationery Office, 1926–1938), 824–838, *WWI Document Archive*, wwi.lib.byu.edu.

23. Charles Tripp, *A History of Iraq* (Cambridge, UK: Cambridge University Press, 2000), 21–22, 24, 27, 28.

24. "Report on the Conditions for Trade in Mesopotamia," ca. Aug 1919: BL L/PS/10/386. G.R. Driver, "The Religion of the Kurds," *Bulletin of the School of Oriental Studies, University of London*, vol. 2 (1922), 197, 210.

25. "Summary of a Pamphlet, 'The Turco-British Campaign in Mesopotamia and our mistakes,' by Staff Bimbashi Muhammad Amin," in Moberly, vol. 1, 352–353. Tauber, 59. See Tripp, 21.

26. See Tauber, 25–26, 29–31, 59–60.

27. al-Fatat, "Resolution," quoted by Tauber, 57. Tauber, 57.

28. "Introduction," "The Hashemites," "The Hashemite Family Tree," official website of King Hussein, www.kinghussein.gov.jo. "New Caliph of Islam is in Power," *WP*, Jun 25, 1916, ES1. See Marquise de Fontenoy, "Turks Long Hated by the Arabians," *WP*, Dec 29, 1914, 6.

29. Secret letter, Lord Kitchener to Sir Edward Grey, Feb 6, 1914: BNA FO6672/6672/14/44 no. 22, quoted in "British Imperial Connexions to the Arab National Movement." See Introduction to "The Husayn-McMahon Correspondence," Hurewitz, 13. See de Fontenoy.

30. Letter, Lord Kitchener to Sir W. Tyrrell, Apr 26, 1914: Grey ms. vol. 9, quoted in "British Imperial Connexions to the Arab National Movement." "Emir Abdullah's Account of His Conversa-tions with Lord Kitchener, transmitted with notes by Mr. G. Antonius," quoted in "British Imperial Connexions to the Arab National Movement."

31. Letter, Sir Louis Mallet to Sir Edward Grey, Mar 18, 1914: BNA FO13871/4688/14/44 no. 103, quoted in "British Imperial Connexions to the Arab National Movement."

32. Letter, Sir Louis Mallet to Sir Edward Grey, Feb 24, 1914: BNA FO9033/7963/14/44 no. 117, quoted in "British Imperial Connexions to the Arab National Movement."

33. See Phillip Willard Ireland, *Iraq: A Study in Political Development* (New York: Macmillan Company, 1938), 67n5. See Isaiah Friedman, "The McMahon-Hussein Correspondence and the Ques-tion of Palestine," *Journal of Contemporary History*, vol. 5 (1970), 83.

34. See "Correspondence between Sir Henry McMahon and The Sherif Hussein of Mecca, July 1915–March 1916 (With a Map)," Cmd. 5957, Miscellaneous No. 3 (1939) (London: H. M. Stationery Office, 1939), 2–18, esp. letters 4–8. See also Antonius, 164–183.

35. Letter, Lord Kitchener to Sharif Hussein, Oct 31, 1914: Israel State Archives 65/2847a: 1, quoted by Tauber, 69.

36. Antonius, 157–158. See map, "The Eastern Arab World," Antonius, 160f.

37. Antonius, 159. See "Memorandum on Proposed Agreement with the French," enclosure to secret letter, Capt. W. R. Hall to Sir Arthur Nicolson, Jan 12, 1916: BNA FO 371/2767.

38. See Tauber, 71–73. See Kitchener to Grey, Feb 6, 1914. See Friedman, 84–87.

39. Letter, Sherif Hussein to Sir Henry McMahon, Jul 14, 1915 (letter 1), "Correspondence," 3–4.

40. Letter, Sir Henry McMahon to Sherif Hussein, Aug 30, 1915 (letter 2), "Correspondence," 4–5.

41. Letter, Sherif Hussein to Sir H. McMahon, Sep 9, 1915 (29th Shawal 1333) (letter 3), "Correspondence," 5–7.

42. Letter, Hussein to McMahon, Sep 9, 1915 (letter 3).

43. Letter, Sir Henry McMahon to Sherif Hussein, Oct 24, 1915 (letter 4), "Correspondence," 7–9.

44. Letter, Sherif Hussein to Sir H. McMahon, Nov 5, 1915 (27th Zil Hijja 1333) (letter 5), "Correspondence," 9–11.

45. Letter, Hussein to McMahon, Nov 5, 1915 (letter 5).

46. See Arnold Toynbee, "The McMahon-Hussein Correspondence: Comments and a Reply," *Journal of Contemporary History*, vol. 5 (1970), 186. Antoinius, 169.

47. Letter, Sir Henry McMahon to Sherif Hussein, Dec 14, 1915 (letter 6), "Correspondence," 11–12.

48. Letter, Sherif Hussein to Sir H. McMahon, Jan 1, 1916 (25th Safar 1334) (letter 7), "Correspondence," 12–14.

49. Briton Cooper Busch, *Britain, India, and the Arabs, 1914–1921* (Berkeley, CA: University of California Press, 1971), 60. Tauber, 65. See Tauber, 88–89, 90–91. See Moberly, vol. 1, 156.

50. Tauber, 80.

51. Tauber, 80. Abdallah ibn al-Husayn, *Mudhakkirati* (Jerusalem, 1945), 105–107, as cited by Tauber, 80. Sa'id, *al-Thawra*, vol. 1, 110–111, as cited by Tauber, 80.

52. Tauber, 80–81.

53. Private letters, Clayton to Jacob, Mar 11, 1916, and Clayton to Beach, Apr 17, 1916: Clayton Papers as cited by Friedman, 87. Friedman, 87.

54. See Tauber, 82, 251. Sa'id, *al-Thawra*, vol. 1, 156, as quoted by Tauber, 251.

55. Arthur Tillotson Clark, *To Baghdad with the British* (New York: D. Appleton & Co., 1918), 1–2. See Petri Liukkonnen, "Who's Who: T. E. Lawrence," *firstworldwar.com*.

56. Private telegram, Sir Percy Cox to the Viceroy, Nov 23, 1914, quoted by Moberly, vol. 1, 133. Moberly, vol. 1, 133–134.

57. Private telegram, Sir Percy Cox to the Viceroy, Nov 23, 1914 quoted by Moberly, vol. 1, 133–134. Letter, Fisher to Asquith, Nov 5, 1915: Asquith ms., 15/124, quoted by Kent, 123.

58. Moberly, vol. 1, 133–141.

59. Moberly, vol. 1, 137–139.

60. Moberly, vol. 1, 137–139.

61. Private letters, Sir A. Hardinge to H. E. Nichols, Jan 6, 1915, Apr 8, 1915, Apr 26, 1915: BNA FO800/377.

62. Wilson, *1914–1917*, 80–83.

63. Moberly, vol. 2, 63–64, 64n. See "The Present and Prospective Situation in Syria and Mesopotamia," Moberly, vol. 2, 467–468, 472–474. See generally Charles Vere Ferrers Townsend, *My Campaign*, vol. 1 (New York: James A. McCann Company, 1920), 249–276, 277–302, 303–332. See "The Battle of Ctesiphon, 1915," *firstworldwar.com*. See "Blunder Made in Mesopotamia Campaign Vigorously Assailed in House of Lords," *WP*, Sep 17, 1916, ES1.

64. Moberly, vol. 2, 282, 439–453, 455, 456–457. Townsend, vol. 2, 95–96, 155–157, 171–172, 203, 205–206, 208–209, 214. Wilson, *1914–1917*, 93–94. Clark, 78–79, 82.

65. Moberly, vol. 2, 282–284. See Letter, Hardinge to Nicholson, Jan 6, 1915: BNA FO800/377, 119.

66. Moberly, vol. 2, 449–450. 451, 452. See Wilson, *1914–1917*, 96, 99.

67. Townshend, vol. 2, 235–237. Moberly, vol. 2, 459, 460n. Wilson, *1914–1917*, 99.

68. Wilson, *1914–1917*, 99–100.

69. Wilson, *1914–1917*, 99–100.

70. Moberly, vol. 2, 461–463. Wilson, *1914–1917*, 130–133, 134–138.

71. Wilson, *1914–1917*, 132.

72. Wilson, *1914–1917*, 132–133.

73. Buchanan, 19.

74. Wilson, *1914–1917*, 136.

75. Wilson, *1914–1917*, 136–137. See photo, "Indian Army Soldier after Siege of Kut," ca. July 1916: BNA IWM Q 79446 (1916).

76. See photos, "British Troops Moving through a Baghdad Street," "Indian Troops Entering Baghdad through a Heavy Dust Storm," Clark, 200f. See "Turkish Armies May Be Surrounded," *NYT*, Mar 18, 1917, XXI. See Wilson, *1914–1917*, 231–234.

77. Moberly, vol. 2, 465.

CHAPTER 7: PROCLAMATION

1. Proclamation delivered by Gen. Stanley Maude to the people of Baghdad, Mar 19, 1917, reproduced in Brigadier General F.J. Moberly, *History of the Great War: The Campaign in Mesopotamia, 1914-1918*, vol. 3 (London: H. M. Stationery Office, 1925), 404–405, and Sir George Buchanan, *The Tragedy of Mesopotamia* (London: William Blackwood & Sons, 1938), 169–172.

CHAPTER 8: INVENTING IRAQ

1. "Tripartite (Sykes-Picot) Agreement for the Partition of the Ottoman Empire: Britain, France and Russia," reproduced in J. C. Hurewitz, ed., *Diplomacy in the Near and Middle East*, vol. 2 (Gerrards Cross, UK: Archive Editions, 1987), 18–22. Philip Willard Ireland, *Iraq: A Study in Political Development* (New York: Macmillan Company, 1938), 68–70. See letter, Sir M. Sykes to Foreign Office, Jan 16, 1916: BNA FO371/2767 no. 11844. See "Negotiations With Arabs," memorandum, Jan 21, 1916: BNA FO371/2767 no. 14106.

2. Letter, Sir T. Holderness to Sir A. Nicolson, Jan 13, 1916: BNA FO371/2767 no. 8117. Sir A. Hirtzel, "Enclosure in Note 1," Jan 13, 1916: BNA FO371/2767 no. 8117.

3. Telegram, Crewe to Hardinge, Nov 12, 1914: *India Sec. War*, May 1915, as cited by Busch, Briton Cooper, *Britain, India, and the Arabs* (Berkeley, CA: University of California Press, 1971), 63.

4. Secret telegram to Sir George Buchanan, Mar 16, 1915: BNA FO371/2627 no. 51288.

5. Marian Kent, *Oil and Empire: British Policy and Mesopotamian Oil 1900–1920* (London: Macmillan Press Ltd., 1976), 121–122.

6. Letter, C. Greenway to Foreign Office (FO), Feb 24, 1916: BNA T1/11952/20174/1916 pt. 1 no. 119238. See confidential letter, de Bunsen to Secretary of the Treasury, Mar 2, 1916: BNA T1/11952/20174/1916 pt. 1 no. 119238.

7. de Bunsen to Secretary of the Treasury. Kent, 129–130.

8. Letter, A. Hirtzel to Under Secretary of State, Apr 1, 1916: BNA FO371/2768 no. 62655.

9. Letter, C. Greenway to the Under Secretary of State for Foreign Affairs, Apr 3, 1916: BNA FO371/2721 no. 63619.

10. C.S. Gulbenkian, "Memoirs of Calouste Sarkis Gulbenkian with Particular Relation to the Origins and Foundation of the Iraq Petroleum Company Limited," Sep 16, 1945: NA RG59 890.G.6363/3-148, 18–22.

11. Gulbenkian, 17.

12. Gulbenkian, 18.

13. Gulbenkian, 18–19.

14. Hurewitz, 19. Stephen H. Longrigg, *The Origins and Early History of the Iraq Petroleum Company, Known from 1912 to 1929 as the Turkish Petroleum Company* (BP Archives, 1968), 55, 88. Gulbenkian, 23.

15. "Laws of War: Laws and Customs of War on Land (Hague II)," Jul 29, 1899, Section III, LoN Archive. "Laws of War: Laws and Customs of War on Land (Hague IV)," Oct 18, 1907, Section III, LoN Archive. Ireland, 80–85.

16. Ireland, 81–82, 87–89. Sir Arnold T. Wilson, *Loyalties: Mesopotamia 1914–1917* (London: Oxford University Press, 1930), 283–284, 321–322. Letter and attached note, J. S Grosland to Craig, Sep 25, 1916: BNA T1/12047/14548 no. 19238. See also Wilson, *1914–1917*, 88.

17. Ireland, 72.

18. Ireland, 81–84.

19. Ireland, 86–87.

20. Ireland, 81. Wilson, *1914–1917*, 66–67.

21. Wilson, *1914–1917*, 290. Ireland, 74–75.

22. "Note on the Future Status and Administration of Basrah," Feb 24, 1915: BNA FO800/377. "The Prospects of British Trade in Mesopotamia and the Persian Gulf," 1919: BL L/PS/RS/386, 41–44. See Sir George Buchanan, *The Tragedy of Mesopotamia* (London: William Blackwood and Sons Ltd., 1938), 276. Wilson, *1914–1917*, 196–198.

23. "Note on the Future Status and Administration of Basrah." "The Prospects of British Trade in Mesopotamia and the Persian Gulf," 41–44.

24. Buchanan, 5–7, 134–138. Wilson, *1914–1917*, 196–198. See telegrams, Feb 1920: BNA T1/12544/18025/1920.

25. "The Prospects of British Trade in Mesopotamia and the Persian Gulf," 41–44. "Note on the Future Status and Administration of Basrah," 2, 7.

26. "The Prospects of British Trade in Mesopotamia and the Persian Gulf," 42. Buchanan, 248–250.

27. "Baghdad Trade and Politics," *Times*, Jun 11, 1910, 7–8, as cited by Mahmoud Haddad, "Iraq Before World War I: A Case of Anti-European Arab Ottomanism," in Rashid Khalidi, et al., eds., *The Origins of Arab Nationalism* (New York: Columbia University Press, 1991), 126. Sir William Willcocks, *Sixty Years in the East* (London: 1935), 72, as cited by Haddad, 126.

28. Letter, W. Graham Greene to Under Secretary of State, Apr 14, 1916: BNA T1/11952/20174/1916 pt. 1 no. 19238. See "H. M. Petroleum Executive," memo, Mar 18, 1918: BNA T1/12144/11109. See telegram, Walter Long to Sir Frederick Black, Mar 14, 1918: BNA T1/12144/11109. R.W. Ferrier, *The History of the British Petroleum Company*, vol. 1: *The Developing Years, 1901–1932* (Cambridge: Cambridge University Press, 1982), 214.

29. Greene to Under Secretary of State. See Kent, 132–139.

30. Ferrier, 218. Letter, C. Greenway to Inchcape, Apr 11, 1917: BNA T1/12054 no. 119238.

31. Ferrier, 218–219. See "Summary of Profits for 18 Months Ended 31st March, 1918, Anglo Persian Oil Company," Dec 17, 1918: BNA T1/12342/26812. Greenway, "Memorandum re: Purchase of British Petroleum Company and Allied Concerns," May 31, 1917: BNA T1/12054 no. 119238. "Finance Arrangements for Purchase of British Petroleum Co. & O.," ca. May 1917: BNA T1/12054 no. 119238.

32. "Oil Interests in Which the Anglo Persian Oil Company Are Concerned Outside of the Area Covered by Their Persian Concern," memorandum, ca. Apr 1918: BNA T1/12366/35297/1919 no. 14799.

33. Letter, L.D. Wakely to the Under Secretary of State, Dec 18, 1919: BNA T1/12544/18025/1920 no. 55286.

34. Letter, C. Greenway to the Secretary of the Treasury, Aug 2, 1918: BNA T1/12366/35297/1919.

35. Greenway to Secretary of the Treasury.

36. Admiral Sir E.J.W. Slade, "The Petroleum Situation in the British Empire," Jul 29, 1918: BNA CAB21/119 no. 5264, 1–6.

37. Slade, 6. See letter, M.P.A. Hankey to Prime Minister, Aug 1, 1918: BNA CAB21/119.

38. Maj. Gen. F.H. Sykes, "Notes by the Chief of the Air Staff on Admiralty Memorandum No. G.T./5267 dated 30th July 1918," Aug 9, 1918: BNA CAB21/119. Letter, M.P.A. Hankey to Sir Eric Geddes, Jul 30, 1918: BNA CAB21/119.

39. Maj. Gen. Charles Vere Ferrers Townshend, *My Campaign* (New York: James A. McCann, 1920), 246–275, 280–282.

40. Sir Arnold T. Wilson, *Mesopotamia 1917–1920: A Clash of Loyalties* (London: Oxford University Press, 1931), 16. Hankey to Asquith, Aug 1, 1918.

41. Wilson, *1917–1920*, 18.

42. Wilson, *1917–1920*, 17–19.

43. Wilson, *1917–1920*, 16, 19–20.

44. Wilson, *1917–1920*, 17, 19–21.

45. Wilson, *1917–1920*, 18–21.

46. Wilson, *1917–1920*, 21, 22–23.

CHAPTER 9: THE PETROLEUM OF PEACE

1. See Sir George Buchanan, *The Tragedy of Mesopotamia* (London: William Blackwood and Sons, Ltd., 1938), 266–267.

2. Letter, Brig. Gen. Macdonough to Sir Arthur Nicolson, Jan 7, 1916, as cited by Efraim Karsh

and Inari Karsh, *Empires of the Sand: The Struggle for Mastery in the Middle East, 1789–1923* (Cambridge, MA: Harvard University Press, 1999), 225.
3. Woodrow Wilson, "Fourteen Points Speech," address to Congress, Jan 18, 1918.
4. Wilson, "Fourteen Points Speech."
5. See Charles Tripp, *A History of Iraq* (Cambridge, UK: Cambridge University Press, 2000), 34–36. See Edwin Black, *The Transfer Agreement* (Washington DC: Dialog Press, 2009), 72–76. See C. Ernest Dawn, "The Origins of Arab Nationalism," in Rashid Khalidi et al., eds., *The Origins of Arab Nationalism* (New York: Columbia University Press, 1991), 3–23. See "League of Nations: Armenia: Correspondence between the President of the Armenian Delegation and the Secretary General," Aug 25, 1921: LoN Archive A. 20. 1921 VII. See Steven W. Sowards, "Lecture 13: Serbian Nationalism from the 'Nacertanije' to the Yugoslav Kingdom," Michigan State University Library, http://staff.lib.msu.edu/sowards/balkan/lect13.htm.
6. Timothy J. Paris, "British Middle East Policy-Making After the First World War: The Lawrentian and Wilsonian Schools," *Historical Journal*, vol. 41 (1998), 773–774, 779–782. J. Marlowe, *Late Victorian: The Life of Sir Arnold Talbot Wilson* (London: Cresset Publishers, 1967), 13. Letter, A. P. Waterfield to Barstow, Apr 9, 1919: BNA T1/112544/18025/1920. Letter, Col. A. T. Wilson to Sir A. Hirtzel, Mar 5, 1920: BL Wilson papers, Add. mss 52455C, as cited by Paris, 779.
7. Private letter, Capt. A. T. Wilson to Col. C. E. Yate, Nov 28, 1914: BNA FO371/2482 no. 12124. See also "Govt's Future Action in Mesopotamia," minute sheet, Jan 28, 1915: BNA FO371/2482 no. 12124. See also letter, Col. Yate to Edward Grey, Jan 28, 1915: BNA FO371/2482 no. 12124.
8. Minutes, Nov 6, 1915: BL L/PS/10/524, as cited by Paris, 779. Paris, 779. See also Sir Arnold T Wilson, *A Clash of Loyalties: Mesopotamia, 1917–1920: A Personal Record* (London: Oxford University Press, 1931), v.
9. Philip Willard Ireland, *Iraq: A Study in Political Development* (New York: Macmillan Company, 1938), 96–97. Briton Cooper Busch, *Britain, India, and the Arabs* (Berkeley, CA: University of California Press, 1971), 22–24.
10. Tripp, 36–37. Ireland, 111–113. "Report on the Conditions for Trade in Mesopotamia Prepared in the Office of the Civil Commissioner in Baghdad," memo, ca. Aug 1919: BL L/PS/10/386. See also "Second Additional Note on the Situation in Kurdistan," memo, Jan 10, 1920: BL L/PS/10/782.
11. Ireland, 74–77.
12. Wilson, 79.
13. Ireland, 94–95. Wilson, 77–79.
14. Ireland, 94–95.
15. Ireland, 76–77. Wilson, 73, 377. Eliezer Tauber, *The Arab Movements in World War I* (London: Frank Cass and Co., 1993), 32.
16. Tauber, 32–33. Wilson, 74–75.
17. Tauber, 33. Wilson, 75. Letter, Gertrude Bell to Lowthian Bell, May 4, 1918: Gertrude Bell Letters. Letter, Gertrude Bell to Lowthian Bell, Sep 13, 1918: Gertrude Bell Letters.
18. Wilson, 75–76.
19. Wilson, 76.
20. Letter, Lord Eustace Percy to Sir George Clerk, Jun 5, 1919: BNA FO368/2095 no. 85781. Letter, Crowe to Curzon, Oct 10, 1919: Lloyd George mss, F/33/2/66, as cited by Marian Kent, *Oil and Empire: British Policy and Mesopotamian Oil 1900–1920* (London: Macmillan Press Ltd., 1976), 141.
21. Letter, French Minister to Secretary of State for Foreign Affairs (trans.), Jan 6, 1919: BNA FO368/2095 no. 3251. See "Agreement for Participation of French and British Interests in World Oil Production," minute sheet, Jan 8, 1919: BNA FO368/2095 no. 3251. "Statement of D'Arcy Exploration Company's Claim to Mesopotamian Oil Concession," Nov 12, 1918: BP 100687.
22. Letter, M. Hankey to Stanley Baldwin, Dec 13, 1918: BNA T1/12442/54465/1919 no. 171.
23. Hankey to Baldwin. Letter, Stanley Baldwin to A. H. Stanley, Dec 21, 1918: BNA BT15/76 no. 119238. See handwritten notes, Dec 21, 1918: BNA T1/12442/54465/1919.
24. Hankey to Baldwin. Baldwin to Stanley. Handwritten notes of Dec 21, 1918.
25. "Agreement for Participation of French and British Interests in World Oil Production."
26. Letter, Clemenceau to President du Conseil, Ministre de la Guerre, and Commissaire General aux Essences & Combustibles, Paris, Jan 30, 1919: BNA FO368/2242 no. 21777.
27. Kent 140–144. Hankey to Baldwin. Baldwin to Stanley. Handwritten notes of Dec 21, 1918.
28. Stephen H. Longrigg, *The Origins and Early History of the Iraq Petroleum Company, Known from 1912 to 1929 as the Turkish Petroleum Company* (BP Archives, 1968), 98–99.
29. Kent, 143–146.
30. Kent, 145.

31. Curzon to Balfour, dispatch 1837, Apr 2, 1919: BNA FO608/231 no. 2642.

32. Longrigg, 97–98. See also C.S. Gulbenkian, "Memoirs of Calouste Sarkis Gulbenkian with Particular Relation to the Origins and Foundation of the Iraq Petroleum Company Limited," Sep 16, 1945: NA RG59 890.G.6363/3-148, 20–24.

33. Gulbenkian, 22.

34. Longrigg, 92, 272–274.

35. Longrigg, 94–96. See Kent, 178–181. Edward Mead Earle, "The Turkish Petroleum Company—A Study in Oleaginous Diplomacy," *Political Science Quarterly*, vol. 39 (1924), 273. See "The Royal Dutch Shell Groups," memo, Oct 4, 1919: BNA T1/12351/30112.

36. Kent, 178.

37. Kent, 178.

38. Kent, 179. See "The Royal Dutch Shell Groups."

39. Kent, 179–180. "The Royal Dutch Shell Groups."

40. Earle, 273.

41. "B. 322. Mesopotamia Oil Policy," memo, Apr 10, 1919: BNA T1/122544/18025/1920.

42. "B. 322. Mesopotamia Oil Policy." Waterfield to Barstow. Office of the Civil Commissioner to the Under Secretary of State for India, Apr 20, 1920: BNA T1/122544/18025/1920. "Anglo-Persian Oil Co., Ltd. Baghdad," memorandum, Jul 30, 1919: BNA T1/122544/18025/1920. "Minutes of an Inter-Departmental Meeting held at the India Office, on Monday, 27th October 1919, to consider Colonel Wilson's proposals regarding the disposal of the Fleet and Oil Barges in Mesopotamia," memorandum, Nov 1, 1919: BNA T1/12544/18025/1920. Letter, L. D. Wakely to the India Office, Nov 19, 1919: BNA T1/122544/18025/1920. See draft letter to the Anglo-Persian Oil Company, Limited, ca. Apr 1919: BNA T1/122544/18025/1920.

43. Longrigg, 94. See also Kent, 152.

44. Kent, 172.

45. Kent, 172–174. See also Longrigg, 272–274.

46. "Covenant of the League of Nations," Article 22.

47. "Covenant of the League of Nations," Article 22.

48. R.W. Ferrier, *The History of the British Petroleum Company* (Cambridge, UK: Cambridge University Press, 1982), 357. Kent, 148.

49. "The Menace of Foreign State Monopolies to the American Petroleum Industry," memorandum, ca. Sep 1919: NA RG59/250/23/25/3 box 7236. Curzon to Cambon, Jul 27, 1919: BNA FO368/2095. Letter, French Chargé d'affaires to Curzon, Aug 12/13, 1919: BNA FO368/2095 no. 115404.

50. Longrigg, 272–274.

51. Longrigg, 274.

52. Longrigg, 92. Letter, H. E. Nichols to M. Tronchiere, Nov 3, 1924: BP 840. Letter, Anglo-Saxon Petroleum Company to H. E. Nichols, Dec 18, 1924: BP 67806.

53. Kent, 149–155.

CHAPTER 1 0: OIL AND THE 1 9 2 0 JIHAD

1. See generally Andrew Wheatcroft, *The Ottomans: Dissolving Images* (London: Viking, 1995), chaps. 7 and 8 ("The Lustful Turk" and "The Terrible Turk").

2. Abram Elkis, "Former Envoys' Remedies for Evil of Turkish Rule," *WP*, Mar 21, 1920, 64.

3. "Imperialism in Turkey," *WP*, Apr 1, 1920, 6.

4. "The Bulgarian Atrocities," *NYT*, Jul 29, 1876, 2. "The Barbarities in Bulgaria," *NYT*, Aug 29, 1876, 1. "Despatch from Mr. Henry Wood, Correspondent of the American 'United Press' at Constantinople; Published in the American Press, 14th August 1915," reproduced in Arnold J. Toynbee, ed., *The Treatment of Armenians in the Ottoman Empire* (London: Hodder & Stoughton, 1916), 2–3.

5. Willard Holcomb, "Abdul a Great Ruler," *WP*, Apr 28, 1909, 2. See "The War on the Danube," *NYT*, Sep 6, 1876, 1. Alan Palmer, *The Decline and Fall of the Ottoman Empire* (New York: M. Evans & Co., 1992), 146.

6. "The Armenian Atrocities," *NYT*, Jan 2, 1895, 5. "The Worst Was Not Told," *NYT*, Jan 14, 1895, 3. Henry Morgenthau, *Ambassador Morgenthau's Story* (Garden City, NY: Doubleday, Page & Co., 1918), 276–277. See "Tales of Horror Retold," *NYT*, May 20, 1895, 3.

7. See photo, "Adana Massacres, April 1909," in Peter Balakian, *The Burning Tigris: The Armenian Genocide and America's Response* (New York: HarperCollins, 2003), 236ff. Balakian, 145–152. "Muslim Massacres Take 5,000 Lives," *NYT*, Apr 21, 1909, 2.

238   NOTES

8. "Greatest Horrors in History Mark Massacres in Armenia, Declares an Official Report," *WP*, Oct 4, 1915, 5. "Turks Are Evicting Native Christians," *NYT*, Jul 12, 1915, 4. Telegram, Henry Morgenthau to Secretary of State, Jul 16, 1915: NA RG59 867.4016/76, reproduced in Balakian, 236ff.

9. Telegram, Henry Morgenthau to Secretary of State. "Armenians Are Sent To Perish in Desert," *NYT*, Aug 18, 1915, 5. "Answer Morgenthau by Hanging Armenians," *NYT*, Sep 16, 1915, 1. "Bryce Asks Us to Aid Armenia," *NYT*, Sep 21, 1915, 3. "800,000 Armenians Counted Destroyed," *NYT*, Oct 7, 1915, 3.

10. "Greatest Horrors in History Mark Massacres in Armenia." See *"New York Times* headlines of 1915," Balakian, 236ff.

11. Morgenthau, 337–338, 339. See D.K. Varzhabedian, "Armenians in Turkey," *WP*, Jan 7, 1895, 2. See poster, "You Won't Let Me Stave, Will You?," reproduced in Balakian, 236ff.

12. Morgenthau, 333–334.

13. Albert Fox, "Ratification Refused; 49 To 35, Senate Vote; Pact Sent To Wilson," *WP*, Mar 20, 1920, 1. James Gerard, "The Mandate for Armenia," *NYT*, Jun 1, 1919, 38. "Why America Should Accept Mandate For Armenia," *NYT*, Jul 6, 1919, 44.

14. "The Balfour Declaration," Nov 2, 1917, reproduced in J. C. Hurewitz, ed., *Diplomacy in the Near And Middle East*, vol. 2 (New York: Van Nostrand Company, 1956), 26.

15. *Encyclopedia Judaica (EJ)*, s.v. "Russia."

16. "Russian Harshness to Jews Increases," *NYT*, Feb 19, 1904, 2. *EJ*, s.v. "Russia." See photo, "Public Hanging in Jerusalem," *EJ*, 300. See *EJ*, 1458.

17. "The Balfour Declaration."

18. See "Resolution of the General Syrian Congress, 2 July 1919," reproduced in Hurewitz, vol. 2, 62–64. See Black, *The Farhud*, chap 5.

19. "Anglo–French Declaration, 7 November 1918," reproduced in Hurewitz, vol. 2, 30. See introduction, "British and Anglo–French Statements to the Arabs, January–November 1918," Hurewitz, vol. 2, 28–29.

20. "Anglo–French Declaration, 7 November 1918."

21. Jan Karl Tanenbaum, "France and the Arab Middle East, 1914–1920," *Transactions of the American Philosophical Society*, vol. 68, pt. 7 (1978), 21, 34, 35. Quai d'Orsay memo, "Note sur la Syrie," Feb 14, 1919: Archives du Ministère des Affaires Etrangères (AAE), série: Levant S-L-C, vol. 10, fol. 46, quoted by Tanenbaum, 27.

22. "Amir Faysal's Memorandum to the Supreme Council at the Paris Peace Conference, 1 January 1919," reproduced in Hurewitz, vol. 2, 38–39.

23. "Amir Faysal's Memorandum to the Supreme Council."

24. "Amir Faysal's Memorandum to the Supreme Council."

25. "Amir Faysal's Memorandum to the Supreme Council."

26. "Amir Faysal's Memorandum to the Supreme Council."

27. Chaim Weizmann, *Trial And Error: The Autobiography of Chaim Weizmann* (New York: Harper & Brothers, 1949), 234–235. "The Faisal–Weizmann Agreement, January 1919," reproduced in George Antonius, *The Arab Awakening: The Story of the Arab National Movement* (New York: Capricorn Books, 1965), 437–439.

28. "The Faisal–Weizmann Agreement."

29. Letter, Clemenceau to Faisal, Apr 17, 1919: AAE, série: Levant, Arabie-Hedjaz, vol. 4, fol. 85, and "Declaration," Apr 17, 1919: AAE, série: Levant, Arabie-Hedjaz, vol. 4 fols. 36–37, as cited by Tanenbaum, 30. Tanenbaum, 29, 30, 31. See letter, Phillip Hitti to the editor, *NYT*, Feb 3, 1919, 32. Generally see Stephen H. Longrigg, *Syria and Lebanon under French Mandate* (London: Oxford University Press, 1958).

30. Letter, Faisal to Clemenceau, Apr 20, 1919: AAE, série: Levant S-L-C, vol. 12, fols. 133–134, quoted by Tanenbaum, 30.

31. "Resolution of the General Syrian Congress at Damascus, 2 July 1919." Tanenbaum, 27–31. Antonius, 297. See letter, Hitti to editor.

32. De Caix, memo, "Esquisse de l'organisation de la Syrie sous le mandat français," Jul 17, 1920: AAE série: Levant S-L-C, vol. 31, fol. 28, quoted by Tanenbaum, 36. Tanenbaum, 31, 36. Longrigg, *Lebanon and Syria*, 75–77, 78, 79, 82.

33. "The Provisional Agreement of January 6, 1920," AAE, série: Levant: 1918-1920, Arabie, vol. 8, fols. 83–86, quoted by Tanenbaum, 44–45. Tanenbaum, 35–36. Longrigg, *Lebanon and Syria*, 82. "General Gouraud on the Second Battle of the Marne, 16 July 1918," *firstworldwar.com*, www.firstworldwar.com. "Who's Who: Henri Gouraud," *firstworldwar.com*.

34. Tanenbaum, 37.

35. Encrypted telegram, Egyptian G. H. Q. to War Office, Mar 12, 1920: BL L/MIL/5/799. Tanenbaum, 37–38. Antonius, 304.

36. Letter, Alexandre Millerand to Paul Cambon, Mar 13, 1920: AAE, série: Levant S-L-C, vol. 25, fol. 5, quoted by Tanenbaum, 38. Letter, Lord Curzon to General Allenby, quoted in letter, Cambon to Millerand, Mar 13, 1920: AAE, série: Levant S-L-C, vol. 24, fol. 55, quoted by Tanenbaum, 38.

37. Letter, Curzon to Allenby, quoted by Tanenbaum, 38. Tanenbaum, 38.

38. "San Remo Meeting to Take Up Turkey," *NYT*, Apr 3, 1920, 3. "The Carving of Turkey," *WP*, Apr 18, 1920, 24. See Edwin James, "Asks British Denial of Turkish Treaty," *NYT*, May 8, 1920, 3. See Secretary of State for India, "Note on the Causes of the Outbreak in Mesopotamia," secret note, ca. Aug 1922: BL L/MIL/5/799. See "Chronology, 1920," League of Nations Photo Archive.

39. "The Mandate for Syria and Lebanon, 24 July 1922," reproduced in Longrigg, *Lebanon and Syria*, 376–380. "The Mandate for Palestine, 24 July 1922," reproduced in Hurewitz, vol. 2, 107–111. See "Treaty of Alliance: Great Britain and Iraq, 10 October 1922," reproduced in Hurewitz, vol. 2, 111–114. See letter, John Davis to Earl Curzon, May 12, 1920: BNA BT15/16/119238.

40. Stefan Wolff, "Long-Term Consequences of Forced Population Transfers: Institutionalized Ethnic Cleansing as the Road to New (In)-Stability? A European Perspective," in Steven Bela Vardy, T. Hunt Tooley, and Agnes Huszar Vardy, eds., *Ethnic Cleansing in Twentieth-Century Europe* (Boulder, CO: East European Monographs, 2003), 773–786. See A. De Zayas, "International Law And Mass Population Transfers," *Harvard International Law Journal*, vol. 207 (1975).

41. Wolff. See De Zayas.

42. "Draft Agreement Concerning Petroleum," confidential attachment to letter, John Davis to Secretary of State, May 7, 1920: NA RG59 800.6363/113.

43. "Memorandum of Agreement between M. Phillipe Berthelot, Directeur des Affaires politiques et commerciales au Ministère des Affaires Etrangères, and Professor Sir John Cadman, KCMG, Director in Charge of His Majesty's Petroleum Department," Apr 24, 1920: BP IPC 168-F4: FO Agreement Correspondence Oct 1912–Oct 1927.

44. "Memorandum of Agreement."

45. "Memorandum of Agreement."

46. "Memorandum of Agreement." Letter, Secretary–General of the Hedjaz Delegation to Secretary-General of the Council of the League of Nations, May 8, 1920: LoN K1 1/4284/4284. Marian Kent, *Oil and Empire: British Policy and Mesopotamian Oil 1900–1920* (London: Macmillan Press Ltd., 1976), 155. See telegram, Department of State to American Embassy, London, May 10, 1920: NA RG59 800.6363/111a.

47. Letter, Secretary-General of the Hedjaz Delegation to Secretary–General of the Council of the League of Nations.

48. Letter, Secretary-General of the Hedjaz Delegation to Secretary–General of the Council of the League of Nations.

49. "Riots in Jerusalem," *NYT*, Apr 8, 1920, 15. See Longrigg, *Syria and Lebanon*, 96–97. See "Note on the Causes of the Outbreak in Mesopotamia." See letter, Millerand to Gouraud, May 11, 1920: AAE, série: Levant S-L-C, vol. 27, fol. 240, quoted by Tanenbaum, 39–40. See T.E. Lawrence, "A Report on Mesopotamia," *Sunday Times*, Aug 22, 1920. See telegram to Wilson, Apr 7, 1919: BNA AIR2/122.

50. See letter, Hardinge to Allenby, Jul 16, 1920, quoted by Tanenbaum, 39. Letter, Curzon to Millerand, May 18, 1920: AAE, série: Levant S-L-C, vol. 28, fol. 35, quoted by Tanenbaum, 40. "Proposition d'une reunion de concertation pour redaction d'instructions au general Gouraud," May 19, 1920: AAE, série: Levant S-L-C, vol. 28, fols. 76–77, quoted by Tanenbaum, 40. Tanenbaum, 39–40.

51. Letters, Millerand to Gouraud, July 23 and 24, 1920: AAE, série: Levant S-L-C, vol. 31, fols. 117 and 164, quoted by Tanenbaum, 41. Longrigg, *Syria and Lebanon*, 101–102.

52. "French Begin War on Feisal in Syria; Columns Moving on Aleppo and Damascus," *NYT*, Jul 17, 1920, 1. "Syria Arms For War," *WP*, Jul 19, 1920, 1. "Feisal Mobilizes Against French in Syria; Gouraud Reported Ready to Move Today," *NYT*, 12. Edwin James, "French Rout Emir; Enter Damascus," *NYT*, Jul 26, 1920, 1. Longrigg, *Syria and Lebanon*, 102–103.

53. "Anglo-French Oil Agreement Is Out," *NYT*, Jul 24, 1920, 7.

54. "Ten Thousand Jews Thank Great Britain," *NYT*, Jul 13, 1920, 12. See "Zionists Elect Brandeis," *WP*, Jul 24, 1920, 4. See photo, "The London Zionist Conference," Jewish Agency for Israel, www.jafi.org.il. See "The Foundation Fund," *Zionist Bulletin*, Jul 26, 1920, 8 reproduced in "The London Zionist Conference 1920 and the Foundation of Keren Hayesod," The Jewish Agency for Israel.

55. Antonius, 312.

56. "Chart Showing Approximate Area Effected by One H. P. Machine Carrying 10–9.45 Gas Bombs," attachment to memo, C. A. S. to R. Brooke-Popham, Dec 13, 1919: BNA AIR2/122.

57. "Churchill Proposes to Guard Mesopotamia by Air Patrol," *NYT*, Mar 23, 1920, 1. "Report on Air Squadrons in Middle East," Nov 4, 1919: BNA AIR2/122. See memo, War Office, Apr 14, 1919: BNA AIR2/122.

58. Secret memo to Air Ministry, Apr 19, 1919: BNA AIR2/122.

59. War Department, "General Orders, No. 62," Jun 28, 1918: U. S. Army Center for Military History. "Weapons of War: Poison·Gas," *firstworldwar.com*, See Edwin Black, *War Against the Weak: Eugenics and America's Campaign to Create a Master Race* (Washington, DC: Dialog Press, 2009), 258.

60. Note to the Flying Office Directorate, Air Board, May 2, 1919: BNA AIR2/122.

61. Churchill, minutes, May 12, 1919, reproduced in Martin Gilbert, *Winston S. Churchill, Companion to Vol. 4* (London: Heinemann: 1977), 649.

62. Churchill, minutes.

63. Memo, R. M. Groves, May 19, 1919: BNA AIR2/122. R. M. Groves, War Office minute sheet B9967, May 24, 1919: BNA AIR2/122.

64. Brooke-Popham, note, Jun 16, 1919: BNA AIR2/122.

65. Brooke-Popham, minute sheet 16A, Jun 16, 1919: BNA AIR2/122

66. Brooke-Popham, memo, Jun 30, 1919: BNA AIR2/122.

67. Brooke-Popham, memo, Jun 30, 1919. "Chart Showing Approximate Area Effected by One H. P. Machine Carrying 10–9.45 Gas Bombs."

68. Eliezar Tauber, "The Struggle for Dayr al-Zur: The Determination of Borders between Syria and Iraq," *International Journal of Middle East Studies*, vol. 23 (1991), 367. Sir Arthur T. Wilson, *A Clash of Loyalties: Mesopotamia, 1917–1920: A Personal Record* (London: Oxford University Press, 1931), 231.

69. Wilson, 232. Tauber, 367.

70. "British Air Service Plan," *WP*, Dec 15, 1919, 4. Wilson, *Clash of Loyalties*, 234. Philip Meilinger, "Trenchard and 'Morale Bombing': The Evolution of Royal Air Force Doctrine before World War II," *Journal of Military History*, vol. 60 (1996), 251.

71. Secret telegram to War Office, Apr 6, 1920: BL L/MIL/5/798.

72. Wilson, *Clash of Loyalties*, 249.

73. "Note on the Causes of the Outbreak in Mesopotamia." Telegram, Wilson to Secretary of State for India, May 8, 1920, reproduced in "Note on the Causes of the Outbreak in Mesopotamia."

74. Telegram, Wilson to Secretary of State for India, May 8, 1920.

75. Amal Vinogradov, "The 1920 Revolt in Iraq Reconsidered: The Role of Tribes in National Politics," *International Journal of Middle East Studies*, vol 3 (1972), 135. Wilson, *Clash of Loyalties*, 253–254.

76. Vinograd, 134–135. Wilson, *Clash of Loyalties*, 253.

77. Vinograd, 135. Wilson, *Clash of Loyalties*, 255.

78. Vinograd, 135–136.

79. Phillip Willard Ireland, *Iraq: A Study in Political Development* (New York: Macmillan Company, 1938), 238–239. Wilson, *Clash of Loyalties*, 273.

80. Wilson, *Clash of Loyalties*, 274.

81. Ireland, 262.

82. Ireland, 259.

83. "Lost 161 in Mesopotamia," *NYT*, Jul 20, 1920, 9. Ireland, 266, 267. Wilson, *Clash of Loyalties*, 277, 278.

84. "Lost 161 in Mesopotamia." Wilson, *Clash of Loyalties*, 278–279, 279n. Ireland, 266, 267–268, 269.

85. Ireland, 268. James, "French Rout Emir."

86. Churchill, "Situation in Mesopotamia, 20th August 1920," secret Cabinet memo, Aug 20, 1920: BL L/MIL/5/799. Wilson, *Clash of Loyalties*, 272, 282, 293.

87. Churchill, "Situation in Mesopotamia, 2nd September 1920," secret Cabinet memo, Aug 2, 1920: BL L/MIL/5/800. Wilson, *Clash of Loyalties*, 294.

88. Ireland, 270–271. Wilson, *Clash of Loyalties*, 292.

89. Wilson, *Clash of Loyalties*, 298. Despatch from High Commissioner, Baghdad, Oct 4, 1920: BL L/MIL/5/800.

90. Wilson, *Clash of Loyalties*, 298. Ireland, 272n3.

91. Secret telegram from Civil Commissioner, Baghdad, Aug 6, 1920: BL L/MIL/5/799.

92. Wilson, *Clash of Loyalties*, 270–271, 277.

93. Wilson, *Clash of Loyalties*, 271.

94. Churchill, "Recent Events in Mesopotamia," secret Cabinet memo, Sep 30, 1920: BL L/ MIL/5/800.
95. "Churchill Proposes to Guard Mesopotamia by Air Patrol." Secret telegram from War Office, Oct 5, 1920: BL L/MIL/5/800.
96. "Situation in Mesopotamia, 2nd September 1920." Secret telegram, General Officer Commanding (GOCM), Mesopotamia to War Office, Aug 28, 1920 quoted in "Situation in Mesopotamia, 2nd September 1920." Secret memo, GOCM to War Office, Sep 30, 1920: BL L/MIL/5/800. Vinogradov, 137.
97. Secret telegram, GOCM, Mesopotamia to War Office, Aug 28, 1920, quoted in "Situation in Mesopotamia, 2nd September 1920." See Secret telegram, GOCM to War Office, Sep 28, 1920: BL L/ MIL/5/800. Secret telegram, War Office to GOCM, Oct 5, 1920: BL L/MIL/5/800.
98. Churchill, "Air Staff Memorandum on the Air Force as an Alleged Cause of the Loss of Popularity of the Mesopotamia Civil Administration," Aug 27, 1920: BL L/MIL/5/800. Meilinger, 244.
99. Meilinger, 244. See "Sir Arthur 'Bomber' Harris (1892–1984)," BBC History, www.bbc.co.uk.
100. Vinogradov, 137, 138–139.
101. Vinogradov, 138.
102. Wilson, *Clash of Loyalties*, 321. Ireland, 277–278, 286–287, 326, 335. See "Churchill's Speech Displeases Paris," *NYT*, Jun 16, 1921, 3.
103. Lovat Fraser, "The War-Mongers," *Daily Mail*, July 12, 1920, quoted by Briton Cooper Busch, *Britain, India, and the Arabs, 1914–1921* (Berkeley, CA: University of California Press, 1971), 409. Antonius, 315. Ireland, 273. See secret telegram, War Office to G. H. Q. Mesopotamia, Sep 8, 1920: BL L/MIL/5/800.
104. Sir Henry Dobbs, "Britain's Work in Iraq and Prospects of the New State," address to the Royal Empire Society, Feb 1933, quoted by Sir George Buchanan, *The Tragedy of Mesopotamia* (London: William Blackwood & Sons, 1938), 285.
105. Buchanan, 285–286.
106. Ferrier, 308–309.

CHAPTER 11: THE RED LINE

1. *Iraq: Treaty with King Feisal*, Cmd. 1757 (1922). "British Conclude Alliance with Irak," *NYT*, Oct 12, 1922, 5.
2. Secret telegrams to War Office, Aug 22, 1920, Aug 24, 1920, Aug 26, 1920, and Aug 26, 1920, reproduced in Churchill, "Situation in Mesopotamia," secret cabinet memo, Sep 2, 1920: BL L/MIL/5/800.
3. *Iraq: Treaty with King Feisal*. "British Conclude Alliance With Irak."
4. See letter to Mead Taylor, Apr 26, 1924: BNA BT15/27/119238.
5. Woodrow Wilson, "Fourteen Points Speech," address to Congress, Jan 18, 1918. Letter, Bainbridge Colby to Earl Curzon, Nov 20, 1920: NA RG59 800.6363/196A, *FRUS* 1920, 669, 670.
6. Letter, Thomas O'Donnell to Robert Lansing, Sep 30, 1919: NA RG59 800.6363/89.
7. See American Petroleum Institute, "The Menace of Foreign State Monopolies to the American Petroleum Industry," ca. Sep 1919, enclosure in O'Donnell to Lansing, Sep 30, 1919.
8. "Memorandum Regarding British Petroleum Policy," ca. Sep 1919, enclosure to confidential memo to the Secretary of State, Oct 10, 1919: NA RG59 800.6363/87.
9. "Imperative Need for Aggressive Foreign Policy as Regards the Oil Industry," Mar 1, 1920, enclosure to letter, Alvey Adee to Bradley Stoughton, Apr 17, 1920: NA RG59 800.6363/95.
10. "The Menace of Foreign State Monopolies to the American Petroleum Industry," 6.
11. "Memorandum on Mesopotamia, and Other Oil-bearing Regions, Affected by the Peace Settlements," ca. Sep 1920: NA RG59 800.6363 S250 R23 C25 box 7236.
12. See "Statement of Mineral Oil Rights Granted in the Ottoman Empire as of January 1st, 1920," enclosure to letter, G. Bie Ravndal to the Secretary of State, Apr 27, 1920: NA RG59 800.6363.16a. *Congressional Record*, vol. 58, pt. 4, 3304–3310, as cited by Habibollah Atarodi, *Great Powers, Oil and the Kurds in Mosul (Southern Kurdistan/Northern Iraq), 1910–1925* (Lanham, MD: University Press of America, 2003), 89. Stephen H. Longrigg, *Oil in the Middle East: Its Discovery and Development* (London: Oxford University Press, 1968), 107, 107n3.
13. Letter, Oscar Heizer to Secretary of State, Dec 9, 1919: NA RG59 800.6363/75.
14. "Minutes of the Conference Held at the India Office on Friday 2nd January 1920:" BNA T1/12544/18025/1920.
15. Draft of telegram, Ambassador Davis to Lord Curzon, May 10, 1920: NA RG59 800.6363/111a.

Confidential letter, Hugh C. Wallad to Secretary of State, May 7, 1920: NA RG59 800.6363/113. Alexander W Knott, "Bainbridge Colby," in Edward S. Mihalkanin, ed., *American Statesmen: Secretaries of State from John Jay to Colin Powell* (Westport, CT: Greenwood, 2004), 141–142.
16. Draft of telegram, Davis to Curzon.
17. Letter, M. L. Requa to Alvey Adlee, May 13, 1920: NA RG59 800.6363/112.
18. Letter, Requa to Adlee.
19. Letter, Davis to Secretary of State, May 18, 1920: NA RG59 800.6363/126.
20. "The Royal Dutch Shell Interests in USA," ca. Oct 1921: BP 72491. See Longrigg, 107n3. See Letter, Ambassador Geddes to Secretary of State, Apr 20, 1921: NA RG59 841.6363/143, *FRUS* 1921, vol. 2, 71. Letter, Thomas O'Donnell to Secretary of State, Sep 30, 1919: NA RG59 800.6363/89. Edward Meade Earle, "The Turkish Petroleum Company—A Study in Oleaginous Diplomacy," *Political Science Quarterly*, vol. 39 (1924), 275. Letter, Earl Curzon to Mr. Davis, Feb 28, 1921, quoted in "Correspondence Between H. M. Government and the United States Ambassador Respecting Economic Rights in Mandated Territories," Feb 1921: BT15/76/119238.
21. John Cadman, "Memorandum of Meeting," Apr 9, 1922, attachment to Foreign Office letter, Apr 21, 1922: BNA POWE33/95.
22. "Memorandum of Meeting."
23. Telegram, Foreign Office to M. Cheetham, Jul 18, 1922: BNA POWE33/95. Letter, Turkish Petroleum Company to H. M. Petroleum Department, Jul 6, 1922: BNA POWE33/95. "Memorandum of Negotiations in London between American Oil Interests and the Turkish Petroleum Company," Jul 21, 1922: NA RG59 890g.6363 T84/48, *FRUS* 1922, vol. 2, 340–342. Letter, Secretary of State to W. C. Teagle, Aug 22, 1922: NA RG59 890g.6363 T84/41a, *FRUS* 1922, vol. 2, 342–344.
24. Telegram, Secretary of State to Ambassador Harvey, Jun 24, 1922: NA RG 59 890g.6363 T84/41, *FRUS* 1922, vol. 2, 337. Letter, A. C. Bedford to the Secretary of State, Jun 27, 1922: NA RG59 800g.6363 T84/46, *FRUS* 1922, vol. 2, 338. Telegram, A. C. Bedford to Charles Greenway, Jun 26, 1922, enclosure to NA RG59 800g.6363 T84/46. Telegram, Ambassador Harvey to Secretary of State, Aug 4, 1922: NA RG59 800g.6363 T84/43, *FRUS* 1922 vol. 2, 339–340. Letter, Secretary of State to W.C. Teagle, Aug 22, 1922: NA RG59 800g.6363 T84/41a, *FRUS* 1922, vol. 2, 342–343. Telegram to Lord Hardinge, Jul 11, 1922: BNA POWE 33/95. Longrigg, 68n1, 69.
25. *Iraq: Treaty with King Feisal*, Article XI.
26. J. C. Hurewitz, introduction to "United States Interests and Conditions of Participation in the Lausanne Conference," in J. C. Hurewitz, ed., *Diplomacy in the Near and Middle East*, Vol. 2 (New York: Van Nostrand Company, 1956), 114. "U.S. *Aide-Memoire* to Britain, France and Italy, 30 October 1922" and "Secretary Hughes' Instructions to U.S. Ambassadors at London, Paris and Rome, 30 October 1922," reproduced in Hurewitz, 114–119.
27. Telegram, Secretary of State to American Mission at Lausanne, Nov 27, 1922: NA RG59 890g.6363/156, *FRUS* 1922, vol. 2, 346.
28. Telegram, Secretary of State to American Mission at Lausanne.
29. Lord Curzon, speech at Lausanne, Jan 23, 1923: BNA CO730/46/4849, quoted by Peter Sluglett, *Britain in Iraq, 1914–1932* (London: Ithaca Press, 1976), 110–111.
30. Lord Curzon, speech at Lausanne, Jan 23, 1923.
31. Minutes, Dec 9, 1922: BNA FO839/10. Letter, Montagau Piesse to W. C. Teagle, Dec 12, 1922, enclosure to telegram, W. C. Teagle to Secretary of State, Dec 13, 1922: NG RG59 890g.6363 T84/62. *FRUS* 1922, 348–349.
32. Letter, Piesse to Teagle.
33. Letter, Piesse to Teagle.
34. Letter, H. E. Nichols to C. S. Gulbenkian, Dec 18, 1922: BP IPC 140-Letter Book, TPC Ltd 2: 1920s.
35. Nichols to Gulbenkian.
36.. Nichols to Gulbenkian.
37. Draft memorandum of Dec 18, 1922: BP 68820.
38. See "At Lausanne," *WP*, Jan 25, 1923, 6. See Lord Curzon, speech at Lausanne, Jan 23, 1923.
39. Turkish Democracy Foundation, "Is Outside Powers' Interest in Kurds Mainly Because Of Humanitarian Concerns?" chap. 14, *Fact Book on Turkey, Kurds, and the PKK Terrorism.*
40. Mustafa Sarımollaoğlu, ed., "Treaty of Lausanne—Chronology of the Treaty," *Türkiye: History of the Republic of Turkey*, http://turkiye.sarimollaoglu.com/history/history-of-the-republic-of-turkey/231-treaty-of-lausanne.
41. Letter, C. S. Gulbenkian to H. E. Nichols, Jan 11, 1923: BP 67810.

42. Letter, C. S. Gulbenkian to H. E. Nichols, Sep 28, 1923: BP 67764. Letter, H. E. Nichols to C. S. Gulbenkian, Oct 4, 1923: BP 67764.

43. Nichols to Gulbenkian, Oct 4, 1923.

44. "Draft Convention of September 1923 between the Government of Iraq and the Turkish Petroleum Company, Limited," Sep 1923, enclosure to letter, W.C. Teagle to the Department of State, Oct 25, 1923: RG 59 890g.6363 T 84/117, *FRUS* 1923, vol. 2, 246–259.

45. Letter, C. S. Gulbenkian to H. E. Nichols, Oct 26, 1923: BP 67764.

46. Gulbenkian to Nichols, Oct 26, 1923.

47. Letter, H. E. Nichols to C. S. Gulbenkian, Oct 31, 1923: BP 67764.

48. See John Lodwick with D. H. Young, *Gulbenkian: An Interpretation of "The Richest Man in the World"* (Garden City, NY: Doubleday & Company, 1958), 151, 254–258.

49. Letter to Clarke, Jan 2, 1924: BP IPC 140-Letter Book, TPC Ltd 2: 1920s. Letter, Turkish Petroleum Company (TPC) to The Registrar, Jan 3, 1924: BP IPC 140-Letter Book, TPC Ltd 2: 1920s. Letter to Clarke, Jan 14, 1924: BP: BP IPC 140-Letter Book, TPC Ltd 2: 1920s. Letter, H. E. Nichols to Sir Henri Deterding, Jan 14, 1924: BP: BP IPC 140-Letter Book, TPC Ltd 2: 1920s. Letter, H. E. Nichols to C. S. Gulbenkian, Jan 14, 1924: BP: BP IPC 140-Letter Book, TPC Ltd 2: 1920s.

50. Letter, H.E. Nichols to N.S. Gulbenkian, Jan 25, 1924: BP 520. *Observer* (1965).

51. Nichols to N.S. Gulbenkian, Jan 25, 1924. Nubar Gulbenkian, *Portrait in Oil: The Autobiography of Nubar Gulbenkian* (New York: Simon & Schuster, 1965), 95.

52. Letter, H.E. Nichols to W.C. Teagle, Jul 29, 1924: BP IPC 140-Letter Book, TPC Ltd 2: 1920s.

53. See Letter, Freshfields, Leese & Munns to H.E. Nichols, Aug 12, 1924: BP 67764. See Longrigg, 115–119.

54. Freshfields, Leese & Munns to Nichols, Aug 12, 1924.

55. Letter, H. E. Nichols to M. Tronchere, Sep 9, 1924: BP IPC 140-Letter Book, TPC Ltd 2: 1920s.

56. See "Draft Letter to be written to Messrs. Freshfields," Sep 16, 1924: BP 67806. Letter, H. G. Brown to Messrs. Freshfields, Leese & Munns, Sep 26, 1924: BP 68820.

57. Brown to Freshfields, Leese, & Munns.

58. Brown to Freshfields, Leese, & Munns.

59. W.C. Teagle et al., memo, Sep 18, 1924: NA RG59 890g.6363 T84/167, *FRUS* 1924, vol. 2, 230, 231.

60. Telegram, Secretary of State to Ambassador Kellog, Sep 20, 1924: NA RG59 890g.6363 T84/162a, *FRUS* 1924, vol. 2, 233–235.

61. Letter, W. Tyrrell to C.S. Gulbenkian, Oct 10, 1924: BP: 27508.

62. Letter, H.E. Nichols to E. Mercier, Nov 12, 1924: BP IPC 140-Letter Book, TPC Ltd 2: 1920s.

63. See letter, Turkish Petroleum Company to C.S. Gulbenkian, Jan 13, 1925: BP IPC 140: Letters from TPC, Jan–Aug 1925. Letter, C.S. Gulbenkian to H.E. Nichols, Feb 16, 1925: BP IPC 174-530A. See Letter H.E. Nichols to C.S. Gulbenkian, Jan 24, 1925: BP IPC 174-530A. "To Fight for Billion and Rich Oil Lands for Sultan's Heirs," *NYT*, Nov 22, 1924, 1. "Riches of 'Abdul The Damned,'" *Daily Express*, Feb 23, 1934: BP IPC 174-530A. See Letter, C.S. Gulbenkian to H.E. Nichols and enclosed press clippings, Feb 26, 1925: BP IPC 174-530A. See *Contract between T.T.H. Heirs of His Majesty Sultan Abdul Hamid II and Mssrs. John Godolphin Bennett & George Maitland Edwards*, ca. Feb 1924: BP IPC 174-530A.

64. Turkish Petroleum Company, *Limited Convention with the Government of Iraq*, Mar 14, 1925: BNA CO730/158/9/119238. "The Omens from Lausanne," *WP*, Jan 25, 1923, 6.

65. John Cadman, "Memorandum of Heads of Agreement Between Sir John Cadman on Behalf of the Anglo-Persian Oil Company Limited's Group and Mr. C. S. Gulbenkian, Subject to Ratification by the Anglo-Persian Co. Ltd.'s Board," Nov 29, 1925: BP 68820. "Synopsis of the Negotiations for American Participation in the Turkish Petroleum Co.," Dec 24, 1924: BP 67809.

66. Draft cable to W.C. Teagle, ca. Sep 1924: BP 68820.

67. Letter, Anglo-Saxon Petroleum Company to TPC, Sep 30, 1925: BP 67808.

68. Montagu Piesse, memorandum on behalf of American group, Oct 6, 1925: BP 67809.

69. Minutes, TPC meeting, Oct 29, 1925: BP 67809.

70. Memo, Dec 2, 1925: BP IPC 166: C2FF. See Longrigg, 114.

71. Telegram, Secretary of State to Ambassador Houghton, Dec 5, 1925: NA RG59 890g.6363 T 84/226, *FRUS* 1925, vol. 2, 239-240.

72. Telegram, Secretary of State to Houghton, Dec 5, 1925.

73. Draft of "Agreement for Payment of Royalty to the D'Arcy Exploration Company Limited and for Making Arrangements Between the Iraq Petroleum Company Limited and Others," May 7, 1925: BP 68820.

74. Letter, C.S. Gulbenkian to Sir John Cadman, Dec 25, 1925: BP 68820.

75. Letter, Henri Deterding to Anglo-Persian Oil Company, Jan 2, 1926: BP 27810.

76. T.R. Ybarra, "War Looms As Turks Raid Christians," *NYT*, Sep 16, 1925, 1. "Turks Lose First Irak Test Despite Threat to Depart," *WP*, Dec 9, 1925, 3. Atarodi, 200–202, 204.

77. Letter, H.E. Nichols to Colonial Office, Apr 1, 1926: BP 68820.

78. Letter, C.S. Gulbenkian to H.E. Nichols, Apr 12, 1926: BP 67810.

79. Letter, Linklaters & Paines to Anglo-Persian Oil Company, May 7, 1926: BP 67810. See draft of "Agreement for Payment of Royalty to the D'Arcy Exploration Company Limited And For Making Arrangements Between the Iraq Petroleum Company Limited And Others."

80. Letter and memorandum, Anglo-Persian Oil Company and Anglo-Saxon Petroleum Company to Linklaters & Paines, Jun 10, 1926: BP 68820.

81. See "An Agreement Between the Turkish Petroleum Company Limited, The D'Arcy Exploration Company Limited, The Anglo-Saxon Petroleum Company Limited, La Comapagnie Française de Petroles and Calouste Sarkis Gulbenkian," ca. Feb 1927: BP 67811. See "Sale of Oil Agreement, La Compagnie Française des Petroles and Participations and Investments Limited and Calouste Sarkis Gulbenkian, Esq," Jul 31, 1928: BP 106287.

82. See "An Agreement." See "Mr. C. S. Gulbenkian and The Turkish Petroleum Company, Ltd., Joint Opinion," Feb 2, 1927: BP IPC 168-F4 FO Agreement Corresp Oct 1912–Oct 1927.

83. Letter, C.S. Gulbenkian to Sir John Cadman, Feb 23, 1927: BP 67811.

84. F.E. Wellings, "Note on the Blow-out of Baba Gurgur No. 1 on 14th October 1927," quoted by Stephen H. Longrigg, *The Origins and Early History of the Iraq Petroleum Company, Known From 1912 to 1929 as the Turkish Petroleum Company* (BP Archives, 1968), 287. "Gas Kills Americans in Turkish Oil Field," *NYT*, Oct 21, 1927, 8. See photos, "Baba Gurgur No. 1 Well—Oil Gushing through Side of Arbor Head," "A River of Oil Flowing from Baba Gurgur No. 1 Well," James Bamberg, *The History of the British Petroleum Company*, vol. 2: *The Anglo-Iranian Years, 1928–1954* (Cambridge, UK: Cambridge University Press, 1994), 160. See "Turkish Petroleum Co. Made Important Find," *WSJ*, Jun 4, 1928, 5.

85. "Note on the Blow-out of Baba Gurgur No. 1 on 14th October 1927."

86. N. Gulbenkian, 98–99.

87. Author's complete copy of the *Redline Agreement*, Jul 31, 1927: BP IPC 354-I8.

88. *Redline Agreement*, 49, 51, 52, 53.

89. *Redline Agreement*, 54.

90. *Redline Agreement*, 21–22.

91. *Redline Agreement*, 54.

CHAPTER 12: NAZI OIL

1. Great Britain, *Treaty of Preferential Alliance: The United Kingdom and Iraq*, Jun 30, 1930, *Parliamentary Papers 1931*, Treaty Series No. 15, Cmd. 3797, reproduced in J. C. Hurewitz, ed., *Diplomacy in the Near And Middle East*, vol. 2 (New York: Van Nostrand Company, 1956), 178–181. Introduction to *Treaty of Preferential Alliance*, Hurewitz, 178. Phillip Willard Ireland, *Iraq: A Study in Political Development* (New York: Macmillan Company, 1938), 413–415, 417–418.

2. Confidential letter, Sir F. Humphreys to Sir John Simon, Jan 28, 1935: BL L/PS/12/2882 v 17. E. Keith Roach, "Pipe Line Across a Desert Will Link East with West," *NYT*, Apr 15, 1934, XXVII. "First Iraq Oil at Mediterranean Port," *WSJ*, Jul 18, 1934, 1. See letter, Emir Abdullah to Sir John Cadman Pasha (trans.), Jan 24, 1935: BP IPC 100-P26: See letter, Sir John Cadman to Emir Abdullah, Jan 25, 1935: BP IPC 100-P26: Political, Transjordan, 1934–39. See confidential letter, High Commissioner for Palestine to H. M. Principal Secretary of State for the Colonies, Feb 15, 1935: BL L/PS/12/2882 v 17. James Bamberg, *The History of the British Petroleum Company*, vol. 2: *The Anglo-Iranian Years, 1928–1954* (Cambridge, UK: Cambridge University Press, 1994), xxvii.

3. Bernard Wasserstein, "Herbert Samuel and the Palestine Problem," *English Historical Review*, vol. 91 (1976), 763–764. See Black, *The Transfer Agreement: The Dramatic Story of the Pact between the Third Reich and Jewish Palestine* (Washington D.C.: Dialog Press, 2009), 91.

4. Philip Mattar, *The Mufti of Jerusalem* (New York: Columbia University Press, 1988), 6–7. See letter, Herbert Samuel to Winston Churchill, Oct 27, 1921: BNA T1/161/146 no. 119238.

5. Mattar, 8–10. Taysir Jbarra, *Palestinian Leader Hajj Amin Al-Husayni, Mufti of Jerusalem* (Princeton: The Kingston Press, 1985), 14.

6. Zvi Elpeleg, *The Grand Mufti: Haj Amin Al-Hussaini, Founder of the Palestinian National Movement*, David Harvey, trans., Shmuel Himelstein, ed. (London: Frank Cass, 1993), 3–4, 5. Mattar, 10–13. Jbarra, 15–16.

7. Mattar, 16, 20. See Wasserstein, 753–754.

8. Mattar, 22–25. Elpeleg, 8. See Jbarra, 41.

9. Note by Samuel, Apr 11, 1921: Israel State Archives 2/245, quoted by Wasserstein, 765. Mattar, 25–27. Elpeleg, 10.

10. See generally see Black, *Transfer Agreement*.

11. "Zionist Leaders: Chaim Weizmann, 1874–1952," Israel Ministry of Foreign Affairs, www.mfa.gov.il. See generally Black, *Transfer Agreement*.

12. See Black, *Transfer Agreement*, 379.See generally Black, *Transfer Agreement*.

13. See Black, *Transfer Agreement*, 379.See generally Black, *Transfer Agreement*.

14. See Sachar, 200. See Black, *Transfer Agreement*, 90.

15. "Two Arabs Killed by Police in Riot," *NYT*, May 2, 1936, 5. "Arabs Reject Plea to Call Off Strike," *NYT*, May 6, 1936, 16. "Arabs Kill 2 in Old Jerusalem," *NYT*, May 14, 1936, 14. "Terror Increases in Palestine Crisis," *NYT*, May 16, 1936. Howard M. Sachar, *A History of Israel, from the Rise of Zionism to Our Time* (New York: Alfred A. Knopf, 1981), 199–201.

16. *Report of the Palestine Royal Commission*, Cmd. 5479 (London: HM Stationery Office, 1937) (Peel Commission Report), chap. 20. "Palestine Inquiry Proves Difficult," *NYT*, Nov 15, 1936, E5. "Palestine Chary of State Domains," *NYT*, Nov 25, 1936, 7.

17. Peel Commission Report, chap. 6.

18. Peel Commission Report, chaps. 21, 22. Mattar, 82. Ferdinand Kuhn, Jr., "British Mark Time on Palestine Issue," *NYT*, Jan 9, 1938, E5.

19. Letter, British Consul to High Commissioner for Palestine, Jul 5, 1937: BNA CO733/326/4.

20. Donald Mallett, secret minutes, Feb 27, 1946: BNA FO 371/27078. British Consul to High Commissioner for Palestine, Jul 5, 1937. Mattar, 28–29, 82, 83. Jbarra, 61–63, 64–65.

21. See letter, W. Ormsby-Gore to Anthony [Eden], Oct 1, 1936: BNA FO954/12B no. 119571. Mattar, 82–83.

22. Mattar, 83. See letter, General Weygand to the Mufti (trans.), Sep 25, 1939: BNA FO371/61926/119288.

23. Weygand to the Mufti, Sep 25, 1939. Mattar, 88.

24. "London Hears Arab Chief Has Escaped to Baghdad," *NYT*, Oct 18, 1939, 3. Telegram, Consul-General, Beirut to Foreign Office, Oct 18, 1939: BNA FO684/12/119288. Mattar, 88, 89.

25. "London Hears Arab Chief Has Escaped to Baghdad." Mattar, 89.

26. "Plan W.A. 6, Appendix A: The Oil Supply Problem in Germany," July 1939: BNA AIR9/122 no. 119738. See "Analysis of German Petroleum Economy," ca. 1939: BNA AIR9/122 no. 119738. "Second Report of the Sub-Committee on the German Oil Position," ca. 1941: BNA CAB77/13.

27. "Oil Allocation and Distribution for Civilian Consumption in Germany," Jul 1944: BP 16548.

28. "Oil Allocation and Distribution for Civilian Consumption in Germany." Olex, "Valuation of Stock End-In-Hand at December 31st, 1937": BP 92868. Letter, W. B. Blackwood to F. G. C. Morris, Sep 3, 1936: BP 72201.

29. British Petroleum, "Report on Germany," Jan 1, 1947: BP 69501. "Valuation of Stock End-In-Hand at December 31st, 1937."

30. Olex, "Shares in and Advances to or from Subsidiary Companies at 31st December 1936": BP 90518.

31. Letter, F.C. Starling to A.C. Hearn, Aug 5, 1936: BP 68318. Olex, "Memorandum: Proposed Barter Transaction: Germany," Feb 6, 1936: BP 68318. Blackwood to Morris, Sep 3, 1936. See generally Black, *Transfer Agreement*.

32. See letter, R. Blackwood to F.G.C. Morris, May 12, 1936: BP 72201. Starling to Hearn. "Proposed Barter Transaction: Germany." Olex-BP, "Anglo-Iranian Oil Company Ltd, London, Claims at 31st December 1936," Mar 15, 1937: BP 90518.

33. Olex, "Anglo-Iranian Oil Company Ltd., London: Claims at 31st December 1938": BP 90492. Letter, "Olex" Deutsche Benzin- Und Petroleum Gesellschaft mit beschrankter Häftung to Anglo-Iranian Oil Co. Ltd., Continental Distribution Department, Oct 28, 1936: BP 64902.

34. See photo, "Pump Installation in Germany, 1926," R.W. Ferrier, *The History of the British Petroleum Company* (Cambridge, UK: Cambridge University Press, 1982), 490. See photo, "'Olex' BP Service Station in Germany, Mid-1930s," James Bamberg, *History of the British Petroleum Company*, vol. 2, 135. Bamberg, 132–133. "Oil Allocation and Distribution for Civilian Consumption in Germany." Memo, N. B. Fuller to Capt. W. J. A. Brown, Jul 7, 1928: BP 64902. "Draft of a Letter to the Automobile Association," Jun 2, 1936: BP 64902. See Ferrier, 489.

35. Olex, "Tale of the Family Tree," ca. 1950: BP 90030. See "Trade Mark Registration Certificate

No. 499538," Jan 27, 1938: BP 97583. See letter, L. Lefroy to F. Mann, Jul 26, 1937: BP 67857. See letter, M. R. Bridgeman to F. G. C. Morris, Jul 25, 1938: BP 67857. See letter, F. G. C. Morris to L. M. Lefroy, Jul 27, 1938: BP 67857.

36. "Standard Oil Co. (N.J.): II," *Fortune*, vol. 21 (1940). "Oil Allocation and Distribution for Civilian Consumption in Germany." See letter, W.B. Blackwood to F.G.C. Morris, Dec 29, 1936: BP 72201. See letter, W.B. Blackwood to F.G.C. Morris, May 31, 1937: BP 72201. See "Trade Mark Registration Certificate No. 511307," May 5, 1939: BP 97574. See "Trade Mark Registration Certificate No. 508749," Mar 13 1939: BP 97585. See "Trade Mark Registration Certificate No. 434021," Mar 10, 1930: BP 97599.

37. "Secret: An Appreciation of the Oil Position in Iran and Iraq," Oct 4, 1941: BNA POWE33/1085 no. 119945. Bamberg, 63–64.

38. See generally Black, *IBM and the Holocaust: The Strategic Alliance Between Nazi Germany and America's Most Powerful Corporation* (Washington, DC: Dialog Press, 2008). "Report on Germany."

39. "Particulars from Custodian of Enemy Property Records," ca. 1941: BNA BT271/592 no. 119571.

40. "Record of a Meeting Held in the Petroleum Department on Monday 29th July 1940, at 4:30 P.M. to Consider the Position of French Interests in the Iraq Petroleum Company," Jul 19, 1940: BNA FO371/24561 no. 119238.

41. Minutes, "Mr. C.S. Gulbenkian," Feb 1, 1944: BNA FO371/40215 no. 119238. Minutes of Feb 10, 1944: BNA FO371/40215 no. 119238. "Communicated to S.o.S. by Sir Kenneth Clark," ca. Feb 1944: BNA FO371/40215 no. 119238.

42. "Report by the Petroleum Department: The Levant Plan," ca. 1940: BNA CAB77/12 no. 358. "Lord Weir's Note of 1st April, 1940": BNA PREM1/434 no. 119738. War Cabinet, "Lord Hankey's Committee on Preventing Oil from Reaching Germany," Jul 14, 1940: BNA CAB77/12 no. 310. See Pilot Officer M. A. ap Rhys Price, "Bombing the Enemy's Fuel Supplies," secret report, Jan 27, 1940: BNA AIR9/122 no. 119738. See "R.A.F. Pours Bombs on Reich to Forestall Invasion Attempt," *WP*, Jun 21, 1941, 1.

43. Martin Gilbert, *The Second World War: A Complete History* (New York: Henry Holt & Co., 1989), 144–147. See generally André Mineau, *Operation Barbarossa: Ideology and Ethics against Human Dignity* (Amsterdam: Rodopi, 2004).

44. "Lord Weir's Note of 1st April, 1940." "Bad Faith Charged," *NYT*, Jun 22, 1941, 1.

45. "Lord Weir's Note of 1st April, 1940."

46. War Cabinet Joint Planning Staff, "Future Strategy Review," Jun 1941: BNA CAB84/31 no. 119945.

47. "Future Strategy Review." "German Activities in Oil Producing Countries of Middle East," secret minute sheet, Dec 11, 1940: BNA FO371/24549. "Extract from D.O. (41) 39th Meeting" Jun 5, 1941: BNA AIR8/497 no. 119945. "Iran to Remain Neutral," *NYT*, Jun 27, 1941, 2. Ray Brock, "Berlin Said to Threaten Rupture with Iran if Germans are Ousted," *NYT*, 3. "The Germans in Iran," *MG*, Aug 18, 1941, 5. Paul Wohl, "Iran: How Nazis Gained Control," *Christian Science Monitor*, Sep. 19, 1941. Chris Paine and Erica Schoenberger, "Iranian Nationalism and the Great Powers: 1872–1954," *MERIP Reports*, no. 37 (1975), 16. See "Iran at the Crossroads," *NYT*, Aug 19, 1941, 20.

48. "Note on Iraq as a Possible Source of Oil Supply to the Enemy," ca. 1940, BP IPC 255: Protective Measures.

49. "Note on Iraq as a Possible Source of Oil Supply to the Enemy."

50. "Feisal of Iraq Dies Suddenly in Berne," *NYT*, Sep 9, 1933, 1, 3. Charles Tripp, *A History of Iraq* (Cambridge, UK: Cambridge University Press, 2000), 80.

51. "Ghazi Is Proclaimed King," *NYT*, Sep 9, 1933, 3. See Majid Khadduri, *Independent Iraq: A Study in Iraqi Politics Since 1932* (London: Oxford University Press, 1951), 47–53 and chaps. 4–8. "Extract from Minutes of Group Meeting Held 17/11/37," Nov 11, 1937: BP IPC 100-45: Pipeline Survey.

52. Tripp, 81, 94–98. Geoffrey Warner, *Iraq and Syria, 1941* (Newark, DE: University of Delaware Press, 1974), 35.

53. Tripp, 98–99. Mattar, 89. Warner, 35. Khadduri, 137–139, 140–142.

54. Warner, 35. Tripp, 98–99. Air Commodore F.W. Walker, "A Review of the Battle of Habbaniya, May 1941," ca. June 1941: BNA AIR8/549 no. 119909, 1. Khadduri, 16. Tripp, 94.

55. Francis R.J. Nicosia, "Arab Nationalism and National Socialist Germany, 1933–1939: Ideological and Strategic Incompatibility," *International Journal of Middle East Studies*, vol. 12 (1980), 363–364. See generally Black, *IBM and the Holocaust*.

56. See Black, *War against the Weak*, 261–277, 279–318. See Black, *IBM and the Holocaust*, 93–96. See Black, *The Transfer Agreement*, 371–380.

57. "Vichy Police Chief Aided Mufti in Syria," ca. June 1940: BNA FO371/61926 no. 119288.
58. Letter, War Office to D.J.M.D. Scott, Nov 24, 1939: BNA FO371/23207 no. 119238. "The Mufti's Bid for Indian Moslem Aid," copy of letter, Mufti to President of All-India Muslim League, Bombay, Mar 2, 1940 (22 Moharrem 1359): BNA FO371/61926 no. 119288. Elpeleg, 58. See Miron Rezun, *The Iranian Crisis of 1941* (Köln; Wien: Böhlau Verlag, 1982), 319. See Harold Denny, "Germans in Iran Worry Russians," *NYT*, Jun 26, 1938, 23. See generally Black, *The Farhud: Roots of the Arab-Nazi Alliance in the Holocaust* (Washington, DC: Dialog Press, 2010), chap. 15.
59. Sir Basil Newton to Lord Halifax, Jun 10, 1940: BNA FO371/24561 no. 119238. Khadduri, 154–155.
60. "Enclosure in Baghdad Despatch No. 238 of 28.5.40: Extracts from the Local Press," May 28, 1940: BNA FO371/24561 no. 119238.
61. Letter, C. J. Edmonds to Sir Basil Newton, May 19, 1940: BNA FO371/24561 no. 119238.
62. Edmonds to Newton.
63. Edmonds to Newton.
64. "A Review of the Battle of Habbaniya, May 1941." Letter, Sir Basil Newton to Viscount Halifax, May 20, 1940: BNA FO371/24561 no. 119238. Letter, C. J. Edmonds to Sir Basil Newton, Jul 1, 1920, enclosure in Baghdad Despatch No. 315: BNA FO371/24561 no. 119238. See confidential letter, Sir Basil Newton to Mr. Eden, Feb 25, 1941: BNA FO371/27100 no. 119904. Mufti al-Amin, "Proposed Draft of an Official Declaration by Germany and Italy with Respect to the Arab Countries," ca. 1940: BNA FO371/61926 no. 119288. Elpeleg, 59. Khadduri, 195.
65. "Proposed Draft of an Official Declaration by Germany and Italy with Respect to the Arab Countries."
66. Heinz Pol, "'German Lawrence' Stirs Revolt," *NYT*, May 18, 1941, E5.
67. "'German Lawrence' Stirs Revolt."
68. Epleleg, 68.
69. See letter, Sir Basil Newton to Viscount Halifax, Oct 9, 1940: BNA FO371/24561 no. 119238.
70. Newton to Halifax, Oct 9, 1940.
71. Newton to Halifax, Oct 9, 1940.
72. Newton to Eden, Feb 25, 1941. War Office, "Iraq: February 1940 to August 1941 and May 1941 to January 1942," ca. Feb 1942: BNA WO32/11437 no. 120130.
73. "Comments on Paragraphs 9–13 of Chiefs of Staff Report of November 1st on an Enemy Advance through the Balkans and Syria to the Middle East," Nov 5, 1940: BNA FO371/24549. Elpeleg, 59–60.
74. Confidential letter, Sir Basil Newton to Mr. Eden, Jan 17, 1941: BNA FO371/27100 no. 119904.
75. Letter, Mufti Hussein al-Amin to Adolf Hitler, Jan 20, 1941, as translated and reproduced in Elpeleg, 202–205 and Khadduri (1960), 378–380.
76. Mufti to Hitler.
77. Mufti to Hitler.
78. Mufti to Hitler.
79. Mufti to Hitler.
80. Secret letter, Ernst Friherr von Wiesacker to Mufti Hussein al-Amin, Mar 1941: BNA FO371/61926 no. 119288.
81. Von Wiesacker to Mufti.
82. "Pro-Axis Leader Ousts the Premier in Iraq," *NYT*, Apr 5, 1941, 2. "Iraqi Coup Denounced," *NYT*, Apr 8, 1941, 7. Khadduri, 180–183. See "Accused of Plot, Regent Quits Iraq," *NYT*, Apr 9, 1941, 12.
83. "New Regent Is Elected," *NYT*, Apr 12, 1941, 5. Khadduri, 182. G.E.R. Geyder, "Syrians Say Nazis Keep Unrest Alive," *NYT*, Apr 5, 1941, 2. Letter to Mr. J. Skliros, Apr 5, 1941, and enclosure, letter of resignation, Taha al-Hashimi to H. R. H. The Regent, Apr 1, 1941: BP IPC 99-M4C: Misc. Correspondence. See "Uprising in Levant Fought by French," *NYT*, Mar 27, 1941, 1, 2.
84. See secret telegram, Baghdad to Foreign Office, Apr 5, 1941: BNA CAB84/28 no. 119909. "Defence of British Embassy and American Legation, Baghdad," memo, Apr 11, 1941: BNA AIR23/5925 no. 119909. "Kirkuk," memo, Apr 13, 1941: BNA AIR23/5925 no. 119909.
85. Telegram, General Wavell to C. I. G. S., May 3, 1941, quoted in "Iraq: February 1940 to August 1941 and May 1941 to January 1942."
86. See secret telegram, Baghdad to Foreign Office, Apr 5, 1941: BNA CAB84/28 no. 119909. "Defence of British Embassy and American Legation, Baghdad," memo, Apr 11, 1941: BNA AIR23/5925 no. 119909. "Kirkuk," memo, Apr 13, 1941: BNA AIR23/5925 no. 119909. War Cabinet Chiefs of Staff (COS) Committee, "Iraq Oil: Note by the Secretary," May 30, 1941: BNA AIR8/497 no. 119945. Major D. Morton, "Iraq Oil: Memorandum by Major Morton," Jun 4, 1941: BNA AIR8/497 no. 119945. See telegram, Commander in Chief, Baghdad to War Office, Apr 15, 1941: BNA CAB85/29 no. 119909.

87. Iraq Petroleum Company, memo, Jul 1, 1940.

88. Most secret and personal letter, Noel Hall to Commodore J. C. Slessor, Jun 26, 1940: BNA AIR9/122 no. 119738.

89. "Note to Petroleum Department: Syria."

90. Dudley Pound, memo, Nov 17, 1940: BNA FO371/24549.

91. "Aide Memoire on Meeting Held at the Petroleum Department on 18th December, 1940."

92. Secret letter, J. Skliros to M. R. Bridgeman, Apr 10, 1941: BP IPC 255: Protective Measures.

93. "British Army Lands in Iraq to Guard Prized Oil Fields," *NYT*, Apr 20, 1941, 1. Secret letter, British Consulate, Basra, to Sir K. Cornwallis, Jul 16, 1941: BNA FO371/27079.

94. Letter, Sir K. Cornwallis to Anthony Eden, Jun 6, 1941: BNA FO371/27077 no. 20157. "A Review of the Battle of Habbaniya, May 1941."

95. Letter, J. Skliros to M. R. Bridgeman, Mar 3, 1942. "Note, Strictly Private and Confidential," Jun 9, 1941: BNA FO371/27078. Generaloberst Franz Halder, *German Use of Arab Nationalist Movements in World War II* (1956), as cited in Historical Division, Supplement Guide to Foreign Military Studies, 1945–1954 (Washington, DC: National Archives, 1959).

96. Walker, 1–2. De Chair, Somerset, *The Golden Carpet* (New York: Harcourt, Brace & Co., 1945), 79. Glubb, Sir John, *The Story of the Arab Legion* (London: Hodder & Stoughton, 1948), 277–278.

97. Walker, 3.

98. Letter to Anthony Eden, Jun 6, 1941: BNA FO371/27077 no. 120157. Walker, 4. Glubb, 278.

99. Walker, 4–5. "Airspeed Oxford Mk I Military Trainer Aircraft," *Military Aircraft*, www.military-aircraft.org.uk/trainers/airspeed-oxford-i.htm.

100. Walker, 5. Douglas Porch, "The Other 'Gulf War'—The British Invasion of Iraq in 1941," The Center for Contemporary Conflict, www.ccc.nps.navy.mil. See generally Robert Lyman, *First Victory: Britain's Forgotten Struggle in the Middle East, 1941* (London: Constable & Robinson, 2006).

101. "Sonderkommando JUNCK," ca. Sep 8, 1952: BNA AIR20/9945 no. 119738. "Reported Killed," *NYT*, May 18, 1941, 4. Gilbert, *The Second World War*, 182. Lyman, *Iraq 1941: The Battles for Basra, Habbaniya, Fallujah, and Baghdad* (Osprey, 2006), 63, 65.

102. "Sonderkommando JUNCK." Secret telegram from Sir K. Cornwallis, "List of Germans who arrived in Iraq from 2nd May, 1941," Jun 26, 1941: BNA FO371/27077 no. 120157. Secret telegram, A. H. Q. Iraq to R. A. F., May 14, 1941: BNA AIR8/549 no. 119909. C.L. Sulzberger, "Nazis at Air Bases," *NYT*, May 15, 1941, 1. C.L. Sulzberger, "Syrian Bases Bombed," *NYT*, May 18, 1941, 1.

103. Telegram, Commander in Chief, Middle East, to War Office, May 3, 1941: BNA AIR8/497.

104. Personal telegram, W.S. Churchill to F.D. Roosevelt, May 4, 1941, quoted by Gilbert, *Winston S. Churchill, Vol. 6: Finest Hour, 1939–1941* (Boston: Houghton Mifflin, 1983), 1078–1079. William Shirer, *Rise and Fall of the Third Reich* (New York: Simon & Shuster, 1981), 829. Walker, 5–6.

105. See Commander in Chief to War Office, May 3, 1941.

106. J. Bowyer Bell, *Terror Out of Zion: The Fight for Israeli Independence* (New Brunswick, NJ: Transaction Publishers, 1996), 55.Yehuda Lapidot, *The History of the Irgun*, Chaya Galai, trans., www.etzel.org.il/english/. Elpeleg, 60.

107. Lapidot.

108. Moshe Dayan, *Moshe Dayan: Story of My Life* (New York: William Morrow, 1976), 63–64. *Encyclopedia Judaica*, s.v. "Palmach."

109. Lapidot. Boyer, 55–56. Elpeleg, 60.

110. Telegram, Major-General Sir H.L. Ismay to War Cabinet, May 22, 1941: BNA AIR8/497.

111. Adolf Hitler, "Order No. 30: Middle East," May 23, 1941: BNA FO371/61926 no. 110288. See Shirer, 829.

112. "A Review of the Battle of Habbaniya, May 1941," 11. "Glubb's Arabs to Parade," *NYT*, Jun 4, 1941, 3. "Mosul is Occupied by British Troops," *NYT*, Jun 5, 1941, 4. "German Flight Reported," *NYT*, Jun 1, 1941, 3. Telegram, Commander in Chief, Iraq, to Foreign Office, May 31, 1941: BNA FO371/27073 no. 120157. Most secret telegram, Assistant Secretary for War to First Sea Lord, May 24, 1941: BNA AIR8/497. Secret telegram, Sir K. Cornwallis to General, Basra, May 30, 1941: BNA AIR8/549 no. 119909.

113. "Sonderkommando JUNCK." "German Flight Reported." Telegram, Sir K. Cornwallis to Foreign Office, May 31, 1941: BNA FO371/27073 no. 120157. "Armistice Ends Revolt in Iraq; Arab Chief Flees," *NYT*, Jun 1, 1941, 1. David Anderson, "War in Iraq Ends; Regent in Baghdad," *NYT*, Jun 1, 1941, 1, 3. Telegram, D. Knabenshue to Secretary of State, Jun 1, 1941: NA RG59 740.0011 European War 1939/11558: Telegram, *FRUS*, 1941, 511.

114. "Extract from minutes of Chief of Staff Meeting held on 31st May, 1941," secret, May 31, 1941: BNA AIR8/497 no. 119945.

115. "Long Allied Columns Drive North in Syria," *NYT*, Jun 9, 1941, 4. John Connell, *Wavell: Scholar and Soldier, to June 1941* (London: Collins, 1964), 490–492.

116. Dayan, 66–68. Shabtai Teveth, *Moshe Dayan: The Soldier, The Man, The Legend*, Leah and David Zinder, trans. (Boston: Houghton Mifflin, 1973), 116–117.

117. Robert Slater, *Rabin of Israel* (New York: St. Martin's, 1993), 46. Teveth, 123–124.

118. "Long Allied Columns Drive North in Syria." "Advance Towards Capitals," *NYT*, Jun 9, 1941, 1. MacRae, James, "Airfields Blasted," *NYT*, Jun 9, 1941, 1. See Connell, 490–492.

119. "War in Iraq Ends." "Bad Faith Charged," *NYT*, Jun 22, 1941, 1.

120. "Iran to Remain Neutral," *NYT*, Jun 27, 1941, 2. Ray Brock, "Berlin Said to Threaten Rupture with Iran if Germans are Ousted," *NYT*, 3. "The Germans in Iran," *MG*, Aug 18, 1941, 5. Wohl, "Iran," 6. Paine and Schoenberger, "Iranian Nationalism," 16. See "Iran at the Crossroads," *NYT*, Aug 19, 1941, 20.

121. Rezun, *The Soviet Union and Iran: Soviet Policy in Iran from the Beginnings of the Pahlavi Dynasty to the Soviet Invasion in 1941* (Leiden: Sijthoff & Noordhoff, 1981), 354, 367. Rezun, *Iranian Crisis*, chap. 2.

122. Naomi R. Rosenblatt, "Oil and the Eastern Front: US Foreign and Military Policy in Iran, 1941–1945," Penn Humanities Forum Mellon Undergraduate Research Fellowship Final Paper, April 2009, 2–5. James A. Bill, *The Eagle and the Lion: The Tragedy of American-Iranian Relations* (New Haven, CT: Yale University Press, 1998), 18, as cited by Rosenblatt, 3. "Iran Refuses to Oust Nazis," *NYT*, Jul 30, 1941, 7. Wohl, "Iran."

123. Rezun, *The Soviet Union and Iran*, 267.

124. Mattar, *The Mufti of Jerusalem*, 96.

125. "Iran Is the Old Meeting Place of Britain and Russia," *NYT*, Aug 25, 1941, 14. "March into Iran," *NYT*, Aug 26, 1941, C18. See "Iranians Expect Showdown," *NYT*, Aug 23, 1941, 3. See Joan Beaumont, "Great Britain and the Rights of Neutral Countries: The Case of Iran, 1941," *Journal of Contemporary History*, vol. 16 (1981), 213–228.

CHAPTER 13: BRITISH PETROLEUM

1. Abdulaziz Bin Salman, "King Abdulaziz Negotiations with Concessionaire Oil Companies in Saudi Arabia," undated, 7–8. James Bamberg, *The History of the British Petroleum Company*, vol. 2: *The Anglo-Iranian Years, 1928–1954* (Cambridge, UK: Cambridge University Press, 1994), 171.

2. Bamberg, *The Anglo-Iranian Years*, 171–172.

3. Abdulaziz Bin Salman, 6. Bamberg, *The Anglo-Iranian Years*, 146, 147–148.

4. "Mr. C.S. Gulbenkian," minutes, Feb 8, 1944: BNA FO371/40215. Stephen H. Longrigg, *Oil in the Middle East: Its Discovery and Development* (London: Oxford University Press, 1968), 118, 174. Bamberg, *The Anglo-Iranian Years*, 335.

5. Minutes of meetings, Sep 16, 1946, Sep 23, 1946, Sep 24, 1946, Sep 27, 1946: IPC 3B 2003, as cited by Bamberg, *The Anglo-Iranian Years*, 335–336. Bamberg, *The Anglo-Iranian Years*, 335–336.

6. Majid Khadduri, *Independent Iraq, 1932–1958: A Study in Iraqi Politics* (London: Oxford University Press, 1960), 262–269, 271. "Britain and Iraq Fix New Alliance," *NYT*, Jan 11, 1948, 2. "Baghdad Riots Threaten Britain-Iraq Pact," *WP*, Jan 23, 1948, 11. "Iraq Regent Balks at British Treaty," *NYT*, Jan 22, 1948. "Iraq Cabinet Quits as People Protest Treaty with British; 70 Killed, 300 Wounded in Riots," *WP*, Jan 28, 1948, 4. "Iraq Premier Flees to Trans-Jordan," *NYT*, Jan 29, 1948, 1.

7. Longrigg, *Oil*, 209–210. Bamberg, *The Anglo-Iranian Years*, 339.

8. Bamberg, *The Anglo-Iranian Years*, 363, 367, 375. See photos, Bamberg, *The Anglo-Iranian Years*, 368–373. Longrigg, *Oil*, 155.

9. Bamberg, *The Anglo-Iranian Years*, 413, 428.

10. Bamberg, *The Anglo-Iranian Years*, 425. See photos, "The Iranian Flag Being Raised Over the Company's Offices at Abadan" and "Husayn Makki Addressing a Crowd at Abadan," Bamberg, *The Anglo-Iranian Years*, 424, 425.

11. Bamberg, *The Anglo-Iranian Years*, 432. Longrigg, *Oil*, 164. See photos, "Iranians Removing the Illuminated Sign" and "Crowd in Teheran Carrying One of the Signs," Bamberg, *The Anglo-Iranian Years*, 432, 434.

12. Longrigg, *Oil*, 163, 165. Bamberg, *The Anglo-Iranian Years*, 438.

13. See photo, "Changing the Plaque at the Entrance to Britannic House, Finsbury Circus, London," Bamberg, *The Anglo-Iranian Years*, 522. Bamberg, *The Anglo-Iranian Years*, 508–509.

14/ Bamberg, *The Anglo-Iranian Years*, 341, 342.

15. Longrigg, *Oil*, 368–369. Abdulaziz Bin Salman, 14.

250   NOTES

16. Harry N. Howard, "The Regional Pacts and the Eisenhower Doctrine," *Annals of the American Academy of Political and Social Science*, vol. 401 (May 1972), 86–90. Khadduri, 298, 299–302. "Planned Revolt 3 Years, Iraqi Says," *WP*, Jul 28, 1958, A10. See "Britain's Palestine Policy Tied to Soviet and Arabs," *WP*, Aug 10, 1947, E5. "Iran Closes the Gap, *NYT*, Oct 13, 1955, 30.

17. "Syria: United Arab Republic," Apr 1987, Library of Congress (LoC) Country Studies, www.loc.gov. "Egypt: Egypt and the Arab World," Dec 1990, LoC Country Studies. Khadduri, 242–243. "Iraqi Premier Sensed Trouble and Appealed to Washington in Vain," *NYT*, Jul 18, 1958, 9.

18. "How Crisis Developed in Iraq," *WP*, Jul 18, 1958, A14. Khadduri, 345.

19. "How Crisis Developed in Iraq." Dispatch, "The Iraqi Revolution of July 14, 1958," Sir Michael Wright to Mr. Selwyn Lloyd, Aug 21, 1958: BNA PREM11/2368, reproduced in Alan de L. Rush, and Jonathan Elliman, eds., *Records of the Hashemite Dynasties: A Twentieth Century Documentary History*, vol. 14 (Slough, UK: Archive Editions, 1995), 801–804. Letter, C. M. Johnson to Foreign Office, Jul 28, 1958: BNA FO371/134201, reproduced in de L. Rush and Elliman, 790–793., Alex Valentine, "King Feisal Arrested, Rebels Say," *WP*, Jul 15, 1958, A1, A4.

20. "Baghdad Regains Quiet after Successful Coup," *WP*, Jul 17, 1958, A8. Johnson to Foreign Office. See photos, "Victims of Baghdad Assassins on Public Display," *Time*, Aug 4, 1958, 20. "Iraqi Premier Sensed Trouble and Appealed to Washington in Vain."

21. "Feisal, 23, Was King 19 Years," *WP*, Jul 15, 1958, A11. "Broadcast by Three Stations," *NYT*, Jul 14, 1958, 1. "Iraq Government Reported Seized by Army Revolt," *NYT*, Jul 14, 1958, 1. "Faisal Vanishes," *NYT*, Jul 15, 1958, 1. "Kassem Tells How He Led Coup," *WP*, Aug 9, 1958, B4. "On This Day–14 July," http://news.bbc.co.uk. "How Crisis Developed in Iraq."

22. "How Crisis Developed in Iraq." "Eisenhower Sends Marines Into Lebanon," *NYT*, Jul 16, 1958, 1. "On This Day–14 July." "British Land in Jordan, Backed by U.S. Jets," *NYT*, Jul 18, 1958, 1. See "Marines in the Mediterranean," http://hqinet001.hqmc.usmc.mil. "British Shift Units to Back U.S. Actions," *NYT*, Jul 16, 1958, 1.

23. James Bamberg, *The History of the British Petroleum Company: British Petroleum and Global Oil, 1950–1975: The Challenge of Nationalism* (Cambridge, UK: Cambridge University Press, 2000), 164–166.

24. Bamberg, *The Challenge*, 166.

25. Charles Tripp, *A History of Iraq* (Cambridge, UK: Cambridge University Press, 2000), 151, 153, 156.

26. Tripp, 158. Bamberg, *The Challenge*, 163-165.

27. Bamberg, *The Challenge*, 165.

28. Bamberg, *The Challenge*, 166.

29. Bamberg, *The Challenge*, 167.

30. Bamberg, *The Challenge*, 167. Tripp, 170.

31. Bamberg, *The Challenge*, 167. Tripp, 180–181.

32. Daniel Yergin, *The Prize: The Epic Quest for Oil, Money & Power* (New York: Free Press, 1991), 515, 521. "Global Trade: Soviet Price Cuts Unite Oil Nations," *WP*, Sep 19, 1960, A16.

33. Yergin, 518, 522–523. "Venezuela Joins Mideast Pact on Oil Stabilization," *WP*, Sep 25, 1960, D24. "Arab Oil Congress Is Expected to Direct Fire at Price Cutting," *NYT*, Oct 8, 1960, 27. "World Oil Cartel May Take Shape," *NYT*, Sep 25, 1960, F1. "Oil Price Propping," *WSJ*, Oct 18, 1960, 1.

34. "About OPEC—OPEC History," www.opec.org. Yergin, 522–523.

35. Bamberg, *The Challenge*, 170–171.

36. Bamberg, *The Challenge*, 171.

Major Sources

Original papers and documents were accessed at several dozen archival repositories, record collections, and unprocessed files in Britain, the United States, Germany, and Israel. The challenging range of repositories spanned the gamut from governmental, military, and organizational archives to corporate and private files. Most of the repositories utilized are listed below, but space precludes a complete roster.

Germany
Berlin Documentation Center   Berlin
Bundesarchiv   Berlin
Institut für Zeitgeschichte   Munich

Israel
Central Zionist Archives (CZA)   Jerusalem
Government Press Office Photo Archive   Jerusalem
Israel State Archives (ISA)   Jerusalem
Weizmann Archives (WA)   Rehovet
Yad Vashem Archives (YVA)   Jerusalem

United Kingdom
Anglo-Iranian Oil Company (AIOC) files   Coventry
Anglo-Persian Oil Company (APOC) files   Coventry
Board of Deputies of British Jews (BDBJ)   London
British Library (BL)   London
British Motor Industry Heritage Trust   Coventry
British Petroleum Company (BP) files   Coventry
Gertrude Bell Papers   New Castle
Iraq Petroleum Company (IPC) files   Coventry
Modern Records Centre, Warwick University   Coventry
National Archives (British) (BNA)   Kew
Turkish Petroleum Company (TPC) files   Coventry

United States
Columbia University Library Lehman Suite   New York, NY
Iraq Foundation Archives   Washington, DC
Jacob Rader Marcus Center, American Jewish Archives   Cincinnati, OH
League of Nations (LoN) Archive, Harvard University   Cambridge, MA
Museum of the Oriental Institute Photo Archive   Chicago, IL
National Archives (NA)   College Park, MD
Rockefeller Family Archives (RF)   Sleepy Hollow, NY
Urman Collection, Justice for Jews from Arab Countries (JJAC)   West Orange, NJ
YIVO   New York, NY

Libraries are crucial to research on oil because each library maintains its own unique and often precious collection of obscure literature and local materials, including personal memoirs of diplomats and military men. In addition, many libraries maintain manuscript collections of original papers or organizational files. Most of the libraries we accessed are listed below, but space precludes a complete roster.

France
Bibliothèque Nationale de France (BF)   Paris

Germany
Berlin State Library   Berlin
Bibliothek der Friedrich-Naumann-Stiftung (BFN)   Königswinter
Library of Contemporary History (LCH)   Stuttgart
Universitätsbibliothek (UBB)   Bonn

Israel
al-Aqsa Mosque Library
National Library of Israel   Jerusalem
Tel Aviv University Central Library   Tel Aviv

United Kingdom
British Library   London
Camden Library, Holborn Branch   London
Camden Library, Swiss Cottage Branch   London
Charing Cross Library, Westminster   London
University of Warwick Library   Coventry
Wiener Library   London

United States
Alvin Sherman Library, Nova Southeastern University   Fort Lauderdale
Asher Library, Spertus Institute of Jewish Studies   Chicago
Blaustein Library, American Jewish Committee   New York
Columbia University Library   New York
Emerson Library, Webster University   St. Louis
Fenwick Library, George Mason University   Fairfax
Gelman Library, George Washington University   Washington, DC
Genesee County District Library   Flint, MI
Hoover Institution on War, Revolution, and Peace   Stanford
Johnson Center Library, George Mason University   Fairfax
Klau Library, Hebrew Union College   Cincinnati
Lamont, Harvard University   Cambridge
Lauinger Memorial Library, Georgetown University   Washington, DC
Library of Congress   Washington, DC
Library of the Simon Wiesenthal Center   Los Angeles
Meriam Library, California State University   Chico
Monterey Institute of International Studies Library   Monterey
Montgomery County Public Libraries   Rockville
Montgomery College Library   Rockville
New York Public Library, Dorot Jewish Division   New York
New York Public Library, General Research Division   New York
New York Public Library, Main Branch   New York
New York Public Library, Science, Industry, and Business Library   New York
Ostrow Library   Bel-Air
Perkins Library, Duke University   Durham
University of Kansas Library   Lawrence
University of Michigan   Flint, MI
U.S. Holocaust Memorial Museum Library   Washington, DC

ELECTRONIC SOURCES

Electronic and digital sources were used extensively. While Internet research is essential to historical investigation, the caveat remains that the web is profoundly unreliable, including some web sites operated by respected academic entities. At the same time, I found certain official organizational and governmental sites important, as were a very limited number of private research sites. Hence, while I consulted and searched through hundreds, perhaps thousands of web sites, only a precious few of the most reliable are listed below. On the other hand, the digital databases of documents and publications that I used were pivotal to my work.

Digital Archives, Libraries, and Databases:
JSTOR, The Scholarly Journal Archive
Lexis-Nexis
MUSE
ProQuest Historical Newspapers: *Atlanta Constitution, Chicago Tribune, Los Angeles Times, Manchester Guardian, New York Times, New York Tribune, Wall Street Journal, Washington Post*
The Times Digital Archive

Web sites
Avalon Law Project, Yale University Law School, http://avalon.law.yale.edu/
Axis History Factbook, www.axishistory.com
Baker College, www.bakeru.edu
BBC News, news.bbc.co.uk
British Library, www.bl.uk
The British Museum, www.britishmuseum.org
Columbia University, Fathom Archive, www.fathom.com
The Gertrude Bell Papers, www.gerty.ncl.ac.uk
The Hashemite Kingdom of Jordan, www.kinghussein.gov.jo
The Holocaust Resource, www.nizkor.org
Holocaust Research Project, www.holocaustresearchproject.org
Indiana University, www.indiana.edu
International Institute of Social History, www.iisg.nl
The Irgun Site, www.etzel.org.il/english/
Israel Ministry of Foreign Affairs, www.mfa.gov.il/MFA
United States Holocaust Memorial Museum, www.ushmm.org
The Jewish Agency for Israel, www.jafi.org.il
The Jewish Virtual Library, www.jewishvirtuallibrary.org
The Knesset, www.knesset.gov.il
The League of Nations Photo Archive, University of Indiana, www.indiana.edu/~league/
Library of Congress, www.loc.gov
Livius: Articles on Ancient History, www.livius.org
Michigan eLibrary, www.mel.org
Michigan State University, www.lib.msu.edu
Midrash ben Ish Hai, www.midrash.org
Military Aircraft, www.military-aircraft.org.uk
Military History Encyclopedia on the Web, www.historyofwar.org
Mt. San Jacinto College, www.msjc.edu.
National Archives and Records Administration, www.archives.gov
New York Public Library, http://legacy.www.nypl.org/research/
Nola.com, www.nola.com
PBS: Frontline, www.pbs.org/wgbh/pages/frontline/
National Archives (UK) Public Records Office, www.nationalarchives.gov.uk
The Royal Air Force, www.raf.mod.uk
State of Kuwait official website, Al-Diwan Al-Amiri, www.da.gov.kw/eng/
State of Kuwait (official website), Al-Diwan Al-Amiri, www.da.gov.kw/eng/
Syrian Social Nationalist Party, www.ssnp.net

Texas A&M, Department of Mathematics, www.math.tamu.edu
Time, www.time.com
Trenches on the Web: An Internet History of the Great War, www.worldwar1.com
Türkiye, http://turkiye.sarimollaoglu.com
U.S. Army Center for Military History, www.army.mil/cmh-pg/
The U. S. Geological Survey, www.usgs.gov
United States Holocaust Memorial Museum, www.ushmm.org
The World War I Document Archive, www.lib.byu.edu/~rdh/wwi/
WKRG, Mobile, Alabama, www.wkrg.com
WorldWarOne.com, www.worldwarone.com

PRINTED AND PUBLISHED MATERIALS

A vast array of printed and published materials was utilized—from diplomatic papers to books, from periodicals to period materials and photographs, from video to audio. Space prohibits a complete list, and the listings here approximate about half of the materials consulted.

Published Diplomatic Papers
Documents in British Foreign Policy (DBFP)
Documents in German Foreign Policy (DGFP)
Foreign Relations of the United States (FRUS)

British Documents on the Origins of the War, 1898–1914. London: H. M. Stationery Office, 1926–1938.
Covenant of the League of Nations. League of Nations (LoN).

Blech, Edward C., and Harry I Sherwood, eds. *British & Foreign State Papers,* vol. 105 (1912). London: H. M. Stationery Office, 1915.
de L. Rush, Alan, and Jonathan Elliman, eds. *Records of the Hashemite Dynasties: A Twentieth Century Documentary History.* Slough, UK: Archive Editions, 1995.
de L. Rush, Alan, and Jane Priestland, eds. *Records of Iraq, 1914–1966,* vols. 8, 9. Slough, UK: Archive Editions, 2001.
Gooch, G. P., and Harold Temperly, eds. *British Documents on the Origins of the War, 1898–1914,* vol. 10, pt. 2: *The Last Years of Peace.* London: H. M. Stationery Office, 1926–1938.
Hurewitz, J. C., ed. *Diplomacy in the Near And Middle East,* vols. I–III. New York: Van Nostrand, 1956; Gerrards Cross, UK: Archive Editions, 1987.
Jarman, Robert L., ed. *Political Diaries of the Arab World: Iraq, vol. 6: 1932–1947.* Slough, UK: Archive Editions, 1998.

Government Documents
Committee on Foreign Relations, U. S. Senate. *A Select Chronology and Background Documents Relating to the Middle East.* Washington, DC: U. S. Government Printing Office, 1969.

Command Papers, Great Britain
Correspondence between Sir Henry McMahon and The Sherif Hussein of Mecca, July 1915–March 1916. (With a map.) Cmd. 5957, Misc. No. 3. London: H. M. Stationery Office, 1939.
Iraq: Treaty with King Feisal. Cmd. 1757. London: H.M. Stationery Office, 1922.
Report of the Palestine Royal Commission. Cmd. 5479. (Peel Commission Report.) London: H.M. Stationery Office, 1937.

Secondary Sources
Literally hundreds of books and journal articles were consulted, from personal memoirs to scholarly works, on a range of topics. It would be impossible to list them all. However, a few hundred of the salient volumes are listed below.

Unpublished Manuscripts
Church, Matthew. "The Imperial Attachment to the Suez Canal from 1914 to 1945."

Kanwar, Ranvir Singh. "States, Firms and Oil: British Policy, 1939–54." Ph D diss., University of Warwick, 2000.

Longrigg, Stephen H. *The Origins and Early History of the Iraq Petroleum Company, Known from 1912 to 1929 as the Turkish Petroleum Company.* BP Archives, 1968.

Books

Ahmed, Akbar S. *Discovering Islam: Making Sense of Muslim History and Society.* New York: Routledge & Kegan Paul, 1988.

Al-Tabari. *History of the World.* Albany, NY: State University of New York Press, 1985.

Antonius, George. *The Arab Awakening: The Story of the Arab National Movement.* New York: G. P. Putnam's Sons, 1946. Reprint, New York: Capricorn Books, 1965.

Ataöv, Türkkaya, ed. *The Armenians in the Late Ottoman Period.* Ankara: The Council of Culture, Arts and Publications of the Grand National Assembly of Turkey, 2002.

Atarodi, Habibollah. *Great Powers, Oil and the Kurds in Mosul (Southern Kurdistan/Northern Iraq), 1910–1925.* Lanham, MD: University Press of America, 2003.

Balakian, Peter. *The Burning Tigris: The Armenian Genocide and America's Response.* New York: HarperCollins, 2003.

Bamberg, James. *The History of the British Petroleum Company: British Petroleum and Global Oil, 1950–1975: The Challenge of Nationalism.* Cambridge, UK: Cambridge University Press, 2000.

Bamberg, James. *The History of the British Petroleum Company, Vol. 2: The Anglo-Iranian Years, 1928–1954.* Cambridge, UK: Cambridge University Press, 1994.

Barnett, Clifford R., et al. *Iran.* Herbert Harold Vreeland and Muriel B. Lechter, eds. New Haven, CT: Human Relations Area Files, 1957.

Bauer, Josef, Robert K Englund, and Manfred Krebernik. *Mesopotamien: Späturuk- und Frühdynastische Zeit.* Edited by Pascal Attinger, Markus Waefler, and Walther Sallaberger. Oxford: Oxford University Press, 1998.

Bell, J. Bowyer. *Terror out of Zion: Irgun Zvai Leumi, LEHI, and the Palestine Underground, 1929–1941.* New York: St. Martin's Press, 1977.

Benderly, Beryl L., et al. *Area Handbook for Iraq.* Washington, DC: U. S. Government Printing Office, 1971.

Betts, Ernest. *The Bagging of Baghdad.* New York: John Lane, 1920.

Black, Edwin. *Banking on Baghdad: Inside Iraq's 7,000-Year History of War, Profit, and Conflict.* Washington, DC: Dialog Press, 2008.

Black, Edwin. *IBM and the Holocaust: The Strategic Alliance between Nazi Germany and America's Most Powerful Corporation.* Washington, DC: Dialog Press, 2008.

Black, Edwin. *Internal Combustion: How Corporations and Governments Addicted the World to Oil and Derailed the Alternatives.* Washington, DC: Dialog Press, 2008.

Black, Edwin. *Nazi Nexus.* Washington, DC: Dialog Press, 2009.

Black, Edwin. *The Plan: How to Rescue Society the Day the Oil Stops—or the Day Before.* Washington, DC: Dialog Press, 2008.

Black, Edwin. *The Transfer Agreement: The Dramatic Story of the Pact between the Third Reich and Jewish Palestine.* Washington, DC: Dialog Press, 2009.

Black, Edwin. *War Against the Weak: Eugenics and America's Campaign to Create a Master Race.* Washington, DC: Dialog Press, 2008.

Bright Jr., Arthur A. *The Electric-Lamp Industry: Technological Change and Economic Development from 1800 to 1947.* New York: Macmillan, 1949.

Buchanan, Sir George. *The Tragedy of Mesopotamia.* London: William Blackwood & Sons, 1938. Reprint, New York: AMS Press, 1974.

Busch, Briton Cooper. *Britain, India, and the Arabs, 1914–1921.* Berkeley, CA: University of California Press, 1971.

Calouste Gulbenkian Foundation. *Calouste Sarkis Gulbenkian, The Man and His Achievements.* Lisbon, Portugal: Calouste Gulbenkian Foundation, 1999.

Carley, Patricia. *Nagorno-Karabakh: Searching for a Solution.* Washington, DC: United States Institute of Peace, 1998.

Cassels, Lavender. *The Struggle for the Ottoman Empire: 1717–1740.* New York: Thomas Y. Crowell, 1967.

Chambers, James. *The Devil's Horsemen: The Mongol Invasion of Europe.* New York: Atheneum, 1985.

Churchill, Randolph S. *Winston S. Churchill, Vol. 2: Young Statesman, 1900–1914* and companion volume. Boston: Houghton Mifflin, 1967.

Clark, Arthur Tillotson. *To Baghdad with the British*. New York: D. Appleton, 1918.
Cleveland, William L. *A History of the Modern Middle East*. Boulder, CO: Westview Press, 2000.
Cohen, Stuart A. *British Policy in Mesopotamia, 1903–1914*. London: Ithaca Press, 1976.
Connell, John. *Wavell: Scholar and Soldier, to June 1941*. London: Collins, 1964.
Dadrian, Vahakn N. *The History of the Armenian Genocide: Ethnic Conflict from the Balkans to Anatolia to the Caucasus*. Providence, RI: Berghahn Books, 1995.
Darrah, William C. *Pithole, The Vanished City: A Story of the Early Days of the Petroleum Industry*. Gettysburg, PA: William C. Darrah, 1972.
Dayan, Moshe. *Moshe Dayan: Story of My Life*, New York: William Morrow, 1976.
De Chair, Somerset. *The Golden Carpet*. New York: Harcourt, Brace, 1945.
Donner, Fred McGraw. *The Early Islamic Conquests*. Princeton, NJ: Princeton University Press, 1981.
Donohoe, M. H. *With the Persian Expedition*. London: Edward Arnold, 1919.
Earle, Edward Mead. *Turkey, the Great Powers, and the Baghdad Railway: A Study in Imperialism*. New York: Macmillan, 1923.
Ellis, Edward S. and Charles F. Horne. *The Story of The Greatest Nations and the World's Famous Events, Vol. 1*. New York: Auxiliary Educational League, 1921.
Elpeleg, Zvi. *The Grand Mufti: Haj Amin Al-Hussaini, Founder of the Palestinian National Movement*. Translated by David Harvey. Edited by Shmuel Himelstein, London: Frank Cass, 1993.
Esposito, John L., ed. *Islam and Politics*. Syracuse, NY: Syracuse University Press, 1984.
Esposito, John L., ed. *The Oxford History of Islam*. New York: Oxford University Press, 1999.
Faroqhi, Suraiya. *Approaching Ottoman History: An Introduction to the Sources*. Cambridge, UK: Cambridge University Press, 1999.
Faroqhi, Suraiya. *Subjects of the Sultans: Culture and Daily Life in the Ottoman Empire*. London: I. B. Tauris, 2000.
Farrington, Anthony. *Trading Places: The East India Company and Asia 1600–1834*. London: British Library, 2002.
Ferrier, R. W. *The History of the British Petroleum Company, Vol. 1: The Developing Years, 1901–1932*. Cambridge, UK: Cambridge University Press, 1982.
Feuerstein, Georg, Subhash Kak and David Frawley. *In Search of the Cradle of Civilization: New Light on Ancient India*. Wheaton, IL: Theosophical Publishing House, 1995.
Foran, John. *Fragile Resistance: Social Transformation in Iran from 1500 to the Revolution*. Boulder, CO: Westview Press, 1993.
Gat, Moshe. *The Jewish Exodus from Iraq, 1948–1951*. London: Frank Cass, 1997.
Gensicke, Klaus. *Der Mufti von Jerusalem, Amin el-Husseini, und die Nationalsozialisten*. Frankfurt am Main: Peter Lang, 1988.
Giddens, Paul H. *The Birth of the Oil Industry*. New York: Macmillan, 1938.
Gilbert, Martin. *Auschwitz and the Allies*. New York: Holt, Rinehart, and Winston, 1981.
Gilbert, Martin, ed. *Britain and Germany between the Wars*. New York: Barnes & Noble, 1967.
Gilbert, Martin. *Winston S. Churchill, Vol. 3: The Challenge of War, 1914–1916* and companion volume. London: Heinemann, 1971.
Gilbert, Martin. *Winston S. Churchill, Vol. 4: The Stricken World, 1917–1922* and companion volume. London: Heinemann, 1977.
Gilbert, Martin. *Winston S. Churchill, Vol. 5: Prophet of Truth, 1922-1939* and 3 companion volumes. Boston: Houghton Mifflin Co., 1977.
Gilbert, Martin. *Winston S. Churchill, Vol. 6: Finest Hour, 1939–1941* and companion volume. Boston: Houghton Mifflin Co., 1983.
Glubb, Sir John. *The Empire of the Arabs*. Englewood Cliffs, NJ: Prentice-Hall, 1963.
Glubb, Sir John. *The Story of the Arab Legion*. London: Hodder & Stoughton, 1948.
Goodwin, Jason. *Lords of the Horizons: A History of the Ottoman Empire*. New York: Picador, 1998.
Gulbenkian, Calouste. *La Transcaucasie et la Peninsule D'Apcheron: Souvenirs de Voyage, 1890*. Paris: Librairie Hachette, 1891. Reprint, Lisbon, Portugal: Calouste Gulbenkian Foundation, 1989.
Gulbenkian, Nubar. *Portrait in Oil: The Autobiography of Nubar Gulbenkian*. New York: Simon & Schuster, 1965.
Heller, Joseph. *British Policy towards the Ottoman Empire, 1908–1914*. London: Frank Cass, 1983.
Hewins, Ralph. *Mr. Five Per Cent: The Biography of Calouste Gulbenkian*. London: Hutchinson & Co. Ltd., 1957.

Hitti, Philip K. *History of the Arabs, from the Earliest Times to the Present*. London: Macmillan, 1937. Reprint, New York: Palgrave Macmillan, 2002.

Holt, P. M., Ann K. S. Lambton, and Bernard Lewis, eds. *The Cambridge History of Islam, Vol. 1*. Cambridge, UK: Cambridge University Press, 1970.

Horovitz, David. *Yitzhak Rabin: Soldier of Peace*. London: P. Halban, 1996.

Hourani, Albert. *A History of the Arab Peoples*. Cambridge, MA: Harvard University Press, 1991.

Imber, Colin. *The Ottoman Empire, 1300–1650: The Structure of Power*. New York: Palgrave Mac-Millan, 2002.

Inalcik, Halil. *The Ottoman Empire: The Classical Age, 1300–1600*. Translated by Norman Itzkowits and Colin Imber. London: Wiedenfeld and Nicolson, 1973.

Ireland, Phillip Willard. *Iraq: A Study in Political Development*. New York: Macmillan, 1938.

James, Lawrence. *The Golden Warrior: The Life and Legend of Lawrence of Arabia*. New York: Paragon House, 1993.

Jbara, Taysir. *Al-□ājj Mu□ammad Amīn al-□usaynī, Mufti of Jerusalem: The Palestine Years, 1921–1937*. [Book print of Jbara's PhD dissertation.] New York: New York University, 1982.

Jbara, Taysir. *Palestinian Leader Hajj Amīn Al-Husaynī, Mufti of Jerusalem*. Princeton: The Kingston Press, 1985.

Jonnes, Jill. *Empires of Light: Edison, Tesla, Westinghouse and the Race to Electrify the World*. New York: Random House, 2003.

Kafadar, Cemal. *Between Two Worlds: The Construction of the Ottoman State*. Berkeley, CA: University of California Press, 1995.

Karsh, Efraim and Inari Karsh. *Empires of the Sand: The Struggle for Mastery in the Middle East, 1789–1923*. Cambridge, MA: Harvard University Press, 1999.

Kelly, Marjorie. *Islam: The Religious and Political Life of a World Community*. New York: Praeger, 1984.

Kent, Marian. *Oil and Empire: British Policy and Mesopotamian Oil 1900–1920*. London: Macmillan, 1976.

Khadduri, Majid. *Independent Iraq: A Study in Iraqi Politics Since 1932*. London: Oxford University Press, 1951.

Khadduri, Majid. *Independent Iraq, 1932-1958: A Study in Iraqi Politics*. London: Oxford University Press, 1960.

Khalid, Rashid, Lisa Anderson, Muhammed Muslih and Reeva S. Simon, eds. *The Origins of Arab Nationalism*. New York: Columbia University Press, 1991.

Khoury, Dina. *State and Provincial Society in the Ottoman Empire: Mosul, 1540–1834*. Cambridge, UK: Cambridge University Press, 1997.

Kinross, Lord J. P. D. B. *The Ottoman Centuries: The Rise and Fall of the Turkish Empire*. New York: William Morrow, 1977.

Köprülü, M. Fuad. *The Origins of the Ottoman Empire*. Edited and translated by Gary Leiser. New York: State University of New York Press, 1992.

Landau, Jacob. *Abdul-Hamid's Palestine*. Jerusalem, Israel: Carta, 1979.

Leland, F. W. *With the M. T. in Mesopotamia*. London: Foster Groom, 1920.

Levin, Itamar. *Locked Doors: The Seizure of Jewish Property in Arab Countries*. Translated by Rachel Neiman. Westport, CT: Praeger, 2001.

Lewis, Bernard. *The Crisis of Islam: Holy War and Unholy Terror*. New York: Modern Library, 2003.

Lewis, Bernard, ed. *Islam and the Arab World*. London: Alfred A. Knopf, 1976.

Lewis, Bernard, ed. and trans. *Islam, from the Prophet Mohammed to the Capture of Constantinople, Vol. 1: Politics and War*. New York: Oxford University Press, 1987.

Lodwick, John, with D. H. Young. *Gulbenkian, An Interpretation of "The Richest Man in the World."* Garden City, NY: Doubleday, 1958.

Longrigg, Stephen H. *Four Centuries of Modern Iraq*. Oxford: Clarendon Press, 1925; Farnborough, UK: Gregg International Publishers, 1968.

Longrigg, Stephen. *The Middle East: A Social Geography*. London: Gerald Duckworth, 1963.

Longrigg, Stephen. *Oil in the Middle East: Its Discovery and Development*. London: Oxford University Press, 1968.

Longrigg, Stephen. *Syria and Lebanon under French Mandate*. London: Oxford University Press, 1958.

MacMillan, Margaret. *Paris 1919: Six Months That Changed the World*. New York: Random House, 2001.

Macqueen, James G. *Babylon*. New York: Praeger, 1965.

Majd, Mohammad Goli. *The Great Famine and Genocide in Persia, 1917–1919*. Lanham, MD: University Press of America, 2003.

Marlowe, John. *Late Victorian: The Life of Sir Arnold Talbot Wilson*. London: Cresset Press, 1967.

Marr, Phebe. *Iraq: A Profile*. Boulder, CO: Perseus Books, 1986.

Marr, Phebe. *The Modern History of Iraq*. Boulder, CO: Westview Press, 2003.

Marr, Phebe. *Revolutionary Regimes in the Middle East: A Comparative Study*. Westport, CT: Greenwood Press, 1982.

Marr, Phebe, and William Lewis, eds. *Riding the Tiger: The Middle East Challenge after the Cold War*. Boulder, CO: Westview Press, 1993.

Marsden, Phillip. *The Crossing Place: A Journey Among the Armenians*. New York: Kodansha International, 1995.

Mattar, Philip. *The Mufti of Jerusalem: Al-Hajj Amin al-Husayni and the Palestinian National Movement*. New York: Columbia University Press, 1988.

McCarthy, Justin. *The Ottoman Peoples and the End of Empire*. London: Arnold, 2001.

Mihalkanin, Edward S., ed. *American Statesmen: Secretaries of State from John Jay to Colin Powell*. Westport, CT: Greenwood, 2004.

Miller, Donald E., and Lorna Touryan Miller. *Survivors: An Oral History of the Armenian Genocide*. Berkeley, CA: University of California Press, 1993.

Miller, Geoffrey. *The Millstone: British Naval Policy in the Mediterranean, 1900–1914: The Commitment to France and British Intervention in the War*. Hull, UK: University of Hull, 1999.

Miller, Geoffrey. *Straits: British Policy towards the Ottoman Empire and the Origins of the Dardanelles Campaign*. Hull, UK: University of Hull, 1997.

Moberly, Brigadier General F. J. *History of the Great War: The Campaign in Mesopotamia, 1914–1918, Vols. I–III*. London: H. M. Stationery Office, 1925.

Morgan, David. *The Mongols*. Oxford, UK: Basil Blackwell, 1986

Morgenthau, Henry. *Ambassador Morgenthau's Story*. Garden City, NY: Doubleday, Page, 1918.

Nakash, Yitzhak. *The Shi'is of Iraq*. Princeton, NJ: Princeton University Press, 1994.

Neff, E. Richard, ed. *Oil History: A Selected and Annotated Bibliography*. Houston, TX: International Association of Drilling Contractors, 1995.

Palmer, Alan. *The Decline and Fall of the Ottoman Empire*. New York: M. Evans, 1992.

Quataert, Donald, ed. *Consumption Studies and the History of the Ottoman Empire, 1550–1922*. Albany, NY: State University of New York Press, 2000.

Quataert, Donald. *The Ottoman Empire, 1700–1922*. Cambridge, UK: Cambridge University Press, 2000.

Quataert, Donald. *Ottoman Manufacturing in the Age of the Industrial Revolution*. Cambridge, UK: Cambridge University Press, 1993.

Rashid, Ahmed. *Taliban, Militant Islam, Oil and Fundamentalism in Central Asia*, New Haven, CT: Yale University Press, 2001.

Ritchie, Berry. *Portrait in Oil: An Illustrated History of BP*. London: James & James, 1995.

Robinson, Francis, ed. *The Cambridge Illustrated History of the Islamic World*. Cambridge, UK: Cambridge University Press, 1996.

Rodengen, Jeffrey L. *The Legend of Halliburton*. Fort Lauderdale, FL: Write Stuff Syndicate, 1996.

Roe, Sir Thomas. *The Embassy of Sir Thomas Roe to India, 1615–1619, Vols. 1 and 2*. William Foster, ed. London: Bedford Press, 1899.

Rogan, Eugene L., and Avi Shlaim, eds. *The War for Palestine*. New York: Cambridge University Press, 2001.

Roth, Martha T. *Law Collections from Mesopotamia and Asia Minor*. Atlanta, GA: Scholars Press, 1997.

Roux, Georges. *Ancient Iraq*. New York: Penguin Putnam, 1992.

Sachar, Howard M. *A History of Israel: From The Rise of Zionism to Our Time*. New York: Alfred A. Knopf, 1981.

Sasson, Jack M., ed. *Civilizations of the Ancient Near East*. New York: Scribner, 1995.

Saunders, J. J. *The History of the Mongol Conquests*. Philadelphia, PA: University of Pennsylvania Press, 1971.

Schechtman, Joseph B. *The Mufti and the Fuehrer: The Rise and Fall of Haj Amin el-Husseini*. New York: Thomas Yoseloff, 1965.

Schonfield, Hugh. *The Suez Canal in Peace and War, 1869–1969*. Coral Gables, FL: University of Miami Press, 1969.

Shaw, Stanford J. *The History of the Ottoman Empire and Modern Turkey, vol. I: Empire of the Gazis, The Rise and Decline of the Ottoman Empire, 1280–1808.* Cambridge, UK: Cambridge University Press, 1976.

Shaw, Stanford J., and Ezel Kural Shaw. *The History of the Ottoman Empire and Modern Turkey, Vol. II: Reform, Revolution, and Republic: The Rise of Modern Turkey, 1808–1975.* Cambridge, UK: Cambridge University Press, 1977.

Sheikh, M. Saeed. *Islamic Philosophy.* London: Octagon Press, 1982.

Shulewitz, Malka Hillel, ed. *The Forgotten Millions: The Modern Jewish Exodus from Arab Lands.* London: Cassel, 1999.

Sicker, Martin. *The Islamic World in Ascendancy: From the Arab Conquests to the Siege of Vienna.* Westport, CT: Praeger, 2000.

Singleton, Solveig, and Daniel T. Griswold, eds. *Economic Casualties: How U.S. Foreign Policy Undermines Trade, Growth, and Liberty.* Washington, DC: Cato Institute, 1999

Slater, Robert. *Rabin of Israel.* New York: St. Martin's Press, 1993.

Sluglett, Peter. *Britain in Iraq, 1914–1932.* London: Ithaca Press, 1976.

Smith, Roy C., and Ingo Walter. *Global Banking.* New York: Oxford University Press, 1997.

Spandounes, Theodore. *On the Origins of the Ottoman Emperors.* Edited and translated by Donald M. Nicol. Rome, 1538. Reprint, New York: Cambridge University Press, 1997.

Stillman, Norman A. *The Jews of Arab Lands: A History and Source Book.* Philadelphia, PA: Jewish Publication Society of America, 1979.

Tarbell, Ida M. *The History of the Standard Oil Company.* New York: Macmillan, 1904. Reprint, Gloucester, MA: Peter Smith, 1963.

Tauber, Eliezer. *The Arab Movements in World War I.* London: Frank Cass, 1993.

Teveth, Shabtai. *Moshe Dayan: The Soldier, the Man, the Legend.* Translated by Leah and David Zinder. Boston: Houghton Mifflin, 1973.

Toynbee, Arnold, J., ed. *The Treatment of Armenians in the Ottoman Empire.* London: Hodder & Stoughton, 1916.

Townsend, Charles Vere Ferrers. *My Campaign, Vols. I & II.* New York: The James A. McCann Company, 1920.

Tripp, Charles. *A History of Iraq.* Cambridge, UK: Cambridge University Press, 2000.

Wall, Bennet H. *Growth in a Changing Environment: A History of Standard Oil Company (New Jersey) and Exxon Corporation, 1950–1975.* New York: McGraw-Hill, 1988.

Wallach, Janet. *Desert Queen.* New York: Anchor Books, 1996.

Warner, Geoffrey. *Iraq and Syria, 1941.* Newark, DE: University of Delaware Press, 1974.

Wasserstein, Bernard. *Britain and the Jews of Europe, 1939–1945.* Oxford, UK: Oxford University Press, 1979.

Weizmann, Chaim. *Trial and Error: The Autobiography of Chaim Weizmann.* New York: Harper & Brothers, 1949.

Wellhausen, J. *The Arab Kingdom and Its Fall.* Translated by Margaret Graham Weir. Beirut, Lebanon: Khayats, 1963.

Wilson, Sir Arnold T. *A Clash of Loyalties: Mesopotamia: 1917–1920, A Personal Record.* London: Oxford University Press, 1931.

Wilson, Sir Arnold T. *Loyalties: Mesopotamia, 1914–1917: A Personal Record.* London: Oxford University Press, 1930.

Wheatcroft, Andrew. *The Ottomans: Dissolving Images.* London: Viking, 1995.

White, Gerald T. *Formative Years in the Far West: A History of Standard Oil Company of California and Predecessors through 1919.* New York: Appleton-Century-Crofts, 1962.

Yapp, M. E. *Strategies of British India: Britain, Iran and Afghanistan, 1798–1850.* Oxford, UK: Clarendon Press, 1980.

Yergin, Daniel. *The Prize: The Epic Quest for Oil, Money and Power.* New York: Free Press, 1991.

Journals and Periodicals

Annals of the American Academy of Political and Social Science
British Journal of Middle Eastern Studies
Bulletin (British Society for Middle Eastern Studies)
Bulletin of the Business Historical Society

Bulletin of the School of Oriental Studies, University of London
Bulletin of the School of Oriental and African Studies, University of London
Business History Review
Economic Geography
The Economic History Review
The English Historical Review
The Geographical Journal
Harvard Journal of Asiatic Studies
Historia Scientarum
The Historical Journal
The Historical Review
Insight: News & Views for the Process, Power and Offshore Industries
International Affairs
International Journal of Middle Eastern Studies
International Organization
Journal of Contemporary History
The Journal of Economic History
Journal of Field Archaeology
The Journal of Military History
The Journal of Modern History
Journal of Near Eastern Studies
The Journal of Political Economy
Journal of the American Oriental Society
Journal of World Prehistory
Military Affairs
Past and Present
Political Science Quarterly
The Quarterly Journal of Economics
The Scientific Monthly
Slavic Review
Smithsonian Magazine
Speculum: A Journal of Mediaeval Studies
Transactions of the American Philosophical Society
Wiener Library Bulletin

Newspapers, Magazines, Wire Services and Other Media
al-Alem al-Arabi (Baghdad)
ABC News
British Broadcasting Corporation (BBC)
Cable News Network (CNN)
CBS News
The Chicago Tribune (Chi Trib)
Christian Science Monitor
The Guardian
Jewish Telegraphic Agency (JTA)
The New York Times (NYT)
The New York Tribune (NY Trib)
Public Broadcasting System (PBS)
Sky News
Time
Times (London)
The Wall Street Journal (WSJ)
The Washington Post (WP)

INDEX

Sazonov, Sergei, 90
Sea Lion, 198
Second General Syrian Congress, 128, 133, 140
Secret societies, 32, 70, 74
Self-denying covenant, 159
Self-denying principle, 166
Self-determination principle, 104
Semites, 186
Serbia, 44, 63
Shah of Iran, 17, 172, 181, 201–202, 207, 214
Shatt al-Arab, 66, 91, 95, 144
Sheikhs, 76, 106–107
Shell Transport Company, 45, 113–114. *See also* Royal Dutch Shell.
Shell Transport and Trading, 16
Shi'a, 18, 71, 107, 133, 138, 203
Shirazi, Imam, 139
"Sick Man of Europe," 20, 22, 33, 69, 100, 123
Simon, Sir John, 57
Six Day War, 213–214
Skliros, J., 195
Slade, Rear Admiral Sir Edmond, 49
Slade Commission, 49
"Small people," 6, 216
Smith, Sir Lancelot, 109, 116
Smith, Sir Llewellyn, 52
Somme, Battle of, 65
Soviet oil industry, 212
Standard Oil, 15, 17, 23, 61, 97, 108, 146–149, 151, 152, 154, 158, 181, 205, 212
Standard Oil of California (Socal), 204
Standard Oil of Indiana (Amoco), 215
Standard Oil of New Jersey, 146, 152, 167–168, 181, 205, 212
Straus, Oscar, 119
Stuart, Captain B., 139
Sublime Porte, 25, 47, 99, 119
Suez Canal, 16, 25, 33, 199
Sunni, 71–72, 101, 133, 138, 184, 203
Suq tribes, 106
Svanberg, Carl-Henric (BP Chairman), 6, 216
Sykes, Mark, 29, 90
Sykes-Picot Agreement, 90–93, 103, 108, 116, 124
Syria, 25, 45, 69–78, 90, 95, 100, 108, 110–111, 115–116, 124–133, 137–138, 140, 146, 152, 171, 177, 188, 190, 191, 193–195, 199–201, 204, 208–211, 213. *See also* Second General Syrian Congress
Syria, Vichy, 186, 192–193, 197, 200–201

Taif province, 19–20
Talaat Pasha, 122
Tapous, 14–15
Teagle,Walter C., 147
Tel Afar, 139
Tel Aviv, 175, 198
Texas, 3, 212
Thatcher, Margaret, 215
Third Reich, 172, 174–175, 180–181, 183–184, 188. *See also* Germany; Nazis
Tigris River, 91, 100. *See also* Euphrates-Tigris delta
Tikrit, 45, 82
Titusville oil strike, 9, 15–16
Toolpusher, 4
Townshend, Charles, 81, 99

Trade Disputes Act, 57
Trading with the Enemy office, 66, 68, 182
"Trading with the Enemy" proclamations, 66
Transferred Territories treaty, 50
Treaty of Lausanne, 155
Trenchard, Hugh, 143
Tripoli refineries, 194
"Trucial Coast States," 204
Turco-Persian Frontier Protocol, 50
Turkey, 15, 20, 22, 25, 32, 33, 36, 40, 42–45, 50–53, 56, 58, 64–67, 69–70, 72, 74, 77–78, 86, 91, 99–100, 120–123, 129, 131, 133, 137, 149, 152–153, 155–156, 158, 162, 165, 169, 188, 202, 209. *See also* National Bank of Turkey; Ottoman; Turks; Young Turks.
Turkey, "carving" of, 129
Turkification, 70, 96
Turkish Mining Law, 58
Turkish Petroleum Company (TPC), 44, 45, 47–48, 51–52, 56, 58, 67–68, 93, 109, 111–113, 116, 152, 154, 156, 160, 163–167, 169
Turks, 26, 48, 52, 55, 58–59, 66, 69, 70, 72, 75, 77–81, 85–86, 101, 103, 106, 120–124, 131, 133–134, 152, 155, 176, 202. *See also* Turkey; Young Turks
Turks, extermination of Armenians by, 121–122
Tutelage, 115, 125, 139, 145
Tyrrel, William, 161

United Arab Emirates, 204
United Arab movement, 73, 127
United Arab Republic (UAR), 209
United States, 8, 13, 15, 23, 31, 47, 68, 89, 99, 122–123, 127, 146–151, 153, 191, 204, 209. *See also* American

"Vart Badrik" family, 12
Verdun, 65
Versailles Peace Conference, 103
Vilayets, 76, 92, 95, 98
von Ribbentrop, German Foreign Minister, 188

Waqf religious trust, 177
al-Wattari, Abdul Aziz, 212
Weir report, 183
von Weizacker, Ernst, 192
Weizmann, Chaim, 126, 174
Weygand, Maxime, 177
Wilhelm II, Kaiser, 25–26, 63
Willcocks, Sir William, 96
Wilson, Woodrow, 104, 110–111, 134, 146, 148. *See also* Fourteen Points
World War I, 6, 65, 70, 89, 97, 123, 137, 166, 189
World War II, 171, 177, 185, 203, 205

Yazidis, 71, 101
Young Turks, 19, 32–34, 36, 42–43, 55, 58, 66, 70, 72, 120–121, 131, 161
Young Turks, alliance with Germans, 55

Zionism, 123–124, 172–173, 187, 203, 213
Zionist Conference, 132–133
Zionist military organization, 198
Zionist state, 126
Zoroaster (oil tanker), 11